TRADE AND MARKET IN THE EARLY EMPIRES

Trade and Market

in the

Early Empires

ECONOMIES IN HISTORY AND THEORY

Edited by
KARL POLANYI, CONRAD M. ARENSBERG,
and
HARRY W. PEARSON

A GATEWAY EDITION
Henry Regnery Company • Chicago

Gateway Edition published by Henry Regnery Company
114 West Illinois Street, Chicago, Illinois 60610
by arrangement with The Free Press, a division of
The Macmillan Company

First Gateway Edition, 1971

Preface

THE senior editors hope to be forgiven for a somewhat lengthy preface. Close cooperation in genuine freedom allowed the present book to take shape as work in progress. Manifold factors, each on its own level, influenced the interdisciplinary plan, structure and form. There were, in the first place, the initiators and their former students who together largely wrote the book, one of the latter, Professor Harry W. Pearson of Adelphi College, acting also as co-editor; the institutions, internal and external to the University, which supported over a decade the various ventures in their overlapping phases; the personal scholarly aims of the editors which they endeavored to bring to fruition on converging lines. The undersigned will therefore speak here in three voices: each for himself, and together for both.

In Spring 1947 Karl Polanyi was appointed Visiting Professor of Economics at Columbia University. Until his retirement in 1953 he taught General Economic History in the Graduate Faculty, redefining the subject in the yearly announcement as "the place occupied by economic life in society." In 1948, the Council for Research in the Social Sciences at Columbia University (C. R. S. Sc.) endowed a research project on the origins of economic institutions, under his direction. Having retired, at the age of sixty-seven, he was given the honorary appointment of Adjunct Professor of Economics. Jointly with Professor Conrad M. Arensberg he then applied to the Ford Foundation, Behavioral Sciences Division, for a grant in support of an Interdisciplinary

v

Project on the economic aspects of institutional growth, to be administered by Columbia University. In accepting the gift, Columbia University pointed to the continuity of effort which linked the C. R. S. Sc. project with the new grant. But while the charter of the C. R. S. Sc. barred students engaged in project work from making use of results towards the attainment of an academic degree, no such restrictions applied to the Interdisciplinary Project; rather it was intended as a center of research benefiting the study purposes both of the senior proponents and of their associates. Polanyi has been serving full-time since 1953 on the Interdisciplinary Project, which in 1956 was continued by the Ford Foundation for another two years. Harry W. Pearson was appointed Executive Secretary. A university Seminar, at faculty level, on the institutionalization of the economic process set up at Columbia University discussed the same general topic from 1953 to 1955.

One by one a number of his 1947 students had joined Polanyi in his inquiries. Theoretical stimulation came from Harry W. Pearson and Rosemary Arnold (Barnard), both also giving valuable literary help; empirical applications were contributed by Charles S. Silberman (Columbia University) and Walter C. Neale (Yale University); George Woodard (Goddard College) uncovered Old Testament data relevant to the Mesopotamian field; Daniel B. Fusfeld (Michigan State University) provided a methodological link with economic anthropology; Roxane Eberlein created an invaluable card index for the total research effort; Laura P. Striker, Ph. D. (History), a guest student, volunteered assistance over several years with the German translations of cuneiform texts. Among later students Terence K. Hopkins (Columbia University) brought to bear a much needed sociological approach to the concept of a substantive economy; Professor Murray C. Polakoff (University of Texas) contributed in the same direction; Abe Rotstein (Sir George Williams College, Montreal) who assisted Polanyi's work in many ways, also wrote the Introductory Note to the present book.

By 1953 definite progress had been made. The distinction between trade and market institutions was proving a potent instrument in rectifying serious misreadings of economic data in early societies. Building on the works of earlier scholars, we had largely solved the problem of money uses in primitive and archaic societies. In regard to prices, the existence of the complex institution of "equivalencies" was revealed. The consequences for our understanding of the manner in which the economic process was instituted in Mesopotamia and classical Greece began to take shape.

At this point Arensberg, whose parallel endeavors at an institutional approach to the problems of sociology and anthropology were laid down in publications reaching back over a period of years, joined forces with Polanyi. Professor A. L. Oppenheim of the Oriental Institute, Chicago agreed to act as consultant in Assyriology. The undersigned then initiated the study of anthropology, economic history, and Assyriology from which this book sprang.

In Arensberg's case, such joint study gave a welcome opportunity to show that anthropology could serve economic history as more than a storehouse of odd data. The approach by which he thinks anthropologists in close collaboration with himself have reached some new understanding of the regularities to be found both in ethnographic and substantive economic data is an operational method recently referred to as "interaction theory."

A few paragraphs may well be devoted to this linking of social arrangements and culture traits on the one hand, institutions on the other. It consists of the systematic use of three operations upon the immediate observations and the generalization of the resultant records —in the form of answers to the question: Who did what to whom, in what order, how often, where? The operations are (1) the specification of the persons acting on one another, (2) the discrimination of the order of the action (initiative and response), (3) the comparison of the events so described in time, as frequencies or rates of recurrence. Economic institutions then take on the appearance of goods-handling and goods-receiving, while ethnographic data may be expected to reveal who passed on goods to whom, in what order, how often, with what response among those listed under "whom." This should, for instance, enable us to link ethnographical data with such a purely empirical classification of parts of the goods-handling and goods-receiving process as are indicated by the terms reciprocative, redistributive, and marketing, as Polanyi has suggested.

The reciprocative sequence among fixed partners AB/BA or AB/BC/CA C indicated similar social arrangements and culture traits whether the institutions formed otherwise part of prestige, kinship, community, religious, or other activities of the peoples who live by reciprocative human action in similar sequence.

In a redistributive world we find only few, if any, simple or complex chains of action and their reversals, or circles of action back upon themselves. Action is instead centripetal movement of many upon one central figure followed by an initiative of that central figure upon the same many. Formally, BA/CA/DA/EA/FA are followed by an event A/BCDEF in unison or repartition. Central authority or focus in human organization has been invented, and it is now a frequent form in which human action occurs. The economics of redistribution, again, has common elements with the other institutions of the epochs in which central authority, the elaboration of "set events," is developing. But the identity of A, the centralizing figure, is still a fixed feature. His identity is not reversible: Temple-god or high priest, or king, or emperor, or even, in republican cases, citizen office-holder in rotation of office still fixed for a day or a year, is a fixed point, round which the others are also bound, liege, and fixed.

We asked the same type of question of the market. Here we asked it, in detail, and again our questioning, which resulted in what we think to be common denominator social arrangements and culture traits, led us to a slightly different pattern of observations than those our economists made. We asked, abstractly and analytically, what social action does the free market entail, and also where in the ethnographic record, can we find such forms of social action prior to modern times.

The economists of our project had difficulty with our question. To them free or moving prices were the earmark of the free market; and production for sale at such prices, fluctuating in its turn against market supply and demand, was the earmark of a market economy. But to the anthropologist that is not enough, since he must connect the specific, developed details of a culture trait, particularly the outward and spectacular features which win it human recognition and acclaim, with the inner features, its social arrangements, its past history, and its functions for men, society, and the maintenance of other institutions than itself. But they finally agreed with us upon the following tentative formulation: In the free market of supply and demand, a man can reverse roles, being supplier or demander as he can or wills. A man can go to this market or that as he sees his advantage; he is free of fixed and static obligation to one center or one partner, he moves at will and at random, or as prices beckon. He can offer to all and any comers, dole or divide among them, "corner the market" so that they all pay his price and so dance to his tune. At another turn of prices, or in a next transaction or market, formally, he is one of a similar "crowd" and dances in unison to the tune called by another who may in his turn have "cornered the market" from them all. Thus the action, judged by our operations, is random as to persons, at the free initiative of any one, formally, and the position of central "authority" in the market goes now to this competitor or cornerer—, now to that. The personal identity of the center, unlike that in redistributions, is fluctuant, moving, reversible, and random, too, a function not of other institutions but of the market itself.

Nowhere in the ethnographic record should we find another such fluid randomizing, so different a pattern of social arrangements to compare with those of reciprocity and redistribution. Here was a pattern reckoned from the will of the actor, giving him only the role he should achieve, not that ascribed to him from outside, forming and reforming the positions of others about him as he himself changed behavior and motive. Now, formally, A/BCDEF took place no oftener than B/ACDEF or F/ABCDE, and somehow human beings had learned, presumably, to accept roles as the movement of the institution itself, the market, dictated, together with a freedom to try to bend the others to their advantage. In the Western world, where this institution had come to emerge and to blossom into extreme elaboration in a Manchester-School England of the 19th century, was it historical accident alone that a "free enterprise," a free and equal democracy, an "open" class system, a free choice of religious and associational membership, and a free choice of mate in a small, ego-reckoned family structure, should all have historically coincided?

In our particular project we could not decide such large matters of history and sociology, but we could ask the second question already mentioned above, Where outside the recent Western world, in the ethnographic record, would we find anything resembling or parallel to this? If it did exist elsewhere, did any parallel connections unite economic behavior and social arrangements and institutions?

To get an answer to the second question we might have turned to several places, perhaps to Japan, Mexico, Melanesia or ancient Greece. For all of them some reporters have claimed free or near-free markets. But we turned instead to Barbary, where the Berber hill tribes have markets that may well be free and where *mutatis mutandis* other free, not to say anarchic, institutions mark a very ancient and interesting civilization of perhaps some common origins with our own but certainly outside it today. A chapter of this book records what seems to be another case of near-free markets there. Let the reader judge for himself, as he will judge the joint efforts of institutional economist and anthropologist in the other treatments of problems in different or alternative economic behaviors, motives, and systems in this book, if we have rightly or wrongly discovered the connections between culture trait, economic institution, and common denominator social arrangement in this case as in the others.

The present work reflects research carried on by the undersigned collectively, in free cooperation, during the 1953–1955 period. The manuscript of a previous work of Polanyi—summing up his 1948–1952 results in a more personal vein—should, however, be mentioned here. It was prepared by him in collaboration with his students, Charles S. Silberman and Rosemary Arnold, then research assistants on the staff of the C. R. S. Sc. project; his wife Mrs. Ilona Polanyi acted as editorial assistant. On leave during the Winter Term 1949–1950, aided by the C. R. S. Sc., Polanyi made studies on Dahomey in the British Museum. In chapters VIII and IX on this subject, by Rosemary Arnold, particular indebtedness to the C. R. S. Sc. has been acknowledged. Chapter VIII consists of passages assembled from previous texts for submission to the University Seminar in 1953; Chapter IX, as it stands, was written by her for the C. R. S. Sc. project. In her case, as in that of Charles S. Silberman, Polanyi welcomes the opportunity to acknowledge the vital contribution of his collaborators in his as yet unpublished work.

We wish to acknowledge our debt to the institutions which made our work possible. We can single out, in grateful memory, the officers of the Behavioral Sciences Division of the Ford Foundation, of the Columbia University Council for Research in the Social Sciences and those of the University administration and of our respective departments of Economics and Anthropology, together with the administration of the University Seminars, particularly Professors Frank Tannenbaum and Arthur R. Burns, all at Columbia University, who gave both material support for the complicated interdisciplinary work of our project and platforms for our many hours of discussion and conference.

Vital encouragement came from Professors Robert M. MacIver, Paul F. Lazarsfeld and Robert K. Merton of the Sociology Department; steadfast support from Professors John M. Clark, Joseph Dorfman,

Carter Goodrich, David S. Landes, and William Vickrey of the Economics Department, all at Columbia. Many others contributed ideas and ideals; moral, intellectual, and technical assistance, running the gamut from the dedicated fellow-scholar to the interested observer; from the authority in his field to the challenging student. Amongst these were Dr. M. I. Finley, Fellow of Jesus College, Cambridge; the Rev. Professor R. J. Williams, University of Toronto; Professor Julius Lewy, Union Hebrew Seminary, Cincinnati; Professor Gregory Vlastos, Princeton University; Professor John Murra, Vassar College; Professor Albrecht Götze, Yale University; Professor Bert F. Hoselitz, University of Chicago, together with Rivkah Harris and R. F. G. Sweet of the Oriental Institute of the University of Chicago; Professor Peter F. Drucker, New York University; Professors Isaac Mendelsohn and Martin Ostwald of Columbia University; Professors Morton Fried and Margaret Mead, together with Sidney Greenfield, Thomas Hazard, Dr. Marshall Sahlins, Donna Chrablow Taylor and Dr. Andrew Peter Vayda, all of the Department of Anthropology, Columbia University; also Drs. Robert Hennion and Cohn-Haft, while at Columbia. Miss Lucy Lowe's able professional services in the way of technical editing also deserve acknowledgement.

Thanks are also due to the Carnegie Institution of Washington for permission to adapt the map from *The Maya Chontal Indians of Acalan-Tixchel: A Contribution to the History and Ethnography of the Yucatan Peninsula*, by France V. Scholes and Ralph L. Roys. We are also indebted to Lee Hunt for his expert assistance in adapting this map and for his beautiful execution of the endpaper maps.

We owe a debt of another kind to Professor Talcott Parsons of Harvard University. If his work is the subject, in essence, of two of our chapters, it is because that work is important and will certainly live in future social science in much of its contribution to our knowledge of institutions and social process. It was possible here to discuss *Economy and Society*, forthcoming almost at the same time as our own book, only because he sent us the manuscript graciously and forebearingly.

Karl Polanyi
Conrad M. Arensberg

November 15, 1956
New York

The Authors

Conrad M. Arensberg
PROFESSOR OF ANTHROPOLOGY
CO-DIRECTOR: INTERDISCIPLINARY
  PROJECT
COLUMBIA UNIVERSITY

Rosemary Arnold
INSTRUCTOR IN ECONOMICS
BARNARD COLLEGE

Francisco Benet
RESEARCH ASSOCIATE IN ANTHROPOLOGY
INTERDISCIPLINARY PROJECT
COLUMBIA UNIVERSITY

Anne C. Chapman
RESEARCH ASSOCIATE IN ANTHROPOLOGY
INTERDISCIPLINARY PROJECT
COLUMBIA UNIVERSITY

Daniel B. Fusfeld
ASSISTANT PROFESSOR OF ECONOMICS
MICHIGAN STATE UNIVERSITY

Terence K. Hopkins
INSTRUCTOR IN SOCIOLOGY
COLUMBIA UNIVERSITY

Walter C. Neale
INSTRUCTOR IN ECONOMICS
YALE UNIVERSITY

A. L. Oppenheim
PROFESSOR OF ASSYRIOLOGY
ORIENTAL INSTITUTE
UNIVERSITY OF CHICAGO

Harry W. Pearson
ASSISTANT PROFESSOR OF ECONOMICS
EXECUTIVE SECRETARY: INTERDISCIPLIN-
  ARY PROJECT
ADELPHI COLLEGE

Karl Polanyi
VISITING PROFESSOR OF ECONOMICS
1947–1953
DIRECTOR: INTERDISCIPLINARY PROJECT
COLUMBIA UNIVERSITY

Robert B. Revere
RESEARCH ASSISTANT IN HISTORY
INTERDISCIPLINARY PROJECT
COLUMBIA UNIVERSITY

Contents

Introductory Note

MOST of us have been accustomed to think that the hallmark of the economy is the market—an institution quite familiar to us. Similarly, our inquiries into general economic history have usually been concerned with market activities or their antecedents.

What is to be done, though, when it appears that some economies have operated on altogether different principles, showing a widespread use of money, and far-flung trading activities, yet no evidence of markets or gain made on buying and selling? It is then that we must re-examine our notions of the economy.

The conceptual problem arises in marketless economies where there is no "economizing," i.e., no institutional framework to compel the individual to "rational" and "efficient" economic activity, or "optimum" allocation of his resources. Economizing action may be present in various aspects of behavior, e.g., in regard to one's time, energy, or one's theoretical assumptions, but the economy need contain no institutions of exchange to reflect these principles in the individual's daily life as they have done in our own day. In that case the economy would not be subject to economic analysis since this presumes economizing behavior with supporting institutional paraphernalia, e.g., price-making markets, all-purpose money and market trade.

Thus the main task of this book is conceptual: it argues that only a small number of alternative patterns for organizing man's livelihood exist and it provides us with tools for the examination of nonmarket economies. These tools are applied in a series of empirical researches, although the underlying theory transcends them.

The aim is not to reject economic analysis, but to set its historical and institutional limitations, namely, to the economies where price-making markets have sway, and to transcend these limitations in a general theory of economic organization.

It is particularly as economists and as economic historians that we may have to revise our traditional assumptions. Some will be inclined to reject as of no interest economies which do not "economize," i.e., have no institutions for economizing action. They may regard the empirical and conceptual work advanced here as presenting no more than unimportant and irrational shards on the fringes of history. Others may even maintain that nothing is advanced here that is not amenable to treatment by economic analysis or some variation of the maximization theorem.

However, many unfortunate consequences follow from an approach that restricts our view of the economy to market activity. It is an impoverished economic history that narrows its concern to markets or market antecedents, for these may be only fragmentary aspects of the economy. The economy would then falsely seem to be in unilineal evolution to our own day, whereas in fact other economies need not be miniatures or early specimens of our own, but may be sharply at variance with it, both as to individual motives and organization.

Technological progress is cumulative and unbounded, but economic organization is not. There are only a few general ways in which the economy may be organized. It is this limitation of the possible patterns of economic organization and their effective combinations which gives to the thoughts and data offered here some topicality. In the receding rule of the market in the modern world, shapes reminiscent of the economic organization of earlier times make their appearance. Of course we stand firmly committed to the progress and freedoms which are the promise of modern society. But a purposeful use of the past may help us to meet our present overconcern with economic matters and to achieve a level of human integration, that comprises the economy, without being absorbed in it.

It is this which makes economic history come alive and throw light on the changing roles of economies in history and society.

PART I

Birth of the Economy

I

The Secular Debate
on Economic Primitivism

———•———

FOR MORE than sixty years a debate has been raging in the field of economic history. Many features have faded out, some were irrelevant from the start. Yet it contained—and still contains—the elements of one of the most significant divergencies in the human sciences. It would not be easy to find a more suitable introduction than this controversy to the interpretive problems involved in the study of archaic economic institutions.

The theorem about which the storm of discussion ultimately centered was first propounded by Rodbertus in the middle 1860's. The actual controversy started some thirty years later between Karl Bücher and Eduard Meyer; it was at its height about the turn of the century. Subsequently Max Weber and Michael Rostovtzeff took their stand. Several others made important contributions.[1]

No more illuminating introduction to this conflict of views could be found than Friedrich Oertel's oft-quoted statement of the issues as he summed them up in 1925:

Are we to conceive of the economy of antiquity as having reached a high level of development, or, on the contrary, as essentially primitive? Should the 5th and 4th centuries B.C. be regarded as an age of national and international business, a receding agriculture, an advancing industry, large scale manufacturing managed on capitalistic lines and growing in scope, with fac-

3

tories working for export and competing with one another for sales in the world market?

Or should we assume, on the contrary, that the stage of the closed "household economy" had not yet passed; that economic activity had not attained a national, even less an international scale; that no organized commerce involving long-distance trading was carried on and that, consequently, no large-scale industry producing for foreign markets existed? In brief, was the character of economic life still agrarian rather than industrial? Was commerce still restricted to a peddling of particular wares, the work of craftsmen producing without the aid of machinery and using the raw materials that were locally available to them?[2]

Oertel termed the first the positive, the latter the negative theory. Johannes Hasebroek, more appropriately, called the first the modernizing, the latter the primitivist view. But careful examination of the terms employed by Oertel to describe the issues involved in the dispute as well as the various attempts to characterize the opposing positions serves well to indicate the lack of conceptual clarity which has dogged the controversy from the beginning. Debates such as this are resolved either by the appearance of new evidence or by the conceptual clarification of the problem so that the previously existing evidence falls into new perspective. In this case, the facts, on what we will call the operational level, can no longer be in dispute. It is, rather, the interpretation of these facts at the institutional level which remains unsettled.

The οικος Theorem: Karl Rodbertus

The origins of this controversy go back to Rodbertus' essay on *Economic Life in Classical Antiquity*, which appeared over the years 1864–1867. The second part of this essay dealt with the "History of Roman Tributes from the Time of Augustus."[3] Here Rodbertus contrasted sharply modern and ancient taxation systems. His approach was highly suggestive. Modern taxation, he wrote, differentiates between personal and property taxes; these latter are either taxes on landed property or taxes on capital; capital, again, is either industrial or commercial, and the latter is invested either in goods or in money (i.e., either in industry or in finance). All these types of property appear as distinct from one another; indeed they appertain to different social classes. Distinctions analogous to those regarding property are also made in regard to incomes. We distinguish purely personal incomes, such as wages or salaries, which are due to the use of labor power, from income that derives from impersonal property, or title to ownership, such as rent; this latter may be either rent from land or profit; profit, again, is split up into interest and entrepreneurial profit.

"This state of affairs," Rodbertus concluded, "resulted in a modern expanding economy."[4] The various stages of production are here linked with one another through the process of buying and selling. In this fashion varying claims to a share in the national dividend are created which take the form of money incomes.

This remarkably modern view of the social function of money has not been sufficiently appreciated. Rodbertus realized that the transition from a "natural economy" to a "money economy" was not simply a technical matter, which resulted from a substitution of money purchase for barter. He insisted instead that a monetarized economy involved a social structure entirely different from that which went with an economy in kind. It was this change in the *social* structure accompanying the use of money rather than the technical fact of its use which ought to be emphasized, he thought. Had this point been expanded to include the varying social structures accompanying trading activity in the ancient world the controversy might have been resolved before it began.

Instead the "household" or "*oikos*" held the center of the stage. With Rodbertus the *oikos* was no more than a logical construct, a kind of anticipation of a Weberian "Ideal type." He invented the term, "lord of the *oikos*"[5] to designate the owner of all the various titles to property and the corresponding incomes listed above. All this was designed to illustrate how, instead of a multitude of differentiated taxes, the ancient Romans knew only one tax, the *tributum* paid by the lord of the *oikos* whose revenue was a compound of all those various kinds of incomes which had been fragmented by the modern "money economy."

For Rodbertus the *oikos* was typified by the vast Roman slave-worked domain, but historical confusion is apparent in a tendency to speak of the *oikos* without reference to any definite period. The term *oikos* thus became merely a peg upon which to hang the concept of economy in kind under which money, markets, and exchange were at a discount, in spite of the existence of an elaborate organization of production.

The essential element in this speculative theory upon which controversy later hinged was Rodbertus' statement that in this *oikos* economy

Nowhere does buying and selling intervene, nowhere do goods change
hands. Since the national dividend never changes hands, it nowhere splits
up into various income categories as in modern times. . . . All this necessi-
tated economy-in-kind. No money was needed to make the national dividend pass from one phase of production to the other, since no change of
ownership was involved.[6]

Karl Bücher and Eduard Meyer

Here the matter might have rested had it not been for Karl Bücher's
path-breaking work, *Die Entstehung der Volkswirtschaft*, first published in 1893. The great achievement of Bücher was to link the study
of economic life in the ancient world with primitive economics. His
aim was to establish a general theory of economic development from
primitive to modern times. He did not equate classical antiquity with
primitive society, but by emphasizing the relatively recent tribal origins
of ancient Greek and Roman society, he suggested that ancient economic life might better be understood if viewed from the perspective
of primitive rather than modern society.

Regarding our specific interest his thesis was that not before the
emergence of the modern state do we find a *Volkswirtschaft*, i.e., a
complex economic life on larger than a city scale. Up to the year 1000
A.D. the economy never passed beyond the stage of closed domestic
economy (*geschlossene Hauswirtschaft*) where production was solely
for one's own needs, involving no exchange between the household
units. The economic life of the Greeks, Carthaginians and Romans, he
said, was typified by this *oikos* economy. (Here he referred to Rodbertus.)[7]

Bücher later conceded that before the development of a large scale
slave economy, there was a much larger amount of free wage labor, professional services, and exchange in general. However he still maintained
his thesis in the following form: Complex economic life of a territorial
character on a large scale (*Volkswirtschaft*) is the result of a development covering a period of thousands of years, and is no older than the
modern state. Prior to this, mankind existed over long stretches of time
without any system of exchange of goods and services that deserves
the name of a complex economic life on a national scale.[8]

By settling on the self-sufficient *oikos* as the central unit of ancient
society and placing this construct in a speculative theory of economic

development, Bücher forced himself into the position of having to deny the significance of trade and money in ancient society. Thus the unfortunate *oikos* theorem cast the die of the controversy which was to ensue, and provided an easy target for Eduard Meyer who vigorously challenged Bücher's position in 1895.[9]

Meyer summed up his opposing thesis in the dictum that, ". . . the later period of antiquity was in essence entirely modern."[10] In support of this he adduced evidence on a number of points which seemed decisive: "The ancient world possessed an articulated economic life with a highly developed system of transportation and an intensive exchange of commodities."[11] "In the ancient Orient we meet from the earliest recorded time with a highly developed manufacturing industry, a general system of commerce, and the use of precious metals as the means of exchange."[12] Here he went on to say that since 2500 B.C. Babylonia produced numerous documents referring to private business transactions in regard to slaves, land and buildings, dividing of property at death, etc. There we find a developed system of accountancy in terms of gold and silver, which spread all over the civilized world and served as a basis for coinage. The central point which seemed to prove the economic modernity of the ancient world was that, "Trade and money were of fundamental importance in the economic life of the ancients."[13]

Meyer's position is what Hasebroek has called the "modernizing" attitude, what Oertel described as the "positive" approach, while Salvioli termed it the historians' view. A more precise designation for this position might be "the market-oriented" view. Our modern world is indeed characterized by an unprecedented development of productive power, an international trade network, and the use of money as a universal means of exchange. By suggesting that the ancient world had begun on the same line Meyer was, of course, adopting a "modernizing" attitude. It was also "positive" in the sense that it attributed these elements to ancient civilization; and it did represent the nineteenth-century historians' traditional view. But these terms do not convey the central feature of Meyer's position. The pivotal institution of the modern economy is the market. It is under its aegis that production, trade and money are integrated into a self-contained economic system. And the crucial point in regard to the position of Meyer and the "modernists" is that in asserting the *existence* of large scale manufacturing, trade and money, they also assumed their *organization* to follow the market pattern. But whether or not these elements of any specific economy are so organized is a point for investigation at least equally as important as the fact of their existence. The fact that the debate turned so much upon the exclusive importance of the *oikos* obscured this point and thereby weakened the position of the "primitivists." The "evidence" clearly turned against them.

The long-distance carrying and exchange of goods and the use of money objects were indeed widely spread features of ancient economic life, and in 1932 Michael Rostovtzeff was able to state that the *oikos* position was then held by almost no one.[14] But this was a pyrrhic victory for the market-oriented position. The *oikos* had been a spurious issue from the start. Once that thesis was thoroughly discredited the argument could move to the level on which it should have begun. On this level there is no disputing the "facts" regarding the physical movements of slaves, grain, wine, oil, pottery; their changing hands between distant peoples, nor can one deny some local exchanges between city and countryside. There is likewise no question of the use of money objects. The question is, how were these elements of economic life institutionalized to produce the continuous goods and person movements essential to a stable economy?

Max Weber and Michael Rostovtzeff

It was the genius of Max Weber which eventually permitted the debate to reach this level. Accepting neither the "primitive" nor the "modern" approach to the problem, Weber admitted that there were some similarities between the economy of the European ancient world at the height of its development and that of the later medieval period, but he emphasized the unique characteristics of ancient culture which for him made all the difference.[15]

The force which moved the Greek and Roman economies in their special direction, according to Weber, was the general military-political orientation of ancient culture. War in ancient times was the hunt for men and economic advantages were won through the ceaseless wars and, in peace, by political means. Even the cities, although superficially like those of the Middle Ages in economic outline, were essentially different in total outlook and organization.

Taken in its entirety . . . the city democracy of antiquity is a political guild. Tribute, booty, the payments of confederate cities, were merely distributed among the citizens. . . . The monopoly of the political guild included cleruchy, the distribution of conquered land among the citizens, and the distribution of the spoils of war; and at the last the city paid out of the proceeds of its political activity theater admissions, allotments of grain, and payments for jury service and for participation in religious rites.[16]

Weber thus opened the way to a new interpretation of the "facts," over which there was now little dispute. No victim of a preconceived stage theory of economic development, his approach showed the possibility of a relatively high level of economic organization existing in a societal framework basically different from that of the modern market system.

It can hardly be said, however, that Weber resolved the issues in this secular debate, for while he sketched in the outlines of a new approach, he did not provide the conceptual tools with which to answer specific questions regarding trade organization, money uses, and methods of exchange. And although Johannes Hasebroek's detailed and masterful elaboration of Weber's thesis in 1931[17] secured an important victory for the so-called "primitivist" side, Michael Rostovtzeff's questioning opposition proved that all the issues had not thereby been resolved.

Rostovtzeff conceded that the class warfare and revolutions which created the democracy of the Greek city states were of a different character than those which established capitalism in the modern western world, and that the ideals of the new society retained the color of the chieftain's society which had preceded it.[18] But in effect this merely moved forward the time setting of the controversy. Rostovtzeff argued that the debate should focus on the high point of ancient economic development, that is, the Hellenistic and early Roman period. And regarding this period, Rostovtzeff stood firm: "As far as I am concerned, the difference between the economic life of this period and that of the modern world is only quantitative, not qualitative."[19] To deny this, Rostovtzeff declared, would be to deny that the ancient world had achieved any economic development over four thousand years.

Like Oertel, Rostovtzeff maintained that the controversy was made up of this dilemma: did the ancient world in its long existence go through a development similar to that of the modern world or was the whole ancient world based upon a primitive stage of economic life? He labeled the closed household theorem an ideal construction which never existed, above all not in Greece where there was an active trade with the highly developed Oriental empires. And did the Ionian Greeks gain nothing from the cities of the Near East where they settled? "Surely something must have happened!"[20]

This statement of Rostovtzeff's view of the issues in the *oikos* controversy appeared in 1932, and thus represented the culmination of nearly forty years of debate since the publication of Bücher's book in 1893. Yet it is remarkable how little clarification of the issues had been achieved; opposing sides still clashed in a conceptual twilight.

The source of the confusion now appears obvious. *Both* sides, with the partial exception of Weber, were unable to conceive of an elaborate economy with trade, money, and market places being organized in any manner other than that of the market system. The "primitivists," who insisted that the ancient world was different from the modern, sought their support in the *oikos*, which to them represented an earlier stage in the development of the self-same market system. The "modernists" saw Greece and Rome resting on a foundation four thousand years in the building, which included the high economic and cultural life of the ancient Near East. Meyer emphasized the high economic development of this area and Rostovtzeff the contact between it and Greek and Roman culture. To them it was inconceivable that such a long period, full of cultural achievement, would not produce an economy at least up to the level of the later medieval period. As Rostovtzeff declared, "Something must have happened!"

But what if those four thousand years of development had moved along different lines than those of the modern world? Then the perspective from which Greece and Rome should be viewed would have to be shifted. Not capitalism, then, but a different organization of economic life would be the model from which to judge the high period of ancient economy. Bücher's primitivist perspective and Weber's military-political approach had suggested this view of the question. But neither Bücher nor Weber had provided adequate conceptual tools for recognizing what had happened, i.e., the institutional foundations of this different sort of economic development.

The following chapters of this work are devoted to this task. Exploring anew the position of trade, money, and market in the Mediterranean empires, a radically new perspective is gained from which to view the economic life of the people of the Old World. This perspective gives a much broader range to the issues of the *oikos* debate. For now the elements of markets and commercial trade which appear in the Greek classical and Hellenistic periods are seen not as the heritage of over four thousand years of Mesopotamian development, but as portentous new inventions seeking a place in Greek culture.

Harry W. Pearson

Notes to Chapter I

1. No attempt has been made in this chapter to summarize all of the contributions to this debate; the intent here is to present only the essential outlines. The best bibliographies are to be found in M. I. Rostovtzeff, *Social and Economic History of the Hellenistic World*, III (Oxford, 1941), 1327–28, fn. 25; and, more recently in Eduard Will, "Trois quarts de siècle de recherches sur l'economie grécque antique," *Annales*, IX (January–March, 1954).

2. Friedrich Oertel, Supplement and comments appended to Robert Pöhlmann, *Geschichte der sozialen Frage und des Sozialismus in der antiken Welt*, 3d ed., III (Munich, 1925), 516–17.

3. Karl Rodbertus, "Zur Geschichte der römischen Tributsteuern," *Jahrbücher für Nationalökonomie und Statistik*, IV (1865), 339 and passim.

4. *Ibid.*, p. 342.

5. *Ibid.*, p. 344.

6. *Ibid.*, pp. 345–6.

7. Karl Bücher, *Industrial Evolution*, English translation (New York, 1912), pp. 96–97.

8. *Ibid.*, p. 88.

9. This challenge was delivered in Meyer's address to the third meeting of the German historians at Frankfort in 1895. The address, "Die wirtschaftliche Entwicklung des Altertums," is published in Eduard Meyer, *Kleine Schriften* (Halle, 1924), pp. 79 ff.

10. *Ibid.*, p. 89.

11. *Ibid.*, p. 88.

12. *Ibid.*, p. 90.

13. *Ibid.*, p. 88.

14. Cf. his review of J. Hasebroek, *Zeitschrift für die Gesammte Staatswissenschaft*, 92 (1932), 334.

15. "Die sozialen Gründe des Untergangs der antiken Kultur," *Gesammelte Aufsätze zur Sozial-und Wirtschaftsgeschichte* (Tübingen, 1924), pp. 289–311. See also *Wirtschaft und Gesellschaft*, ch. 8 (Tübingen, 1922).

16. Max Weber, *General Economic History* (Glencoe, Illinois, 1950), p. 331.

17. *Griechische Wirtschafts-und Gesellschaftsgeschichte* (Tübingen, 1931).

18. *Op. cit.*, p. 337.

19. *Ibid.*, p. 335, n. 1.

20. *Ibid.*, p. 338.

II

Marketless Trading in Hammurabi's Time

———•———

AT one stage or another in the history of almost any field of study, the condition may obtain that the more ample the facts that come to our cognizance the less do they appear to fit into a pattern. In regard to the Babylonian economy, Max Weber showed himself conscious of deep-seated difficulties as early as 1909, but never returned to the issue. Among the Assyriologists themselves symptoms of *malaise* were noticeable only comparatively late, but then all the more significantly. Paul Koschaker, who time and again warned against some of the assumptions made by the earlier pioneers, eventually complained that his own efforts had reached a dead end. His study on economic administration in the Old Babylonian state (1942) closed, in his own words, "on a discordant and sceptical note." It had not been found possible, he intimated, satisfactorily to apply transactional terms to the process of governmental trading as it was recorded in the documents of Larsa; we might, he added, for the time being have to resign ourselves to the inadequacy of rational concepts to cope with the administrative irrationalities of what he arraigned as hyperbureaucratic trading methods. In this particular phrasing, a policy bias may be deemed to have interfered with that great scholar's clarity of vision. However such a view would bypass the heart of the matter. The anything but anti-socialist V. Gordon Childe also failed to disperse the obscurities surrounding the early form of economic life in that area. His theory of an "urban revolution," reflecting the results of the spectacular advance of the archaeology of prehistory, nevertheless, offers no answer to the question how production and trade were organized. It should be assumed, therefore, that the obstacles to a deeper insight transcended any preferences of historical philosophy or economic policy. Indeed, there may be strong reasons to believe that the frustration with which the inquiring mind has met in the field of the Babylonian economy is only the latest phase of that secular perplexity which for almost a century went under the name of *oikos* controversy, as presented in the previous chapter. The issue was roughly, whether at the highest point of its development the society of classical Greece and Rome in its economic aspects was essentially modern or primitive.

Pseudo-economy and Inverted Perspective

In retrospect it is not too difficult to see why, even where there was broad agreement on the facts, interpretation remained elusive. Actually, the question at issue was the extent to which the economy, in its various spheres, was organized through markets. Evidence of functioning markets is not so readily available as might be supposed. Even under modern conditions it is often a delicate matter to ascertain whether at a definite time and place a supply-demand-price mechanism for a definite good or service is in operation or not. For the distant past direct evidence may not be at hand. We are then forced back to relying on such indirect evidence as those culture traits that commonly denote the presence of markets and market activities in a society. But this type of evidence is deceptive. Traits superficially recalling a business men's culture may occur independently of markets and even of the economy altogether. Famous instances of pseudo-economies, such as the potlatch or the Kula trade, details of which sometimes are almost a mimicry of stock-jobbers' activities, abound with the Manus of the Great Admiralty Islands, the Tolowa-Tututni of California or the Kwakiutl of the North West Coast. Habits not intrinsically economic, such as the urge of gambling, competition in auctioneering, rigid accountancy, the lure of risk, pride in a public turnover, which occur in modern business life, also play a vital part in the social fabric of primitive communities. Obviously, the presence of such pseudo-economic traits is not proof of functioning markets. Moreover—yet another ambiguity—some genuine economic institutions that in their elaborate form we justly regard as having arisen only in modern times are found to have occurred under archaic conditions as well. However, while as to its structure the institution may be similar, its function may be very different. In its early, premarket form it acted as a substitute for markets; in its market form it is, on the contrary, *supplementary* to the existing market. Examples: In recent centuries business life produced complex credit structures and clearing systems, elaborate forms of brokerage, and special purpose moneys. All of these must be regarded as new. Yet, in much less complex forms similar institutions had existed before, in early societies. The explanation is simple. Where barter is widespread, credit, brokerage, clearing or money used as a standard help to carry on barter and thus make up for the absence of exchange-money and markets.

To use modern terms, it may be said that in these cases the lack of functioning markets calls for a substitute for markets. In the absence of money employed as a means of exchange there is often a large-scale public storage of staples with the concomitant practice of carrying debt accounts of individuals, and accompanying clearing practices. Though money is not used as a means of exchange, it may well be employed as a standard as well as a means of payment, different goods being used for the different purposes. Brokerage and auction are then the usual devices of arranging for exchange. With the development of markets such practices, of course, become superfluous and tend to disappear, until much later they reappear again, only this time in a sophisticated form and in the new role of assisting the functioning of highly developed markets. Typical of such a recurrence of institutional traits and operational devices which made their reappearance in our days, is the field which we call banking. Historically the appearance of money-changers, these earliest bankers, *preceded* the general use of coined money. Even branch banking reached a high development in Ptolemaic Egypt, where it served as a means of running an advanced planned economy in kind, without markets or money as a means of exchange. Actually, the clearing of obligations between traders' accounts appears to have been general fifteen hundred years prior to Ptolemaic Egypt, in the "early Assyrian" trade, in the absence not only of price-making markets, but even of coined money.

To sum up: The elusive element in the *oikos* controversy was the role of the market on which in reality the issues centered even though with no sufficient awareness of this circumstance on the part of the disputants. Translated into these terms, Rodbertus stressed that in the absence of a market system taxation in the Late Roman Empire would naturally be based on a general property tax put on the practically self-sufficient households of the big slave-owning landowners. Bücher, again in these terms, recognized that modern economies were integrated through national markets, themselves largely creations of the state, a development that had never occurred before. Finally, Weber's position on capitalism in antiquity as well as that of Rostovtzeff boiled down to the factual question to what extent, large or small, was the economic process in ancient Rome at other times and in its other aspects instituted through markets. But in asserting the presence of markets we must carefully avoid a dangerous pitfall. Economic acitivities under advanced market conditions may resemble similar activities under premarket conditions while their function is quite different. The distinction between pre- and postmarket should help to avoid that "inverted perspective," as it might be called, which sometimes induced historians to see strikingly "modern" phenomena in antiquity where in fact they were faced by typically primitive or archaic ones.

Problems of the Babylonian Economy

Paul Koschaker in 1942 was indeed much less confident of our grasp of the Babylonian economy than Eduard Meyer had been in 1895. The underlying reasons will now become apparent.

Shortly after Bücher's and Meyer's clash of views, the find was made of the obsidian stele on which the Code of Hammurabi was displayed. To all intents and purposes it contained a commercial code of law which was (at the time) dated about twenty-five centuries before our era.* The significance of the sheaves of clay tablets relating to business matters that had been previously unearthed now stood revealed. Civilization, so much seemed evident, had been born from man's commercial instincts; and the cradle of our own world, that of a businessmen's culture, had been uncovered in Babylonia; to argue the primitive character of the economic life of antiquity in the face of these facts was no more than a fad. A series of scholars whose critical faculties

---

* More recently dated around the second half of the XVII century B.C.

have been rarely surpassed in any field of learning testified to the collective findings. There was no lack of differences between them on detail, nor of the recognition of important lacunae—but as to the general character of the economy, the ethos of the participants, the attitudes and value scales on which they oriented their behavior, no doubt could prevail. We had here before us the very essence of a capitalistically minded business community, in which king and god alike engaged in profiteering, making the best of their chances in lending money at usury and imbuing a whole civilization with the spirit of money-making over millennia. It is against this climate of opinion that the doubts here voiced in regard to the actual organization of the economic life of the ancient Near East should be viewed.

In terms of our interpretation of the *oikos* controversy the impasse can be succinctly formulated. Babylonian economic life had necessarily appeared as a complex of activities ultimately depending on the functioning of an underlying market system. Markets were the rock bottom on which rested with axiomatic assurance the determination of forms of trade, money uses, prices, commercial transactions, profit and loss accounts, insolvency, partnership, in short, the essentials of business life. It follows that in the absence of such markets these explanations of the economic institutions and their way of functioning must fall to the ground.

We submit that this precisely is the case. Babylonia, as a matter of fact, possessed neither market places nor a functioning market system of any description.

This recognition, which supplies the main thesis of this chapter arises out of a number of mutually supporting groups of facts:

(1) Herodotus, who visited Babylon some time between 470 and 460 B.C., asserted with the greatest possible emphasis that "the Persians do not frequent market places and in effect, do not possess in their country a single market place." (Her. I, 153.) This passage was consistently ignored by economic historians of Mesopotamia.

(2) Even a superficial survey of the legal character of economic transactions from the Old Babylonian period down to Persian times showed the soundness of the accepted view that in spite of the intervening "Dark Ages" no striking change in the nature and character of these transactions had ever occurred.

(3) It appeared as a matter of common sense that market places, had they been present to any extent in Hammurabi's time, would

hardly have disappeared so thoroughly as to be beyond reviving during that upsurge of business activities which took place a thousand years later, and in the wake of which Herodotus was visiting Babylon.

(4) According to reliable archaeological evidence the walled towns of Palestine (with the single exception of Hellenistic Jerusalem) possessed right down to their destruction no open spaces whatsoever.

(5) The chief market place of Babylon would offer a landmark not easily overlooked. Yet contemporary literary records of the names, sites and layout of temples and avenues of that city which were discovered in the library of Ashur-banipal indicated no open space of this kind.

(6) Some half dozen different words occurring in various cuneiform documents and translated in different contexts as "market" turned out on closer inquiry either not to mean "market place" at all or at least to be doubtful.

(7) Eventually, partial confirmation was received in February, 1953, from A. L. Oppenheim, in these terms: "As to your specific questions: Archaeological evidence speaks against the existence of 'market places' within the cities of the Ancient Near East."*

An Early Assyrian Trading Post

A rough outline of accounts of an early Assyrian trading post that existed over a century in the period of Hammurabi in the center of Asia Minor shall provide us with a generalized version of how Assyriologists only a few decades ago conceived of the organization of trade in this admittedly specific case. Such a broad survey shall throw into relief the problems that must arise if the traditional view—based on the assumption of markets is to be replaced by another resting on the same data yet barring that assumption. It will hardly be possible to avoid some repetitiousness, when contrasting the composite scene as it emerges from our sources—the two main publications, that of Landsberger in 1925, and Eisser-J. Lewy in 1935—with the tentative picture we here suggest as an alternative. The first publication was admittedly conjectural—unavoidably so, in view of the gaps in the evidence; also it justly claimed the right to a free rendering of the selected illustrative material, so as to round off the original texts where meticulous precision could have produced but inarticulate fragments. The

* See below, pp. 30–31.

second publication, a decade later, comprised the bulk of the then transliterated tablets, and was roughly in accordance with the first, from which it differed, apart from detail, mainly in literal accuracy and legal elaboration. Landsberger had offered a brilliant sequence of life-like scenes, suggestive of the drama of business; Eisser-J. Lewy supplied philological comment and juridical systematization. We will keep this brief and inevitably elliptic sketch of their presentations to three points: personnel and incentives; the nature of the goods; the character of the activities.

Near Kanish, on the river Halys, we have a settlement of Assyrian merchants, members of the so-called *karum*, businessmen who make profit on buying and selling, partnership, loaning and investing. The records are ample; they cover some three generations and end abruptly. The merchants act as middlemen between the distant city of Assur, to which they themselves belong by race, religion and language, and be-tween the subjects of a native prince (or princes) of central Anatolia. Whatever its origin, the *rationale* of the trading post as actually or-ganized is the procurement of copper for the City. Profit is made on the sale-purchase of goods, on loans—short or long—on participations and as between the members of the firm, on a share in the profit. The firm is a family affair, though not exclusively so. Frequently a journey-man or junior partner, in reward for his services as a traveler, is accorded an interest-free loan, in money or goods, which he is permitted to use for trading on his own account (*be'ulatum*). The main driving force in business is the big man in Ashshur (*ummeanum*), who provides the goods, lends the money, invests sums over a long term against interest or participation or both. However, some of the more successful gild merchants in Kanish may be doing likewise. Transportation is organ-ized through a special group of carriers, on a commercial basis. Besides these, the anonymous figure of the *tamkarum* is in evidence, whose function, interests and activities are not clear, but evidently important. The goods are, primarily, copper, as we said, which is handled as a monopoly by the *karum* as such. Second, consignment ware such as lead (tin?) and fine cloths from the capital. From Kanish, native cloth and other goods are exported. Silver bars move both ways. Third, "free" goods are mentioned, which are neither subject to "monopoly" nor to consignment. The main activity is sale-purchase, mostly in regard to goods on consignment, on which the merchant can claim a commis-sion. For the rest, his job is to find a customer for the goods and to make the best of the chances of the market. Prices and interest rates fluctuate almost in the stock-exchange manner, so he must keep an eye on them. Dealings amongst the merchants give rise to disputes, often brought to a head by arbitration. In other cases, severe penalties, moral as well as physical, seem to threaten the defaulter at the hand of the authorities. All this would accord well with a system of market trading before coined money was invented and executive organs were set up capable of enforcing court decisions.

Other points appeared to fit in less well with these assumptions. Landsberger did not fail to remark that profits are hardly ever explicitly mentioned, losses practically never, prices are not the center of interest, and dealings amongst merchants are not secured by surety or pledge, as usual in archaic trade. Also the data implied that there was a prohibition on other than cash transactions, at least in regard to consigned goods. Moreover, it was noted that rules were sometimes enforceable under the threat of the death penalty.

So far, the bare outline of the traditional presentation.

Risk-free Trading

It is unavoidable, then, that we take another look at the Assyrian trade settlement and suggest methods of trading suitable in the general circumstances as we see them. Yet in the main we will be merely reinterpreting the above data.

Nonmarket trade—this is the crucial point—is in all essentials different from market trade. This applies to personnel, goods, prices, but perhaps most emphatically to the nature of the trading activity itself.

The traders of the *karum* of Kanish were not merchants in the sense of persons making a living out of the profit derived from buying and selling, i.e., price differentials in regard to the transaction in hand. They were traders by status, as a rule by virtue of descent or early apprenticeship, in other cases maybe, by appointment. Unless the appointment was accompanied by a substantial land grant—as we may assume in the case of the *tamkarum*, but not in that of the members of the gild— their revenue derived from the turnover of goods on which a commission was earned. This was the original source of all "profit," i.e., that pool of goods, including silver, in which eventually the internal members of the firm as well as the external ones, i.e., creditors and partners shared.

The goods were trade goods—storable, interchangeable and standardized, or, as Roman law has it, *quae numero, pondere ac mensura consistunt*. Apart from standard cloths, the chief staples were metals —probably silver, copper, lead and tin, all goods reckoned according to their silver equivalent. Silver, besides functioning as standard, was also, up to a point, a means of payment. The role of gold was much more restricted in both these uses.

"Prices" took the form of equivalencies established by authority of custom, statute or proclamation.* The necessaries of life were supposed to be subject to permanent equivalencies; actually they were subject to long-range changes by the same methods by which they had been established. This need not have affected the trader's revenue, which did not depend on price differentials. In principle there was always a "price," i.e., the equivalency at which the trader both bought and sold. But rules regarding the application of equivalencies were hardly the same for monopoly goods, consignment ware and "free" goods. The numerous qualifying adjectives which accompany the term equivalency refer to the various rules and their effects. The equivalency for copper, "a monopoly," was fixed by treaty over a long term. Copper mining, as organized by the natives, would involve assurances by their chiefs that at least a part of the equivalencies, presumably in goods coveted by the people, would be forthcoming in definite amounts. As to consignment ware, mainly fine cloths manufactured in Assur and imported lead (or tin?), "prices" were similarly fixed and the goods bought and sold at that "price." "Prices" for free goods are especially important, for eventual departures towards market trading were likely to originate from here; in other words, the present meaning of "price" might have developed from equivalencies for "free" goods. The many different adjectives attaching to equivalencies in the Sumerian formulary (also found in Ugarit) as well as the peculiar terminology of Larsa documents indicate that the handling of "equivalencies" must have been subject to administrative rules of an intricate kind. In the twentieth century A.D., this should surprise no one.

However, the chief difference between administrative or treaty trade on the one hand and market trade on the other lies in the trader's activities themselves. In contrast to market trade, those activities are here

* See below, p. 32.

risk-free, both in regard to price expectation and debtor's insolvency.

Price risk is excluded by the absence of price-making markets with their fluctuating prices, and the general organization of trade which does not depend for profit on price differentials, but rather on turnover. Hence that relative lack of concern with prices; absence of the mention of profits on the business in hand; and even more important, mention of losses. In effect, participation in business is participation in profits. This has far-reaching consequences for the forms of trade partnership, which cannot be understood at all unless the discounting of loss on prices, as a general rule, is kept in mind.

There is no risk of debtor's insolvency, and consequently hardly any mention of losses on bad debts. This fact is as incisive in regard to the organization of trade as the absence of risk on prices.

In contrast with modern society, the archaic state makes obligations towards the public hand *stricti juris*, while obligations toward the private need not always be so. He to whom public goods are entrusted must unfailingly be able to produce either the goods themselves or their equivalent. This fits in well with the practice of *in rem* transactions (Zug um Zug, didontes kai labontes) and the exclusion of credit. Several known features of Karum-trading follow: (1) No sale except for cash. (2) The Kanish trader receives his consignment of goods against security to the value of the goods. (3) Obligations against third parties must be registered with the competent authority, City, Karum or Palace (in the case of natives); hence, in principle, all obligations are guaranteed by the public hand. Under treaty trade this rule is widely attested. (4) The public hand assumes here no risks, since it would refuse to guarantee obligations beyond the security in hand.

In case of fraud or the infringement of the rules of law, the severest penalties are applied.

Taken together all this explains why apparently no default on debt occurs; why arbitration awards are self-executing; how it comes about that the account-keeping authority can simply charge the defaulter's account with the amount awarded to the other party; why membership of the *Karum* and a good standing with the *City* is a precondition of trading; why no pledges to ensure payment are met with; why the interest-free loan employed by the journeyman for trading on his own account, the *be'ulatum*, is never lost; why business knows only profit, not loss.

Under such circumstances of no-risk business along administrative lines, the term "transaction" hardly applies; we will therefore designate this type of activity as "dispositional."

The traders' activities were manifold: copper procurement desigvolved a mining of the ore; its collection and transportation; refinement; storage and payment. The trader's job was to stimulate native mining activity through advances and, perhaps, long-term investments, up to several years duration; to ensure delivery and deposit the copper with the gild office in Kanish. But his main job was to make payment for the copper or whatever else he had bought. Some may have been paid for in refining the copper, some in silver, tin or imported high-grade cloth. The rest of the copper and native cloth were exported, the latter maybe, after having been finished on the spot. All that which was bought with consignment goods went to Assur.

Although the principles of "fixed price," "cash delivery," "legal surety," and "commission on turnover" obtained throughout, the trader's job was far from simple: to make the right contacts among the natives; correctly to judge their requirement of goods; make his financial arrangements in time; conform strictly to rule and regulation; dispose with precision the goods entrusted to him; see to the quality of the wares, either way; procure funds with which to make advances to prospective suppliers, and for deposit with the government; as well as many other matters. Mistakes or omissions meant delay; difficulty in raising loans; small procurement; unnecessary expense; domestic unpleasantness; loss of authority in the family firm; trouble with colleagues and authorities; a reduced turnover. Yet, in this marketless trade there was no loss on prices, no speculation, no failure of debtors. It was exciting as an occupation, but risk-free as a business.

Transactions and Dispositions

This dispositional mode of dealing was the main characteristic of early Assyrian trade. The essential element in the trader's behavior was not a two-sided act resulting in a negotiated contract but a sequence of one-sided declarations of will, to which definite effects were attached under *rules of law* which governed the administrative organization of the treaty trade he was engaged in. It is easy to deduce from this the criteria of dispositional trading.

(1) Acquisition of goods from a distance—the criterion of all au-

thentic trade—was the constitutive element. The procurement of useful objects ran in a peaceful way, goods going in both directions. There was a large professional personnel employed in the acquisitional activities and the actual physical carrying of the wares. The traders derived a revenue from their activities, in which they had a direct financial interest.

(2) Although acting within the frame of a governmental organization and a network of official and semi-official institutions, the trader remained an independent agent. He was in no one's employ, under the orders of no superior, free to expand and contract his business at will, or to discontinue it altogether. If unskilled, lazy or unwise, his earnings would drop. But he need not fear the summons of any employer or higher authority—as long as he kept within the law. The principle of *rule of law* was paramount.

(3) Nevertheless, not even in principle could transactions or *private deals* be banned. The *rationale* of "rule of law" therefore was the institutional separation of the trader's dispositions relating to public business from his private transactions. The trader needed capital to be provided in the form of short or long term loans, or of partnerships; associates, as members of the firm; employees to travel for him and do the neighborhood carrying; he was free to buy and sell non-consigned ware; to loan money to firms and to participate in their profits. Yet at no time was there to be any doubt about the "public" as distinguished from the "private" character of the deal—whether the trader had acted in his public capacity in the course of the copper procurement involving consignments of government ware or apart from this public business, that is, privately. In the former sphere, his steps were formalized and his acts were phrased as dispositions; in the latter sphere, they were informal and could be described as transactions. But of what kind the institutions were, which in the various fields of economic activity permitted such a separation to become effective, is still largely hidden from our view. Did the separation run on the lines of the different kinds of goods in question, the quantities involved, or rather according to the origin of the funds employed, or maybe combinations of these criteria? We do not yet know.

(4) Documents were recorded by public scribes, made out under the supervision of public officials, a copy of the document presumably filed in the official archives, under readily identifiable headings. The state of affairs in regard to any item of business could then at all times

be ascertained at headquarters. The documents themselves were set out with a brevity and precision which enabled the public trustee—the *tamkarum*—to take action at all times if enjoined by an interested party in legitimate possession of a copy of the relevant document.

The Tamkarum

The key to the functions of the *tamkarum* lies in the methods and organization of trading. And vice versa: the key to the understanding of those methods lies in the office of the *tamkarum*. His figure and function are *sui generis*. His primary duties are those of a public trustee; he takes action under the law as soon as an authorized person produces (or rather has read out to him) the appropriate clay tablet, probably leaving a copy; according to the case and the situation, his duty is to advance fares or other small expenses; to accept pledges, as, e.g., of a slave that may have been handed to the gild merchant on the default of his native debtor; to be instrumental in having goods from the City purchased by the gild merchant and (although this does not clearly appear) to deliver on the trader's behalf goods to the City; to facilitate transportation by accepting responsibility for money and goods entrusted to carriers, and also for the safety of the goods bought in the City for the account of the gild trader (in these latter cases a document was made out, addressed to the *tamkarum*, which the creditor could transfer to another gild merchant if he happened to be in need of cash); to have goods auctioned at the trader's request, crediting him with the sum thus recovered, whether it happened to be "more or less" than the equivalency. Other minor services were in the nature of legal advice and legal intervention with the *karum* especially if differences with the natives arose. Also, in case of sudden death of an important gild trader the sequestration of goods and monies as well as liquidation of the firm was done through his immediate intervention. The *tamkarum* derived no revenue from the business in hand, although he may have charged small service fees to the traders according to some fixed scale. His living was ensured through the landed property with which he was invested at his appointment.

If the figure of the *tamkarum* can be outlined only conjecturally, that of the *ummeanum* must frankly be described as obscure. The suggestion made here is no more than a tentative construction that might fit the pattern of risk-free marketless trading, organized in the public interest, primarily on behalf of governmental war material procurement. The financing of such imports would be a public service. While the trade aspects of the matter may be left to the *karum* and the *tamkarum*, respectively, who between them would take care of its efficient performance, the financial side would be seen to by the *ummeanum*. There is, first, the handling of the accounts of the gild traders, including transfers from debtor's to creditor's accounts; secondly, direct investments into this branch of foreign trade so as to increase supply and make it more regular. The *ummeanum*—that much should be taken for granted—was a public figure similar to the *tamkarum*. His investments and partnerships are what we might call treasury advances; these are usually made in round sums of gold ounces (employing units of two ounces) which may indicate the prestige character of the transaction, since gold was treasure. Whether the "big men" of the land were given a chance to invest into this privileged business and thus benefit from the manufactures of dependent labor (particularly female) we cannot be sure. Much speaks for such an extension of palace business to the favored few. Cleomenes of Naukratis compensated the big landholders of Egypt for his introducing of the corn export monopoly by allowing them a profitable share in the governmental syndicate. The King of Dahomey treated his environment with a similar liberality in matters of the royal slave trade, of which he remained, of course, the chief beneficiary.*

When all is said, this type of organization of trade and business was probably unique in history. To what extent it may have served as a model for the port of trade** of late Ugarit, and eventually Sidon, Tyre and Carthage can as yet only be conjectured. So much already appears certain: contrary to traditional notions, Babylonian trade and business activities were not originally market activities.

The next chapter offers a bird's-eye view of Mesopotamian economic history which in more than one regard brings unexpected simplifications. The absence of marketplaces from this picture provided by an expert may be taken as supporting at a vital point the tentative assumptions that underlie our presentation. Admittedly, in no detail does the new prospectus support the many conjectures that were drawn upon in this chapter to give life and plausibility to the views presented here.

If our interpretation is borne out by the facts, the question arises, How, when and where did market trade, fluctuating prices, profit and loss accounts, commercial methods of business, commercial classes and all the paraphernalia of a market organized economy originate? The history of market trade may be found to have shifted by a thousand years downwards and several degrees of longitude westwards, to the Ionia and Greece of the first millenium B.C.

Karl Polanyi

* See below, Ch. VIII.   ** See below, Ch. IV.

III

A Bird's-Eye View of Mesopotamian Economic History

———•———

brevis esse laboro,
obscurus fio; sectantem levia nervi
deficiunt animique; professus grandia turget
Ars Poetica, 25–27

IF ample documentary evidence alone sufficed to serve as a basis for the writing of the economic history of a dead and distant civilization, the very number of cuneiform texts dealing with all aspects of the economic life of Mesopotamia should certainly enable the historian to accomplish this task. Few if any periods of history prior to the flowering of the European Middle Ages are as well documented with regard to private business activities and the dealings of the administrative offices of temples and palaces as certain eras of the history of Babylonia and Assyria. Nowhere else—China and India perhaps excepted— can the rise and development of economic institutions be observed for far more than two millennia.

The number of clay tablets dealing with these matters increases by the thousands every year, and the number of published and unpublished documents approaches the hundred thousand mark with no end in sight. The practically imperishable nature of the writing material combines with the custom of recording administrative as well as private transactions in writing to yield as bountiful a harvest as any economic historian might hope for. What, then, are the reasons for the failure of Assyriologists and economic historians alike to make the utmost of this source of information?

There is, for one, the very number of texts available, with which only a few scholars are willing and able to deal adequately. More important an obstacle, however, is the conceptual barrier which hampers full understanding of both the real nature of a recorded transaction and its many-sided institutional background. Steeped in the economic theories of the nineteenth century, which affect even the Assyriologist most naive in matters of economic theory, we are bound to locate every economic situation within the traditional coordinates of money, market, price, etc., as these have been defined and have found acceptance within the last hundred years of our civilization. We constantly apply this frame of reference without even realizing that we distort the Mesopotamian picture in its most essential aspects, by basing our analysis on a set of assumptions which we take for granted are universally applicable.

But this barrier is by no means insuperable. The few students of the legal institutions and of the religion of Mesopotamia came to realize some time ago—even if they have not always been able to achieve this goal—that any attempt at understanding the complex and basically alien phenomena in an archaic civilization must be oriented along the lines in which this civilization itself conceived of them. In dealing with a literate civilization, the most efficient means of reaching this understanding is to study the semantics of selected key terms rather than to use modern categories of organization as the avenues of approach. This is admittedly extremely difficult when one has to handle a dead language whose full utilization by the historian is restricted by the nature of the accidentally preserved text material.

The reaction against the thought patterns evolved in the nineteenth century in the fields of history of religion, linguistics, sociology, etc., have taught us to respect alien civilizations and sharpened our faculties for self-observation in those areas; but this, unfortunately, is not the case with regard to economics. There, epistemological discussions, traditional or otherwise, have created an atmosphere in which there is no understanding of any economic pattern beyond that which has grown out of the spectacular economic development of Western Europe since the eighteenth century. The resulting attitude of the economic historians, be their background that of historic materialism or of traditional liberalism, is characterized by a markedly inadequate treatment of the economies of so-called primitive peoples as well as by a complete disregard for the essentials of the economics of the ancient great civilizations.

A new approach to this problem has been opened up by the Interdisciplinary Project at Columbia University, and has been tested in several areas with considerable success.

The basic advantage of this approach is that it provides us with a new set of concepts which can be used to describe large sections of the complex and varied array of data which the Assyriologist culls from the economic texts. These concepts serve primarily descriptive purposes and succeed in revealing certain structurally relevant features of Mesopotamian economics. They provide adequate categories in which to organize and present a number of important observations which would otherwise remain meaningless; the most important of these concepts is that of "redistribution." This is not meant to imply that any given period or area attested in cuneiform documents can be fully or even adequately characterized by this term; in fact, the entire development of Mesopotamian economy is marked by continuous shifts in emphasis which bring now one and now another form of economic integration to the foreground without the others completely disappearing at any time. The investigation of the exact relationship between the concept of "redistribution" and others, such as "reciprocity," consequently becomes the primary task of research, which has to extend, moreover, into the realm of social history, since such forms of economic integration are deeply imbedded in the social fabric of the country.

Of course the new approach will multiply the problems rather than offer easy solutions, but under its impact the line of investigation is bound to shift to new points of attack, and may even compel the Assyriologist to abandon the convenient excuse that lack of evidence hampers his chances to solve the problems. Under these circumstances the necessity of a re-evaluation and re-examination of the entire evidence bearing on matters economic becomes imperative. This process, moreover, should not only be applied to all text material directly concerned with the problem but also to historical, religious and literary documents. Obviously such a project is too far-reaching to be dealt with adequately by one individual, and too novel and difficult to promise easy success. For this reason the following pages represent solely an attempt to point out the possibilities of the new interpretation and are meant to illustrate the approach rather than to demonstrate its effectiveness.

Three main factors will be singled out here as having contributed towards the shaping of the unique socio-economic basis of Mesopotamian civilization as it emerges into the limelight of the literary period. Each of them recurs severally or in different combinations in other civilizations of the ancient Near East, but nowhere else appears the specific constellation which arose in Southern Babylonia.

There is, first, cereal agriculture based on irrigation, able to produce reliable harvests independent of rain and capable of extension in space to support an ever-increasing population. The advantages of this type of agriculture—a crop that can easily be stored and exactly divided for distribution, yielding the greatest amount in return for the effort required under the given climatic and technological conditions—coincide with the second factor: a unique settlement pattern. Thus a situation is created which differs unmistakably from Egypt, where under apparently similar circumstances the relatively primitive type of integration that characterizes a storage-economy can be observed. The decisive difference seems to lie in the nature of the urbanization which materialized in Mesopotamia quite early, producing a city concept *sui generis*. In these cities, however small they be, a communal bond had so completely replaced all loyalties of the inhabitants beyond those toward the immediate family that not even their traces can be found. This relationship between individuals finds expression in the way in which the city administers itself and acts towards its own citizens, other cities, and central authority. The essential and unique feature of urbanization in Southern Mesopotamia is the fact that a city could grow there into a center of cultural activity without the stimulus or the presence of social conditions inherent in political power.

The internal economic organization of these cities is still quite obscure, but it seems admissible to posit that it did not differ essentially from that of the village communities which we find all over the ancient Near East including those regions where agriculture relied on rain. Within a compass of fields in a commons near the city where the harvest ripened for the farmers and the few essential craftsmen, such villages could offer their populations an adequate living, necessitating but few contacts with other cities and only marginal money uses. It is essential to note that each of these towns consisted of the town proper (u r u), the suburb (u r u . b a r . r a) and the port (k a r). The absence of a market place is exactly as revealing of the internal economic structure of the city as is the presence of a special extramural district called the port for intercity economic relations. Here enters the third and most decisive factor: in a number of cities of this type there existed a second and separate economic system centered in a sanctuary, or later—due to a secondary development—in the palace of a king. This factor clearly represents a redistributive system of varied complexity and magnitude.

Into that center were channelled for storage or conversion into manufactured objects the products of the labors of a complex hierarchy of personnel working for and within the organization. The center used the stored wealth as a source of social and economic power, for prestige purposes as well as—by means of special channels of redistribution—for the support of a second hierarchy of personnel, from priests and scribes to warriors and merchants. Thus deriving income in agricultural products and labor from its own land and using it for the maintenance of a plethora of officials, as well as for such mainly social purposes as the decoration of sanctuaries and palaces, such an organization was bound to grow in size and power and to extend its holdings. The two interwoven production and distribution cycles were administered from the center by a bureaucratic staff using highly complex systems of bookkeeping and accounting which have left us many documents still to be fully evaluated. Their number has created the impression that this organization represented the entire economic set-up of the city-states. However, the continuous existence of an urban tradition which had grown out of Sumerian folk society and maintained its vigor up to the Seleucid period, demonstrates that coexistence of the two systems marks the entire course of Mesopotamian social, and hence economic, history. Due to lack of information, the relationship between the city, on the one hand, and temple or palace on the other cannot yet be described, but there are indications that it varied greatly from city to city because of special conditions or accidental developments which may remain unknown forever.

The symbiosis between a city organized, at least originally, along the lines of a village community, and the temple or palace, in point of social structure and economic potentialities, so different, provided a satisfactory and fruitful arrangement. It fostered the accumulation of staples in the royal or divine household, compelling it to evolve bureaucratic methods to deal with those accumulations by stock-taking, budgeting, and assigning income and expenditures on a large scale. An elaborate system of equivalences was developed to manage in an efficient way the array of different foodstuffs, materials for manufacturing, payments in kind to the personnel, etc. These techniques—especially the use of equivalences—influenced all contacts of the redistributive system with the outside world and developed into an important means of exercising the political power which is inherent in such an economic situation. In the control of the prices of staples, of the rate of interest and of weighing standards, exercised or at least attempted by temple or palace, an essential aspect of the mentioned symbiosis is revealed. More difficult to understand is the readiness of the city to acquiesce in such a symbiosis and at the same time to keep a communal spirit alive through all the vicissitudes of recurrent wars and invasions and even, in the course of the development, to exercise considerable political influence on both palace and sanctuary. At times, this spirit blossomed into a conscious civic pride that is unparalleled in other urban societies of the ancient Near East and created spurts of commercial activity based primarily on individual initiative which likewise have few analogies. Above all, it assured the longevity of the cities, which maintained themselves over periods of foreign domination and the steady decline of the importance of the temples. Many of these cities eventually became no more than empty shells in which a handfull of inhabitants kept a millennial tradition alive, though others still continued as prosperous centers famed throughout the world.

Within the symbiosis, however, the balance of power was far from stable, shifting from king to city and back in reflection of political changes, which affected the entire region, or of the relative efficiency of the individual rulers. In spite of these changes, an atmosphere of social peace characterizes Mesopotamian history (and literature) in contrast with that of Egypt.

The region's lack of suitable timber and stones for building purposes and for ornamentation, as well as of metals, served as a stimulus for an economic activity transcending the scope of the redistributive system. Palaces and temples sought those materials for prestige reasons, and this led to trade with foreign countries which was restricted to luxury goods and carried on exclusively on an official level by royal emissaries. The need to produce goods for export purposes, goods which could be easily transported and were likely to find a ready market in countries which produced or trafficked in the coveted metals, stones, etc., created industrial activities utilizing the abundant staples stored in the palaces and temples. The implications of this aspect of Mesopotamian economics are still far from clear; the king's trade was either based on some kind of reciprocity between rulers or on treaties fixing the nature of the goods, their price, etc. Equally undefined remains the status of the persons manipulating the exchange of goods, when and under what circumstances private citizens could or did replace royal officials, and many related problems.

The interaction between the two independent variables, palace and city, determined the entire course of the economic—and political—history of Babylonia. The palace enlarged its basis of operation through various intermediate stages, changing from tax income to tribute. The ensuing increase in economic power influenced the preferred behavior pattern of the ruling group and resulted in a change of inter-city relations. The original city-state concept gave way to that of a territorial state composed of numerous village communities and new settlements, protected by royal fortresses, all feeding staples into the redistributive organization of the palace. Conflicts for hegemony between rulers caused new cities to become capitals decorated with imposing palaces and temples, and resulted in a political structure based upon a feudalism imposed from above. The preservation of a territorial state under these circumstances required a sustained military effort in the form of a standing army made up of a segment of the population taken out of their economic and social context. Since the palace organization was by function and political aspiration beyond the orbit of the community which formed the city, it was easily open to outside influence and liable to look for its personnel among people of different ethnic or cultural backgrounds. These in turn were likely to seize power and to make use of their warlike compatriots to maintain themselves at the center of the redistributive system. Repeated foreign invasions caused feudalistic fragmentation which tended to replace any central government, and the inevitable antagonism between the old cities and their cultural and civic traditions and the new rulers led to the creation of new capitals that were in the nature of military camps.

The development just outlined as typical by no means materialized in all its stages in any of the states which vied with each other in Southern Mesopotamia ever since the rise of the empire of Sargon of Akkad. A number of atypical developments caused by the signal successes of individual rulers or as a consequence of foreign invasion con-

tributed to blur the pattern without, however, succeeding in destroying an impressive array of recurring sequences of historical events
which underly the reconstruction offered above.

The emergence of some of the larger cities of Babylonia with renewed vigor and economic strength towards the first half of the first
millennium B.C., after a prolonged period during which royal power
had declined, presents the most tantalizing mystery in Babylonian
economic history. The few centuries separating the short-lived post-
Kassite dynasties from the conquest by the Persians, who found Babylonia to be their richest satrapy, must have witnessed an economic
upsurge which, in view of the economic conditions and possibilities
of the entire region, could only be the direct consequence of international trade, manipulated in this instance either by the cities acting
through some form of commercial organization or—less likely—by individuals or the palace itself. The fact that trading with the East begins at about this period after a pause of nearly half a millennium supports this explanation. One should not contest such an interpretation
on the ground of total lack of any pertinent documentary evidence.
Although texts recording private business transactions and the affairs
of the few large sanctuaries are quite frequent in this period, one has
to assume that it was not customary in the Neo-Babylonian time to use
written records to any large extent in the realm of foreign trade. Apparently we will have to differentiate two practices in the large-scale
commercial activity of the ancient Near East. One, such as that of the
Assyrian trade settlements in Asia Minor and the copper importers
from overseas into Old-Babylonian Ur, was patently under the influence of the bureaucratic techniques of the Sumerian temple administrations, with their complex bookkeeping and multilateral accounting.
The other seems to have preferred oral agreements supplemented by a
variety of operational devices, upon which Near Eastern merchants,
from the Phoenicians on to the Nabataeans, primarily relied. To the
second practice must have adhered those inhabitants of Babylon to
whom Esarhaddon granted, as a demonstration of their return to
power, the right to trade with all the regions of the world, after his
father Sennacherib had destroyed their city and sold them into slavery.

This reveals, accidentally, two rather important bits of information:
the inhabitants of Babylon were engaged in long-distance trading
which had become the source of their riches and their power, and the
Assyrian kings normally tolerated such activity and, most likely, profited

therefrom. Their interest in this type of carrying trade is furthermore documented in a passage of a historical inscription of Sargon II (grandfather of the mentioned Esarhaddon). In this recently published text a statement is made which reflects with remarkable clarity the essential role trade occupied in the finances of the Assyrian empire. Sargon lists among his military achievements the fact that he was the first king to have compelled Egypt—which he apparently attacked during his Palestinian campaign—to establish trade relations with Assyria. That the Egyptian frontier is here characterized as being "sealed" illustrates the fundamentally different attitudes of the two adversaries towards trade. The autarchy of the Egyptian monolithic storage economy clashed with the Mesopotamian interest in international trade which was the direct expression of the unique fusion between the two economic systems which we observed in Babylonia.

This leads us to an important problem in Assyriology: the understanding and evaluation of the nature of the Assyrian form of Mesopotamian civilization.

In the wide arc of territory which surrounds Southern Mesopotamia to the north and west, agriculture had to rely exclusively on rainfall. This assured, as a rule, the livelihood of smaller communities as they were scattered through the piedmont regions and the valleys of the Zagros and throughout Upper Mesopotamia, including the coastal regions of the Mediterranean Sea, etc. Cities in this arc required a special stimulus to grow, such as a sanctuary, a seat of royal power, or trade routes, which were quite rare. The villages contained a number of families which supported themselves by cultivating adjacent fields and gardens, paying taxes collectively either to a ruler residing in a fortified palace or to an absentee owner connected by birth or feudal status with some sort of central power. The village units themselves, or the income derived from them, were negotiable within certain restrictions which varied according to time and region. They thus served as the economic basis of a feudal organization attached to ephemeral carriers of political power. By its contribution in taxes, the entire set-up readily supported superimposed power groups which, as a rule, showed little stability, extended rapidly under the leadership of an individual, were taken over smoothly by invading foreign groups, and collapsed easily whenever the faculty of the central organization to collect taxes vanished. The village community remained remarkably stable, and the obligation to pay taxes collectively counteracted individual defections, although craftsmen often seem to have been attracted to the king's court thus helping towards the type of industrialization for which all kings of that region strove in order to strengthen their economic basis.

From Assur, a city which seems to represent the northernmost exponent of the Babylonian type of city organization, native as well as foreign dynasties built up a series of short-lived empires of the socioeconomic structure just described, but they were supplied in ever-increasing measure from the spoils gathered in apparently institutionalized annual war expeditions and the income from ventures of internal colonization and international long-distance trade. The projects of internal colonization sprang from the royal initiative; Assyrian kings constantly founded new cities and peopled them with prisoners of war. These were ruled by royal officials and paid taxes to the king. All this and a road system built for policing, as well as for the collecting of taxes and tributes, served to support the king's household and his army.

It should be pointed out in this context that Assyrian political power was based essentially on a policy of forced urbanization imposed upon those regions which were outside the relatively small area of genuine and spontaneous urbanization in the South which forms the "heart-land" of Babylonian civilization. A certain amount of forced urbanization was also applied by some of the more energetic and militarily successful figures among the Babylonian kings, but a conscious and ruthless execution of the political concept of forced urbanization can be said to have created the Assyrian empire. And the very same policy was later on applied by all the conquerors who laid their hands on the same regions of the Near East from the Persians to the Sassanians.

Assyrian internal politics seem to have been extremely complex. The old and charter-protected cities thrived due to exemption from taxation and military levy; they may well have had their share in commercial activity, but this cannot be documented for the later period. Different interests dictated the activities of the redistribution system centered in the palace, which needed the booty and the human raw material coming from the endless campaigns to support and to extend the royal household, while the feudal organization, with its secondary and tertiary redistribution systems spread its influence from manors and village communities to the officials of the court. All these powers vied for political influence to increase their strength, and this makes Assyrian history a difficult, while most fascinating field of investigation.

By singling out certain basic patterns of economic integration we have in this somewhat reckless oversimplification of nearly three millennia of economic history by no means intended to discount the interwoven and ubiquitous ideological influences at work nor the fact that local and ephemeral conditions constantly exercised pressure to dislocate these patterns. Still, there is a definite tendency within the evolution of the social and economic institutions of Mesopotamia to return to a relatively small number of typical configurations of political and economic situations, whatever disturbing factors may have moved across the historical scene. This strange faculty to reverse the course of development accounts to a large extent for some of the unique features of the picture outlined in this "bird's-eye view" of Mesopotamian economic history.

A. L. Oppenheim

IV

"No Man's Coast": Ports of Trade in the Eastern Mediterranean

IN the ancient Near East, particularly in Asia Minor, Syria and Palestine, we have before us two separate territorial entities inhabited by different peoples: coast and continent. The narrowness of the coastal strip makes their co-existence almost paradoxical. Yet a mere handful of Greeks were able to establish themselves in what proved to be some of the most strategic and economically important areas of the Mediterranean and the Black Sea. They proceeded to enjoy an independent existence spanning hundreds of years, despite the presence of great empires in their backyards. Indeed, ever since the middle of the third millennium trading cities were established peacefully on the Syrian coast. They flourished and remained unmolested by the military powers of the hinterland over many centuries.*

The reasons for these coastal settlements remaining relatively undisturbed are complex. In certain areas, they were military, in others economic. Apart from fortified spots, especially walled off peninsulas or rocky islands, the coast was an indefensible and eminently unsafe area. Thus the military dangers of a coastal location may have produced the "no man's coast" that invited the Greek colonizations, while

---

* The thesis developed in this chapter was suggested by Professor Karl Polanyi in Memo. No 1, Interdisciplinary Project, Columbia University, 1954 (mimeographed) under the title "Archaic Thalassophopia."

mainly economic factors, as we will see, accounted for the spectacular independence of the Phoenician cities.

Significantly, we hardly ever hear of inland states offering any sustained resistance to coastal settlements. The Greeks are not the only instance. In southern Palestine the Philistines, participators in an unsuccessful invasion of Egypt, subsequently made good their settlement on the coast within the very confines of the Egyptian empire. Nor did the Israelites make any attempt to disestablish the Philistines when under David and Solomon they gained considerable military power over the hinterland.

Higher up on the coast, Sidon and Tyre present a similarly undisturbed development of even longer duration, with Al Mina and Ugarit as their predecessors further north. That they remained safe from their continental neighbors cannot in this case be attributed solely to military considerations. These wealthy cities happened to fit into an economic context fundamental to the international organization of trade, comprising that of the continental powers themselves; hence their relative safety.

If this state of affairs is to us astonishing, it is because it violates our accustomed notion of the behavior of empires. Illustrations of their rapacity on land and sea form the very links of modern history: witness the rivalry between England, Spain and Holland to control the Channel; the Russian drive for warm water ports from Peter the Great's fumbling campaigns against Sweden for dominance of the Baltic shore to Nicholas II's excursion into Manchuria. Modern history reflects a constant awareness on the part of the powers that without a strong navy and the possession of strategic coastal areas full status as a nation cannot be achieved.

It would seem that in defiance of this allegedly universal law an opposite principle was at work in the ancient world. Indeed, well into the first millennium B.C. it seems to have lived under a law of its own, namely, a continentalizing attitude on the part of the inland powers ranging from an outright avoidance of the coast, which was the rule, to a cautious co-existence and, in some cases, remote control.*

To refrain from occupying coastal areas appears to have been the policy followed by the Mesopotamian empires and Egypt, as well as by the Hittite (or Hatti) empire of Asia Minor. We will first discuss Mesopotamia and Egypt; supplementing this by some new evidence

* See below, pp. 162–4.

on Hatti. There follows a survey of the Phoenician coast, drawing upon our more recent knowledge of Al Mina and Ugarit. Finally, an attempt will be made to show how shunning of the coast gives way, about the second quarter of the first millennium B.C., to a symbiosis between the empires and the trading cities of the coast.

Mesopotamia and Egypt

The broad fact which in itself should establish a *prima facie* case of a kind of archaic thalassophobia was the persistency with which the city state areas of Sumer, Babylonia, Assyria, Mitanni, etc., refused to shift their centers of gravity towards the coast. The same applies to Egypt. The location of the majority of these areas was riverain, yet none seemed to make any effort to gain access to the sea. The vicissitudes of history brought about a variety of power configurations in the area between the Lakes Van and Urmia in the north, the Persian Gulf and the Red Sea in the south, the Mediterranean in the west; nevertheless at no time was a sustained effort made that would serve as proof of a seaward tendency on the part of the continental powers. This is the immutable framework of Mesopotamian history against which the shifting events should be judged which sometimes seem to point in the opposite direction.

Several inscriptions are extant which record ambitious far-western conquests of Mesopotamian rulers. There is the inscription about Sargon I of Akkad which speaks of Yarmuti and Ibla having been subdued. Similar, but more authentic data refer to almost identical expeditions by his successor, Naram-Sin. In different contexts Gudea of Lagash and later Dungi of the third dynasty of Ur mention their Western exploits; and an inscription of Shamshi-Adad II of Assyria runs: "My great names and my stele I set up in the land of Laban on the shore of the Great Sea."[1] Tukulti Urta made claim to the Bahrein Island and Melukha in the South.[2]

What broadly was the nature of these claims to the coast? And do they justify a belief that the third and second millennium Mesopotamian empires intended to acquire, hold, and keep these coastal areas? Did they institute military garrisons, appoint governors or others officers, set up a religious hierarchy, administer foreign trade, or exact regular tribute payments? As far as our records go, there is but little evidence for either.

The inscriptions of Gudea of Lagash[3] help us to spell out the nature of some of his coastal adventures:

> From Amanus the mountain of cedar trees whose length was 60 cubits, cedar trees whose length was 50 cubits, *ukarinu* trees whose length was 25 cubits, he made into logs and brought down from the mountain. . . . Gold dust from Mount Kahkhu he brought down. . . . Gold dust from the mountain of Melukha he brought down. . . . With living ewes he brought living lambs; their shepherds he made to serve.

The details point to expeditionary procurements, often indistinguishable from raids, to secure material for temple building, such as huge stones or logs of rare timber, or to pan gold in mountain streams. It is a highly ambiguous form of trading. The goods that may be carried to gain the goodwill of the local inhabitants, need not be the *ultima ratio* of these armed caravans. The organization would rather be that of forays to obtain booty or slaves, maybe to exact ransom payments from weak settlements, but mainly to facilitate expeditionary trade. A raid is made on a herd of cattle or sheep, if they happen to be about. Mule drivers are taken along with their mules, the ewes with their lambs, and the shepherds to tend the flocks. Occasionally, a town is destroyed if its people offer resistance to this kind of indiscriminate quarrying, cutting of timber and general procurement. It is a mixed undertaking.

There seems to be here nothing that would force us to conclude that other ventures emanating from Mesopotamia and Assyria were essentially different from such expeditionary raids and forays of supply. Such evidence as Shamshi-Adad I's statement of setting up a stele holds nothing to indicate that he ruled rather than visited, administered rather than intimidated. Tukulti-Urta mentions places widely separated from the heartland of Assyria. To incorporate them in his empire, he would have had to be the ruler of Babylon and also of the Sea-Lands. There has not been found any evidence pointing in that direction.

It would appear then, that the early Mesopotamian empires never established permanent control of the coast nor intended to do so. Hardly any of the conditions listed above and indicating control were, to our knowledge, fulfilled.

Three regions enter into Egyptian coastal policy: the Delta of the Nile; the Phoenician and Philistine cities; the Red Sea and the Mediterranean, as the scenes of the maritime activities of the Egyptians.

Since the time Egypt was first unified, she comprised the Delta of the Nile. However, a sharp distinction should be made between the inland Delta and the coastal strip, which alone is relevant to the argument. H. R. Hall has noted that in early times the people of the coastal Delta were regarded as foreigners. Its marshes had always been a place apart from Egypt proper.[4] The invading Hyksos were able to consolidate their power in the Delta, set up their capital Avaris and, making use of the fens, strike out for the south. Ipower, the Egyptian prophet, wailed: "Behold it (the Delta) is in the hands (?) of those who knew it not like those who know it. The Asiatics are skilled in the arts of the marshlands. Even outside of the Delta the foreigners have taken root."[5] During Egypt's decline, reflected in the Wen-Amon story, the Delta would tend to be governed by independent princes.[6] The Libyans at several occasions infiltrated it and Libyan chiefs eventually established themselves there.[7] The marginal character of the fens was still in evidence as late as the seventh century B.C., at the time of Psamtik's alliance with the "bronze men" of Ionia.[8]

If Lower Egypt had had a strong intent to hold this area securely, it seems unlikely that the splitting off of the coastal delta would so often have been successful. That area must have been somewhat of an unclaimed land, repeatedly harboring fugitives or foreigners, and in general, at a discount with the Egyptians.

After the expulsion of the Hyksos, Egypt marched into Asia, organizing in the wake of her armies the coastal Phoenician cities as satellites. These cities had to accept military garrisons and were put under native rulers friendly to Egypt.

Yet Egyptian interest in these maritime sites remained limited. They were not incorporated, but retained their sovereignty. The Egyptians, we are told, paid well for the favors of the native rulers,[9] and the military garrisons were frequently composed of non-Egyptian mercenaries.[10] It can then be inferred that the interest of the Egyptians in these cities was primarily to furnish their growing empire with military supply depots and to have their flanks protected when marching into the interior.[11] The hinterland, and not the coast, set unswervingly the direction for their military efforts.

The Red Sea and the Mediterranean, it was stated, were the scenes of Egyptian maritime trade activity. It comprised such notable achievements as the expedition to Punt; the Nile-to-Red Sea Canal as well as continuous trading in the eastern Mediterranean.

Despite their seafaring exploits, the Egyptians managed to by-pass the coast. No permanent Egyptian settlement or port on the Red Sea or the Mediterranean is on record. Regular trade would have been greatly facilitated by the establishment of coastal ports or settlements; that none was made, suggests that Egyptian trade was of an adventitious, occasional, expeditionary nature. As in the case of the Mesopotamian raids to the West, these expeditions were aimed at procuring specific materials, e.g., aromatic woods and exotic animals as in the Hatshepsutut expedition to Punt.

This is all the more surprising since Egypt was situated on two seas, both having a considerable amount of trade. However, this was largely passive trade, carried in foreign bottoms. Her position in regard to seaborne trade was broadly the same as that—with the possible exception of Ur—of the Mesopotamian, the Hittite or, later, the Persian empires.

In summary: the comparatively weak hold on the Delta, the vacuum of power on the coastal strip, the continental line of Egyptian military expansion in Asia, the relative independence of the Philistine and Phoenician cities even in times of Egyptian ascendency, the absence of Egyptian coastal settlements in the north and east, the expeditionary nature of trade—all this argues for a shunning of coastal possessions during most of the 2600 years of pre-Hellenistic Egyptian antiquity.

The Hittites

Both politically and culturally, the Hittite empire was the ruling force in the Asia Minor of the second millennium. At the height of its expansion, it bordered on Egypt in the south, the Mesopotamian empires in the east. Its constitutional ideas, its codes of law, and the level of its political thought in general make it the immediate predecessor of the Greek and Persian empires, together with which it bridged the gap between the early civilizations of Mesopotamia, Crete and Egypt, on the one hand, Rome on the other.

The heartland of Hatti was Anatolia, the central part of Asia Minor. Situated in the middle of a large peninsula, its boundaries related in three directions to the coast. Landlocked towards the East and Northeast by high mountain ranges, its only line of expansion, except towards the coast, was to the Southeast, being led by the Upper Euphrates even further into the heart of the Asiatic continent. As a matter of fact, this precisely was the line Hittite expansion followed. It provides, in effect, an extreme case of the relation between coast and continent in antiquity.

Aware of their peninsular situation, the Hittites appear to have consciously settled on a continentalizing bent. Endowed with the faculty of conceiving comprehensive political ideas and of relating these to moral and juridical norms, they reveal in their documents a clear reflection of that national policy.

Our interpretation of the evidence must, admittedly, often remain doubtful as long as it is merely grounded on translations, without first-hand knowledge of the originals. However, even at this stage of the inquiry an attempt at collating some of the available instances may be permissible.[12]

1. RELEGATING AN ENEMY TO THE COAST

One of the most important of these documents, the *Telepinush Text*[13] (c. 1650) describes the traditional Hittite policy of forcing the defeated enemy towards the coast. Telepinush, among the latest of the early set of rulers, ascribes, in his *Annals*, this policy to the three founding kings—Labarnash, Hattushilish and Murshilish. This is probably done in order to lend the authority of historical precedent to his own policy.

Telepinush Text[14]

Art. 1.   1   Thus speaks the Tabarna Telepinush, the great king
          2   At one time Labarnash was Great King. . . .
Art. 2.   5   And the land was small; but wherever he went to war
          6   he ruled the enemy country with a (strong) hand (?).
Art. 3.   7   And again and again he harassed their country and devastated (??) it.
          8   And *he made them to border on the sea** [machte sie zu Grenz (nachbarn) des Meeres]. But when he came home from the campaign, 9 wherever each of his sons went, to
Art. 4.   10 Hupish, Tuwanuwa, Menashsha, Landa, Zanlar . . . they administered the land 12 and the big towns were given over into their hands.
Art. 5.   13 After him reigned (?) Hattushilish . . . he went to war, he, too, 16 held the enemy country down with a (strong) hand (?).

* Italics are mine.

Art. 6. 17 And again and again he harassed their country and devastated (??) it.
Art. 8. 24 When Murshilish ruled in Hattushash. . . .
         27 And he harassed. the country and *made them to* border on the sea.
Art. 9. 28 And he marched to Halpa (Aleppo) and razed Halpa. . . . After this he marched on Babylon and razed Babylon, he also
         30 attacked the Harrites (Hurrites). . . .

The need for expansion was given because "the land was small."[15] Cattle and horses require suitable pastures. Raids and harassment are followed by devastation. "And again and again he harassed their country and devastated it."[16] The formerly sedentary victims give way to the pressure of the Hittites, only to find themselves pursued by their enemies and driven off the plateau and towards the coasts. "And he made them to border on the sea."[17]

Nowhere in the *Telepinush Text* do we read of a Hittite move to seize the coast or even to drive the dispossessed into the sea. The typical ways of disposing of the vanquished, best known to us from Old Testament, Hellenic and Far Eastern sources, was the massacre of the population (sometimes of adult males only), their subjugation on the spot; selling them into slavery abroad. Expelling vanquished peoples from their towns and driving them in the direction of the coast appears to have been the early Hittites' alternative means. Towns were not razed, but taken over intact; pastureland was enlarged; the peoples were not destroyed; the borderlands were not left empty; international relations with the defeated were continued, and empire building proceeded. In the light of Hittite practice these implications may well have been obvious. At any rate, the verbatim repetition of the principles of policy allegedly followed by the empire builders is singularly impressive.

2. PEJORATIVE REFERENCES TO THE COAST

The *Madduwattash Text*[18] gives us an appraisal, on the official level, of the relative values of coastal lowland and continental highland locations.

Madduwattash was the chief of a people who were defeated by the Ahhiyawa and were fleeing from their conquerors towards the highlands. He was rescued by Shupiluliumash, Great King of Hatti, whose official title was The Sun. Madduwattash was permitted by Shupiluliumash to enter the hill country of Zippashta, thus escaping with his people both from his enemy and from deadly famine.

There is but little doubt that the Ahhiyawa were the Achaians of Homer; their ruler Attarshshiyash is being identified with the Atreus, who may have been the father of Agamemnon.

In return for being rescued Madduwattash swore an oath of fealty to the Hittite king. But later in the reign of his son, Arnuwandash IV, he united with Arzawa and the Ahhiyawa to seize Cyprus. In the text the Hittite king expresses his displeasure of Madduwattash's ingratitude and accuses him of treason:

The accusations against Madduwattash

Art. 1. Front	1	Attarshshiyash the Ahhiyawa has chased /you/, Madduwattash, from your country
	2	After that he pursued you and hounded you and wished for your, Madduwattash's /dire/ death
Art. 1. Front	3	and /would/ have killed you. But you, Madduwattash took refuge with the Father /of the Sun/; and the Father of the Sun
	4	rescued you from death and kept Attarshshiyash away from you.
Art. 2. Front	6	As the Father of the Sun 7 . . . took you . . . together with your wives, your children, your troops (and) your chariot fighters, and he gave you chariots . . . grain (and) seeds to overflow,
	8	and he gave you also ale (and) wine . . . (and) malted loaves . . . and cheese to overflow. And you . . . 9 kept alive by the Father of the Sun in your hunger.
Art. 3. Front	10	And the Father of the Sun rescued you . . .
	11	. . . . But for him the dogs would have devoured you in all your hunger.
	12	Had you escaped from Attarshshiyas with your bare lives, you would have starved to death.
Art. 4. Front	13	Thereupon the Father of the Sun came (and) took you . . . into an oath, and defended /you/ and made an oath
	14	. . . "Behold, I, the Father of the Sun, have rescued /you/, Madduwattash /from the sword/ of Attarshshiyash.
	15	"Therefore you shall (belong) to the Father of the Sun and the country of Hatti. And behold: I have given /you/ the hill country of Zippashta /to rule/.
	16	"/and/ you, Madduwattash, together with your /peo-

ple/ shall live in the hill country of Zippashta; and so have in the hill country of Zippashta

17 "your mainstay (??)."

19 . . . "behold I have given you the hill country of Zippashta. . . .

20 "But do not then on your own further occupy any other vassal's (land), nor any other's land (at all) and be the Hill country of Zippashta your boundary.

Art. 4. Front 21 "Thus be you my servant; also be your troops my troops."

Art. 5. Front 22 . . . "/you/ have given /me/, my /lord/, the hill country of Zippashta to live in.

23 "Thus /I/ am /in these countries/ an outpost and a gu/ard. And who /so even speaks to/ my face a word of enmity.

24 "(and) from whatever country I hear a word of enmity, I shall /not hide/ from you such man and such country

25 "but rather write you of them."

For the Hittites, the lowland towards the coast was a wasteland: "Had you escaped from Attarshshiyash with your bare lives you would have starved to death." To be forced to sojourn there included the probability of death from starvation, enslavement by coastal raiders, and eventually becoming carrion for wild dogs—these were the alternatives awaiting him. Although neither the word "coast" nor lowlands is mentioned, it may be permissible to infer, in view of the *Telepinush Text* that what is meant are the desert lands lying towards the west. The area must have been a notoriously arid one since the possibility of starvation is mentioned three times. The few fertile valleys would have been occupied by their conquerors. The reference to the wild dogs which devour corpses is also to be found in Homer, where the area in question is the coastal strip lying opposite Troy. The hill country is contrasted to the lowland as a land of bounty and Zippashta is referred to as a "mainstay."

The dating of the two documents—Telepinush ca. 1650 and Madduwattash ca. 1350—shows that a similar attitude towards the coast prevailed for at least three centuries. However, the ascribing of such a policy to much earlier rulers and its obvious survival to the end of the empire extends its ascendency to rather double that stretch of time.

3. BANISHMENT TO THE COAST

Further confirmation of the marginality of the coast is to be found in the *Hattushilish Text*,[19] the autobiography of a Hittite king. Hattushilish raised himself to the throne at the expense of the legitimate sovereign, his brother, whom he desposed. Having defeated his rival he "sends him off to the side of the sea." A chief supporter of the exiled king is allowed "to cross the border and escape," as the context would indicate, presumably also to the coast (which incidentally can be identified as the north or Black Sea coast). In another case banishment is to the south coast or an island off that coast. The disaffected persons "are sent to Alashiyash,"[20] which is commonly thought to be Cyprus, lying opposite Cilicia.

This important episode appears to indicate that any person exiled (or self-exiled) to the coast would have been thereby rendered harmless to the Hittite realm—whether for lack of resources or on account of the political weakness of the peoples among whom he would have to live.

4. COASTAL BUFFER STATE POLICY OF THE HITTITES

The economic needs of the Hittite empire made, of course, a complete insulation from the coast impracticable. As we have seen in the case of Cyprus, some contact was unavoidable, particularly in order to ensure the flow of copper from the island. As a solution, the Hittites appeared to have favored leaving the coast in weak, semi-independent hands. Such a policy was apt to mitigate both the military disadvantages of coastal possessions and the economic drawbacks that would have resulted had they occupied the area themselves.

The political status of such a coastal area is documented in *The Shunashshura Treaty*,[21] which concerns the relations between Kizzuwatna and the two great neighboring powers, the Hurrites to the east, the Hittites to the north. Convincingly located by A. Goetze in the strategically vital area of Eastern Cilicia,[22] Kizzuwatna controlled the shortest route from Cyprus and the southern coast to Boghazköy via the Cilician gates. Situated on the coast opposite Cyprus, it was the chief natural point of entry for copper to the Anatolian plateau.[23]

Under modern conditions the political independence of such a commercially and militarily strategic area under the shadow of a vastly superior great power, would be a practical impossibility, or to say the least, it would be most precarious. Hence its relatively independent status, securing immunity from military attack, more than 3000 years ago, becomes most significant, especially since it was grounded on freely concluded treaties, and supported by experience.

The *Shunashshura Treaty* opens with a statement which comes very near the principle of what, in modern terms, woud be called the self-determination of small countries. It begins:

> 5. Previously in the days of my grandfather, the country Kizzuwatna
> 6. had become (part) of the Hatti country. But afterward . . .
> 7. seceded . . . and shifted (allegiance) to the Hurri country.

We are then told how the shift in allegiance of such a strategic territory was possible in terms of international usage. Three generations before, a neighboring people, the Ishuwa, had sought asylum from the Hittites and had fled to the neighboring land of the Hurrites. When the Hittites objected to this and said:

> 12. to the Hurrian: "Extradite my subjects!" . . . the Hurrian sent word back
> 13. to the Sun as follows: "No."
> 17. . . . the cattle 18 have chosen their stable, they definitely
> 19. have come to my country.

The Hittite king then asked the question

> 26. . . . If some country 27 would secede from you (and) would shift . . . to the Hatti country
> 28. How would such a thing be? The Hurrian 29 sent word to me . . . as follows: "Exactly the same."

It was therefore on the basis of international usage, reciprocity and precedent, that Shunashshura, king of Kizzuwatna, arranged the transfer of allegiance of his state from the neighboring Hurrites to their enemies, the Hittites.

The treaty reflects a careful delimitation of boundaries. Access to the sea was to be guaranteed to the continental great power at one point of entry, Lamiya. The Hittites agreed, in turn, that Lamiya would not be fortified.

> 40. Toward the sea Lamiya belongs to the Sun. . . .
> 42. The Sun will not fortify Lamiya

In this delimitation of boundaries by the two kings, all areas are measured out cooperatively and then halved.

> 49. . . . the mountain of Zabarashna 50 belongs to Shunashshura, they will measure out the territory together 51 (and) divide (it)

59. The river Shamri (is) his boundary. The great king will not cross the river Shamri.

As regards other non-maritime fortifications in general the Hittites— the Great Power—explicitly limit themselves to the places they may fortify. No such restrictions are made on Kizzuwatna, the much smaller and weaker state.

45. The Sun must not fortify Aruna.
51. The Sun may fortify Anawushta.

These elaborate diplomatic methods seem to have served the purpose of enabling the Hittites to avoid coastal occupation by keeping a small friendly state on their coastal flank, permitting them access to the sea while the weaker state acted as a buffer zone between sea and hinterland.

5. EARLY MIGRATION AND LINE OF EXPANSION

The Hittites, an Indo-Germanic people, probably entered Anatolia via the Black Sea coast. The cultic seats of the oldest gods in their pantheon are found to the north in Kashka territory, which probably included the southern coast of the Black Sea. In the historical period we find the Hittites in Central Anatolia: in other words, their national movement must have been initially inland, starting from somewhere on the northern coast. It should be stressed, that no monument has been yet found in the neighborhood of the west coast which can unquestionably be called a proof of Hittite expansion in that direction.[24] On the contrary, the line of expansion has been consistently south-east, i.e., further towards the main Asiatic inland.

In the *Telepinush Text* we learn that the first efforts made by the Hittites are towards consolidation in the interior of the Anatolian plateau. Later they moved into northern Mesopotamia, attacking the ancient cities of Aleppo and Carchemish and actually raiding southeastward as far as Babylon. The Black Sea region became for them a back door, permanently closed to new entrants. The Kashka peoples, conglomerate of "barbaric" tribes, were left in occupation of the area.[25] They were tolerated despite their harassing of the Hittite Empire, to the point of burning Boghazköy.[26] Significantly, there is no evidence that the Hittites ever retaliated against them in force.

6. CULTURAL FRONTIER BETWEEN EAST AND WEST

According to Albrecht Goetze there was over some two millennia a permanent cultural and political boundary line in Asia Minor west of the River Halys separating Anatolia proper on the east from the early Aegean and—later—Greek culture on the west.[27] This boundary of land running roughly in a north-south direction remained intact through all historical vicissitudes. Goetze traced it as far back as the first invasion from the European continent of which we have knowledge,[28] surviving the sway of third millennium Aegean culture, Minoan thalassocracy, and even subsequent Greek settlement. Rostovtzeff asserted its presence right up to late Achemenid times.[29] No quite satisfactory explanation has ever been offered for the persistence of this nonpolitical frontier.

Yet such a borderline would be a logical outgrowth of the policy of keeping away from the coast and orienting oneself inland which we have posited with the Hittites. Not only does it lend additional support to the idea that the Hittite Empire of the second millennium held policies of this kind, but it suggests that a similar principle held sway over a much longer period of time, and for many more peoples. The remarkable cultural frontier running behind and along the coast which Goetze found in Western Asia Minor was, in effect, general—if to a lesser extent—along the whole Eastern Mediterranean and the Black Sea. The relative safety of coastal cities which we instanced for the Philistine and Phoenician ports, bears this out. All along the Syrian coast a padding of smaller and weaker states separated the port cities proper from the continental powers. This suggests that deeper causes were here in play than the military and cultural drawbacks of such possessions for the inland powers. They were, as we mentioned to begin with, of an economic order.

Port of Trade Policies

The port of trade belonged to an organization of trading fundamentally different from that of the nineteenth century. Trading did not depend primarily upon markets but had a history and logic of its own, stemming from the principle of a politically neutral meeting place.

In "silent trade"—mainly for reasons of safety—agreement was reached without either party communicating directly with its opposite number. This form of primitive trade may have lingered on in the Eastern Mediterranean into pre-historic times as the archaeological remains of some walled coastal sites indicate. Such enclosures, right on the coast, and yet outside of the towns proper, have been unearthed. They were provided with an altar to ensure the safety of men and goods.

Neither a place for silent trade, nor a neutral sanctuary provides of itself the authority required for transacting trade in any other than a haphazard and ephemeral manner. Permanent guarantees of safety and more elaborate facilities are needed to make trade possible under archaic conditions.

The complex instrument which fulfilled these conditions was the port of trade. Seen from inland, the port of trade was an "epineion" as Lehmann-Hartleben called "the coastal approach of a definite region, be it that of a tribe, a countryside or a city."[30] The port of trade was such a place, though not necessarily on the coast, but quite often on a great river or where desert and mountain meet. There goods could be exchanged under the non-military protection of shrine, monastery or a weak political authority. Its inner organization would vary greatly according to the social context in which the administration of trade was embedded.

Its main function was to guarantee neutrality. Continuity of the supply of goods was essential, since it could not be expected that traders —under the difficult conditions of archaic long distance travel—would come to an outlying place unless they knew for certain that a safe exchange of goods was possible. The presence of a strong military power on the spot would unfailingly frighten them away. Political neutrality, guarantee of supplies, protection of the lives and property of strangers had to be assured before trade could start. A prior understanding between the corporate parties was therefore needed, usually based on regular treaties. Such an understanding, no doubt, would include facilities for disembarking, lading, portage, storage, grading of goods and the fixing of equivalencies backed by the coastal authority. Without this mechanism of the port of trade, there could be no regular trading.

Here, in our view, lies the key to the lasting independence of the coastal towns of antiquity. It is too early to say how far the mainly agricultural settlements of the Greek colonists, e.g., on the north Black

Sea coast performed such a function for the corn trade. Anyway the Eastern Mediterranean ports of trade had distinguishing marks which set them aside from the common run of such outlets for regional produce. There is evidence of the existence of two outstanding ports of trade in Syria that antedate the Hittite empire by many centuries. Recent excavations have unearthed Al Mina, north of the mouth of the Orontes, and Ugarit, less than a hundred miles south of it. The first has been given currency by Sir Leonard Woolley in his booklet on the Kingdom of Alalakh, the second, by the writings of Claude Schaeffer, head of the French expedition at Ras Shamra.

When Woolley excavated Al Mina, he found a city with a large group of warehouses and only a very few residences or burial sites. The city, as far as we are able to ascertain, was devoted exclusively to trade between the Aegean and the Syrian hinterland, with evidence available that Aegean traders did settle there. But the actual habitations were situated off the marshy coast on a hillside, at some distance.

This high degree of specialization was sometimes part of an even more complex setup which comprised a small neighboring state acting as middleman between the distant empires and the port of trade proper. This seems to have been true of the relations between the kingdom of Alalakh and Al Mina.[31]

In excavating Al Mina's parent city, Alalakh, Woolley noted that the Hittites had occupied and administered that town. However, he offers no evidence of the Hittites ever having seized Al Mina. More conclusive evidence for the neutrality of Al Mina is the fact that this city neither suffered siege nor occupation in the second millennium in which the Egyptian and Hittite Empires clashed in its immediate neighborhood.

If we turn to Ugarit—operating in the Egyptian sphere of influence, as did Al Mina in the Hittite—the same singular phenomenon is manifest.

Ugarit was an independent kingdom which probably combined the function of a port of trade with that of the neutral state to which it belonged. It has been found to be one of the richest sites in the ancient world. The royal palace had three times the area of the one at the Hittite capital of Boghazköy. Yet Ugarit had no territory to speak of. We must infer that its wealth came to it from the trade in which it specialized. Evidence of a scribe-school teaching four different languages;[32] texts and inscriptions; a multilingual dictionary using three languages; groups of foreign residents, and the administration of an equivalency system based on the shekel, show beyond the shadow of a doubt that this area was designed to perform the functions of a port of trade.[33]

And, again: Ugarit was neither besieged nor suffered occupation during the imperial rivalries. It was seized between the eighteenth and sixteenth centuries contemporaneously with the Hyksos period in Egypt. Schaeffer offers evidence that this conquest was by a nonliterate, military, "barbaric" people. This would confirm the view that the politically more sophisticated powers followed a "hands-off" policy in regard to ports of trade.[34]

The geographic proximity and exposed strategic location of these eminently important trading centers must force us to the conclusion that during centuries of the second millennium Hittites and Egyptians were tacitly agreed to respect the neutrality and inviolability of each other's *epineion*. Further confirmation of the neutrality of such ports of trade comes from the traditional pattern of Hittite avoidance of the coast, of which we have already spoken. Their main route into Syria ran past the Gulf of Adana, yet the Hittites are not known ever to have touched upon the coast. That this pattern did not merely reflect military considerations is confirmed by a letter of the king of Babylon to Hattushilish III in which he complains of the loss of a caravan ambushed on the way from Babylon to Ugarit. Hattushilish, asked to investigate, replied that the locality was not under his control.[35] The event took place after the fall of the Mitanni Empire and subsequent to the eclipse of Egyptian power in northern Syria. To our knowledge, one power alone remained in control of the area at this time: the Hittites. Yet they neither claimed control over the coastal cities, nor did they seem in practice to interfere with their political life.

Protection for trade was deemed a concern of the highest order, as we can see from the fact that the king of Babylon would correspond with the king of the Hittites in the interest of trade. According to Schaeffer other correspondence and treaties from Ugarit confirmed such a mutual interest in the security of traders.[36] In the Hittite law code the killing of a trader amounts to murder; the killing of others, to manslaughter.[37]

Up to the turn of the first quarter of the first millennium ports of trade functioned in this manner. About that time there are signs of a recession in the neutrality of the ports of trade, and the principle of "hands off" the coast weakens.

Important changes were taking place in the Near East.

Symbiosis

The great expansion of trade in the second quarter of the first millennium had an incisive effect upon the relationship between coast and continent. The Powers of the hinterland could no longer afford to indulge in their continental bias of ignoring the coast whenever possible. They were now reluctantly moving towards a new balance which was to have far-reaching consequences for the course of history in the Eastern Mediterranean.

Tyre, the leading port of trade of the period, now operates on a world-wide scale; the administration of trade brings in distant political powers as her agents in the exchange of goods. Ionia, the Persian Gulf, the Black Sea, Arabia and the Atlantic coast of Spain are now all part of a network which may have extended as far as India and Central Africa. This is the picture drawn in Ezekiel 27, on the trade activities of Tyre in the early part of the sixth century:

12. Tarshish was thy merchant . . . with silver, iron, tin and lead they traded in thy fairs.
13. Javan, Tubal, and Meshech . . . they traded the persons of men and vessels of brass in thy market.
14. They of the house of Togarmah traded in thy fairs with horses and horsemen and mules.
15. The men of Dedan were thy merchants; many isles were the merchandise of thine hand; they brought thee for a present horns of ivory and ebony.
22. The merchants of Sheba and Raamah they were thy merchants; they occupied in thy fairs with chief of all spices, and with all precious stones, and gold.
25. The ships of Tarshish did sing of thee in thy market: and thou wast replenished, and made very glorious in the midst of the seas.

Phoenician manufacture appears to have been universally in demand and to have been bartered for diverse goods—slaves, livestock, metals, prestige goods, and so on. The increasing volume and variety of the turnover no doubt went with extended treaty relations. While the Tyrian ships themselves carried a large amount of cargo, other ships, as well as land caravans, were coming into Tyre all the time. To secure a supply of merchandise for such far-flung trade, to arrange for the disposal of goods and for the safety of ships and caravans must have required a diplomatic activity spanning almost the whole inhabited world, as far as then known.

Thus, along with the growth of trade, the ports of trade were bound to become political factors. Part of the reason for this, again, may lie in the strategic importance of iron, the flow of which they controlled. Of this no direct evidence is available to us. There is ample proof, however, of the increasing importance of navies as a military factor. Combined naval-land operations were on record since the Peoples of the Sea and continued to grow in the first millennium. In the seventh century we find the Ionian amphibious troops hired by Psamtik acting as the catalyst in the overthrow of the power of Assyria in Egypt. Allied with the Lydians, the Phoenician cities also engaged in similar politico-military intrigues.

Thus one of the vital attributes of the ports of trade—their neutrality—tended to disappear, not as if they had lost their independence to the hinterland powers; rather, they themselves had become powers to be reckoned with.

This change of role was reflected in the attitude of the inland powers. Warily and reluctantly, they saw themselves compelled to move against the ports of trade. Straight conquest and subjugation was out of the question. This would have altogether done away with their value as a channel of entry for foreign goods. Other responses had to be devised.

One answer was demilitarization. This interpretation may be put on the policy of Assyria towards Sidon, when that city was transferred from a reef to the mainland, and resettled with Assyrian colonists; similarly, on the policies of Lydia against the Ionian cities, when the walls of Smyrna were torn down. In a milder form, the Lydian policy of making annual raids against the coastal cities had the same purport. These moves appear to have been as nondestructive as possible, while nevertheless rendering those cities militarily helpless on land.

A basic change of role was taking place which combined a more active policy of the empires towards the coast with maintenance of much of the traditional continental bias. Often this manifested itself in a show of force, even in transitory control, followed by a withdrawal.

Sometimes this led to a symbiotic relationship (as Rostovtzeff called it) growing into a closer cooperation between coast and continent than ever before. Again, we are forced to ignore the important differences which subsisted between the simple *emporia* of a local range, and the elaborate organizations of foreign trade we called ports of trade. The situation, in somewhat greater detail, was this:

In the northern Black Sea area, Scythia and the Greek colonies achieved a firm symbiosis, avoiding overt military pressure. Rostovtzeff describes how the Scythians exchanged their surplus goods for products of Greece and Ionia:

> . . . the Scythians favoured the Greek colonies, left them unmolested, entered into personal relations with them, and probably contented themselves with levying a nominal tribute as a sign of sovereignty. Neither from Herodotus nor from other 6th or 5th century sources do we hear of any conflict between the Greek colonies and the Scythians.[38]

In Lydia, Gyges moved against Miletus (ca. 663), Colophon, and Magnesia ad Siplum.[39] That this was merely a military demonstration and an assertion of nominal suzerainty is apparent, since Gyges did not seem to aim at capturing citadels. He raided only the fields of Miletus and did not attack the two nearest coastal cities, Cymē and Ephesus. Eventually, his military activities against the coastal cities came to a halt. In a significant move, Lydia permitted Miletus to colonize Abydos on the Hellespont, on plainly Lydian soil. Gyges, himself, in the latter part of his reign, turned openly philhellene. The coastal cities and Lydia later cooperated in the face of the Cimmerian invasion.

Gyges' successors, too, followed a policy of mild pressure, essentially aiming at a symbiosis. Alyattes devastated the Milesian fields every year, but left farmsteads unmolested. He destroyed the walls of Smyrna in an evident attempt at demilitarizing the city, yet did not occupy it. He concluded a treaty favorable to Miletus and, in the second half of his reign, a mutually advantageous relationship was fostered by the strong cultural affinity that was springing up between Lydia and Ionia. Herodotus declared there was but little difference between them.

Croesus, following in the traditions of Alyattes, had the hill forts of Ephesus destroyed. The other cities were left unmolested after they allowed peaceful entry to his troops. While they had to pledge annual payments, and military aid in extraordinary cases, they were not garrisoned, nor were their domestic affairs interfered with. Croesus was

out and out friendly towards the Greek ports of trade. Last of the
Lydian monarchs, he was the most thoroughly hellenized of them all.

So far, in talking about the symbiosis of empire and port of trade,
we had in mind the region of the northern Black Sea and Western
Asia Minor, directing our attention to the Scythian and the Lydian
empires respectively. In either instance the Greek ports of trade such
as Miletus, Ephesus, or Theodosia were in the center of interest.

In turning south toward the Syrian coast where history started more
than a thousand years earlier, two periods compete. Al Mina and
Ugarit, the first ports of trade, had been faced by the inland empires of
Assyria, Babylon, the Hittites, and Egypt. Their successors, Sidon and
Tyre, had to deal with the Neo-Assyrian Empire, Chaldean Babylonia,
and the Persians. In following up the changes that occurred in the first
millennium in the policies of these latter continental powers we will
have to substitute for Kanaanite Al Mina and Ugarit, their much later
successors, the Phoenician cities of Sidon and Tyre.

At first sight there is a striking change in Assyrian policy. The
western military escapades of the Mesopotamian rulers of the third and
second millennium now turn into regular warfare, which seems to aim
at the permanent conquest of the West with a Mediterranean coast as
its ultimate object. In this move Assyria, with its almost yearly campaigns, has the lead. The inhuman cruelties committed against their
prisoners reveal a deliberate policy of intimidation.

Delving deeper it seems doubtful whether in regard to the coast
the change is really as big as it appears on the surface. Up to about 782,
though Assyria collected tribute from the coastal cities, her interference
was tentative in character. Shamshi-Adad V visited the Mediterranean
region only twice during his reign. These visits were booty raids and
military demonstrations rather than campaigns of conquest. Adad-
Nirari also assured himself of the tribute of Tyre, Sidon, Israel and
Philistia, but did not repeat his visit to the coast. Shalmaneser III and
Tiglath-pileser III both exacted annual tribute while otherwise leaving
the Phoenician cities alone except for Philistia, which was raided
though not then incorporated. A policy of fierce aggression starts with
Sennacherib who occupied Phoenicia in 701, with the sole exception
of Tyre. Esarhaddon and Ashurbanipal following in his footsteps destroyed Sidon and exacted heavy tribute from Tyre. No doubt, the end
of the eighth century saw a new Assyrian policy, much more reminis-

cent of the nineteenth century A.D. than of the nineteenth century B.C. Military pressure against the coastal cities was now constant.

Nevertheless, it would be easy to exaggerate the "modernness" of the neo-Assyrian drive toward the coast. Tyre was made to pay tribute and some attempt was made to subject her foreign policy. Yet her relationship with Assyria was for the most part one of cooperation. Assyrians had right of entry into Tyrian territories, but Tyrian traders were granted full reciprocity by Esarhaddon.[40] Though Tyre had an Assyrian resident magistrate watching her rulers she was otherwise independent. Later, Nebuchadnezzar kept Phoenicia under subjection, and tried to take Tyre, but was defeated. Neo-Assyrian and neo-Babylonian policies broadly amounted to an economic activation of the coast through the ports of trade, which, however, were not incorporated, pressure being mostly exerted by methods of remote control.

Persia represented entirely new principles of empire building. To use a minimum of coercion was among its tenets. Herodotus credited its rulers with professing a remarkable principle of empire government, according to which their interest in peoples diminished in proportion to the distance from the center of the country.[41] This may well have held out to the coastal towns a promise of autonomy. Its fulfillment seems to have depended on whether or not the cities were willing to accept Persian suzerainty. Miletus was treated mildly, other Ionian cities harshly—obligation of military service, payment of tribute and native rulers chosen by the Persians were imposed. To call these rulers tyrants is essentially misleading. Over the whole of the Hellenic world the fashionable monarchy of the nontraditional type went under the name of *tyrannis*. But the sinister overtones that the term later acquired are thoroughly anachronistic. Seventh and sixth century tyrannies were anything but unpopular; the typical self-made ruler arose from the ranks of the aristocracy with the help of the populace to rid them of oppression from oligarchic class rule. In metropolitan Greece, by the middle of the fifth century the new monarchy had been generally superseded by free forms of popular rule and the *tyrannis* was now under a cloud. Yet the ambiguity is still apparent in Herodotus. The Ionian tyrants of his grandfathers' time often owed their positions to the Persians who preferred to deal with monarchs rather than with assemblies, and to that extent the Ionian "tyrants" were justly dubbed Persian puppets. Herodotus mentioned that the Ionian kings during the Scythian wars did not cut the bridge on the Danube which Darius had entrusted to their care because they felt they would only be in power as long as the Persians were present. Persian *tyrannis* was then often merely a method by which popular but sympathetic satellite governments were established. In preparation for the second invasion of Greece the Persians, who nourished no ideological preferences, replaced the *tyrannis* in all Ionian cities by democratic regimes. When the wars were over, a return to the old policy of almost complete political independence occurred, yet with a closer approximation to a symbiotic relationship between coast and continent.

The Phoenician cities did not go through the same sharp fluctuations of Persian policies as those of Ionia. They retained their native kings, free to join or refuse to join Persian expeditions. There was a break in the mutual good-will when Xerxes beheaded some Phoenician officers for poor conduct. The Phoenicians thereupon withdrew their fleet from Persian service for approximately fifteen years. The bitter revolt of 352 in which many Sidonians immolated themselves in their city was not severely punished: the city was rebuilt and Phoenicia continued to enjoy a fair measure of independence and prosperity under Persia, which seemed to be tolerant of all but open rebellion. Co-operation was based on a smoothly functioning trade organization of the coast which the Persians implemented by contributing a metallic standard, an efficient road system, and a secure hinterland.

When in the last third of the first millennium, Macedonia cut across Europe, Asia, and Africa to create a world empire, the demise of the port of trade seemed imminent. Both the strategic and the cultural perils of the coast had lost substance and actuality. The coastlines, now lying for the first time *within* the boundaries of the all-inclusive empire, were left without political and military significance, and the hellenization of the *oecumenē* was the order of the day. Symbolic of the change was the defeat of Tyre at the hands of Alexander the Great. The man who embodied the novel idea of a universal civilization, had possessed himself of the impregnable rock which harbored Ezekiel's admired and hated Mistress of the Seas, and which had braved the might of Assur and Babylon. A vast expansion of peaceful trade was on, fusing the hitherto separated continents and transforming the Eastern Mediterranean into an Hellenic lake.

It is all the more remarkable to find instead a revival of the early port of trade almost in its classic form. For a long time to come, the port of trade with its neutral administration of transactions between many foreign peoples proved indispensable. To channel the commerce of the Orient which would flow through the Indian Ocean and the Red Sea, Cleomenes of Naucratis was commissioned by Alexander the Great to plan a city at the point of entry to the west. The outcome was the port of trade *par excellence*, Alexandria. Neutrality was its *raison d'être*.[42] Although situated on Egyptian soil, and erected under a Greek government, neither the Egyptians, nor even the Greeks themselves were to wield power in it. It was built outside the administrative boundary of the Egyptian *chora* and its autonomy was to prove indestructible. Its neutrality was guaranteed by settling there Jews and Egyptians in large numbers, so as to reduce the preponderance of the Greeks themselves. The security of trade under the municipal authority was assured by business transactions being sworn to before the altar of Hephaestion,[43] the defied friend of Alexander. The great king who bestowed his genius on these details had ordered two temples to be erected to Hephaestion, and all business documents to invoke the sanction of the guardian god.

Alexandria was the model to which, in Hellenistic times, many other ports of trade conformed, whether on the Phoenician coast, in Greece, or in Asia Minor. Ports of trade now had an informal status of their own. Tyre, Byblus, Sidon enjoyed the same independence as did the Greek cities of the coast; but the same independence was not granted to the Greek *poleis* of inland Babylonia.[44] Thus the transcontinental empires of the Hellenistic age, far from discarding the concept of the port of trade, rather strengthened and renewed it. But the shunning of the coast that the ancient world had known was now overcome. And the time was near when, in the Western Mediterranean an utterly novel constellation of power in relation to coast and continent would arise to revolve around the Roman axis.

Robert B. Revere

Notes to Chapter IV

1. A. T. Olmstead, *History of Assyria* (New York, 1923), p. 28,—CAH, I, 568.
2. *Ibid.*, p. 54.
3. G. A. Barton, *The Royal Inscriptions of Sumer and Akkad* (New Haven, 1929), p. 181 ff.

4. H. R. Hall, *The Ancient History of the Near East* (London, 1913), p. 97 ff.

5. Robert Engberg, *The Hyksos Reconsidered* (Chicago, 1939), p. 10.

6. Breasted, *CAH*, II, 192. "As Wenamon was obliged to pass through the territory of Nesubeneded, who now ruled the Delta, Hrihor supplied him with letters to the Delta prince, and in this way secured him passage in a ship. . . ."

7. *Ibid.*, p. 167.

8. H. R. Hall, *CAH*, III, 295.

9. Breasted, *op. cit.*, p. 193.

10. Cook, *CAH*, II, 306.

11. Breasted, *op. cit.*, p. 78.

12. In this section we closely follow J. Friedrich's and A. Goetze's translations. Cf. "Hittite Policies in Regard to Coastal Areas," by Karl Polanyi, Columbia University, March, 1955. (Mimeographed.)

13. Polanyi, *op. cit.*, J. Friedrich, *Aus den hettitischen Schriften*, A. O. 24, 3 (1925), The Telepinush Text, *op. cit.* (trans. into English).

14. *Ibid.*

15. *Ibid.*, Art. 2, Line 5.

16. *Ibid.*, Art. 3, Line 7.

17. *Ibid.*, Art. 3, Line 8.

18. A. Goetze, "Madduwattash," *MVAeG*, 32, 1 (1928), *Accusations Against Madduwattash.*

19. A. Goetze, "Hattushilish," *MVAeG* (1925).

20. *Ibid.*, III (28).

21. A. Goetze, *Kizzuwatna and the Problem of Hittite Geography* (New Haven, 1940), "The Shunashshura Treaty," p. 36 ff.

22. *Ibid.*

23. R. Dussaud, *Prélydiens, Hittites et Achéens* (Paris, 1953), fig. I.

24. *Ibid.*, p. 62.

25. A. Goetze, *Klein Asien* (1936), p. 168.

26. Dussaud, *op. cit.*, p. 59.

27. A. Goetze, *op. cit.*, p. 168, "The old border line that separated the West from the East remained all through the Hittite period, that is, almost through the whole of the second millennium."

28. *Ibid.*, p. 31.

29. M. Rostovtzeff, *Social and Economic History of the Hellenistic World* (Oxford, 1941), I, 81. "These cities, though subjects of Persia in the 4th century B.C., in fact belonged not to the Oriental but to the Greek world. They were, so to speak, fragments of the Western world on the fringe of the Eastern, serving as connecting links between the two. Behind them, however, the interior of Anatolia and the adjoining parts of north Syria remained essentially Oriental."

30. Lehmann-Hartleben, *Die antiken Hafenanlagen des Mittelmeeres* (Leipzig, 1923), p. 24.

31. Sir Leonard Woolley, *A Forgotten Kingdom* (Harmondsworth, 1953), p. 151.

32. Claude Schaeffer, *Cuneiform Texts*, p. 38.

33. Claude Schaeffer, "Reconstructing an Ancient Civilization," *The Listener*, Vol. 53 (June 30, 1955), 1162. "And here were sets of weights based on the shekel, that is one-third of an ounce. There are many small weights for fractions of a shekel, probably for the silversmith, and others for two, three, five, ten, twenty, thirty and fifty shekels. These are in bronze or in haematite. The heavy stone weights for 300, 500 and 1,000 shekels are in stone. One, which is cut with particular

care in hardstone, corresponds to one talent, that is, 3,000 shekels. These weights show that at Ugarit a decimal system was in use different from the system in vogue in Mesopotamia or in Egypt at the same time, which was based on multiples of sixty."

34. *Ibid.*, p. 1163.

35. Claude Schaeffer, *Cuneiform Texts*, p. 25. This letter is confirmed by the extraordinary lack of objects from Anatolia on the site of Ugarit. There are a sufficient number to indicate that there was trade, but an insufficient number to postulate an occupation.

36. Claude Schaeffer, *The Listener, op. cit.*, p. 1163.

37. O. R. Gurney, *The Hittites* (Harmondsworth, 1952), p. 97. "It is curious that the only case which we should describe as wilful murder is mentioned in connection with a merchant, who seems to be treated rather in a class by himself, and is associated with the motive of robbery."

38. M. Rostovtzeff, *Iranians and Greeks in South Russia* (Oxford, 1922), p. 41.

39. Hogarth, *CAH*, II, whom we follow for this period.

40. Olmstead, *op. cit.*, p. 375 ff.

41. Herodotus, I, 134. See also Rostovtzeff, *Social and Economic History of the Hellenistic World*, I, 83.

42. Cl. Préaux, *L'économie royale des Lagides* (1939), p. 432 ff.

43. Arrian, *Anabasis*, XXIII. "Hephaestion's name was to be engraved on all the legal documents with which the merchants entered into bargains with each other."

44. M. Cary, *A History of the Greek World from 323 to 146* B.C. (London, 1951), p. 268.

V

Aristotle Discovers the Economy

—————•—————

IN perusing the preceding chapters the reader may have sensed that some significant conclusion was pending. The *oikos* debate and our discussion of the Assyrian trading methods together with that of the ports of trade in the Eastern Mediterranean seemed to suggest that the study of the Old World, out of which civilization broke forth into the radiance of Greece, had a surprise in store. Such an expectation would not have been quite unjustified in view of the weighty implications that the recognition of the absence of markets from Hammurabi's Babylonia obviously holds for the appraisal of Greek economic history.

The familiar picture of classical Athens will have to absorb what might appear as a criss-cross of contradictions. The dominant conclusion must be that Attica was not, as we firmly believed, heir to commercial techniques that were supposed to have developed in the East; rather, she may herself have been a pioneer of the novel method of market trading. For if Babylon and Tyre were not, as it now appears, the ancient homes of the price-making market, then the elements of that seminal institution must have come from the Hellenic sphere, some time in the first millennium B.C. Sixth and fifth century Greece was, therefore, in essential respects, economically more naïve than even the extreme "primitivist" would have it, while in the fourth century these very Greeks initiated the gainful business practices that in much later days developed into the dynamo of market competition.

This brings into focus an aspect of the *oikos* controversy which only now becomes apparent. The "primitivists" asserted no more than that, up to the time of the Persian Wars, Attica was not a mercantile community. They did not deny that by the fourth century the Phoenicians had been ousted from their former maritime preeminence by the Hellenic seafarers, whose enterprising spirit backed by sea-loans gave them the lead over their erstwhile masters. For the rest, it was taken for granted that the Lydians had passed on to their Hellenic pupils the arts of gainful trading which they themselves had acquired from their Mesopotamian neighbors of the East.

All this falls to the ground if, as seems beyond dispute, Sumeria, Babylonia and Assyria as well as their Hittite and Tyrian successors practiced trade primarily through the dispositional actions of status traders. But whence then did the Hellenes, or for that matter the Lydians, derive their arts of individual business initiative, risky and gainful, which they hence certainly began to apply to some extent in their proceedings? And if, as it appears almost impossible not to conclude, they drew mainly upon themselves for the new attitudes, what evidence does the Greek literary record offer of the inevitable crisis of values which must have resulted?

To dramatize the cultural event of Greece at the climactic point of her awakening from a heroic to a semi-commercial economy, would be beyond our capacity, even if the attempt were not barred by the scope of this work. Yet it appears appropriate, indeed, it is imperative to follow up in the light of our newly gained knowledge the peripety in the social thinking of that encyclopaedic mind in the Greek orbit, Aristotle, when he first encountered the phenomenon we have become used to calling the "economy."

The contempt into which Aristotle's "Economics" has fallen in our day is a portent. Very few thinkers have been listened to on a greater diversity of subjects over so many centuries as he. Yet on a matter to which he devoted a signal effort and which happens also to be reckoned among the issues vital to our own generation, the economy, his teachings are judged inadequate by the leading spirits of the time to the point of irrelevance.[1]

Aristotle's influence on medieval city economy exerted through Thomas Aquinas was as great as later that of Adam Smith and David Ricardo on nineteenth century world economy. Naturally, one might say, with the actual establishment of the market system and the subsequent rise of the classical schools, Aristotle's doctrines on the subject went into eclipse. But the matter does not rest here. The more outspoken among modern economists seem to feel as though almost everything he had written on questions of man's livelihood suffered from some baneful weakness. Of his two broad topics—the nature of the economy and the issues of commercial trade and just price—neither had been carried to any clear conclusion. Man, like any other animal, was presented by him as naturally self-sufficient. The human economy did not, therefore, stem from the boundlessness of man's wants and needs, or, as it is phrased today, from the fact of scarcity. As to those two policy issues, commercial trade sprang according to Aristotle from the unnatural urge of money-making, which was of course unlimited, while prices should conform to the rules of justice (the actual formula remaining quite obscure). There were also his illuminating, if not altogether consistent remarks on money and that puzzling outburst against the taking of interest. This meager and fragmentary outcome was mostly attributed to an unscientific bias—the preference for that which ought to be over that which is. That prices, for instance, should depend upon the relative standing in the community of partners in the exchange seemed indeed an almost absurd view to take.

This sharply circumscribed breaking away from the body of thought inherited from classical Greece deserves more attention than it has hitherto received. The stature of the thinker and the dignity of the subject should make us hesitate to accept as final the erasing of Aristotle's teaching on the economy.

A very different appreciation of his position will be sustained here. He will be seen as attacking the problem of man's livelihood with a radicalism of which no later writer on the subject was capable—none has ever penetrated deeper into the material organization of man's life. In effect, he posed, in all its breadth, the question of the place occupied by the economy in society.

We will have to reach far back to explain why Aristotle thought as he did of what we call "the economy," or what impelled him to regard money-making in trade and the just price as the chief policy questions. Also we agree that economic theory cannot expect to benefit from Book I of *Politics* and Book V of the *Nichomachian Ethics*. Economic analysis, in the last resort, aims at elucidating the functions of the market mechanism, an institution that was still unknown to Aristotle.

To go to the root of our approach, classical antiquity was altogether wrongly placed by economic historians along the time scale which led up to market trade. In spite of intensive trading activities and fairly advanced money uses, Greek business life as a whole was still in the very first beginnings of market trade in Aristotle's time. His occasional vagueness and obscurities, not to speak of his alleged philosopher's remoteness from life, should be put down to difficulties of expression in regard to what actually were recent developments, rather than to the supposed insufficient penetration by him of practices allegedly current in contemporary Greece and nourished by a millennial tradition of the civilizations of the East.

This leaves classical Greece, however definitely some of her eastern states were already advancing towards the market habit, still considerably below the level of commercial trading with which she was later credited. Thus the Greeks may not have been, as was so confidently assumed, simply latecomers picking up the commercial practices developed by the Oriental empires. Rather, they were latecomers in a civilized marketless world, and compelled by circumstances to become pioneers in the development of the novel trading methods which were at most on the point of turning towards market trade.

All this, far from diminishing, as might superficially appear, the significance of Aristotle's thought on economic questions must, on the contrary, very greatly enhance their importance. For if our "nonmarket" reading of the Mesopotamian scene is true to fact, which we have no more cause to doubt, we have every reason to believe that in Aristotle's writings we possess an eye witness account of some of the pristine features of incipient market trading at its very first appearance in the history of civilization.

The Anonymity of the Economy in Early Society

Aristotle was trying to master theoretically the elements of a new complex social phenomenon in *statu nascendi*.

The economy, when it first attracted the conscious awareness of the philosopher in the shape of commercial trading and price differentials, was already destined to run its variegated course toward its fulfilment some twenty centuries later. Aristotle divined the full-fledged specimen from the embryo.[2]

The conceptual tool with which to tackle this transition from name-lessness to a separate existence we submit, is the distinction between the embedded and the disembedded condition of the economy in relation to society. The disembedded economy of the nineteenth century stood apart from the rest of society, more especially from the political and governmental system. In a market economy the production and distribution of material goods in principle is carried on through a self-regulating system of price-making markets. It is governed by laws of its own, the so-called laws of supply and demand, and motivated by fear of hunger and hope of gain. Not blood-tie, legal compulsion, religious obligation, fealty or magic creates the sociological situations which make individuals partake in economic life but specifically economic institutions such as private enterprise and the wage system.

With such a state of affairs we are of course fairly conversant. Under a market system men's livelihood is secured by way of institutions, that are activated by economic motives, and governed by laws which are specifically economic. The vast comprehensive mechanism of the economy can be conceived of working without the conscious intervention of human authority, state or government; no other motives than dread of destitution and desire for legitimate profit need be invoked; no other juridical requirement is set than that of the protection of property and the enforcement of contract; given the distribution of resources, of purchasing power as well as of the individual scales of preference the result will be an optimum of want satisfaction for all.

This, then, is the nineteenth century version of an independent economic sphere in society. It is motivationally distinct, for it receives its impulse from the urge of monetary gain. It is institutionally separated from the political and governmental center. It attains to an autonomy that invests it with laws of its own. In it we possess that extreme case of a disembedded economy which takes its start from the widespread use of money as a means of exchange.

In the nature of things the development from embedded to dis-embedded economies is a matter of degree. Nevertheless the distinction is fundamental to the understanding of modern society. Its sociological background was first mooted by Hegel in the 1820's and developed by Karl Marx in the 1840's. Its empirical discovery in terms of history was made by Sir Henry Sumner Maine in the Roman law categories of *status* and *contractus*, in the 1860's; finally, in the more comprehensive terms of economic anthropology, the position was restated by Bronislaw Malinowski in the 1920's.

Sir Henry Sumner Maine undertook to prove that modern society was built on *contractus*, while ancient society rested on *status*. *Status* is set by birth—a man's position in the family—and determines the rights and duties of a person. It derives from kinship and adoption; it persists under feudalism and, with some qualifications, right up to the age of equal citizenship as established in the nineteenth century. But already under Roman law *status* was gradually replaced by *contractus*, i.e., by rights and duties derived from bilateral arrangements. Later, Maine revealed the universality of *status* organization in the case of the village communities of India.

In Germany, Maine found a disciple in Ferdinand Toennies. His conception was epitomised in the title of his work *Community and Society (Gemeinschaft und Gesellschaft)*, 1888. "Community" corresponded to "*status*," "society" to "*contractus*." Max Weber frequently employed "*Gesellschaft*" in the sense of contract-type group, and "*Gemeinschaft*" in that of status-type group. Thus his own analysis of the place of the economy in society, though at times influenced by Mises, was molded by the thought of Marx, Maine and Toennies.

The emotional connotation, however, given to *status* and *contractus* as well as to the corresponding "community" and "society," was widely different with Maine and Toennies. To Maine the pre-*contractus* condition of mankind stood merely for the dark ages of tribalism. The introduction of contract, so he felt, had emancipated the individual from the bondage of *status*. Toennies' sympathies were for the intimacy of the community as against the impersonalness of organized society. "Community" was idealized by him as a condition where the lives of men were embedded in a tissue of common experience, while "society" was never to him far removed from the *cash nexus*, as Thomas Carlyle called the relationship of persons connected by market ties alone. Toennies' policy ideal was the restoration of community, not, however, by returning to the pre-society stage of authority and paternalism, but by advancing to a higher form of community of a postsociety stage, which would follow upon our present civilization. He envisaged this community as a co-operative phase of human existence, which would retain the advantages of technological progress and individual freedom while restoring the wholeness of life.

Hegel's and Marx's, Maine's and Toennies' treatment of the evolution of human civilization was accepted by many continental scholars as an epitome of the history of society. For a long time no advance was made on the trails they blazed. Maine had dealt with the subject chiefly as pertaining to the history of law, including its corporate forms as in rural India; Toennies' sociology revived the outlines of medieval civilization. Not before Malinowski's fundamental stand on the nature of primitive society was that antithesis applied to the economy. It is now possible to say that *status* or *gemeinschaft* dominate where the economy is embedded in noneconomic institutions; *contractus* or *gesellschaft* is characteristic of the existence of a motivationally distinct economy in society.

In terms of integration we can easily see the reason for this. *Contractus* is the legal aspect of exchange. It is not surprising, therefore, that a society based on *contractus* should possess an institutionally separate and motivationally distinct economic sphere of exchange, namely, that of the market. *Status*, on the other hand, corresponds to an earlier condition which roughly goes with reciprocity and redistribution. As long as these latter forms of integration prevail, no concept of an economy need arise. The elements of the economy are here embedded in noneconomic institutions, the economic process itself being instituted through kinship, marriage, age-groups, secret societies, totemic associations, and public solemnities. The term "economic life" would here have no obvious meaning.

This state of affairs, so puzzling to the modern mind, is often strikingly exhibited in primitive communities. It is often almost impossible for the observer to collect the fragments of the economic process and piece them together. To the individual his emotions fail to convey any experience that he could identify as "economic." He is simply not aware of any pervading interest in regard to his livelihood which he could recognize as such. Yet the lack of such a concept does not appear to hamper him in the performance of his everyday tasks. Rather, it is doubtful whether awareness of an economic sphere would not tend to reduce his capacity of spontaneous response to the needs of livelihood, organized as they are mainly through other than economic channels.

All this is an outcome of the manner in which the economy is here instituted. The individual's *motives*, named and articulated, spring as a rule from situations set by facts of a noneconomic—familial, political or religious—order; the site of the small family's economy is hardly more than a point of intersection between lines of activities carried on by larger kinship groups in various localities; land is either used in common as pasture or its various uses may be appropriated to members of different groups; labor is a mere abstraction from the "solicited" assistance offered by different teams of helpers, at definite occasions; as a result, the process itself runs in the grooves of different structures.

Accordingly, before modern times the forms of man's livelihood attracted much less of his conscious attention than did most other parts of his organized existence. In contrast to kinship, magic or etiquette with their powerful keywords, the economy as such remained nameless. There existed, as a rule, no term to designate the concept of economic. Accordingly, as far as one can judge, this concept was absent. Clan and totem, sex and age-group, the power of the mind and the ceremonial practices, custom and ritual were instituted through highly elaborate systems of symbols, while the economy was not designated by any one word conveying the significance of food supply for man's animal survival. It can not be merely a matter of chance that until very recent times no name to sum up the organization of the material conditions of life existed in the languages even of civilized peoples. Only two hundred years ago did an esoteric sect of French thinkers coin the term and call themselves *économistes*. Their claim was to have discovered the economy.

The prime reason for the absence of any concept of the economy is the difficulty of identifying the economic process under conditions where it is embedded in noneconomic institutions.

Only the concept of the economy, not the economy itself, is in abeyance, of course. Nature and society abound in locational and appropriational movements that form the body of man's livelihood. The seasons bring around harvest time with its strain and its relaxation; long-distance trade has its rhythm of preparation and foregathering with the concluding solemnity of the return of the venturers; and all kinds of artifacts, whether canoes or fine ornaments are produced, and eventually used by various groups of persons; every day of the week food is prepared at the family hearth. Each single event contains necessarily a bundle of economic items. Yet for all that, the unity and coherence of those facts is not reflected in men's consciousness. For the series of interactions between men and their natural surroundings will, as a rule, carry various significances, of which economic dependence is only one. Other dependences, more vivid, more dramatic, or more emotionalized may be at work, which prevent the economic movements of forming a meaningful whole. Where these other forces are embodied in permanent institutions the concept of the economic would be more confusing than clarifying to the individual. Anthropology offers many examples:

1. Where the physical *site* of a man's life is not identifiable with any ostensible part of the economy, his habitat—the household with its tangible environment—has but little economic relevance. This will be so, as a rule, when movements belonging to different economic processes intersect in one site, while the movements forming part of one and the same process are distributed over a number of disconnected sites.

Margaret Mead described how a Papuan-speaking Arapesh of New Guinea would envisage his physical surroundings:

A typical Arapesh man, therefore is living for at least part of the time (for each man lives in two or more hamlets, as well as in the garden huts, huts near the hunting bush, and huts near his sago palm) on land which does not belong to him. Around the house are pigs which his wife is feeding, but which belong either to one of her relatives or to one of his. Beside the house are coconut and betel palms which belong to still other people, and the fruit of which he will never touch without the permission of the owner, or someone who has been accorded the disposal of the fruit by the owner. He hunts on the bushland belonging to a brother-in-law or a cousin at least part of his hunting time, and the rest of the time he is joined by others on his bush, if he has some. He works his sago in others' sago clumps as well as in his own. Of the personal property in his house that which is of any permanent value, like large pots, well carved plates, good spears, has already been assigned to his sons, even though they are only toddling children. His own pig or pigs are far away in other hamlets: his palm trees are scattered three miles in one direction, two in another: his sago palms are still further scattered, and his garden patches lie here and there, mostly on the lands of others. If there is meat on his smoking rack over the fire, it is either meat which was killed by another, a brother, a brother-in-law, a sister's son, etc.— and has been given to him, in which case he and his family may eat it, or it is meat which he himself killed and which he is smoking to give away to someone else, for to eat one's own kill, even though it be only a small bird, is a crime to which only the morally, which usually means with the Arapesh mentally, deficient would stoop. If the house in which he is, is nominally his, it will have been constructed in part at least from the posts and planks of other people's houses, which have been dismantled or temporarily deserted, and from which he has borrowed timber. He will not cut his rafters to fit his house, if they are too long, because they may be needed later for someone else's house which is of a different shape or size. . . . This then is the picture of a man's ordinary economic affiliations.[3]

The complexity of the social relations that account for these every-day items, is staggering. Yet it is only at the hand of such relations, familiar to him, articulated and meaningfully deployed in the course of his own personal experience, that the Arapesh is able to find his bearings in an economic situation, the elements of which are jigsawed into dozens of different social relationships of a non-economic character.

So much for the locational aspect of the economic process where reciprocity prevails.

2. Another broad reason for the absence in primitive society of an integrating effect of the economy is its *lack of quantitativity*. He who possesses ten dollars does not, as a rule, call each by a separate name, but conceives of them rather as interchangeable units that can be substituted one for another, added up or subtracted. Short of such an operational facility on which terms like fund or balance of profit and loss depend for a meaning, the notion of an economy would mostly be devoid of any practical purpose. It would fail to discipline behavior, to organize and sustain effort. Yet the economic process does not naturally offer such a facility; that matters of livelihood are subject to reckoning is merely a result of the manner in which they are instituted.

Trobriand economy, for instance, is organized as a continuous give-and-take, yet there is no possibility of setting up a balance, or of employing the concept of a fund. Reciprocity demands adequacy of response, not mathematical equality. Consequently, transactions and decisions cannot be grouped with any precision from the economic point of view, i.e., according to the manner in which they affect material want satisfaction. Figures, if any, do not correspond to facts. Though the economic significance of an act may be great, there is no way of assessing its relative importance.

Malinowski listed the different kinds of give-and-take, from free gifts at the one extreme, to plain commercial barter at the other. His grouping of "gifts, payments, and transactions" came under seven headings, which he correlated with the sociological relationships within which each occurred. These numbered eight. The results of his analysis were revealing:

(a) The category of "free gifts" was exceptional, since charity was neither needed nor encouraged, and the notion of gift was always associated with the idea of adequate counter-gift (but not, of course, of equivalency). Even actual "free gifts" were construed as counter-gifts, given in return for some fictitious service rendered to the giver. Malinowski found that "the natives would undoubtedly *not* think of free gifts as being all of the same nature." Where the notion of "dead loss" is lacking, the operation of balancing a fund is not feasible.

(b) In the group of transaction, where the gift is expected to be returned in an economically equivalent manner, we meet another confusing fact. This is the category which according to our notions ought to be practically indistinguishable from trade. Far from it. Occasionally the identically same object is exchanged back and forth between the partners, thus depriving the transaction of any conceivable economic purpose or meaning! By the simple device of handing back, though in a roundabout way, the pig to its donor, the exchange of equivalencies instead of being a step in the direction of economic rationality proves a safeguard against the intrusion of utilitarian considerations. The sole purpose of the exchange is to draw relationships closer by strengthening the ties of reciprocity.

(c) Utilitarian barter is distinct from any other type of mutual gift giving. While in ceremonial exchange of fish for yam there is, in principle, adequacy between the two sides, a poor haul or a failure of crops, e.g., reducing the amount offered, in barter exchange of fish and yam there is at least a pretence of higgling and haggling. It is further characterized by an absence of special partnerships, and, if artifacts enter, by a restriction to newly manufactured goods—second-hand ones might have a personal value attached to them.

(d) Within the sociologically defined relationships—of which there are many—the exchange is usually unequal, as befits the relationship. Appropriational movements of goods and services are thus often instituted in a manner that renders some transactions irreversible and many goods noninterchangeable.

Thus quantitativity can hardly be expected to operate in that wide domain of livelihood which comes under the heading of "gifts, payments and transactions."

3. Another familiar concept that is inapplicable in primitive con-

ditions is that of property as a right of disposing of definite objects. Consequently, no straight inventory of possessions is practicable. We have here a variety of rights of different persons in regard to the same object. By this fragmentation, the unity of the object under its property aspect is destroyed. The appropriational movement does not as a rule have the complete object, for instance a piece of land, as its referent, but only its discrete uses, thus depriving the concept of property of its effectiveness in regard to objects.

4. *Economic transactions* proper hardly crop up in kinship-organized communities. Transactions in early times are public acts performed in regard to the status of persons and other self-propelling things: the bride, the wife, the son, the slave, the ox, the boat. With settled peoples changes in the status of a plot of land, too, were publicly attested.

Such status transactions would naturally carry important economic implications. Wooing, betrothal and marriage, adoption and emancipation are accompanied by movements of goods, some of them immediate, some to follow in the long run. Great as the economic significance of such transactions was, it ranked second to their importance in establishing the position of the persons in the social context. How, then, did transactions in regard to goods eventually separate off from the typical kinship transactions in regard to persons?

As long as only a few status goods, such as land, cattle, slaves were alienable there was no need for separate economic transactions since the transfer of such goods accompanied the change in status, while a transfer of the goods without such a change would not have been approved of by the collectivity. Incidentally, no economic valuation could easily attach to goods the fate of which was inseparably linked with that of their owners.

Separate transactions in regard to goods were in early times restricted to the two most important ones, namely, land and labor. Thus precisely the "goods," which were the last to become freely alienable were the first to become objects of limited transactions. Limited, since land and labor for a long time to come remained part of the social tissue and could not be arbitrarily mobilized without destroying it. Neither land nor freemen could be sold outright. Their transfer was conditional and temporary. Alienation stopped short of an unrestricted transference of ownership. Amongst the economic transactions in fourteenth century tribal-feudal Arrapha on the Tigris, those which refer to land and labor illustrate the point. Property, both in land and persons, belonged with the Nuzi to collectivities—clans, families, villages. Use alone was transferred. How exceptional in tribal times the transfer of property in land was, may be seen from the dramatic scenario of the episode of Abraham purchasing a family vault from the Hittite.

It is a peculiar fact that the transfer of "use alone" is rather more "economic" than would be the transfer of ownership. In the exchange of ownership, considerations of prestige and emotional factors may weigh heavily; in the alienation of use the utilitarian element prevails. In modern terms: interest, which is the price of use over time, may be said to have been one of the earliest economic quantities to be instituted.

Eventually, the thin economic layer may "peel off" from the status transaction, the referent of which is a person. The economic element may then change hands alone, the transaction being camouflaged as a status transaction which, however, is to be fictitious. Sale of land to non-clan members being prohibited, the residual rights of the clan to reclaim the land from the purchaser may be voided by legal devices. One of these was the fictitious adoption of the buyer or, alternatively, the fictitious consent of clan members to the sale.

Another line of development toward separate economic transactions led, as we saw, through the transference of "use only," thus expressly maintaining the residual property rights of the clan or family. The same purpose was served by a mutual exchange of "uses" of different objects, while pledging the return of the objects themselves.

The classical Athenian form of mortgage (*prasis epi lysei*) was probably such a transference of "use alone," but (exceptionally) leaving the debtor *in situ* while pledging to the creditor by way of interest a part of the crop. The creditor was safeguarded by the setting up of a boundary stone inscribed with his name and the amount of the debt, neither the date of repayment nor interest being mentioned, however. If this interpretation of the Attican *horos* holds good, the plot of land was, in a friendly way, mortgaged for an indefinite period against some participation in the crop. Default with a subsequent distraint would occur only quite rarely, namely, on a confiscation of the debtor's lands or the ruin of his entire family.

Almost in every case the separate transference of "use" serves the purpose of strengthening the bonds of family and clan with its social, religious and political ties. Economic exploitation of the "use" is thus made compatible with the friendly mutuality of those ties. It maintains the control of the collectivity over the arrangements made by their individual members. As yet the economic factor hardly registers its claims in the transactions.

5. Services, not goods make up wealth in many archaic societies. They are performed by slaves, servants, and retainers. But to make human beings disposed to serve as an outcome of their status is an aim of political (as against economic) power. With the increase of the material against the nonmaterial ingredients of wealth, the political method of control recedes and gives way to so-called economic control. Hesiod the peasant was talking thrift and farming centuries before the gentlemen philosophers, Plato and Aristotle, knew of any other social discipline than politics. Two millennia later, in Western Europe, a new middle class produced a wealth of commodities and argued "economics" against their feudal masters, and another century later the working class of an industrial age inherited from them that category as an instrument of their own emancipation. The aristocracy continued to monopolize government and to look down on commodity production. Hence, as long as dependent labor predominates as an element in wealth, the economy has only a shadowy existence.

6. In the philosophy of Aristotle *the three prizes of fortune* were: honor and prestige; security of life and limb; wealth. The first stands for privilege and homage, rank and precedence; the second ensures safety from open and secret enemies, treason and rebellion, the revolt of the slave, the overbearing of the strong, and even protection from the arm of the law; the third, wealth, is the bliss of proprietorship, mainly of heirloom or famed treasure. True, utilitarian goods, food and materials, accrue as a rule to the possessor of honor and security, but the glory outshines the goods. Poverty, on the other hand, goes with an inferior status; it involves working for one's living, often at the bidding of others. The less restricted the bidding, the more abject the condition. Not so much manual labor—as the farmer's ever respected position shows—but dependence upon another man's personal whim and command causes the serving man to be despised. Again, the bare economic fact of a lower income is screened from view.

7. The *agatha* are the highest prizes of life, that which is most desirable and also rarest. This is indeed a surprising context in which to encounter that feature of goods which modern theory has come to regard as the criterion of the "economic," namely, scarcity. For the discerning mind when considering those prizes of life must be struck

by the utterly different source of their "scarcity" from that which the economist would make us expect. With him scarcity reflects either the niggardliness of nature or the burden of the labor that production entails. But the highest honors and the rarest distinctions are few for neither of these two reasons. They are scarce for the obvious reason that there is no standing room at the top of the pyramid. The fewness of the *agatha* is inherent in rank, immunity and treasure: they would not be what they are if they were attainable to many. Hence the absence in early society of the "economic connotation" of scarcity, whether or not utilitarian goods sometimes also happen to be scarce. For the rarest prizes are not of this order. Scarcity derives here from the noneconomic order of things.

8. The *self-sufficiency* of a body of humans, that postulate of bare life, is ensured when a supply of the "necessaries" is physically available. The things that are here meant are those that sustain life and are storable, that is, which keep. Corn, wine and oil are *chrēmata*, but so are wool and certain metals. The citizenry and the members of the family must be able to depend upon them in famine or war. The amount that the family or the city "needs" is an objective requirement. The household is the smallest, the polis is the largest unit of consumption: in either case that which is "necessary" is set by the standards of the community. Hence the notion of the intrinsically limited amount of the necessaries. This meaning is very near to that of "rations." Since equivalencies, whether by custom or law, were set only for such subsistence goods which actually served as units of pay, or of wages, the notion of the "necessary amount" was associated with the commonly stored staples. For operational reasons a boundlessness of human wants and needs—the logical correlate of "scarcity"—was a notion quite foreign to this approach.

These are some of the major reasons that so long stood in the way of the birth of a distinctively economic field of interest. Even to the professional thinker the fact that man must eat did not appear worthy of elaboration.

Aristotle's Probings

It may seem paradoxical to expect that the last word on the nature of economic life should have been spoken by a thinker who hardly saw its beginnings. Yet Aristotle, living, as he did, on the borderline of economic ages, was in a favored position to grasp the merits of the subject.

This may explain incidentally why in our own day, in the face of a change in the place of the economy in society comparable in scope only to that which in his time heralded the oncoming of market trade, Aristotle's insights into the connections of economy and society can be seen in their stark realism.

We have therefore every reason to seek in his works for far more massive and significant formulations on economic matters than Aristotle has been credited with in the past. In fact, the *disjecta membra* of the *Ethics* and *Politics* convey a monumental unity of thought.

Whenever Aristotle touched on a question of the economy he aimed at developing its relationship to society as a whole. The frame of reference was the community as such which exists at different levels within all functioning human groups. In terms, then, of our modern speech Aristotle's approach to human affairs was sociological. In mapping out a field of study he would relate all questions of institutional origin and function to the totality of society. Community, self-sufficiency and justice were the focal concepts. The group as a going concern forms a community (*koinonia*) the members of which are linked by the bond of good will (*philia*). Whether *oikos* or *polis*, or else, there is a kind of *philia*, specific to that *koinonia*, apart from which the group could not remain. *Philia* expresses itself in a behavior of reciprocity (*anti-peponthos*),[4] that is, readiness to take on burdens in turn and share mutually. Anything that is needed to continue and maintain the community, including its self-sufficiency (*autarkeia*) is "natural" and intrinsically right. Autarchy may be said to be the capacity to subsist without dependence on resources from outside. Justice (contrary to our own view) implies that the members of the community possess unequal standing. That which ensures justice, whether in regard to the distribution of the prizes of life or the adjudication of conflicts, or the regulation of mutual services is good since it is required for the continuance of the group. Normativity, then, is inseparable from actuality.

These rough indications of his total system should permit us to outline Aristotle's views on trade and prices. Trade is "natural" when it serves the survival of the community by maintaining its self-sufficiency. The need for this arises as soon as the extended family grows overpopulous, and its members are forced to settle apart. Their autarchy would now be impaired all round, but for the operation of giving a share (*metadosis*), from one's surplus. The rate at which the shared services (or, eventually, the goods) are exchanged follows from the requirement of *philia*, i.e., that the good-will among the members persist. For without it, the community itself would cease. The just price, then, derives from the demands of *philia* as expressed in the reciprocity which is of the essence of all human community.

From these principles derive also his strictures on commercial trading and the maxims for the setting up of exchange equivalencies or the just price. Trade, we saw, is "natural" as long as it is a requirement of self-sufficiency. Prices are justly set if they conform to the standing of the participants in the community, thereby strengthening the good-will on which community rests. Exchange of goods is exchange of services; this, again, is a postulate of self-sufficiency and is practiced by way of a mutual sharing at just prices. In such exchange no gain is involved; goods have their known prices, fixed beforehand. If exceptionally gainful retailing there must be for the sake of a convenient distribution of goods in the market place, let it be done by noncitizens. Aristotle's theory of trade and price was nothing else than a simple elaboration of his general theorem of the human community.

Community, self-sufficiency and justice: these pivots of his sociology were the frame of reference of his thought on all economic matters, whether the nature of the economy, or policy issues were at stake.

The Sociological Bent

On the nature of the economy Aristotle's starting point is, as always, empirical. But the conceptualization even of the most obvious facts is deep and original.

The desire for wealth, Solon's verse had proclaimed, was unlimited with man. Not so, said Aristotle, in opening up the subject. Wealth is, in truth, the things necessary to sustain life, when safely stored in the keeping of the community, whose sustenance they represent. Human needs, be they of the household or of the city, are not boundless; nor is there a scarcity of subsistence in nature. The argument which sounds strange enough to modern ears, is powerfully pressed and carefully elaborated. At every point the institutional reference is explicit. Psychology is eschewed, sociology imposed.

The rejection of the scarcity postulate (as we would say) is based on the conditions of animal life, and is thence extended to those of human life. Do not animals from their birth find their sustenance waiting for them in their environment? And do not men, too, find sustenance in mother's milk and eventually in their environment, be they hunters, herdsmen, or tillers of the soil? Since slavery to Aristotle is "natural," he can without inconsistency describe slave raids as a hunt for peculiar game and consequently represent the leisure of the slave-owning citizenry as supplied by the environment. Otherwise, no need save that for sustenance is considered, much less approved of. Therefore, if scarcity springs "from the demand side," as we would say, Aristotle attributes it to a misconceived notion of the good life as a desire for a greater abundance of physical goods and enjoyments. The elixir of the good life—the elation of day-long theater, the mass jury service, the holding in turn of offices, canvassing, electioneering, great festivals, even the thrill of battle and naval combat—can be neither hoarded nor physically possessed. True, the good life requires, "this is generally admitted," that the citizen have leisure in order to devote himself to the service of the *polis*. Here again, slavery was part of the answer; another and much more incisive part lay in the payment of all citizens for the performance of public duties, or else, in not admitting artisans to citizenship, a measure Aristotle himself seemed to commend.

For yet another reason the problem of scarcity does not arise with Aristotle. The economy—as the root of the word shows, a matter of the domestic household or *oikos*—concerns directly the relationship of the persons who make up the natural institution of the household. Not possessions, but parents, offspring and slaves constitute it. The techniques of gardening, breeding or other modes of production Aristotle excluded from the purview of the economy. The emphasis is altogether institutional and only up to a point ecological, relegating technology to the subordinate sphere of useful knowledge. Aristotle's concept of the economy would almost permit us to refer to it as an instituted process through which sustenance is ensured. With a similar liberty of phrasing, Aristotle may be said to put down the erroneous conception of unlimited human wants and needs, or, of a general scarcity of goods, to two circumstances: first, the acquisition of foodstuffs through commercial traders, which introduces money-making into the quest for subsistence; second, a false notion of the good life as a utilitarian cumulation of physical pleasures. Given the right institutions in trade and the right understanding of the good life, Aristotle saw no room for the scarcity factor in the human economy. He did not fail to connect this with the existence of such institutions as slavery, infanticide and a way of life that discounts comfort. Short of this empirical reference his negation of scarcity might have been as dogmatic and as unfavorable to factual research as the scarcity postulate is in our days. But with him, once and for all, human needs presupposed institutions and customs.

Aristotle's adherence to the substantive meaning of "economic" was basic to his total argument. For why did he have to probe into the economy at all? And why did he need to set in motion an array of arguments against the popular belief that the significance of that dimly apprehended field lay in the lure of wealth, an insatiable urge common to the human frame? To what purpose did he develop a theorem comprising the origins of family and state, solely designed to demonstrate that human wants and needs are not boundless and that useful things are not, intrinsically, scarce? What was the motive behind this orchestration of an inherently paradoxical point which, moreover, must have appeared too speculative to be quite in keeping with his strongly empiricist bent?

The explanation is obvious. Two policy problems—trade and price —were pressing for an answer. Unless the question of commercial trade and the setting of prices could be linked to the requirements of communal existence and its self-sufficiency, there was no rational way of judging of either, be it in theory or in practice. If such a link did offer, then the answer was simple: first, trade that served to restore self-sufficiency was "in accordance with nature"; trade that did not, was "contrary to nature." Second, prices should be such as to strengthen the bond of community; otherwise exchange will not continue to take place and the community will cease to exist. The mediating concept was in either case the self-sufficiency of the community. The economy, then, consisted in the necessaries of life—grain, oil, wine, and the like —on which the community subsisted. The conclusion was stringent and no other was possible. So either the economy was about the material, substantive, things that sustained human beings, or else there was no empirically given rational link between matters such as trade and prices on the one hand, and the postulate of a self-sufficient community, on the other. The logical necessity for Aristotle's insistence on the substantive meaning of "economic" is therefore evident.

Hence also that astonishing attack on the Solonic poem in an overture of a treatise on economics.

Natural Trade and Just Price

Commercial trade, or, in our terms, market trade, arose as a burning issue out of the circumstances of the time. It was a disturbing novelty, which could neither be placed, nor explained, nor judged adequately. Money was now being earned by respectable citizens through the simple device of buying and selling. Such a thing had been unknown, or rather, was restricted to low-class persons, known as hucksters, as a rule metics, who eked out a living by retailing food in the market place. Such individuals did make a profit by buying at one price and selling at another. Now this practice had apparently spread to the citizenry of good standing, and big sums of money were made by this method, formerly stamped as disreputable. How should the phenomenon itself be classified? How should profit, systematically made in this manner, be operationally explained? And what judgment should be passed on such an activity?

The origin of market institutions is in itself an intricate and obscure subject. It is hard to trace their historical beginnings with precision and even harder to follow the stages by which early forms of trade developed into market trade.

Aristotle's analysis struck to the root. By calling commercial trade *kapēlikē*—no name had yet been given to it—he intimated that it was nothing new, except for the proportions it assumed. It was hucksterism written large. The money was made "off" each other (*ap'allēlōn*), by the surcharging methods so often met with in the market place.

Aristotle's point, inadequate though such a notion of mutual surcharge was, reflected a crucial phase of transition in the history of the human economy: the juncture at which the institution of the market began to move into the orbit of trade.

One of the first city markets, if not the very first, was no other than the *agora* in Athens. Nothing indicates that it was contemporaneous with the founding of the city. The first authentic record of the *agora* is of the fifth century when it was already definitely established, though still contentious. Throughout the course of its early history the use of small coin and the retailing of food went together. Its beginnings in Athens should therefore coincide with the minting of obols sometime in the early sixth century. On Asian territory it may have had a precursor in Sardis, the Lydian capital, to all accounts a thoroughly Greek type of city. Here again pioneering in small change marks the trail, especially if we include as we should, the use of gold dust. On this point Herodotus leaves little doubt. The Midas legend dates the presence in Phrygia of large amounts of river gold about 715, while in Sardis the market place itself was crossed by a gold-bearing stream, the Pactolus. In Herodotus' birthplace, Halicarnassus, stood that huge monument to Alyattes to the cost of which the love trade of Lydian girls had so generously contributed, while Gyges, founder of the Mermnade dynasty, appears to have initiated the coinage of elektron. Alyattes' son, Croesus, adorned Delphi with the splendor of his massive gold gifts. No beads or shells that might be employed as money stuffs are known from Asia Minor; the mention of gold dust is therefore crucial. The probability is strong that the twin Lydian innovations of coinage and the retailing of food were introduced together in Athens. They were not yet inseparable by any means. Aegina, which preceded Athens in matters of coinage, may have used coins only in foreign trade. The same might be true of the Lydian coins, while gold dust circulated in the food market and in love deals. Up to this day the market place in Bida, capital of Nupe, in Nigeria, is said to turn after midnight into a place of mercenary sociability, with gold dust presumably circulating as money. In Lydia, too, the presence of gold dust may have induced the retailing of food in the market. Attica followed in its wake, but replaced the specks of gold by fractions of obols of silver.

Broadly, coins spread much faster than markets. While trade was abounding and money as a standard was common, markets were few and far between.

By the end of the fourth century Athens was famous for her commercial agora, where anyone could buy a meal cheaply. Coinage had spread like wildfire, but outside of Athens the market habit was not particularly popular. During the Peloponnesian War fleets of sutlers accompanied the navy, for the troops could only exceptionally rely on subsisting from local markets. As late as the beginning of the fourth century the Ionian countryside possessed no regular food markets. The chief promoters of markets were at that time the Greek armies, notably the mercenary troops now more and more frequently employed as a business venture. The traditional self-equipping hoplite army had been engaged only in brief campaigns on a sack of barley meal brought along from home. By the turn of the fifth century regular expeditionary forces were formed, only the cadres of which consisted of Spartan or Athenian citizens while the bulk was recruited from abroad. The employment of such a force, especially if it was supposed to cross friendly territory, raised logistic problems, on which scholarly generals were fond to comment.

Xenophon's tracts offer many instances of the actual and the ideal role assigned to the market in the new strategy. The food market from which the troops could provision themselves from the hand money due to them from their C. O. (unless local requisitioning was practicable) formed part of a broader issue—the sale of booty, especially slaves and cattle, as well as provisioning from sutlers who followed the army in the hope of profit. It all boiled down to so many market problems. Concerning each we have evidence of organizational and financial activities initiated by kings, generals or governments responsible for the military undertaking. The campaign itself was quite often no more than a rationalized booty raid, if not of the renting out of an army to serve some foreign government for the benefit of the home country that financed the venture on business grounds. Military efficiency, of course, was the paramount requirement. An expedition's sale of booty, if only for reasons of military tactics, formed as much part of efficiency as did the regular provisioning of the troops, while it avoided, as far as could be, the antagonizing of friendly neutrals. Go-ahead generals devised up-to-date methods of stimulating local market activities, financing sutlers to wait upon the troops, and engaging local craftsmen in improvised markets for the supply of armaments. They boosted market supply and market services by all means at their disposal, however tentative and hesitant local initiative sometimes may have been. There was, in effect, but little reliance on the spontaneous business spirit of the residents. The Spartan government sent a civilian commission of "booty sellers" along with the king who commanded the army in the field. Their task was to have the captured slaves and cattle auctioned on the spot. King Agesilaos busied himself to have markets "prepared," "set up," and "offered" to his troops by the friendly cities along his prospective itinerary. In the Cyropaedian utopia, Xenophon described how any trader who wished to accompany the army and needed money for supplies, would go to the commander and, after giving references as to his reliability, would be advanced money out of a fund kept for that purpose. (*Cyr.* VI ii 38 f). Around that time Timotheus, the Athenian general, heedful of the sutlers' financial needs, acted on lines similar to Xenophon's educational novel. In the Olynthian war (364 B.C.), having substituted copper for silver in paying his soldiers, he persuaded the traders to accept it from the soldiers at that value, firmly promising them that it will be accepted from them at that rate for the purchase of booty, and that anything left over after purchasing booty would be redeemed in silver. (Ps. Arist. *Oecon.* II 23 a). It all goes to show how small the reliance on local markets still was, both as a means of provisioning and as a vent for booty unless fostered by the military.

Local markets, then, in Aristotle's time were a delicate growth. They were put up on occasion, in an emergency or for some definite purpose and not unless political expediency so advised. Nor does the local food market present itself in any way as an organ of long-distance trade. Separation of trade and market is the rule.

The institution which eventually was to link the two, the supply-demand-price mechanism, was unknown to Aristotle. It was of course the true originator of these commercial practices which were now becoming noticeable in trade. Traditionally, trade carried no taint of commerce. In its origins a semi-warlike occupation, it never cut loose from governmental associations, apart from which but little trading could take place under archaic conditions. Gain sprang from booty and gifts (whether voluntary or blackmailed), public honors and prizes, the golden crown and the land grant bestowed by prince or city, the arms and luxuries acquired—the *kerdos* of the Odyssey. Between all this and the local food market of the *polis* there was no physical connection. The Phoenician *emporos* would display his treasures and trinkets at the prince's palace or the manorial hall, while the crew would settle down to grow their own food on foreign soil—a yearly turnover. Later forms of trade ran in administrative grooves, smoothed by the urbanity of port of trade officialdom. Customary and treaty prices loomed large. The trader, unless compensated from commission fees, would make his "gain" from the proceeds of the imports that were the trophy of the venture.

Treaty prices were matters of negotiation, with much diplomatic higgling-haggling to precede them. Once a treaty was established, bargaining was at an end. For treaty meant a set price at which trading took its course. As there was no trade without treaty, so the existence of a treaty precluded the practices of the market. Trade and markets had not only different locations, status and personnel, they differed also in purpose, ethos and organization.*

We can not yet tell for certain, when and in what form higgling-haggling and gain made on prices entered the realm of trade, as implied in Aristotle. Even in the absence of international markets gain made in overseas trade had been normal. There can be no doubt however, that the sharp eye of the theoretician had discerned the links between the petty tricks of the huckster in the *agora* and novel kinds of trading profits that were the talk of the day. But the gadget that established their kinship—the supply-demand-price mechanism—escaped Aristotle. The distribution of food in the market allowed as yet but scant room to the play of that mechanism; and long-distance trade was directed not by individual competition, but by institutional factors. Nor were either local markets or long-distance trade conspicuous for the fluctuation of prices. Not before the third century B.C., was the working of a supply-demand-price mechanism in international trade noticeable. This happened in regard to grain, and later, to slaves, in the open port of Delos. The Athenian *agora* preceded, therefore, by some two centuries the setting up of a market in the Aegean which could be said to embody a market mechanism. Aristotle, writing in the second half of this period, recognized the early instances of gain made on price differentials for the symptomatic development in the organization of trade which they actually were. Yet in the absence of price-making markets he would have seen nothing but perversity in the expectation that the new urge for money making might conceivably serve a useful purpose. As to Hesiod, his famous commendation of peaceful strife had never transcended the prizes of premarket competition on the manorial level—praise for the potter, a joint for the lumberman, a gift to the singer who won.

Exchange of Equivalencies

This should dispose of the notion that Aristotle was offering in his *Ethics* a theory of prices. Such a theory is indeed central to the understanding of the market, the main function of which is to produce a price that balances supply and demand. None of these concepts, however, was familiar to him.

* See below, Ch. IV.

The postulate of self-sufficiency implied that such trade as was required to restore autarchy was natural and, therefore, right. Trade went with acts of exchange which again implied a definite rate at which the exchange was to take place. But how to fit acts of barter into a framework of community? And, if barter there was, at what rate was it to be performed?

As to the origin of barter, nothing could appeal less to the philosopher of *gemeinschaft* than the Smithian propensity allegedly inherent in the individual. Exchange, Aristotle said, sprang from the needs of the extended family the members of which originally used things in common which they owned in common. When their numbers increased and they were compelled to settle apart, they found themselves short of some of the things they formerly used in common and had therefore to acquire the needed things from amongst each other.[5] This amounted to a mutual sharing. Briefly,[6] reciprocity in sharing was accomplished through acts of barter.[7] Hence exchange.

The rate of exchange must be such as to maintain the community.[8] Again, not the interests of the individuals, but those of the community were the governing principle. The skills of persons of different status had to be exchanged at a rate proportionate to the status of each: the builder's performance exchanged against many times the cobbler's performance; unless this was so, reciprocity was infringed and the community would not hold.[9] *

Aristotle offered a formula by which the rate (or price) is to be set:[10] it is given by the point at which two diagonals cross, each of them representing the status of one of the two parties.[11] This point is formally determined by four quantities—two on each diagonal. The method is obscure, the result incorrect. Economic analysis represented the four determinative quantities with correctness and precision by pointing out the pair of indices on the demand curve, and the pair of indices on the supply curve, which are determinative of the price that clears the market. The crucial difference was that the modern economist was aiming at a description of the *formation of prices* in the market, while such a thought was far from Aristotle's mind. He was busied with the quite different and essentially practical problem of providing a formula by which the *price was to be set.*

Surprisingly enough, Aristotle seemed to see no other difference between set price and bargained price than a point of time, the former

* See, e.g., below, Ch. XI.

being there before the transaction took place, while the latter emerged only afterwards.[12] The bargained price, he insisted, would tend to be excessive because it was agreed to when the demand was not yet satisfied. This in itself should be sufficient proof of Aristotle's naiveté concerning the working of the market. He apparently believed that the justly set price must be different from the bargained one.

The set price, besides its justness, also offered the advantage of setting natural trade apart from unnatural trade. Since the aim of natural trade is exclusively to restore self-sufficiency, the set price ensures this through its exclusion of gain. Equivalencies—as we will henceforth call the set rate—serve therefore to safeguard "natural" trade. The bargained price might yield a profit to one of the parties at the expense of the other, and thus undermine the coherence of the community instead of underpinning it.

To the modern market-adjusted mind the chain of thought here presented and ascribed to Aristotle must appear as a series of paradoxes:

It implies the ignoring of the market as a vehicle of trade; of price formation as a function of the market; of any other function of trade than that of contributing to self-sufficiency; of the reasons why set price might differ from market-formed price, and why market prices should be expected to fluctuate; finally, of competition as the device that produced a price unique in that it clears the market and can therefore be regarded as the natural rate of exchange.

Instead, market and trade are here thought of as separate and distinct institutions; prices, as produced by custom, law or proclamation; gainful trade, as "unnatural"; the set price, as "natural"; fluctuation of prices, as undesirable; and the natural price, far from being an impersonal appraisal of the goods exchanged, as expressing the mutual estimation of the statuses of the producers.

For the resolution of these apparent contradictions the concept of equivalencies enters as crucial.

In the key passage on the origin of exchange (*allagē*) Aristotle gave perfect precision to that basic institution of archaic society—exchange of equivalencies. The increase in the size of the family spelt the end of their self-sufficiency. Lacking one thing or another, they had to rely on one another for supply. Some barbarian peoples, Aristotle said, still practice such exchange in kind "for such people are expected to give in exchange necessaries of life for other necessaries of life, for example, wine for corn, as much as required in the circumstances and no more, handing over the one and taking the other in return, and so with each of the staples of the sort. The practice of barter of this manner and type was not, therefore, contrary to nature, nor was it a branch of the art of wealth-getting, for it was instituted for the restoring of man's natural self-sufficiency."[13]

The institution of equivalency exchange was designed to ensure that all householders had a claim to share in the necessary staples at given rates, in exchange for such staples as they themselves happened to possess. For no one was expected to give away his goods for the asking, receiving nothing in return; indeed, the indigent who possessed no equivalent to offer in exchange had to work off his debt (hence the great social importance of the institution of debt bondage). Thus barter derived from the institution of sharing of the necessities of life; the purpose of barter was to supply all householders with those necessities up to the level of sufficiency; it was institutionalized as an obligation of householders to give of their surplus to any other householder who happened to be short of that definite kind of necessary, at his request, and to the extent of his shortage, but only to that extent; the exchange was made at the established rate (equivalency) against other staples of which the householder happened to have a supply. In so far as legal terms are applicable to so primitive conditions, the obligation of the householder was directed towards a transaction in kind, limited in extent to the claimant's actual need, performed at equivalency rates by exclusion of credit, and comprising all staples.

In the *Ethics*, Aristotle stressed that in spite of the equivalency of goods exchanged, one of the parties benefited, namely, the one who felt compelled to suggest the transaction. Nevertheless, in the long run, the procedure amounted to a mutual sharing, since at another time it was the other's turn to benefit by the chance. "The very existence of the state depends on such acts of proportionate reciprocity . . . failing which no sharing happens, and it is the sharing which binds us together. This is why we set up a shrine of the Graces in a public place to remind men to return a kindness; for that is a special characteristic of Grace, since it is a duty not only to repay a service done one, but another time to take the initiative in doing a service oneself."[14] Nothing, I feel, could show better the meaning of reciprocity than this elaboration. It might be called reciprocity on the square. Exchange is here viewed as part of reciprocity behavior in contrast to the marketing view which invested barter with the qualities which are the very reverse of the generosity and grace that accompanied the idea of reciprocity.

But for these strategic passages, we might still be unable to identify this vital institution of archaic society, in spite of the sheaves of documentary evidence unearthed by archaeologists within the last two or three generations. Figures representing mathematical rates between units of goods of different kinds were throughout translated by Orientalists as "price." For markets were assumed as a matter of course. Actually those figures connoted equivalencies quite unconnected with markets and market prices, their quality of fixedness being an inborn one, not implying any antecedent fluctuations brought to an end by some process of "setting" or "fixing" as the phrase seems to imply. Language itself betrays us here.

The Texts

This is not the place to elaborate on the numerous points at which our presentation differs from previous ones. However, in brief we must refer back to the texts themselves. Almost inevitably an erroneous view had been formed of the subject matter of Aristotle's discourse. Commercial trading, which was taken to be that subject, was, as it now appears, just only beginning to be practiced in his time. Not Hammurabi's Babylonia, but the Greek-speaking fringe of Western Asia together with Greece herself were responsible for that development— well over a thousand years afterward. Aristotle could not, therefore, have been describing the working of a developed market mechanism and discussing its effects on the ethics of trade. Again, it follows that some of his key terms, notably *kapēlikē, metadosis* and *chrēmatistikē,* were misinterpreted in translation. Sometimes the error becomes subtle. *Kapēlikē* was rendered as the art of retail trade instead of the art of "commercial trade," *chrēmatistikē* as the art of money-making instead of that of supply, i.e., the procuring of the necessaries of life in kind. In another instance, the distortion is manifest: *metadosis* was taken to be exchange or barter, while patently meaning its opposite, namely, "giving one's share."

Briefly, in sequence:

Kapēlikē, grammatically denotes the art of the *kapēlos.* The meaning of *kapēlos* as used by Herodotus in the middle of the fifth century, is broadly established as some kind of retailer, especially of food, a keeper of a cook shop, a seller of foodstuffs and cooked food. The in-

vention of coined money was linked by Herodotus with the fact that
the Lydians had turned *kapēloi*. Herodotus also recounts that Darius
was nicknamed *kapēlos*. Indeed, under him military stores may have
begun the practice of retailing food.[15] Eventually *kapēlos* became
synonymous with "trickster, fraud, cheat." Its pejorative meaning was
congenital.

Unfortunately, this still leaves the Aristotelian meaning of the word
kapēlikē wide open. The suffix *-ikē* indicates "art of," and so makes
kapēlikē signify the art of the *kapēlos*. Actually, such a word was not in
use; the dictionary mentions only one instance (apart from Aristotle)
and in this instance it designates, as one would expect, the "art of
retailing." How, then, did Aristotle come to introduce it as the heading
for a subject of the first magnitude noways restricted to retail trading,
namely, commercial trade? For that and no other is without any possible doubt the subject of his discourse.

The answer is not hard to find. In his passionate diatribe against
gainful trading Aristotle was using *kapēlikē* with an ironical overtone.
Commercial trade was of course, not huckstering; nor was it retail
trading; and whatever it was, it deserved to be called some form or
variant of *emporia* which was the regular name for seafaring trade,
together with any other form of large-scale or wholesale trade. When
Aristotle referred specifically to the various kinds of maritime trade,
he fell back on *emporia*, in the usual sense. Why, then, did he not do
so in the main theoretical analysis of the subject but use instead a new-
fangled word of pejorative connotation?

Aristotle enjoyed inventing words, and his humor, if any, was
Shavian. The figure of the *kapēlos* was an unfailing hit of the comic
stage. Aristophanes in his *Acharnians* had made his hero turn *kapēlos*
and in that guise earn the solemn praises of the chorus which lauded
him as the philosopher of the day. Aristotle wished drastically to convey his unimpressedness with the *nouveaux riches* and the allegedly
esoteric sources of their wealth. Commercial trade was no mystery.
When all is said, it was but huckstering written large.

Chrēmatistikē was deliberately employed by Aristotle in the literal
sense of providing for the necessaries of life, instead of its usual meaning of "money-making." Laistner rendered it correctly as "the art of
supply," and Ernest Barker in his commentary recalled the original
sense of *chrēmata*, which, he warned, was not money, but the necessaries themselves, an interpretation also upheld by Defourny and by

M. I. Finley in an unpublished lecture. Indeed, with Aristotle the stress on the nonmonetary meaning of *chrēmata* was logically unavoidable, since he held on to the autarchy postulate which was pointless outside of a naturalistic interpretation of wealth.

The signal error in rendering *metadosis* as "exchange" in the three crucial passages of the *Politics* and the *Ethics* cut deeper still.[15] In the case of *metadosis* Aristotle kept to the common meaning of the word. It was the translators who brought in an arbitrary interpretation. In an archaic society of common feasts, raiding parties, and other acts of mutual help and practical reciprocity the term *metadosis* possessed a specific operational connotation—it signified "giving a share," especially to the common pool of food, whether a religious festivity, a ceremonial meal, or other public venture was in question. That is the dictionary meaning of *metadosis*. Its etymology underlines the unilateral character of the giving, contributing, or sharing operation. Yet we are faced with the astonishing fact that in the translation of these passages in which Aristotle insisted on the derivation of exchange from *metadosis*, this term was rendered as "exchange" or "barter," which turned it into its opposite. This practice was sanctioned by the leading dictionary, which recorded *s. v. metadosis* those crucial three passages as exceptions! Such a deviation from the plain text is understandable only as an expression of the marketing bias of latter-day translators, who at this point were unable to follow the meaning of the text. Exchange to them was a natural propensity of men and stood in no need of explanation. But even assuming it did, it certainly could not have sprung from *metadosis* in its accepted meaning of "giving a share." Accordingly, they rendered *metadosis* by "exchange," and thus turned Aristotle's statement into an empty truism. This mistake endangered the whole edifice of Aristotle's economic thought at the pivotal point. By his derivation of exchange from "giving one's share" Aristotle provided a logical link between his theory of the economy in general and the practical questions at issue. Commercial trade, we recall, he regarded as an unnatural form of trade; natural trade was gainless since it merely maintained self-sufficiency. In support of this he could effectively appeal to the circumstance that, to the limited amount needed to maintain self-sufficiency, and only to that amount, exchange in kind was still widely practiced by some barbarian peoples in regard to the necessaries of life, at set equivalences, benefiting at one time the one, at another time the other, as chance would have it. Thus the *derivation* of exchange from contributing one's share to the common pool of food was the linchpin that held together a theory of the economy based on the postulate of self-sufficiency of the community and the distinction between natural and unnatural trade. But all this appeared so foreign to the marketing mind that translators took refuge in turning the text upside down, eventually losing their hold of the argument. Perhaps the most daring thesis of Aristotle, which up to this day must stagger the thinking mind by sheer force of originality, was in this manner reduced to a platitude that, had it carried any definite meaning at all, would have been rejected by him as a shallow view of the ultimate forces on which the human economy rested.

Karl Polanyi

Notes to Chapter V

1. J. A. Schumpeter, *History of Economic Analysis* (New York, 1954), p. 57, "Aristotle's performance is . . . decorous, pedestrian, slightly mediocre and more than slightly pompous common sense." Schumpeter had no doubt that Aristotle was engaged in "analyzing actual market mechanisms. Several passages show . . . that Aristotle tried to do so and failed" (p. 60). The latest detailed study is no less negative on the merits of the case. Cf. C. J. Soudek, "Aristotle's Theory of Exchange," *Proceedings of American Philosophical Society*, V, 96, NR, 1 (1952). Joseph J. Spengler's "Aristotle on Economic Imputation and Related Matters," *Southern Economics Journal*, XXI (April, 1955), 386, fn. 59, is the lone exception: "Aristotle did not concern himself with how prices are formed in the market."
2. Cf. Karl Polanyi, *The Great Transformation* (New York, 1943), p. 64.
3. *Cooperation and Competition* (New York and London, 1937), p. 31.
4. Aristotle, EN 1132b 21, 35.
5. Aristotle, *Pol.* 1257a 24.
6. *Ibid.*, 1257a 19.
7. *Ibid.*, 1257a 25.
8. Aristotle, *EN* 1133b 16, 1133b 8.
9. *Ibid.*, 1133b 29.
10. *Ibid.*, 1133a 8.
11. *Ibid.*, 1133a 10.
12. *Ibid.*, 1133b 15.
13. Aristotle, *Pol.*, 1257a 24–31.
14. Aristotle, *EN* 1133a 3–6.
15. Ps.-Arist., *Oec.* II, 1353a 24–28.
16. *Ibid.*, 1133a 2; *Pol.* 1257a 24; 1280b 20.

PART II

Aztec-Maya; Dahomey; Berber; India

VI

Anthropology as History

————•————

A BOOK on the economy in early societies must call upon the data of cultural and social anthropology along with those of history. In both fields man's experience with substantive economies finds its record. The varied and often strange patterns of economic action described in Part One of this book have already suggested rethinking of some concepts and definitions in economic theory, signaling as they do the inappropriateness of that theory outside the marketing system of the classical Western nineteenth century.

The Empirical Approach

For its part, but without the written documents of history, anthropology has amassed an immense record of scattered and haphazard data about man's behavior with things for use, subsistence and consumption and about his relationships with his fellows over such things. It is well to know something of the lessons that the field work of anthropologists teaches and to explore the implications of that work for any new economic discipline which should analyze and generalize their data. Gathering of empirical data in the field, picking up economic facts without separation from other information, treating them in the technical or social context in which they were met, covers a hundred years or more of experience in anthropology. Its theorizing, busy with the processes, the similarities and differences among cultures, addressed itself thus to what it found rather than to deducible consequences of any first principles of human nature. Anthropology, as we learn in another chapter of this book,* felt no need for economic theory and did not seek to discover any of those principles of human action such as economic theory's rationalizing, or economizing, to establish them as central. It turned instead to the dynamics of the emergence of cultural content.

This experience of first recording and next trying to understand man's endlessly multifarious behavior and his many systems of motives, products of his various cultures and civilizations, confirms anthropology in its kinship with such an empirical discipline as history. Empiricism continues to separate them among the social sciences from such eminently conceptualizing disciplines as economics, political science or sociology. It means for both anthropology and history that the burden of proof is shouldered by him—a Kroeber, a Darwin, a Toynbee—who should assert a comparison or identify a common process or claim discovery of a universally unfolding law working out many times in the record. It has made further them kin in that both disciplines must deal in time sequences, must treat past and present, must seek recurrences, parallels, convergences. Both deal with events and occurrences, not with man's nature or the timeless necessities.

The comparative, temporal, empirical and processual bent of modern anthropology makes it nevertheless complementary to a comparative sociology and social psychology of the world's peoples, past and present. It is pressing upon its neighbor disciplines the recognition of the sweeping force and pervasive results of cultural process and thereby transcending traditional sociology's and psychology's concentration on contemporary Western man and his society. The same empirical bent also nourished anthropology's essential kinship with history and prehistory. Anthropology's great archeological branch treats trends and processes in the cultural record of peoples whose achievements lie not in writing but in the mute artifacts of the ruins they have left behind. That elder branch of the subject still continues today to extend backward the so-called "ethnographic present," the time of first European contact with the world's non-Western peoples, and so to join the present to the past history of all mankind. Anthropology, indeed, maintains its original three branches intact even today. Cultural anthropology, archeology, and physical anthropology—the original interest in man's

* See below, Ch. XVII.

evolution up from the animals—still interfertilize. It is this very processual and temporal concern, this comparison of past and present, which keeps them together.

This triple experience of the three branches of anthropology, scanning processes in past and contemporary peoples for parallels, differences and convergences in the record of man's cultural achievement, needs to be connected to the difficulties for economic theory to which nonmarket systems give rise. Much already partly tested theory is to be won from the work of anthropologists to date on this record of man's behavior. If it mostly does not distinguish man's "economic" activity from his action in other fields, nevertheless it is specifically relevant, since it touches upon those alternate substantively economic patterns which concern us in this book. Much of what anthropologists have discovered about man's culture apart from economic institutions is directly in point when we turn to the particular questions which arise out of his many different ways of treating goods and goods-handlers and receivers.

Admittedly, there is as yet no body of generalizations that treats "economic" behavior from the specifically anthropological point of view. Instead, we possess a vast body of diverse data about the various behaviors and motives with which non-Western peoples' livelihood is made and in which goods pass from hand to hand, move into distribution among new persons, and in new modes of consumption. Karl Polanyi has already devised an at least tentative classification of these diverse ways of goods-handling; in broad outline, reciprocative, redistributive, and marketing systems can be distinguished.* They are by no means mutually exclusive, nor do they claim to be exhaustive. Yet this empirical classification for descriptive purposes is useful; it is a first breakthrough from nonempirical and a *priori* interpretations, and its implications and ramifications, as well as its limitations, will occupy us in many sections of this book.

Were anthropologists in their turn to attempt even the first step in conceptualizing the data, they too would probably turn to consideration of social arrangements, forms of interpersonal relationship, and self-contained logics based on them. In this lies a most important convergence among the empirically-minded social sciences of the present day. And if anthropologists were to move in this direction, they too would be forced to read those "economic" patterns of behavior and

* See below, Ch. XIII.

motive against the same general view of society that another chapter of this book has elevated to a central tenet of modern sociology.* They would start with society as a system in which "the units . . . are not individuals, but patterns of interaction"** of persons with one another. Not free human nature, nor free individuals, nor even any hard and fast psychological attributes of man, within his biological and physiological limits as an animal, give the anthropologist his starting point. In treating any culture patterns, even those of economic institutions, the anthropologist selects these "patterns of interaction" to begin with, not because they are logically prior, but because they are empirically decisive in those comparisons of present and past to which he subjects his data.

Not many anthropologists have yet begun to take this step explicitly in regard to economic data. Chapple and Coon in *Principles of Anthropology*, 1942, seem to be the first to attempt it. Firth seems to sense its necessity, as it is implicit in the efforts of British social anthropology. "Economic anthropology," to date, is not yet a reality. It is still freeing itself from the belief that other chapters in this book demolish, that economic theory itself already has something to offer for an easy explanation of other economic systems than the market system of the recent West. The first generalizer, Herskovits, now asserts allegiance to formal economic theory and has tried a reduction of the data in that direction, away from the attempts of Mauss, after Durkheim, in which the early French ethnologists discovered empirical regularities in the reciprocities of gift-giving. But even Herskovits must continually stop to point out how little the categories of economic theory and the concerns of rationalizing and economizing which it follows out to their logical end help with ordering the ethnographers' data and how different, deviant, and quite outside the motivational categories of rational action in the market are the behaviors and motives with which he must deal.***

Yet anthropology is deeply committed to this priority of social patterns in any scheme for the understanding of the substantive economies of the human record. Our discipline is preconditioned to derive specific motivations, whether "economic" or otherwise, from such arrangements rather than from abstract human nature or needs. But it also sees these patterns and arrangements as historically achieved

* See below, Ch. XIV.   ** See *ibid.*, p. 279.   *** See below, pp. 348 ff.

rather than as consequences of the play of general forces of human nature or circumstance, as the economist might view them. Anthropology expects the social arrangements underlying economic behaviors and motives to be particular human inventions of historical times and places. It expects social and economic inventions, like technical and artistic ones (of which we have a better record so far), to have spread and combined in diffusions, evolutions and convergences and to continue to do so today and in the future, rather than simply to prove responsive to the effects of universal processes of association, as sociology sees them. This processual bent of anthropology has substantial implications, as we shall see. It makes of the interpretation of non-Western economic data a vitally historical, even "culturological" pursuit rather than a psychological, economic, or sociological one.

For the anthropologist must not only identify the social arrangement of human interaction and organization as invented and patterned into culture that explains economic behaviors and motives, but he must also account for its presence. For him a common denominator of economic action, such as reciprocations or redistributions, with their attendant mechanisms of trade or forms of money use, is both an arrangement of human interactions and an institutional import of a new emergence among the people where he happens to find it. He must account for its being there, historically and geographically. He must account for it functionally, that is, for its connection with the other patterns of the people's culture of that time and place. He must add to the reasons for its presence the functions it performs and the values it embodies for those who act it out and by which it is kept alive, sanctioned as custom, and transmitted as *Kulturgut* of their cultural inheritance. He must account for its continuation then and there, as well.

He cannot always do the first accounting, of course. Ethnographic records are haphazard and even written history must be finely sifted before our knowledge of the presence of any particular institution or culture pattern grows firm. For many of the inventions and institutions which interest us today, "origins" are lost in the mists of time and in the endless successions and transformations of cultural evolution. But the anthropologist must try. For a culture pattern is a concrete thing, whose presence or absence is an historical fact and whose emergence is an historical event.

He cannot always do the second thing either; but he can try to spell out its contemporary functions. For a culture pattern coexists with others and it supports or opposes the others in some sort of integration or lack of it. Such integration possesses details and has a structure that is important for the continuation of a culture and society and the integration has form and laws of being which the social sciences are uncertainly exploring. An imperative rests upon an anthropologist, whether or not he is explicitly a social anthropologist committed to functionalism or other special theories of cultural or social integration, to spell out in faithful, empirical detail all observable and checkable dovetailing of transmitted action, interaction, meaning and context which makes up any culture pattern, social, lingual, or technical.

And he cannot always do the third thing: account historically for the continuation of a pattern he has identified and interpreted. Yet here again he must continue to try, for human culture, like other animals' behavior, is adaptive, functional for survival, and presumably even rewarding. Its continuance rests upon its successful transmission to the new generations who must use it and pass it on in turn. Its further elaboration seems at least in good part to come from the further gains it yields. The anthropologist exploring culture patterns, including those behind variant non-Western economic behaviors, must treat the rise and fall of his subject matter as an historian accounts in his field for the growth and decline of institutions and empires.

To see social arrangements, then, as prior to economic actions, institutions, and value and motive schemes, and to see them specifically as culture patterns, that is, as contrivances and devices man has achieved with the human material given by the existence and the characteristics of his fellow human beings, is not merely the bias with which anthropology will take its next steps into the explanation of the record of substantive economics. It is not merely the occupational bias which anthropologists bring to any experience, as one might perhaps surmise. It is one grand view imposed on all social science analysts, from the discovery of the three first categories of substantive economies prior to this book,[1] through the sociologists here, to the work of others here and yet to come. It may well be, moreover, *the* view to which empirical discoveries are impelling us all.

Note that sociologists often write as if the priority of the presence or absence of particular social arrangements over economic actions and motivations of a particular kind were a matter of logical premise in the world-view of their discipline. So it is, of course, when a theory of the social system, or of the economic system, "embedded" in the social system, is under construction. In another view, however, particular social arrangements are the empirical controlling elements, and their priority is one of relevance, perhaps even of causation. The real issue between the deductive theories deriving economic action from man's rational or gain-seeking faculties and the findings of the newer social science is only half stated when the sociologist limits himself to insisting that his science has taught him to see economic behaviors dependent upon the social systems in which they are "embedded." For anthropology finds these systems in turn dependent upon, and serving to integrate, particular patterns or inventions of human interactional and social arrangement and its symbolization, achieved in time and place, in the way that technology or science also depend upon and unite the other particular inventions of mankind's variously unfolding development.

Using social arrangements as a frame of reference, then, and seeking them out by an operational method that extracts them as common denominators in the data of action and motive, are not merely biases or philosophical premises in anthropology and the newer social science now turning to the comparative record. They are discoveries already achieved about the relevant priorities of phenomena in our science. The institutionally operational method working with nonmarket economic data is very much akin, as we shall see, to other contemporary analyses in social science. It makes the same path as has anthropology to a discovery of the common-denominator patterns of arrangement, structure, and form in human interpersonal action.

In other branches of social science today these patterns seem to turn out to be the things controlling human motives and human institutional action. I have tried elsewhere to show their force in the small group and short-term attitude and behavior of industrial relations,[2] while George Homans has documented their determination of group behavior and attitude in the wide range of studies of social behavior already accomplished by observational and empirical methods,[3] and Hopkins* reminds us of the central place of these arrangements in current social system theory with Parsons and its other formulators. It is a confirmatory discovery, indeed, that in the non-Western economic data we have before us here the same priority of relevance faces us.

* See below, Ch. XIV.

In the Berber markets, in the Indian redistributions, in the African and American "ports of trade" which find review here, we have had again and again to seek out these patterns and to dig down into the arrangements of action between persons before we could go on to search for an explanation of the motives of our actors, the values which prompt them, the circumstances they cope with, or the gains they win. We had again and again to connect these backward to common-denominator patterns of action before we could structure all these things into a representation and interpretation of the institutions the record gives us.

And we have had to do all this *comparatively*. Our common, emerging social science is not an endless excavation of particular details alone, but like all science, a generalizing of probes, propositions, and proofs. If Arnold, Revere, and Chapman here find a common form of early trade in "the port of trade," in "weak hands" (to use Polanyi's apt phrases), in eighteenth century Dahomey, in Asia Minor three thousand years earlier, and pre-conquest Mesoamerica, or if Benet finds elements of "free markets" in an anarchic Barbary, we can be sure of these findings only because we can, in the end, demonstrate that common patterns exist behind these things our authors describe and because we can check the record for the known and specified arrangement of interpersonal action applying to any two of them despite their differences of setting and detail. Priority of one kind of datum over another is not a matter of disciplinary or philosophical affection for one kind of phenomenon over another. It is a matter of just such comparison, discovery and check among the observers of the run of cases. Just such comparison pushes us to the "scientific fact."

Stated baldly thus, and if our proofs are accepted and our "facts" are "true," there seems little to argue with in the discovery that social arrangements serve as a frame of reference to economic actions and motives. But to see these arrangements as culture, as human inventions, with anthropology, presents continuing difficulties, even in sociology. It finds it sometimes difficult to decide between the claims for prior relevance between these arrangements and "values" in the scheme of social system theory. We touch here on a great debate still raging everywhere in social science as it did once in philosophy. But the view of common denominator, social arrangements as culture patterns, derived from the experience of anthropology, comes to our rescue. In that view social arrangements make their own values in the process of becoming culture patterns, or "instituted." The evolution of a culture pattern is just such an emergence of summary and symbolizing values, meaning, vocabulary and concept about a new pattern of action, making it ready for recognition, sanction, and transmission. Action comes first, in anthropology's view of culture, whether it be the wheel, or divine monarchy, or parallel cousin marriage, and values come second in the usual evolutionary or diffusionary problems with which the science has had to deal. In this anthropology repeats the discoveries of small group and industrial studies, where new group norms and new shared attitudes likewise arise out of changes in interpersonal and group action. And a culture pattern is not complete, any more than an "institution" is fully emerged, until the summarization, symbolization, and evaluation which crystallizes the connection between the new action and its resultant values is achieved in a configuration which has won the instant recognition and the long term habit of the human actors who "carry the culture trait."

Read properly, then, social science's experience with "culture" and with "institutionalizing" a process, here the substantive goods-handlings of the "economic process," offers no difficulties in giving both historical and methodological priority to action over values. Much of the trouble with this discovery lies in our semantic training (we say we "act out" a value) and in our philosophical tradition of idealism ("In the beginning was the Word."). The long squabble of idealism and realism haunts us unnecessarily. Anthropological experience with culture shows the same phenomena of emergence as does sociological experience with group process, though the data are different. What stands in the way of acceptance of the common finding seems to be a tendency to read the anthropologist's term "culture" as a synonym for the sociologists' own word "values." Thus it is easy for sociologists, often assuming out of philosophic tradition that values ("common meanings" they sometimes call them) are prior to social action—a tautology of long standing since "social" action is in turn the action based on "common meanings"—[4] to think the anthropologist is also claiming values to rule action when he speaks of "culture" and the "cultural determination" of a bit of behavior.

By the same route it is easy for sociologists—and many anthropologists as well—to take another finding of our common social science, one equally important to our understanding of the nonmarket economies under examination here, for an obstacle to following the his-

torical and evolutionary emergence of culture patterns out of common-denominator arrangements in the determination of economic
(and other) institutions and values. Anthropology has discovered in its
record of man's doings the process of cultural diffusion, by which two
peoples come to share a trait or institution out of their contact with
each other, and its counterpart, the process of cultural convergence or
cultural parallelism, in which two peoples, in no contact, come to share
a very like trait, too, but by a quite different route. Comparison of
traits and patterns from people to people and time to time and place
to place, the very comparison which yields us similar social arrangements behind widely separated civilizations in these pages, like the
common "ports of trade" in distant Mesoamerica and Syria, has led
us to these discoveries in dealing with all sorts of doings of man. It is
not surprising that comparison has led to analogous discoveries once
again when we have turned to explore the record of his economic acts.
But too often both sociologists and anthropologists forget these processes of culture and jump logically from the specificity of particular
culture patterns to the uniqueness and integration of cultures as wholes.
They read the discoveries of anthropology about "culture" or "values"
to bar comparison or to license neglect of it, and to reify integrated
"cultural wholes" and "social systems" into unique entities whose
essences and consequences have no parallels anywhere. To some of
them, then, in this context to say that the prior social arrangements
behind economic motive and behavior are culture patterns is tanta-
mount, erroneously, to saying that no connections can be drawn at all
between one people's institutions and the next.

There seems to be a tendency in social science today to condemn
as idealistic and to impute to anthropologists a view according to which
whole cultures are unique and the economic arrangements springing
up in them without parallel. This is the reading of culture which
we are presently expounding as fallacious. We have already described
how anthropology must of course explore the instant case and unravel
the functional and other interconnections and integrations of traits
within a culture, just as sociologists must always look from particular
norms or processes to the whole social system before them. But to
work out the place of a phenomenon *in situ* is another thing than to
compare it with others; both things must be done in science and both
yield knowledge. The experience of anthropology has always comprised both. The discoveries of convergent evolution and diffusion in

man's doings could not have taken place without ethnographic and historical comparisons.

Now the main point of anthropology, and of the work which has taught us to handle economic action and value as culture patterns, lies in this comparison of the common-denominator social arrangements and this discovery of the processes leading to the evolution of institutions from out of them. It is not any finding that economic institutions, whether market ones or nonmarket ones, are culture traits (which they are), or that culture traits are expressions of values (a happy tautology which delights some anthropologists still), or that patterns of social action are prior to values (which they are), or that social arrangements and culture traits are the independent variables (which is true). It is rather that each term of the analysis leading to these findings must have particular, empirical, historical documentation. Moreover, once this proof can be provided we can at once go on further to depicting the processes which have given us the actual events of the past emergence of these institutions. It is in this way alone, in treating them as culture traits, that we can legitimately spell out the cultural dynamics and reconstruct the true history of economic institutions. This dynamics and this rewon history is the best account we will ever have of their "origins."

Methodological Conclusions

The usefulness of the historical bent of anthropology and its experience with culture traits and processes is easy enough to see when we treat institutional origins and history. Its insistence that action is prior to values is perhaps easier to accept in that context than is the comparable discovery in social and group dynamics. Examples come readily enough from well-known history, where the painful searches required here are in the long past. After all, a use of gold for personal enrichment rather than for collective worship had to exist in Europe and in Spain before conquistadores should sack the New World for it and should corrupt "innocent" Indians to their gold lust. The course of historical civilization and the diffusion of pecuniary values ran from East to West, not the other way, as we all know. But the consequences of this historical bent and the cultural experience for methods of research, indeed in the very analysis and comparison of diverse data of behavior and motive which fills the ethnographic and historical record, is not so easy to grasp or to accept. Nevertheless, a temporal, processual view of social arrangements, culture traits, and resultant institutions pervades the most basic operations of anthropological research and dominates the methods which have brought ethnographic data into accord with those of substantive economic analysis in these pages. In their most basic methods both anthropology and historical-institutional or substantive economics, at least as developed here, are processual and operational. They share a realization that their comparison, their synthesis, their structuring of their data must always reflect the particular observations of persons, times, and actions which their data-gatherers actually make. To demonstrate the existence of an economic institution of nonmarket kind, for example, Polanyi here and elsewhere must show both what was done and when and with and by whom. He must also show explicitly what was not there and when and by whom an action we might expect to take place did not occur, as he does in showing that "sales" are not made to random demanders but only to recognized trading partners in reciprocal systems and that reciprocity exchanges involve merely appropriate and worthy, not equivalent unit-reckoned returns.* And he must show that these specifics of time, place, person, action, and quantification recur, repeat, grow standard, or come to be supplanted by others.

Anthropology's method with culture traits is equally specific, observational, operational and processual. For traits of human social organization it must also specify who and who not does a thing, where and when, and where and when not, with what and without what else, at what rates of occurrence. It must also establish the regularities, the limits, and the restoring sanctions upon deviations, in order to demonstrate patterns of existence. And when it treats changes, it must touch the changes in these particulars as they arise, in new time and new circumstance.

This careful documentation of detail of observation and this empirical handling of events in time and this painful documentation of regularities of recurrence reflects not only the kinship of anthropology and institutional history but it also marks as well their common divergence from the formal and often timeless logic of economic theory and sociology alike. The doctrine of culture trait, like the concept of institution, rests upon experience which asks questions about function, gain, conformity to man's nature, powers or needs, *after* and not *before* the details of observation about man's behavior have been taken up, compared, ordered, synthesized, classified and recognized.

This is an especially important theoretic and methodological point. When we come to the problem of functional equivalency among traits and institutions in different societies and cultures, it may become crucial. To the anthropologist a social arrangement ("real culture," e.g., *de facto* polygyny), a culture pattern (i.e., one of "ideal" culture, e.g., *de jure* but not rigorously observed monogamy), an institution (e.g., sororate, bride-price, usury) exists in its own right and has form, structure, and characteristics independent of functions and relationships among other social or cultural data. Such real things—concrete inventions ordering persons, acts, symbols, etc., into patterns of unique existence—change in function, take on or lose functions from time to time, people to people, just as they accrete or slough off their other defining elements. A social arrangement, a culture trait, an institution is not defined exclusively or even primarily by its function, and the first thing to know about it is not what it does for men or society. The first thing to know is how it operates within itself and how it came to be. Only then can one ask what its functions are now, were once, and may yet be in the future. Moreover, of course, not its functions but its forms give it the character by which the observers (ourselves) and the actors ("the natives") recognize and value it, and the question of just what function it performs is an empirical one to be solved by further research, not an answer deduced from the essence of the thing.

Thus in anthropology and history to analyze an institution as a concrete event rather than—as in economics or sociology—to explore it in general terms as a functional equivalent for doing what is done by something else in another society or other circumstances is to ask different questions and to work toward different answers however complementary the ultimate knowledge may prove to be.

For the anthropological view of the evolution of traits, like the historical view of institutions, is that the functions they perform and the rewards they bring do not in themselves call these things into being or account for their continuance. Necessity is not the mother of invention, nor is reward its father. The two together may remain childless. Inventions are rather events of discovery or creation, whether they be technical or institutional, and they make good their new trending or trial arrangement of persons, materials, and actions *per saltum* into the new configurations of achieved form which make of culture traits new emergences. Once the jump is made, and the new form attained, then functional serviceability and sometimes unexpectedly huge gain confirm the existence of the new trait and work strongly to elaborate and to extend it. But the record is replete with trends not so consummated and with jumps approached but never made.

Consciousness of emergence, and the combination of temporal and formal observations which have yielded it out of ethnographic data, is another of the empirical discoveries of anthropology which make it different from the system-building disciplines of sociology and economics. It is a discovery, too, which enforces, as we shall see presently, the quite other than simply functional method which the research of this book on the ethnographic record of man's substantive economic behavior has had to carry out.

Thus the search for the ordering similarities in economic matters of ethnographic and historical record which is the latter-day equivalent of the old-fashioned study of the origins of economic institutions, and which has motivated our studies is not by any means merely a search for alternate ways in which man has solved his universal problems. It is not a study of the functional equivalents of our economic institutions in other cultures and societies. It is doubtful indeed whether beyond subsistence man has had any universal economic problems; rather his problems arise, like his values, from his institutions and their evolutions. To restrict a study of economic institutions to the functional equivalents among societies, and to neglect the discovery that they are also in part culture patterns and behave like these, would be to falsify the facts. Rather, the facts of economic evolution resemble in great measure the facts of cultural evolution.

The facts of cultural evolution are not, as it may seem, that most cultures and most societies have developed alternate ways of doing much the same thing and that different economic institutions are nothing but different cultural devices for winning a livelihood, meeting scarcities, spreading goods about, effecting necessary exchanges. There is danger here of meekly surrendering to empty truisms, since all cultures survive for a time in an environment and most of their people stay alive on the goods somehow brought to them. The facts of cultural evolution instead tell us that some peoples in some real past events by chance and hard thought have combined specific prior actions and relationships in new ways or experimented with new ones. Their new combination of old ways, their new invention out of former materials bequeathed or diffused to them, was not independent of their old custom, but it was nevertheless a jump into the unknown. Culture patterns, like all inventions, recombine both old and new; they have both a history which is specific and limited, and a future of uncharted dimensions and promises. A new pattern, newly emergent, of course, soon takes on functions, established connections with the older social and cultural order, brings gains and rewards which confirm its discoverers in its use. Each new advance in mastery of it, each rewarded further use, brings greater and greater reward, for a time, and in this sense culture is functional in the adaptive sense as well as in the integrative one. The people among whom our innovation spreads soon come to experience and value unexpected consequences in greater and greater rewards as they also begin to encounter unexpected pains and restrictions in their expanding use of a new technique, a new art or ceremonial device, a new social or economic institution. Who could foresee that domesticating grains and herd animals would bring first a many-fold increase of population and then a desiccation and destruction of the land? Who could see that sacrificial blood-offering would lead to human sacrifice and brittle empires of warfare and hate, or harnessing machines to mine pumps and clothmill looms in England would lead to an industrial and technical revolution over the whole globe?

The history and ethnography of human culture is full of examples of such emergence, elaboration, and revolution. A people evolving a new culture, or inventing a new culture trait or a complex of them, from minor technique to major economic institution, has often found heady riches in its hand. Such peoples have often entered upon long and deep elaborations of such a new pattern. They have often flourished with it as it has flourished for them. They have built upon it, explored it and embroidered it, mined and exhausted its resources. We need not animize the process with a Spengler for whole civilizations, or hypostatize the resources into motive forces with such clichés as ascribe England's nineteenth century glory to her coal and iron or Plains Indians' riches to the horse. Here again what cultural innovation gives command over what absolute or relative new riches and power is a question of empirical discovery and exploration, a something to be learned both by the men on the spot and by the commentators who come afterwards palely to record the accidents of history. Suffice it to say that the story of culture is also the story of man. Man is the animal (maybe the chief animal) who has hit upon the device of culture for achieving mastery of the environment by freeing himself of slavish dependency on it. He is one animal, perhaps the chief one, who explores and exploits his habitat by a device, the cultural one, which creates for him successive environments both natural and artificial. And he is no fool; he can quickly see and use up his advantage while it lasts.

Certainly the concept of functional equivalents among culture patterns and institutions is useful. But its usefulness ceases where the sweep of cultural evolution and variation starts. Certainly, in these pages and in others, we can find that gift-giving does the same things for human individual and social life as does the market. Both are mechanisms of distribution and survival. But they are different mechanisms, based on very different social arrangements, in many ways opposite cultural and institutional elaborations. Presumably as well they have very different antecedants, advantages, and limitations. Certainly they have very different distributions among the world's times, places, and peoples. To understand them we must know not only these circumstances, but also the relative order of their historical emergence, and the necessary precursors and preconditions they must have had.

The experience of anthropology with culture patterns, then, teaches us not only this processual thinking which extends beyond functionalism and system-building relyings on putative needs of individual or society. It commits us as well to a humble descent to operational methods in which both analysis and synthesis are bound to consistency with the observations, descriptions, and eliminations shown by the record. Where, as with both culture patterns and social arrangements, specificities of time occurrence and recurrence go into the data-gathering and data-ordering, the operations treating these must be reflected in the models and the definitions we construct for what we find. Where specification of persons, listing who acts and who does not, is a necessary part of the recording of the behaviors we are examining, this operation, too, must continue to appear in the classifications of data we erect and the building of alternate institutions or systems we carry out. Where determining the order of action or initiative between persons is part of the observation which goes into discriminations of status and relationship, that operation also must carry over into our models of institution, social arrangement, economic system, etc. In this way, if we find, as we do in some of them, that common-denominator social arrangements underlie convergences and parallelisms of economic institutions, then we must be very clear that we derive these comparisons from regularities in the data themselves and not from an *a priori* bias of our own. It is the consistent use of these operations basic to so many of the modern social sciences[5] that give us this power of control and clarity.

Conrad M. Arensberg

Notes to Chapter VI

1. Cf. Karl Polanyi, *The Great Transformation* (New York, 1943).

2. Conrad M. Arensberg, "Behavior and Organization: Industrial Studies," ch. XIV in Muzafer Sherif and John Rohrer, eds., *Social Psychology at the Crossroads* (New York, 1952), and in Conrad M. Arensberg and Geoffrey Tootall, "Plant Sociology: Real Discoveries and New Problems" in Paul Lazarsfeld and Mirra Komarovsky, eds., *Common Frontiers of Social Research* (Glencoe, Ill., forthcoming).

3. George Homans, *The Human Group* (New York, 1952).

4. As opposed to symbiosis or physical collision, for example.

5. See E. D. Chapple and Conrad M. Arensberg, *Measuring Human Relations*, Genetic Psychology Monographs (Provincetown, 1940). Also, E. D. Chapple and Carleton S. Coon, *Principles of Anthropology* (New York, 1942). Also, Conrad M. Arensberg in Rohrer and Sherif, eds., *Social Psychology at the Crossroads, op. cit.*

VII

Port of Trade Enclaves in Aztec and Maya Civilizations

The Problem of Aztec-Maya Trade

MUCH of the obscurity that has veiled the contacts of the Aztec and the Maya and prevented an understanding of the economic relations obtaining among the peoples of Mesoamerica now appears to be lifting.[1] Trade carried on over long distances, more than any other activity, bound together the two great culture areas of Mesoamerica. Yet this trade that so intimately linked the Aztecs of the Basin of Mexico and the Maya of Yucatan had to overcome very considerable physical and perhaps even more formidable organizational obstacles. The distance between the centers of these metropolitan areas was great. As the crow flies, Tenochtitlan (on the site of Mexico City) was more than 500 miles removed from the Maya heartlands in the Yucatan peninsula. The length of the traject over high mountains and primeval forest may have been almost twice as much. Yet over most of this area not only the empires, but also numerous tribes and tribal confederacies were frequently at war with one another; slave raiding was constant; feuds, massacres and border violence the rule.

How, then, were these difficulties surmounted? What was the operational nature of this trade between the different and distinct cultures? These are the questions to which this chapter is devoted.

114

Our subject is restricted geographically to the Aztec empire and the Maya states; institutionally it comprises only long distance trade as distinguished from market institutions, from which trade was to a remarkable degree separate.

To the modern mind this may sound paradoxical. But long-distance trade was an institution apart: geographically, it was trade beyond the borders; its personnel formed a distinct social group; its members only exceptionally made their appearance in markets; both the organizing of caravans and the negotiating of exchange in foreign countries formed part of this specialized occupation. This particular form of administered trade should not then be confused with any other form of exchange, such as the important local market complex itself, corner food-stalls, peddlers, the sale of services, or the variants of neighborhood trade.

To return to the long-distance trade between Aztec and Maya, three factors will recur in our analysis: the commodities imported and exported; the personnel engaged in the foreign economy; and the geographical locations where the meetings of the long-distance traders took place.

Luxury wares and their raw materials formed the main items of trade. It did not as a rule directly concern the common people as consumers. This was an added reason why the democratic exchanges of the home market places, where everyone with a few cacao beans in his pocket was welcome, had no room in a trading system reserved to the élite, and the needs of the state.

Even more significant was the person of the trader. At no time does the trade over these vast areas appear as random activity of individuals; certainly it is not simply an extension of the face to face exchanges common in the metropolitan market places. Rather it was the highly structured occupation of persons dedicated to performing their duties under the authority of their professional organizations. It emerges, especially among the Aztecs, as an institution of characteristic social, economic, and ecological configuration. To a large extent this trade determined the type of contact maintained between civilizations across geographical and political boundaries.

The locational focus of the exchange transactions was the "port of trade," the name introduced in this book to denote those towns or cities whose specific function was to serve as a meeting place of foreign traders. The word "port" as employed here, need not imply a coastal or riverain site, although ports of trade were usually thus situated. Transshipments naturally developed from the earliest times on the borders of ecological regions, such as highland and plain, desert and jungle, forest and savannah. Prior to modern days, the port of trade should therefore be regarded as the main organ of long-distance commerce. Trade was here treaty-based, administered, as a rule, by special organs of the native authorities, competition was excluded, prices were arranged over long terms. Ports of trade usually developed in politically weak spots, such as small kingdoms near the coast, or chieftains' confederacies, since, under archaic conditions, strangers shunned territories that were incorporated in military empires. To the hinterland empires the "ports" served as a "bread basket," that is, as a source of supply.* Even powerful rulers were wary of laying their hands on the "port," lest foreign traders and strangers shy off and trade suddenly dry up. Independent trade areas of this kind, harboring numbers of warehouses, storing the goods of distant trading peoples, while the local population of the area itself did not engage in trading expeditions have been found to exist in widely different parts of the globe.

We submit that the key to the volume and intensity of long-distance trading between Aztec and Maya should be sought in the existence of such port of trade territories—whether enclaves or buffer states—which served as intermediaries to the trade of militarily powerful metropolitan units. To such areas outside of their political boundaries both the Aztecs of Mexico and Maya of Yucatan traveled to exchange goods. The ports of trade had their setting mainly on the lagoons and rivers of gulf areas. Situated to the south of the Aztec Empire and beyond the cultural province of Yucatan Maya, these areas extended westward from Yucatan on the Gulf of Mexico as well as eastward to the Gulf of Honduras, and even to points further south. It happened that these were also the regions where cacao cultivation was predominant, a significant fact, since the cacao bean was the universal money in the Mesoamerican and Central American regions.

Port of trade areas (see map, p. 118) probably benefitted from their relative neutrality and enjoyed a fair measure of independence. Admittedly, they were occasionally to some extent controlled by Aztec colonists or factors, that is, by Nahuatl-speaking people who had established themselves in a ward or quarter of the neutral trading towns; the Yucatan Maya also had their factors living in some of the ports of

* See below, p. 160.

trade; moreover various ports had their own agents in other ports. Such resident agents or factors did undoubtedly wield considerable power, and may often have been, wholly or partly, rulers of the port towns or provinces. However, with the exception of Xoconusco, none of the ports of trade paid tribute to the Aztec state or to the Maya. For the most part the port of trade areas were autonomous.

Another notable fact appears to be that no traders native to these ports of trade traveled to the Basin of Mexico to trade, although some may have visited Yucatan. The documents indicate that the active trade ran from the metropolitan centers to the ports of trade, the exchange taking place in the ports of trade themselves, of which a dozen or so existed in the neutral enclaves.

The Aztec of the Basin of Mexico

The Aztec Empire[2] at the beginning of the Spanish conquest, extended from northern Veracruz on the Gulf coast to the state of Guerrero, on the Pacific; and south, above the Isthmus of Tehuantepec. It can be loosely described as a wide belt stretching across central Mexico, with the capital lying well in the north.[3]

The seat of the Empire was the Basin of Mexico, in the southernmost part of the Central Mexican Plateau. Its floor in this area reaches an altitude of some 7,400 feet. At the time of the conquest the Basin of Mexico comprised a number of cities and towns on the edge and on islands of several connecting salt and fresh water lakes, which have since almost entirely dried up. The capital of the Empire—ruins of its ceremonial buildings can still be seen in the central plaza or *zocalo* of Mexico City—was Tenochtitlan. Its "twin city" to the north on the same island was Tlatelolco. Together they had a population of about one million, while in the entire valley there lived perhaps as many as two million people.[4]

Here, in Tenochtitlan and Tlatelolco, lived the Culhua-Mexica.[5] The less precise but more familiar name Aztec will be used to refer to the Nahua-speaking inhabitants of Tenochtitlan.

Their culture was an ancient heritage, parts of which can be traced back to the classical period of Teotihuacan (300 to 900 A.D.). Its great pyramids still look down on the northern part of the Basin of Mexico.

The structure of Aztec society has baffled historians and ethnologists for generations.[6-10] The Aztecs, Nahuatl speakers, were in a po-

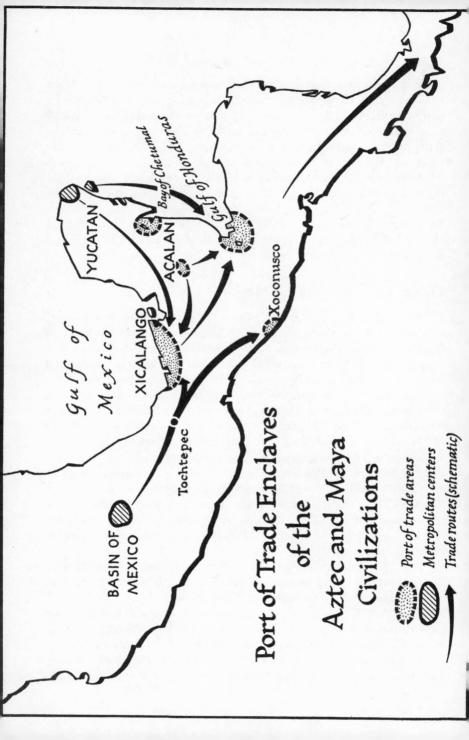

Port of Trade Enclaves
of the
Aztec and Maya
Civilizations

Port of trade areas

Metropolitan centers

Trade routes (schematic)

Gulf of Mexico

BASIN OF MEXICO

Tochtepec

XICALANGO

ACALAN

YUCATAN

Bay of Chetumal

Gulf of Honduras

Xoconusco

litico-historical sense a new people. Their empire, which, most likely, had a state structure, was less than a hundred years old at the time of the conquest. Theirs was a highly stratified and complex society, based on agriculture. Intense religiosity was expressed in the pageantry of their rituals. Almost every public act was sanctified by an appeal to the gods, an appeal which sometimes culminated in human sacrifice and ritual cannibalism. The splendor of its capital, Tenochtitlan, was described by its conqueror, Herman Cortés, in these terms:

This great city of Temistitan is built on a salt lake, and from the mainland to the city is a distance of two leagues, from any side from which you enter. . . . The city has many squares where markets are held, and trading is carried on. There is one square, twice as large as that of Salamanca, all surrounded by arcades, where there are daily more than sixty thousand souls, buying and selling, and where are found all the kinds of merchandise produced in these countries.[11]

The metropolis fell to the Spaniards in August of 1521 after nearly three months of siege; then it was "a vast charnel-house, in which all was hastening to decay and decomposition."[12]

The basis of the regime of the Spanish conquest was the usurpation of political power and economic control achieved through military victory. Deliberately, the Spaniards utilized those of the aboriginal institutions that would further their own ends, attempted to destroy those which opposed their objectives, and let those disintegrate for which they had no need. Accordingly, they utilized such aboriginal institutions as the ancient system of tributes and status, slavery, forced labor, tenantry and cacao bean money. However, temples were demolished, idols smashed and religious codices burned. As to long-distance trade, they had no use for it and allowed it to disintegrate. They had other means of acquiring goods; during the conquest by plunder and confiscation, later by tribute and in the markets. The Aztec long-distance traders were an anomaly in them. Their trade goods were different from the Spanish, and so were their ports, their methods of transportation, and motivations. Markets were another matter. The Spaniards were highly dependent upon the markets during the early years, principally for food. These circumstances taken together explain the striking paucity of data, in the writing of the *conquistadores* and in later reports to the Spanish Crown, on an institution of enormous importance in the aboriginal society, namely, the system of long-distance trade.[13]

For the purpose at hand the different fate of trade and markets is in itself significant. The fact that the markets remained in existence and, even though in modified form, continued to be a major focus of interest to the Spaniards, while the whole system of long-distance trade suffered rapid disintegration, goes to show that even prior to the conquest trade and markets were separate institutions, for had they been closely interdependent it would have been hardly possible for the Spaniards to continue one without the other.

The long-distance trader among the Aztecs was called *pochteca*. This term will be used generically to refer to the various types of full-time professional traders who carried on trading relations exclusively with peoples *beyond the frontier of the Aztec Empire*.[14] The only exception to this was the trade with the isolated province of the Empire, the enclave of Xoconusco in the Guatemala region. Although Xoconusco definitely formed part of the empire, goods flowed to the center not only as tribute or tax, but also were traded by the pochteca.

Precisely where the *pochteca* fit into the Aztec status structure is not easy to determine. They did not belong to the "nobles" (*pilli*) nor to the commoners (*macehualli*) but neither do they appear to have constituted somehow a "middle class." Actually, they were closely associated with the *pilli*. Sahagún, referring to some honored pochteca, calls them "nobility by fantasy."[15] They invited the *pilli* to their sumptuous feasts as honored guests. There is a reference to individual pochteca as having been granted private ownership of a piece of land, traditionally a prerogative of the *pilli*, although it was not extensively practiced at the time of the conquest.[16] Some of the pochteca, the top ranking officers and especially the slave traders, are repeatedly referred to as persons of great wealth and as highly esteemed by the sovereign. Certain of the pochteca traded in distant ports on behalf of the sovereign for the coveted elite goods. On the other hand, they were obliged to present gifts and pay tribute in kind, although not in service,[17] thus differing from the *pilli* who may be economically classed as receivers of tribute.[18] Also the sovereign cautioned the pochteca not to appear too haughty in presumption of their wealth, lest they lose the esteem in which he held them, have them killed, and their goods confiscated.[19]

For the rest, their status seems most nearly to approximate that of some skilled craftworkers. The latter paid tribute with their finished product; the pochteca, with their wares. Alike they were exempt from personal services or labor for the state and from service in the army, except in times of emergency. Also both groups dealt largely in luxury items. The pochteca brought the raw materials from the distant tropics such as quetzal and macaw feathers, animal skins, and precious stones with which the craftsmen made their wares, and then carried some of the finished products back to the foreign ports. Yet there was no close linkage between this trade and the crafts, for just as the pochteca also exported other commodities, such as slaves and fine fabrics, craftsmen were probably often directly commissioned for some of their work by the sovereign and the *pilli*.[20] Nevertheless, it is significant that of all the craftworkers, the pochteca were most closely identified with the feather workers, the *amanteca*, whose status was comparable in Western terms to that of jewelers. Sahagún states that their *barrios* (quarters) were together, their principal gods coupled, that they reciprocated at feasts and were almost equal in wealth.[21]

Apparently the pochteca of the Aztec domain formed a definite type of organization through which they were in association. The traders of at least eighteen towns, most of which were in the Basin of Mexico, were known to have traveled together. They also jointly organized for war from various towns.[22] Their occupation was hereditary. Sahagún states repeatedly that the pochteca of Tenochtitlan and Tlatelolco, twin towns of the capital, live in their own barrios. Again, the term needs explanation. In common parlance, it means simply quarter or ward of a town. The Spaniards, however, used it also to refer not only to a quarter, but also to an entire town, in still other cases to a subdivision of a quarter, termed, in Nahuatl, *calpulli*, i.e., clan owned land; sometimes even only a subdivision of clan land, i.e., land owned by a lineage or extended family, *Tlaxilacalli*. One ethnologist (A. Monzón) maintains that in this context they (barrios) were clan lands and that the pochteca were organized as a kin unit.[23] Others have interpreted it simply as a quarter and held that the pochteca were organized as guilds or even only as a socio-economic class.[24] Again, the pochteca structure has been thought to contain elements of both clan and class.[25] Whatever their barrios were, and they might well have been the territory of stratified clans as Monzón believes, there are on record names for seven of them dispersed and repeated over a wide area of the Aztec Empire. And often more than one of these barrios existed in the same town.

Be this as it may, the pochteca possessed a tight-knit structure, with their own hierarchy, special gods, distinctive rites, particular feasts and religious celebrations, unique insignia and a strict moral code, as well as an ethical point of view on the hazards and rewards of the profession, and a high regard for honesty and group solidarity.[26] They had courts to judge their own members. Yet, as we know, the pochteca were not a separate, autonomous body, rather they formed part of the community very close to the *pilli*, and had strong ties with the craftsmen, especially the feather workers. They also sacrificed and ate slaves in honor of the main god of Tenochtitlan-Tlatelolco, the so-called Aztec tribal god, Huitzilopochtli.[27] Nor, indeed, was their role in Aztec society confined to trading. As they pushed beyond the political frontiers into enemy, that is non-tribute-paying territory, they were frequently assaulted, robbed, imprisoned or slaughtered, whereupon in retaliation the Aztecs declared war on the offenders.[28] Once a territory was conquered and thereby subjected to tribute payments, the pochteca ceased to trade there.[29] The exception to this rule, as we noted, was the geographically isolated province of Xoconusco, far to the south on the Pacific coast. It is significant, if true, that the pochteca themselves conquered this province.[30] In most cases where trade preceded tribute, once a province had been conquered and began to pay its tribute, long-distance trading ceased. In this sense, then, trade was followed by tribute; commerce by administration. For an example of the type of goods paid in tribute, these were paid by Quiauteopan and its five towns, as recorded in the Codex Mendoza. Admittedly, this province is not typical because the list does not include the usual quota of maize, beans, and other foods. Every six months the following was paid to Tenochtitlan: 400 large mantles, 40 large copper bells, 80 copper axe blades, 100 jars of bees' honey; and yearly, 1 war dress with its shield of rich feathers and 1 pan of turquoise stones. As we shall see, most of these items were exported by the pochteca, which suggests that trade preceded tribute.[31]

There is no doubt that the pochteca differed in rank; also, as stated, the profession was hereditary.[32] Yet it called for considerable ability, courage, and training. Young men making their first expedition were counseled and admonished by their elders. The top-ranking officers were old men who no longer went on expeditions.[33] But whether age-grading was basic to the ranking system is another question. The interrelationship of the different status groups remains a problem, as does that of the different towns and barrios in which the pochteca lived. If, as has been suggested, the pochteca were organized in stratified clans then the various ranks may have constituted separate clans or sub-clans.[34]

It has been possible to discern the following four or five ranks, some of which may have been localized, that is, may have existed only in a few barrios or towns of the pochteca.

1. Top-ranking officers. For the highest rank there are several terms, one of which is *pochtecatlatoque*, literally, a senior or principal person of the pochteca.[35] Sahagún implies that such persons were appointed by the sovereign; if so, undoubtedly from among the old pochteca of prestige. They inhabited one or several of the barrios of Tenochtitlan and Tlatelolco. These were highly esteemed old traders who stayed at home, bidding farewell to the outgoing expeditions with words of encouragement and admonishment. They commissioned the expeditionary pochteca with goods to be exchanged for them in the ports of trade, and upon whose return the gain would be shared by both parties. There is even a mention of women commissioning goods, this case being the only reference known to the writer to women as pochteca.[36] The *pochtecatlatoque* presided at the important feasts and ceremonies and probably provided also the judges among the pochteca.[37]

2. Slave traders. This group ranked very high, but just what their relationship was to the *pochtecatlatoque* is not clear. Sahagún says that they were, "the major and most principal of all the merchants, their wealth being in men themselves." Slave traders domiciled in Tlatelolco actually resided also in Tochtepec, in Oaxaca near the southern frontier of the Empire. These frontier residents were so important that the pochteca from Tenochtitlan and Tlatelolco made special visits there to take part in certain of their rituals and to extend to these members among the slave traders their personal invitations to attend the yearly celebration in the capital.[38]

3. King's traders. These were called the *teucunenenque* (*teuctli* —lord, noble, person of quality; *nenenqui*—traveler, passenger). They were dearly loved by the sovereign. It is clear from the data given by Sahagún that these were royal administrative trade officials. He describes them as going to the Gulf coast area and exchanging goods there on behalf of the sovereign and also for themselves with the lords of Xicalango (also Coatzocoalcos and Cimatan).[39] He also tells us that they were honored for having conquered the outlaying province of Ayotla, in which was located the trading port of Xoconusco, mentioned earlier.[40] However, Hernando Alvarado Tezozomoc,

writing at the close of the sixteenth century, gives credit for the conquest to the emperor Ahuizotl and his troops.[41] This same chronicler relates that Moctezuma the Younger summoned the *Teucunenenque* and ordered them to go with other principle señores to collect tribute from the Gulf coast towns of Ahuilizapan and Cuetlaxtlan. Upon their arrival they were attacked, smothered with chile smoke, disemboweled, stuffed with straw, seated upon handsome benches and cursed in farcical obsequiousness by their slayers. When Moctezuma received news of this affront, he was incensed. He declared war and the towns were reconquered in quick order.[42] Significantly, in all of these varied activities there is a very close relationship between the *Teucunenenque* and the emperor, while at the same time there is no mention of them as top officers, nor slave traders, nor spies.[43]

4. Trader-spies. These, the *naualoztomeca*, were described by Sahagún as "not so principal." He mentions them only in the role of trader-spies and this may well have been their exclusive function. In this capacity they are described as entering enemy territory with a knowledge of the local dialect or language, disguised as natives, to seat themselves in the market place, ostensibly to exchange their wares, but really listening, observing and inquiring for vital information. Upon their return they reported all to the emperor. As would be expected, these "trader spies" did not trade in luxury goods for which the other pochteca were famous, but in common goods such as knives and combs of flint.[44] The Nahuatl-Spanish dictionary of Molina written in the sixteenth century gives further evidence for the existence of this rank. In it *naualcalaquini* is defined: to enter a place in dissimulation with caution and in secret, while *oztomeca* is defined as *harriero* and in derivations as walking merchant.[45]

5. *Oztomeca* or "walking merchants" are mentioned by Tezozomoc and may have been the same as the *naualoztomeca*, although he does not describe them as trader-spies but rather in two instances as the traders whose slaughter was motive for war.[46] But it may have been merely a general term for trader, synonymous with pochteca.[47]

The caravan or expedition was led by a "captain" pochteca, and included non-pochteca, the slaves and *tamemes* or porters. The parents of young men on their first trip were solicitous that the captain look after their boys. Certainly the slave traders and king's traders also went on expeditions and it is probable that all kinds of pochteca ventured out jointly, as it was always a perilous journey. Thus there would be among the usual expeditionary crew both age grading and differences of rank.[48]

How did the pochteca obtain the commodities which they exported? Sahagún describes a trip in which the king supplied them with 1600 *quachtli* (cotton cloths) which they took to Tlatelolco and divided there equally with the Tlatelolcan pochteca. Thereupon both groups took the cloths to the market in Tlatelolco and purchased rich clothing with which to trade on behalf of the sovereign as well as jewelry and finery "for their own trading."[48a] Upon arriving in the ports of trade of the Xicalango area, they exchanged these goods again with the local rulers.[49] In another instance Sahagún quotes a trader as saying that he had purchased stone knives, bells, needles, cochineal and *piedra de lumbre* with which to trade.[50] This same source gives several accounts of the slave traders buying slaves in the market of neighboring Azcapotzalco for the purpose of ceremonial sacrifice, a part of the pochteca yearly celebration.[51] They may also have purchased slaves for export. Slaves were sold in various markets, one of the most important being that of the just mentioned Azcapotzalco. But the home of the slave traders was, as we may recall, Tlatelolco. Masters certainly sold their slaves in the market and a person could sell his children and even himself. A slave could even purchase a slave. But there is no mention of the pochteca selling slaves in the markets of the Basin of Mexico.[52] Evidently those who sold slaves in the market were not the pochteca who traded slaves over long distances. But as to exports in general, a comparison of the items sold in the markets of the Basin of Mexico with the goods exported by the pochteca reveals that all of the latter goods were available in the local markets.[53]

Thus is can be asserted that some pochteca did purchase goods in the markets of Tenochtitlan-Tlatelelco which they traded in foreign ports. However, they may also have had other sources, one of them being the royal cloths supplied by the palace, and other treasures.

The most frequently mentioned types of goods exported are: slaves (men, women and children); richly worked garments for men and women (there is one reference to clothes "for the common people"); ornaments of gold and precious stones; skeins of rabbit fur; copper bells. Copper and obsidian ornaments, needles, combs and knives of obsidian, red ochre and cochineal dyes, sweet smelling herbs and *piedra de lumbre* are also mentioned.

Garments and ornaments seem to be by far the most important items as they are frequently mentioned and many different kinds are described.[54] It is significant that most of these goods are manufactured articles, and most of the raw materials out of which they were made were not found in the Basin of Mexico but came in partly as tribute from outlying provinces, perhaps also with local vendors and certainly with the pochteca on their return trips. The extent to which exports relied on markets is not yet clear.

The commodities most frequently described as imported by the pochteca are: rich feathers; precious and semi-precious stones. Cacao, cacao stirrers, gold, animal skins and fans are also mentioned.[55] Thus in contrast to exports, imports mostly consisted of raw materials. This is qualified by "mostly" not because of the fans or stirrers which probably were not very important, but because there is occasional mention of some of the imported precious stones and animal skins as having been "worked." This undoubtedly means polished and tanned as there is no account of actual manufactured objects in either case.[56]

Given the great importance of gold and copper objects in the Aztec society, absence of the mention of copper and the infrequent references to gold as imported would seem to indicate that most of it was obtained either in the local markets or through tribute payment. The present states of Oaxaca and Guerrero were known sources of gold and most of this region had been conquered by the Aztecs.[57] However, the pochteca are known to have traveled as far south as the present Costa Rica-Panama border for gold.[58] We can only suggest, however, that the question of gold, its sources, forms, and uses merits a study in itself.

Here attention should be drawn to the extraordinary importance of feather objects. Feather working was an ancient and, as we have seen, a highly respected craft. There were numerous types of feathers. The most highly prized came from birds of the highlands of the south, those of the quetzal bird being outstanding. Apparently it was an extremely arduous task to hunt or capture these birds. Some conservation of the species was practiced; sometimes the captured bird was carefully held while its best feathers were plucked and the bird then set free in order to give another supply.[59] Among the amazing variety of objects made or adorned with the feathers were head gear, mosaics on shields and helmets used in ceremonies, garments and cloths, ornaments, standards and banners.[60]

Surprisingly, there are only a few mentions of cacao as having been imported by the pochteca. This is baffling because cacao was very important as the principal money of the various cultures and as the main ingredient of the people's favorite chocolate drinks. Cacao beans, along with other objects, were used both in exchange and for payment of fines, debts and tribute.[61] It was cultivated or in use all the way from the Basin of Mexico to Costa Rica, although it may not have been employed throughout this entire area. A recent dissertation entitled "When Money Grew On Trees" shows that its principal areas of cultivation were central Veracruz, northern Oaxaca and the Xoconusco exclave far to the south, yet forming part of the empire. Beyond the frontiers it was grown in the Xicalango region of the Gulf coast, southwestern Guatemala and the Gulf of Honduras.[62] It will be noted that two of these areas were the central regions of the great ports of trade. Among the Aztecs, then, if cacao was not a principal trade import, it may have been because the 900 loads received annually in tribute payment supplied most of their needs.[63] Should this be so, the importance of Xicalango and the Gulf of Honduras as Aztec ports of trade may have indirectly been due to cacao production. Indirectly, since wealth in cacao might well have attracted from the hinterlands and regions inaccessible to the pochteca, the fine feathers and precious stones which they sought.

Other money in use with the Aztecs were a particular kind of small cotton cloth, gold dust in transparent quill containers, "rich feathers" and perhaps small copper axes and pieces of tin.[64] Just how these moneys circulated and what might be paid for with each will necessitate special research. Although barter also obtained, the various money objects, and especially cacao, were extensively used in the markets. Like cacao, some were also used in payment. It is not possible to say with assurance whether cacao served as a standard, that is, whether all other moneys had established equivalencies in relation to cacao. This writer is acquainted with only one reference which definitely stipulates an exchange equivalency between cacao and cloth. Sahagún writes that a canoe was worth one *quachtli* (cloth, and presumably money) or one hundred cacao beans.[65] This equivalency need not have obtained universally, of course, as the exchange values of the moneys were known to vary in different regions. Nevertheless, the existence of equivalencies between objects used as money appears established and of money objects cacao was certainly the most widely spread, and thus, practically, must have served as a standard.

For the relation between long-distance trade and the markets, it is a most suggestive fact that we have not come across any mention of the pochteca using money of any description in the ports of trade. Money as a means of exchange was employed, of course, primarily in the market. Trade, as carried on by the pochteca was directed towards ports of trade in which transactions were performed in kind, whether with the intervention of the administration of the store houses where the staples were deposited, or through direct acts of exchange in kind.

In principle, all foreign trade was barter, and the method of operation was barter. The description referred to above of the pochteca *teucunenenque* receiving cloths from the emperor and going to Tlatelolco where they shared them with other pochteca "and spoke of the business which the king had entrusted them with" is evidence of administered trade, that is, trade between politically independent entities. This is further substantiated by this same chronicler's account of their arrival at the ports of trade:

> When the traders arrived at the province of Anahuac Xicalango, they gave the rulers that which the ruler of Mexico had sent them and they greeted them on his behalf, and the ruler of rulers of this same province, of the town of Xicalanco, and the town of Cimatecatl (Cimatan), and Quatzaqualco (Coatzacoalco) gave them large polished green stones, and other long polished *chalchiuites* (turquoise), and red stones and other emeralds . . . and other stones. . . . They also gave them shells and red and yellow fans, and cacao stirrers . . . rich feathers . . . tanned skins of wild beasts . . . all these things were brought back by the traders from that province of Xicalanco for the ruler of Mexico; and when they returned and arrived at Mexico they immediately presented them to the ruler.[66]

Sahagún further says that the traders took goods to Xicalanco "for the common people" consisting of earnings of copper and flint, flint combs, small knives, bells, needles, cochineal and sweet smelling herbs. He does not say how this ware was exchanged. However, in the entire account by Sahagún of the pochteca trading in these foreign provinces there is *no mention of prices or markets* or of their exchanging with anyone but the rulers. The only exception is the spy traders, the *naua-*

loztomeca, who went, not to the ports of trade, but into enemy territory where they sat in the markets disguised as natives—a strong indication of the local ethnic character of markets, as contrasted with trade.

There are no data on how the *slave traders* carried on exchange. The rulers and other nobles who bought slaves in the ports of trade must have either sacrificed them, or put them to work as domestics or in the cacao fields.

The pochteca also exchanged the goods which had been commissioned by the *pochtecatlaloque* with whom they shared the "gain" upon return. There is no direct indication of what this gain consisted in, but, as will be evident from the passage cited below, it must have been in goods.[67] Where barter prevails gain must necessarily take that form.

Just how the pochteca returned with their precious ware is of great interest. The crucial point is that their goods were not destined for the market. They made sure of returning on a good luck day. They waited until night-time before entering the capital and came in secretly so that no one should notice them. They did not go directly to their houses, but to that of a relative or some person of confidence where they deposited their goods. If anyone inquired there about what they had brought back they would say:

> . . . this wealth that I bring, take care of it for me but don't think I entrust it with you because it is mine, it belongs to the señores, the principal merchants, they recommended that I bring it here.[68]

And only after reporting to the pochteca officers did they go home to sleep.

The Maya of Yucatan

We now enter the world of the Maya. The paucity of data on trade is striking. Yet the little that the Spanish documents reveal is suggestive. By taking advantage of modern research on related subjects, in particular the organization of the pochteca and the use of cacao money and comparing them with accounts of the Basin of Mexico we can piece together a fragmentary image of the preconquest situation. The degree to which it has been possible to attain some clarity is due chiefly to the excellent studies of Roys, Scholes, and Chamberlain.

The absence of the mention of trade in the Spanish eye witnesses' accounts on Yucatan after its discovery, in 1517, has two very different reasons: The one was the indifference of the *conquistadores* to this obviously non-gold-bearing area. Once the Spaniards were resigned to the lack of gold in a region, they were little interested in observing native trading customs. The other was the almost immediate disappearance of the native trading system after the conquest of the Aztec capital in the north, in 1521. Actually, the entire area under consideration had had a very active and tightly knit trade organization, based on regional ecology, agricultural specialization and localized manufacture. Consequently, the entire network of trading relationships, from the Basin of Mexico south to Yucatan and Honduras and even to Panama, was drastically affected by the fall of Tenochtitlan, the center of economic and political power. A few years after that event the basis of the Indian societies had shifted and the delicate web of trade relations had become torn or tangled; by the 1540's it had all but disappeared.

The accounts of some of the participants of the first three expeditions directed towards the western mainland (1517–1519) and of later *entradas* into the unexplored inland regions deserve close scrutiny for what they may reveal of trade and markets.

We will enumerate certain isolated facts in regard to trade in Yucatan taken from these records, mostly written by the *conquistadores* and early missionaries, and compare them with accounts of the Basin of Mexico and other areas.

By coincidence the very spot where the Spaniards first touched the mainland, the northeastern corner of Yucatan, was one of the few commercial centers of the entire peninsula. The conquerors were much impressed with the richly dressed Indians who greeted them at Ecab (Belma), in northeastern Yucatan. In their enthusiasm they called it "el Gran Cairo." Ecab and the neighboring inland towns of Cachi and Cahuacha were described as having large markets.[72] At Cachi there was a market court on one corner of the square, where disputes were settled by certain officials.[73]

In 1527 the Adelantado of Yucatan, Francisco de Montejo, sailed down the eastern coast to the Bay of Chetumal. Here he found the town of Chetumal two leagues inland from the bay. He described it as having two thousand houses, stone walls facing the coast for defense(!), fertile lands, highly developed bee culture and as being an important trading center. It was also the only extensive cacao-producing area of the entire peninsula. Later his lieutenant Alonso Dávila came to the same area and was so favorably impressed with the many maize fields, the populous settlements and the strategic location that he established the Spanish town of Salamanca there. This was one of the few places, the other being the northeastern tip, where the Spaniards found gold objects. In this same bay region was the town of Bacalar. It was also reported to have had a thriving commerce. Situated on a lake of the same name, it was joined by a river to the Bay of Chetumal.[74]

The land around the Bay of Chetumal region, in some essential respects, appears closely comparable to the coastal strips of the Gulf of Mexico and the Gulf of Honduras. This point of embarkation for overseas trading and for receiving goods from the hinterland was, like the Xicalango-Gulf of Mexico, a land of bays, lagoons, rivers, lakes and marshes, all of which made for extensive canoe travel. It also had cacao cultivation. But the similarity to the other two areas becomes even more striking when we see that, despite several eye witness reports, there is no mention of markets or market places. (See map, p. 118)

In contrast to the Basin of Mexico with its unified imperial government, Yucatan at the time of the conquest, according to Roys, was divided into eighteen politically autonomous entities, which he describes as follows:

Certainly each of these subdivisions was independent of its neighbors. Some of them possessed a well-organized political system headed by a single ruler: others were more or less closely knit confederacies of towns or groups of towns; still others seem to have been merely collections of towns in a given area, whose relations with one another are largely a matter of conjecture.[75]

The greater part of the northern peninsula was limestone with only a thin layer of humus on top and it was covered with a shrub or thick brush growth. Only the northeast had sufficient rainfall to permit of forest growth. The center of the peninsula was traversed from east to west by a low mountain range. This country would have presented great difficulties for living were it not that the underground water table was sufficiently near the surface to make water accessible through natural or artificial wells, called *cenotes*. It was therefore around these cenotes that the farming communities were located. Maize, beans, squash, cotton and cassava were the most important crops. There were settlements along the coast dedicated exclusively to

fishing. Here salt gathering was also important. Apiculture was extensively practiced. Game, and especially deer, was plentiful. But metals
were entirely lacking, although flint was to be found, and apparently it
was even mined along the foothills of the sierra. Flint was the material
used for cutting implements and weapons.[76]

Notwithstanding the apparent simplicity of its basic neolithic pattern, the Maya-Yucatecan society was highly stratified, ritualistic and
commercial.

The long-distance trader in Yucatan was a person of noble status
and wealth. He trafficked mainly in slaves, cloth and salt, to a lesser
extent in honey and flint, i.e., mostly in raw materials. His principal
ports of trade were about Xicalango in the Gulf of Mexico to the
southwest, and on the Gulf of Honduras to the southeast. In the latter
area he had warehouses and factors (agents). There apparently was a
manner of distinction among the traders, between what Roys calls
the "professional merchant," the ppolom, and "those who traveled,"
the ah ppolom yoc.[77]

There does not seem to have existed in Yucatan the same sharp
definition of the traders as a group which obtained among the Aztecs.
Nor is there any mention of their occupation of a special section of a
town or city. Nor is there evidence, as we saw, of a comparable degree
of internal ranking and differentiation of types of traders. Nor do we
find any such complex ritual and ceremonial activities as characterize
the Aztec traders. It is not by any means suggested, however, that
Yucatecan-Maya trading institutions represented simply a watered
down version of the Aztec, or a simpler commercial system than was
theirs. Trade in Yucatan was a vitally important activity. The Maya
social and political stratification, internecine warfare, as well as the
economics of production and consumption, was to a large extent dependent on the maintenance of trade relations beyond their ethnic
frontiers.

Indeed, the Yucatecan trader was apparently much more closely
identified with his political rulers than was the Aztec trader. In at
least one case, dating back to the middle of the fifteenth century, the
son of the ruler of Cocom is referred to as a trader.[78] A close connection of, if not identity with, the rulers and traders, coupled with
the absence of any indication of trading in the market places of foreign ports, points towards the practice of administered trade carried on
by chieftain's clans through warehouses in the ports of trade.

As we have noted, the main export commodities at the time of the conquest were slaves, cloth and salt. Flint and honey ranked second. In contrast to the Mexican exports, none required specialized labor in manufacture. Nearly every woman wove cloth. Anyone living near the coast could generally obtain permission to gather salt. Flint was readily available and easily made into tools or weapons; and most families possessed bee hives. Slaves, of course, are a special case. Their acquisition for trade both within Yucatan and abroad was a primary cause for raids and wars between the provinces. They were also bought and sold in Yucatan.[79]

Because the cultivation of cotton and its spinning and weaving were universal in Yucatan, cloth may not have been an important item of trade within Yucatan proper. The same may have been true of honey. Certainly slaves, salt and flint were traded internally. Many other articles were also traded "domestically," such as fish, pottery, canoes, dyes, copal gum for incense, maize, game, fruit, wooden idols and small amounts of native cacao.[80]

It is clear, then, that long-distance trade dealt only in certain specific goods. At the time of the conquest, only a relatively few types of articles were being exported.

Turning now to the imports, we will recall that the Spaniards were never weary of complaining of and continually disheartened by the small amounts of gold to be had in Yucatan and that all of it had been imported. The lure of richer plunder from the various regions of the Aztec Empire was an important factor in the relatively late conquest of the peninsula. Yucatan was not definitely conquered until after the suppression of the Great Maya Revolt of 1546–47. For our purposes it is significant that the largest amounts of gold objects acquired by the Spaniards were from the region of the large market towns on the northeastern coast and from the important trading area of the Bay of Chetumal on the East coast. About the time of the conquest gold articles were imported from the Xicalango region, having been brought there by pochteca from the Basin of Mexico where the ornaments and ritual paraphernalia were made. Bells, axes or celts, plates and thin sheets of copper and skeins of dyed rabbit hair seem to have followed the same route. Precious and semiprecious stones including jade and jadite turquoise, crystalline green stones, yellow topaz, obsidian and the fine quetzal and macaw feathers that originated in the southern highlands and were traded in via the Gulf of Honduras as well as the Gulf of Mexico. A type of red shell, *Spondylus princeps*, was relayed to Yucatan via Honduras from the Pacific coast of Nicaragua. Cacao was also imported in large quantities. Of all the above-mentioned items only cacao was native to the two main ports of trade areas, the Gulf of Mexico and the Gulf of Honduras.[81]

Money, in the sense of quantifiable objects used in exchange, was common in Yucatan. Cacao was the most important, but cotton cloths of a standard size, strings of red shells (*spondylus princeps*), copper hatchets, and bells as well as jade beads and salt were also used as money. Of these, only the cotton cloth and salt were native to Yucatan. As in the case of the Nahua area, this matter calls for further research. However, as suggested above, in view of the extensive use of the cacao money and its predominance over other money, it may well have been a standard against which all other commodities were equated throughout the entire area of central and southern Mexico and Central America. As among the Aztecs, it was also used to make a kind of chocolate drink.[82]

The long-distance traders used only the cacao bean as money. The traders carried a kind of pocketbook filled with cacao beans. These may have been used as cash to pay for lodgings on the journey. One of the early chroniclers, Gasper Antonio Chi, asserts that the Yucatecans, being a hospitable people, gave shelter to all traveling strangers, except the traders, who had to pay.[83]

The goods were transported by human caravans and canoe fleets. Overland the noble *ah ppolom yac* led his slave porters single file along the foot trails through the underbrush and forest, which had been cleared just enough to allow the passage of one man with a pack. The mounted Spaniards later complained of these trails that they had not been cleared for a man on a horse and that consequently a rider often got himself entangled in the overhanging vegetation. The traders led, the porters followed. The porters were slaves, destined to be sold in the foreign ports. This was a convenient arrangement for the traders, because the goods which they exported were bulkier than those which they brought back. At their destinations they exchanged all of their goods, including their slaves, mostly for manufactured items, and so simplified the problem of portage on the return trip. Apparently the Maya did not pay their porters as did the Aztecs their *tamemes*. The Maya may have had a corps of slaves who always accompanied them on trading expeditions and simply augmented the number of this corps of porters going out with the slaves to be sold. Like the *pochteca*, however, they stopped along the trails at shrines, in this case those of their god Ekchuan, who was also the god of cacao.[84]

But by no means did all their travel go overland. From the Bay of Ascencíon on the east coast they journeyed by canoe to the Gulf of Honduras and perhaps around the peninsula and down the west coast as well. The porters then became rowers. The canoes were made from a hollowed out tree trunk and were traded from the Chetumal Bay area. Some were reported to be very large, holding as many as forty to sixty men.[85]

Aztec *pochteca*, Mayan *ppolom*, in either case persons of the upper class, enter on a long-distance carrying service on behalf of the community. The *pochteca* of the Nahua are a highly elaborated gild, probably of communally settled clan origin; the *ppolom*, though perhaps of even higher rank, are less specialized because their exports are not luxury wares but raw materials. We know their gods, their porters, their routes, their military and political status, but what was the journey's aim? How would the *pochteca* and the *ppolom* trade in the absence of markets? Obviously nothing but barter in kind was feasible, and it would be transacted even while their respective countries may have been engaged in hostilities.

Pochteca as well as *ppolom* were moving toward definite geographical areas organized to serve just that purpose. The actual exchange of goods took place in ports of trade. We now turn to the discussion of their locations.

Gulf of Mexico—Xicalango

The ports of trade on the Gulf of Mexico extended from a point in the State of Veracruz to the westernmost section of the Laguna de Términos, i.e., the "lagoon at the border," the town of Xicalango proper.[86] (See map, end pages)

This was (and is) a hot alluvial plain covered by a network of rivers, lagoons, swamps and bogs interspersed with tropical rain forests and grassy savannahs. From the lagoon of Tupilco, just east of the Coatzalcoalcos River through this entire region there predominated a people of Maya stock, the Chontal. It was, as we have noted, one of the principal cacao-producing areas. Within the region there were a number of small señorios, politically autonomous entities, each with its lords and nobles, working population and a varying number of subject tributary towns.[87] Neither politically nor militarily was there any strong concentration of power present.

Many and far-flung routes come together here at the various ports of trade. People and goods traveled by canoe, almost exclusively. From the north came the famous pochteca of the Aztec with their luxury wares. Inland, down from the southern and eastern sierras came people with precious stones and feathers, from the Zoque and Tzeltal-Tzotzil towns and mines. Traders following other riverain routes west came down the Candelaria River from Acalan and across the base of Yucatan from the Gulf of Honduras as well. Up the Gulf Coast towards the east the canoes traveled at least as far as the town of Campeche. There is no direct evidence that the traders spanned the entire distance around the Yucatecan peninsula by canoe to the east coast. Roys assumes that they did so because it is known that traders from Xicalango made pilgrimages to the shrine of the merchant god on the Island of Cozumel. He admits, however, they may have traveled up the eastern coast from the Gulf of Honduras instead.[88]

As we have seen, this Xicalango enclave was perhaps most important for Aztecs in their long distance trade. Sahagún documents the journey of the pochteca to this region.

Cargoes of richly worked fabrics and clothing, ornaments and spindle whorls of gold, copper bells, obsidian knives and combs, and skeins of dyed rabbit hair all firmly secured on the backs of their porters, which the pochteca of the various cities of the Basin of Mexico assembled, in making ready for their departure overland, were destined for these two main ports of trade: Xicalango on the Gulf coast and Xoconusco on the Pacific.[89]

Some of the pochteca, perhaps each one of them, carried a black wooden staff, symbol of their god, Yiacatecutli. They also carried fans, corn mash and other dried foods for the journey. Some of the porters were slaves and others the lowly tamemes, clothed in rags and subsisted as human beasts of burden.[90] Writing some hundred odd years after the conquest, the English missionary, Thomas Gage, made notes on this same rank of men, now working for the Spaniards:

    . . . they will make those wretches to carry on their backs a whole day, nay some two or three days together, which they do by tying the chest on each side with ropes, having a broad leather in the middle, which they cross over the forepart of their head, or over their forehead, hanging thus the weight upon their heads and brows, which at their journey's end hath made the blood stick in the foreheads of some, galling and pulling off the skin, and marking them in the fore-top of their heads, who as they are called *tamemes*, so are easily known in a town by their baldness, that leather girth having worn off all their hair.[91]

Each porter and slave carried approximately fifty pounds. There is no indication of how much the pochteca themselves may have carried. They trotted single file over mountain trails. If, as Bernal Díaz reported, they averaged five leagues a day, it must have taken many days to cover the first lap.[92] At night they stopped to sleep in any cave, gorge or ravine, beside a large boulder or under a tree. Each night they tied their black staffs together, thus improvising the image of their god Yiacatecutli. To it they offered their blood by piercing their tongues, ears, legs or arms, and in burning incense in its honor they felt assured of a safe journey. Sometimes also they worshipped at shrines of their god along the trail. A strange proscription was laid upon them: during the entire journey until the return home, they could not bathe nor wash nor cut their hair. It was, however, permissible to wash the neck.[93]

The first lap of the journey was terminated in the town of Tochtepec, near the southern border of the Empire, in the northeastern section of the present state of Oaxaca. Tochtepec was the chief frontier trading center and the home of a colony of rich slave traders who had originally come from Tlatelolco. It was the gateway into the enemy territory through which the pochteca passed to reach those two great trading centers to the south,[94] that of Xicalango, to the east, Xoconusco, to the west. At Tochtepec the caravan split, some going over the sierra to the isolated Aztec province of Xoconusco, that Aztec exclave on the Pacific coast. The others went instead down the sierra to the marshy swamp lands of the Gulf coast. As enemy territory lay ahead, upon departing the pochteca took to swords and shields, and even armed their slaves, marching cautiously and only at night.[95] Those headed towards the Pacific had the protection of a line of Aztec garrisons along the sierra trail until they reached Xoconusco. Those headed toward Xicalango, on the Gulf, did not have so far to go and although they had no garrisons to protect them, the local rulers of the ports of trade would send emissaries to greet them and give them safe conduct at the final part of their journey. Upon arrival, as has been described, the pochteca presented themselves to the rulers of Coatzal-coalco, Cimatan and Xicalango.[96]

There were apparently five major groups of ports of trade in this Gulf of Mexico area; (1) the settlements at the mouth of the Coatzal-coalco River, (2) the inland towns of Cimatan and (3) those of the Chontalpa, (4) the town of Potonchan at the mouth of the Grijalva River and (5) the famous Xicalango at the western end of the Laguna de Términos.

1. Coatzalcoalco was a coastal town just beyond the frontiers of the Aztec Empire but in the vicinity of an Aztec garrison. The pochteca arrived here bearing greetings and goods from their ruler. At the time of the conquest it was known to have been Nahuatl-speaking. The Spaniards described this country as rich and populous.[97]

2. Inland from the coast, further east, lay the Nahuatl town of Cimatan with its two closely allied neighboring towns. Cimatan con-trolled vital trade routes from both the inland sierras and the Basin of Mexico due to its strategic position near the great rivers which flowed down from the highlands and its accessibility to the Aztec traders coming from Tochtepec. It was the most powerful of the eight Mexican or Nahua speaking towns in Tabasco. It had conquered several Zoque towns to the south.[98] Scholes and Roys write that,

> There can be little doubt that the temples of a town of such importance were set on pyramids, and the more important buildings, on raised plat-forms, presumably of earth in this locality.[99]

Bernal Díaz described the palisades which surrounded it for defense but made no mention of a market.[100]

3. To the east of Cimatan and nearer the coast lay the Chontalpa, a thickly populated region and rich in cacao. In the lowlands between the Río de Dos Bocas (present Río Seco) and the Río Nuevo ó Gonzales lay at least twenty-three Chontal speaking towns. According to a docu-ment recently discovered, there were five other towns to the west of the Río de Dos Bocas and five more to the east of the main group of twenty-three. This entire group of towns was called the Chontalpa. Here the Aztecs had factors and warehouses in the towns of Mecoacan, Chila-teupa and Teutitlan Copilco (modern Copilco). Scholes and Roys say the Aztecs sold their goods to local traders. Nevertheless, they infer that this region was not a commercial center because, according to a document of 1541, there was no market, although as the presence of

factors and warehouses testify, it was an important trading center.[101] The point is of eminent importance for a clearer understanding of the nature of long-distance trading. As we shall see, it is precisely the separation of markets and trading in the ports of trade, that seems to typify long-distance trading among the Nahua and Maya.

4. Next in order was Potonchan, near the mouth of the Grijalva River. Like its neighbor to the east, Xicalango, it had traffic with Acalan, the Usumacinta Valley and the Gulf of Honduras and hence up the east coast of the peninsula of Yucatan. Although there is no direct evidence, Scholes and Roys believe the traders also went up the west coast and across to the island of Cozumel and the trading towns of that area. Potonchan was inhabited by Chontal speakers and thus contrasted with Xicalango where there were at least some Nahua speakers. As Sahagún and other sources fail to mention Potonchan as a port of trade for the pochteca and as it was inhabited by a Maya people, this writer suggests that it traded exclusively with Mayas and not with the pochteca at all. Although the town is described at some length in the sixteenth century sources, there is no record of a market.[102].

5. The port of trade of Xicalango was the leading commercial site for the Aztecs. As we know, they called this entire Gulf area, Anahuac-Xicalango. The town itself was situated near an inlet on the western side of the Laguna de Términos. Scholes and Roys suggest that "the Mexican merchants with their employees and slaves occupied a quarter of the town. . . ." The ruling class, including the important local merchants, spoke Nahuatl while the native inhabitants spoke Chontal.[103] This is a situation which was quite common, if not typical, in the Aztec ports of trade. It raises in a concrete way the question of the relationship between the Nahua colonists-traders and the local rulers. Given a Nahua ruling class which included the traders and given the vital importance of trade for the community, it can be surmised that the Nahua traders were the actual rulers. The close tie if not identity between the traders and rulers was described for Yucatan and will be seen even more clearly in the province of Acalan and Naco on the Gulf of Honduras. Therefore this pattern may perhaps tell us something of an ethno-historical interest. Xicalango differs from both Yucatan and Acalan but is similar to Naco in that the trader-rulers were foreigners, that is, Nahua colonists. The chronicler Ixtlilxochitl men-

tions a "feria" (fair) in Xicalango but does not describe it nor associate it with the pochteca.[104]

Scholes and Roys recognize that just as Cimatan was favorably situated to handle long-distance trade from the highlands to the south and west, Xicalango enjoyed a similar advantage in regard to Acalan, the Usumacintla Valley and hence the Gulf of Honduras up to Yucatan. As we know, they may also have taken the coastal route to northeastern Yucatan. Xicalango shared all this traffic with its neighbor, Potonchan. But it contrasted to Potonchan not only on account of Nahua residents, but also because it was the preferred port of trade for the pochteca.

It is for Xicalango, that Sahagún gives his most detailed description of administered trade.[105] Some features of its concrete organization emerge. Hence our knowledge that no local traders from Xicalango went north to the Basin of Mexico. This trade was apparently handled exclusively by the pochteca. The Xicalango traders did however travel southward, to Acalan and the various ports of the Gulf of Honduras. They also may have gone to Yucatan as noted since there is indication that they went to the island of Cozumel to worship at the shrine of a merchant god. Cortés, in 1524, during his march to Honduras acquired a cloth map from the traders of Xicalango which he is said to have followed as far as Acalan.[106]

The inland sierras to which we have referred were also inhabited by peoples of the Maya linguistic stock; among them the Zoque, and the Tzeltal-Tzotzil. The other large group, the Chiapaneca, were an Otomangue speaking people.

The foothills and sierra of the present states of Tabasco and Chiapas were the home of the Zoque. Here the people are described in the sixteenth century, some years after the conquest, as wearing tufts of feathers and skeins of green birds for ornaments, with necklaces and nose and ear plugs of wood, gold, topaz and other stones. Roys comments: "We know little of their political or social organization, except that there was among them an upper class which prided itself on its noble status."[107] At least four of its principal towns were subject to Cimatan, while others were subject to the Chiapanec (the Otomangue group) and there were many independent towns and villages. This province, too, produced some cacao in the lowlands towards the Gulf coast, and manufactured cloth. It had mines of amber or so-called yellow topaz and produced cochineal which was used to make a red dye.[108] The English missionary, Thomas Gage, visiting in 1625, describes it as the richest part of Chiapas and comments on its important connections with Tabasco and Yucatan. He names the chief commodities as silk, which was certainly post-hispanic, and cochineal which, although used in pre-hispanic times, may have increased in production after the conquest.[109]

In the Tzeltal-Tzotzil region lay the town of Zinacantan, in the highlands of Chiapas. Amber was obtained in trade by the Aztecs from this area. This product was much desired by the Culhua as well as the Maya for lip and nose beads. It was probably exported to the Gulf of Mexico and hence to Yucatan as well as the Basin of Mexico.[110]

To the Aztecs, to whom this was enemy territory, Zinacantan was well known as a town of "merchants." Sahagún reports that spy traders came here to sit in the market place disguised as natives. We have already noted that their wares were not the luxury goods for which the pochteca were famous, but rather goods which the common people could buy.[111] *This is the only mention by Sahagún of pochtecas actually trading in a market.* It took place in unfriendly territory, in a town which, despite it being a trading town, cannot be called a port of trade. In other words, a port of trade, although located in a foreign territory, must be a friendly site, that is, *safe for the traders.* In some cases the friendliness of the Culhua ports of trade consisted in the circumstance that by some means Nahua traders had usurped political and economic power from the local inhabitants.

Zinacantan, site of a Mexican garrison, was one of the strong points that protected the Culhua traders as they passed through enemy territory and along the sierra down to the outlying Culhua province of Xoconusco, near the present-day frontier between Mexico and Guatemala.[112]

Pacific Coast—Xoconusco

The province of Xoconusco—an enclave on the Pacific coast—was conquered by the Aztecs about 1486.[113] Just how this conquest was carried out is not clear. While Sahagún states that pochteca conquered it, Tezozomoc names Aztec troops as the victors. He connects the traders with the conquest only in the sense that their slaughter in Xoconusco was the cause for an Aztec reprisal.[114] In any event the fertile cacao fields, for which Xoconusco was renowned, must have exerted a great attraction on the Aztecs.[115]

There is very little information on trade with this region. Sahagún mentions the pochteca setting out for Xoconusco, called Anahuac-Ayotlan, but proffers no description of their arrival nor of what was traded.[116]

The cacao and perhaps quetzal feathers and other products of the inland sierras offered a sufficiently rich reward for the Aztecs to warrant their passing through enemy territory.[117] Nevertheless this area appears not to have been comparable in importance to either the Gulf of Mexico or that of Honduras; it had very few navigable rivers, so that trade movements were of necessity restricted.[118]

As in the ports of trade on the Gulf coast, this region was inhabited by some Nahua elements. Yet there is no evidence of the role they may have played as traders.[119]

In general, Xoconusco presents a problem. It is the only known area where long-distance trade was continued after subjugation to the Aztecs as a tribute-paying province. In all other instances long-distance trade was carried on outside the Aztec empire as well as beyond the provinces of the Mayan confederacies.

Inland—Acalan

Of first importance for the study of the region of Acalan is the discovery of a sixteenth century Chontal text in the Archives of Seville by Scholes. It has been recently published in a study by the finder and Roys. They have definitely located this province on the upper Candelaria River, draining into the Laguna de Términos. The Chontal text names seventy-six towns belonging to the province but Scholes and Roys found it impossible to locate or identify most of them. Concerning the capital, Itzamkanac, however, we know that it was situated south of the Candelaria near the junction of the Arroyo Caribe and the San Pedro tributaries in the present state of Campeche.[120]

Situated on the main river routes between the Gulf of Mexico and the Gulf of Honduras, Acalan was a focal point of trading. Its very name, derived from the Nahuatl acalli, means "the place of canoes." Since travel was mostly by canoe its settlements were probably near navigable waters.[121]

There is clear evidence here of the trader-ruler pattern. Scholes and Roys say in so many words that Acalan was ruled by "merchants," that is, by what we have termed traders. They go on to say that the wealthiest of them, a lord named Poxbolonacha, was the supreme ruler of the entire province.[122]

The Acalan traders occupied a ward or quarter in Nito, on the Gulf of Honduras, where they also had factors and warehouses. They likewise traded inland to the northeast with the Cehache and to the southeast in the region of the Itzas. Our authors write that Itzamkanae, the capital of Acalan,

> seems to have been an outlet for the commerce of the Sarstoon, Polochic and Montagua valleys, all of which were rich in cacao; and from its location we may well infer that there was also much trade with Chetumal and the commercial centers of Northeastern Yucatan.[123]

It will be recalled that Cortés followed a map to Acalan which was given to him by traders of Xicalango. Itzamkanac witnessed a tragic episode, the execution of Cuauhtemoc. Cortés considered it perilous to leave Cuauhtemoc in Tenochtitlan in his absence, fearing that he would become the rallying point of an Indian insurrection. He thus took him and other Aztec rulers as prisoners on the march to Honduras in 1524 only to have them beheaded in Acalan.

On approaching Itzamkanac, hungry and destitute on the march, Cortés and his men received canoes loaded with food from the Acalans. Upon his arriving at the town the ruler greeted him bearing gifts of honey, turkeys, maize, copal and fruit. Cortés described Itzamkanac as a large place with many temples, a rich and flourishing town. Yet he, as well as Bernal Días and the later Dávila, fails to mention any market or market place. As we have seen from examining the ports of trade, this is no longer surprising. Although markets may have been held for the local inhabitants, they were not necessary for the long distance trading and therefore they were probably either quite small or infrequently held.

It was largely because of the enthusiastic reports of Cortés and other of his *conquistadores* praising Acalan as a prosperous and populous region, that the Adelantado of Yucatan, Montejo, planned in 1529 to use Acalan as a military base for his attack on the still unconquered peninsula of Yucatan. This same year, only five years after Cortés had passed through, Montejo sent his lieutenant Dávila to inspect the region with this plan in mind. However, although Dávila describes Itzamkanac as having from nine hundred to a thousand very good buildings of stone and white stucco, he considered that it could not be used as a basis for military operations. His reasons were, in effect, that it was not as prosperous as both he and Montejo had been led to believe. Not only was it lacking in gold but the agricultural products were limited and *its former thriving commerce had fallen away.*[124]

In a lapse of only five years, from 1524 to 1529, Acalan had suffered a marked decline in its prosperity. Yet the Spaniards had not as yet attempted to subject the region to tribute. Nor had they, until Dávila's arrival, established encomiendas. It is quite probable that the decline was due to the very rapid disintegration of the pre-hispanic trade structure. Even as an important trading center, Acalan may well have been merely a point of transit with little besides agriculture, copal gum and perhaps dyes of its own. The town must have been drastically affected by any lessening of the flow of goods from the far richer areas of Honduras and the Gulf of Mexico. The wealth of Acalan depended upon its strategic trade position between the two Gulfs. Once the network of trading relations was disturbed, its location made it highly vulnerable.[125] As traders, the Acalans depended on the port.

On their route to the Gulf of Honduras the traders of Acalan passed through the swampy region of the Itzas, who inhabited five islands in Lake Peten in what is now northern Guatemala. Their territory extended west to the Cehache and southward perhaps to the Río de la Pasión. Here among the Itzas and in contrast to Acalan, the ruler was not a merchant or trader, rather he shared his rule with the high priests.[126] The Itzas undoubtedly traded with Acalan and probably also with the Cehache, and the ports of trade on the Gulf of Honduras. Here, however, we can surmise that the lack of mention of the importance of traders is related to the fact that the ruler was closely allied to the priest. This obviously was not a port of trade area.

Another province, known as Verapaz during the colonial period, and situated in western central Guatemala, was described by the chronicler Ximénez as having many markets and as being particularly important because it was a habitat of wild animals and birds, whose skins and feathers were a very important trade item. Despite these economic resources and the considerable commercial activity, there is no mention of native long-distance traders nor of any localities which might have been ports of trade.[127]

The Mesoamerican ports of trade were specific localities, of typical organization and trade relations such as those of the two Gulf areas. In this context Acalan was not only a port of trade but also a community of traders.

Gulf of Honduras

The role of the Gulf of Honduras, to the south east of the broad base of Yucatan, shows a startling functional similarity to the Xicalango area on the Gulf of Mexico, described above (see map p. 118). Even topographically the two coastal areas, left and right of the peninsula present a symmetrical picture: in the Xicalango region there were, as we have seen, at least four long distance trading centers: Cimatan, the Chontalpa, Pontonchan and Xicalango, each closely related to riverain routes. In the Honduras region there were likewise at least four trading centers, each in close proximity to the four large rivers: the Sarstoon, the Rio Dulce and the inland Lake Izabal, the Montagua and the Ulua.

Instead of a detailed presentation of the Honduran trading centers, we will conclude this chapter by listing significant resemblances between the two coastal regions, east and west of Yucatan, i.e., the Gulf of Honduras and the Gulf of Mexico. While this latter lay between the Maya and Aztec main areas, the Gulf of Honduras represented a link in the opposite direction, i.e., a trading bridge connecting Mesoamerica with Central America. In either case—to conclude the argument—the essential resemblance of topographical traits and economic organization is apparent:

1. Topographically they are similar in that both are tropical coastal regions watered by a number of rivers whose basins lie in the inland sierras. Although the Gulf of Mexico area is more swampy, both were traveled almost exclusively, in pre-hispanic times, by canoe. This fact is relevant to trade and may also have been an important source of a demand for slaves as rowers. There was a need in both regions for slaves imported from the Basin of Mexico and Yucatan. Slaves were probably also used in the cacao "plantations." Scholes and Roys insist that cacao is unusually suited to slave labor in that it demands year round care.[128]

2. Both regions were among the largest cacao producers of the entire area under consideration. Alike, they lacked precious metals, stones, feathers and obsidian. Yet they exported (i.e., re-exported) most

of these items, and all their exports, with the exception of their cacao, were brought down by canoe from the sierras.

3. Both Xicalango and Honduras imported not only slaves but also cloth, garments and ornaments of precious stones and metals from the Basin of Mexico and cloth as well as salt, honey and flint from Yucatan.

4. According to various authorities, a basic Maya linguistic and cultural affinity existed among the non-Nahua population all the way from the Copilco River on the Gulf of Mexico across to the Ulua River on the Gulf of Honduras.[129]

5. Of great interest is the parallel in the trading activities of the two regions under consideration. There are references stemming from the conquistadores testifying to the existence of factors and warehouses, both of which were notably lacking within the Aztec Empire proper as well as in Yucatan. In this context, the scattered Nahua settlements were undoubtedly very important for long distance trading with the Basin of Mexico. As in the Gulf of Mexico region, so likewise here in Honduras, did the trading routes converge from distant areas. The two regions were moreover linked through the Acalan and the Usumacintla river routes.

6. The Spaniards described both these regions as rich and populous during the first years of the conquest period. But their initial enthusiasms for them faded as little gold was found. The prosperity of either region was quickly undermined, as trade ceased. The early encomenderos, harassed by insurrections, attacks, mute refusal of the Indian to pay tribute responded with cruel reprisals, and the flight of the natives into the as yet unconquered regions of the interior set in.[130]

Anne M. Chapman

Notes to Chapter VII

1. The anthropologist Paul Kirchhoff (1952) first used the term Mesoamerica to define a culture area of central and southern Mexico and northern Central America. On the north it is bounded by the mouth of the Panuco River on the Gulf of Mexico, the Sinaloa River through to the mouth of the Lerma on the Pacific; to the south by the Montagua River on the Gulf of Honduras and extends further to the south to the Gulf of Nicoya on the Pacific. It refers to Indian cultures as they existed just prior to the Spanish conquest. The area is defined by the prevalence of certain diagnostic traits of high culture such as step pyramids, hieroglyphic writing, calendars of 365 and 260 days, specialized markets, trader spies and so forth. The

validity of Mesoamerica as a culture area has been amply confirmed by specialists in the fields of archaeology and ethnology.

2. The data on the Aztecs have been drawn principally from the great work of Fray Bernardino de Sahagún, a Franciscan monk who arrived in New Spain in 1529. Versed in Nahuatl and a scholar of extraordinary merit, Sahagún may be described as the first American ethnologist. Beginning in 1538 and for a period of several decades he wrote, in collaboration with Indian informants, the twelve books of the *Historia de las Cosas de Nueva Espana* (Jimenez Moreno, 1938).

Other early sources have been consulted but not exhausted. The directly descriptive data have been given precedence over general statements. Modern studies have been extensively used; outstanding among these is that of Acosta Saignes.

3. Barlow, 1949.

4. Cook and Simpson, 1948, pp. 27–28.

5. Barlow, 1949.

6–10. Until Bandelier published his three famous studies on the Aztecs in the 1870's (Bandelier, 1877, 1878, 1878a) their society had been, even in the empirical descriptions by very competent historians, considered comparable to feudal Europe. Bandelier provoked a controversy which still has not ended by contending that here was a democratic egalitarian tribal society similar not to feudal Europe, but to the Iroquois of aboriginal North America. Since Bandelier, and especially in the last few decades, the Aztec society has been characterized as having a class structure (Moreno, 1931), as being a "tribal" society (Vaillant, 1950, ch. 6), as based on kinship relations in the from of stratified clans (Monzón, 1949, ch. 10), or, as seems most likely, as having a state structure (Caso, 1954).

11. Cortes, 1908, Second Letter, *passim*.

12. Prescott, n. d., p. 599.

13. McBryde, 1933, p. 110; Hendrichs, 1940–41, p. 193; Scholes and Roys, 1948, p. 165; Borah, 1951, p. 2; Tax and others, 1952, ch. 12. Gibson, 1952, pp. 190–194; Zavala and Miranda, 1954, *passim*; Borah, 1954, *passim*.

14. Cunow, 1926, Vol. I, pp. 275–78; Acosta Saignes, 1945, pp. 9–10.

15. Sahagún, 1946, Book 9, ch. 2.

16. Acosta Saignes (1945, p. 16) quotes Gonzalo Fernández de Oviedo y Valdés, *Historia general y natural de las Indias, islas y tierra-firme del Mar Océano*, 4 vols. Madrid, 1851–55).

17. Herrera y Tordesillas, n. d., decade 3, bk. 4, ch. 17; Veytia, 1826, pp. 227, 230, 232; Zurita, 1941, pp. 142, 147–148.

18. Monzón, 1949, ch. 2.

19. Sahagún, 1946, bk. 9, ch. 6.

20. Herrera y Tordesillas, n. d., decade 3, bk. 4, ch. 17; Veytia, 1826, pp. 227, 230, 234; Suarez de Peralta, 1878, p. 21; Torquemada, 1943, Vol. 2, bk. 13, ch. 34; Sahagún, 1946, bk. 9, chs. 15–21; Caso, 1954, p. 24.

21. Sahagún, 1946, bk. 9, ch. 19.

22. Acosta Saignes, 1945, *passim*; Dahlgren de Jordan, 1954, pp. 246–49; Caso, 1954, p. 23.

23. Monzón, 1949, *passim*.

24. Cunow, 1926, Vol. 1, p. 278; Moreno, 1931, pp. 43–44; Vaillant, 1950, p. 122; Caso, 1954, p. 21.

25. Acosta Saignes, 1945, p. 21.

26. Herrera y Tordesillas, n. d., decade 3, bk. 2, ch. 17; Sahagún, 1946, bk. 9, chs. 3, 6.

27. Sahagún, 1946, bk. 4, chs. 17–18; bk. 9, chs. 5, 10–14.

28. Ixtlilxochitl, 1891–92, Vol. 2, pp. 272, 279–81; Tezozomoc, 1944, chs. 27, 23, 31, 33, 34, 37, 75, 78, 88–92.

29. Acosta Saignes, 1945, pp. 10–11.

30. Sahagún, 1946, bk. 9, ch. 2.

31. Codex Mendoza, 1938, vol. I, p. 75.

32. Zurita, 1941, p. 142.

33. Sahagún, 1946, bk. 9, ch. 3.

34. Monzón, 1949, passim.

35. Simeón, 1885.

36. Sahagun, 1946, Bk 9, Ch. 3.

37. Ibid., bk. 9, chs. 3, 10.

38. Ibid., bk. 9, chs. 4, 10. In one passage Sahagún calls them tealtianime and tecoanime, but otherwise refers to them simply as slave traders. These Nahuatl words are not found in Molina (1585) while Simeón (1885) defines them in the context of Sahagún.

39. Simeón, 1885; Sahagún, 1946, bk. 9, ch. 4.

40. Sahagún, 1946, bk. 9, ch. 2.

41. Tezozomoc, 1944, ch. 75.

42. Ibid., ch. 34.

43. Ibid., chs. 89–91.

44. Sahagún, 1946, bk. 9, ch. 5.

45. Molina, 1585.

46. Tezozomoc, 1944, chs. 75, 78.

47. Simeón, 1885; Acosta Saignes, 1945, p. 13.

48. Sahagún, 1946, bk. 9, ch. 3.

48a. One of the few indications of how private profit splits off public service in trade.

49. Ibid., bk. 9, ch. 2.

50. Ibid., bk. 9, ch. 3.

51. Ibid., bk. 9, ch. 10.

52. Torquemada, 1943, Vol. 2, bk. 14, ch. 17; Bosch García, 1944, passim.

53. Cortés, 1908, Second Letter, passim; Conquistador Anónimo, 1941, pp. 43–44; Díaz del Castillo, 1947, ch. 92.

54. Sahagún, 1946, bk. 9, passim.

55. Ibid.

56. Ibid., bk. 9, ch. 1.

57. Saville, 1920, pp. 102–3, 143, 187; Aguilar Piedra, 1946, passim; Lothrop, 1950, p. 76; Dahlgren de Jordan, 1954, pp. 138–140.

58. Lothrop, 1950, p. 87.

59. Herrera y Toresillas, n. d., decade 4, bk. 10, ch. 11.

60. Cervantes de Salazar, 1914, Vol. 1, p. 19; Torquemada, 1943, Vol. II, bk. 13, ch. 34; McBryde, 1945, p. 72, note 115; Sahagún, 1946, bk. 9, chs. 18–21.

61. Suarez de Peralta, 1878, pp. 21, 166–67; Bastow, 1897, passim; Codex Mendoza, 1938, Vol. I, passim; Acosta, 1940, bk. 4, ch. 22; Torquemada, 1943, Vol. II, bk. 14, chs. 24, 33; Clavijero, 1945, Vol. I, bk. 1, ch. 9; Vol. II, bk. 7, ch. 36; Vol. 4, disertación 6, no. 1. Clavijero is the only early source known to this writer who states that of the four known species of cacao, the smallest bean, the tlalcahuatl, was commonly used as ingredient for the drink while the other species were more often used as money. See also Bastow, 1897, p. 51.

62. Millon, 1955, ch. 10.

63. *Ibid.*, ch. 6.
64. Bastow, 1897, pp. 50–51; Acosta Saignes, 1945, p. 11; Clavijero, 1945, Vol. 2, bk. 7, ch. 36.
65. Sahagún, 1946, bk. 9, ch. 10.
66. *Ibid.*, bk. 9, ch. 4. Translation A.M.C.
67. *Ibid.*, bk. 9, ch. 3.
68–71. *Ibid.*, bk. 9, ch. 6. Translation A. M. C.
72. Roys, 1939, pp. 60–1; Roys, 1943, p. 51; Chamberlain, 1948, pp. 47, 50–2.
73. Roys, 1943, pp. 51–2.
74. Tozzer, 1941, note 26; Chamberlain, 1948, pp. 47, 60–1, 100–1; Scholes and Roys, 1948, pp. 83–6.
75. Roys, 1943, p. 11.
76. *Ibid.*, ch. 1.
77. Roys, 1939, p. 61.
78. Landa, 1941, p. 39.
79. Mendizabal, 1946–7, Vol. I, pp. 296–302, 317; Roys, 1943, ch. 8.
80. Roys, 1943, ch. 8.
81. Boekelman, 1935; Landa, 1941, pp. 94–7; Tozzer, 1941, notes 19, 23, 171, 415, 433; Roys, 1943, ch. 8; Thompson, 1954, pp. 21–2, 183–5.
82. Blom, 1932; Tozzer, 1941, notes 417, 418, 421; Chi, 1941, p. 231; McBryde, 1945, p. 84.
83. Chi, 1941, p. 231.
84. Blom, 1932; Thompson, 1929; Roys, 1943, ch. 8.
85. Roys, 1943, ch. 8.
86. Roys, 1943, p. 57; Scholes and Roys, 1948, p. 31.
87. Scholes and Roys, 1948, ch. 2.
88. *Ibid.*, pp. 33–4.
89. Sahagún, 1946, bk. 9, ch. 4.
90. *Ibid.*, bk. 9, chs. 4, 6.
91. Gage, 1929, p. 233.
92. Díaz del Castillo, 1947, ch. 45.
93. Sahagún, 1946, bk. 9, ch. 3.
94. Cooper Clark, 1938, Vol. 1, note on p. 95; Sahagún, 1946, bk. 9, ch. 11; Barlow, 1949.
95. Sahagún, 1946, bk. 9, ch. 4.
96. *Ibid.*; Barlow, 1949, map.
97. Blom and LaFarge, 1926–27, Vol. 1, p. 68; Sahagún, 1946, bk. 9, ch. 4; Scholes and Roys, 1948, p. 91.
98. Scholes and Roys, 1948, pp. 31–3, 318.
99. *Ibid.*, p. 32.
100. *Ibid.*, p. 32.
101. *Ibid.*, pp. 24, 31–2.
102. *Ibid.*, pp. 33–4, 36.
103. *Ibid.*, 34–6.
104. Ixtlilxochitl, 1891–92, Vol. 2, p. 345; Cortes, 1908, Fifth Letter.
105. Sahagún, 1946, bk. 9, ch. 4.
106. Scholes and Roys, 1948, pp. 3, 57, 93.
107. Roys, 1943, pp. 110–11.
108. Scholes and Roys, 1948, pp. 32, 39.
109. Gage, 1929, p. 167.
110. Roys, 1943, p. 107.

111. Sahagún, 1946, bk. 9, ch. 5.
112. Barlow, 1949, map.
113. Kelly and Palerm, 1950, pp. 275–76.
114. Tezozomoc, 1944, ch. 78; Sahagún, 1946, bk. 9, ch. 2.
115. Millon, 1955, chs. 3, 10.
116. Sahagún, 1946, bk. 9, ch. 4.
117. Ibid., bk. 9, ch. 2.
118. Relación de Soconusco, 1882, pp. 426–27.
119. Lothrop, 1939, p. 44.
120. Scholes and Roys, 1948, p. 48.
121. Ibid., pp. 50–1.
122. Ibid., p. 4.
123. Ibid., p. 58.
124. Chamberlain, 1948, p. 88.
125. Scholes and Roys, 1948, p. 165.
126. Thompson, 1951.
127. Herrera y Tordesillas, n. d., decade 4, bk. 10, ch. 13; Relaciones . . . de
América Central, 1908, pp. 447–48; Ximenez, 1929–31, Vol. I, pp. 93–4.
128. Scholes and Roys, 1948, p. 29.
129. Ibid., pp. 3, 316–17; Chamberlain, 1948, p. 151; Stone, 1941, p. 15.
130. Scholes and Roys, 1948, ch. 5; Chamberlain, 1953, ch. 1.

Bibliography to Chapter VII

Acosta, José de, Historia natural y moral de las Indias. Mexico, 1940.
Acosta Saignes, M., "Los Pochteca." Acta Antropológica, Vol. 1, no. 1, Mexico, 1945.
Aguilar Piedra, C. H., "La orfebrería en el México precortesiano." Acta Antropológica, Vol. 2, no. 2. Mexico, 1946.
Bandelier, A. F., "On the art and mode of warfare of the ancient Mexicans." Peabody Museum. Harvard University, 10th Annual Report, 95–161. Cambridge, 1877.
——, "On the distribution and tenure of lands, and customs of with respect to inheritance, among the ancient Mexicans." Peabody Museum, Harvard University, 11th Annual Report, 385–448. Cambridge, 1878.
——, "On the social organization and mode of government of the ancient Mexicans." Peabody Museum, Harvard University, 11th Annual Report, 557–669. Cambridge, 1878a.
Barlow, R. H., "The Extent of the Empire of the Culhua Mexica." Ibero-Americana, 28. Berkeley and Los Angeles, 1949.
Bastow, J. W., "Comercio, moneda y cambio de los antiguos pueblos de México." Congreso Internacional de Americanistas, XI reunión; 47–63. Mexico, 1897.
Berlin, H., "Relaciones precolombinas entre Cuba y Yucatan." Revista Mexicana de Estudios Antropologicas, nos. 1–2: 140–160. Mexico, 1940.
Blom, F., and O. La Farge, Tribes and temples. A record of the expedition to Middle America conducted by Tulane University of Louisiana in 1925. 2 Vols. New Orleans, 1926–27.
Blom, F., "Commerce, trade and montary units of the Maya." Middle American Research Series, No. 4: 531–566. Tulane University of Louisiana, New Orleans, 1932.

Boekelman, H. J., "Ethno- and archeo-conchological notes on four Middle American shells." *Maya Research*, 2: 255–277. New Orleans, 1935.

Borah, W., "New Spain's century of depression." *Ibero-Americana*, 35. Berkeley and Los Angeles, 1951.

——, "Early colonial trade and navigation between Mexico and Peru." *Ibero-Americana*, 38. Berkeley and Los Angeles, 1954.

Bosch García, C., *La esclavitud prehispánica entre los Aztecas*. Mexico, 1944.

Caso, A., "Instituciones indígenas precortesianas." *Memorias del Instituto Nacional Indigenista*, VI; 13–27. Mexico, 1954.

Cervantes de Salazar, Francisco, *Crónica de Nueva Espana*. Madrid, 1914.

Chamberlain, R. S., *The conquest and colonization of Yucatan. 1517–1550*. Carnegie Institute of Washington, Publication 582. Washington, 1948.

——, *The conquest and colonization of Honduras: 1502–1550*. Carnegie Institute of Washington. Publication 598. Washington, 1953.

Chi, Gaspar Antonio, *Relación*. In Landa's *Relación de las cosas de Yucatán*. A translation edited with notes by A. M. Tozzer. Papers Peabody Museum. Harvard University, Vol. 18: 230–232. Cambridge, 1941.

Clavigero, Francisco Javier, *Historia antigua de México*. 4 Vols. Mexico, 1945.

Codex Mendoza, A translation edited with notes by J. Cooper Clark. 3 Vols. London, 1938.

Columbus, Ferdinand, *The history of the life and actions of Admiral Christopher Colon. A General Collection of . . . Voyages and Travels*. John Pinkerton edition, Vol. 12. London, 1812.

Conquistador Anónimo, El, *Relación de algunas cosas de la Nueva Espana y de la gran ciudad de Temestitan Mexico. Escrita por un companero de Hernán Cortés*. Mexico, 1941.

Cook, S. F. and L. B. Simpson, "The population of central Mexico in the sixteenth century." *Ibero-Americana*, 31. Berkeley and Los Angeles, 1948.

Cooper Clark, J., See Codex Mendoza, 1938.

Cortés, Hernán, *Letters of Cortés; the five letters of relation to the Emperor Charles V*. Translated and edited by F. A. MacNutt. 2 Vols. New York, 1908.

Cunow, H., *Allgemeine Wirtschaftsgeschichte*. 4 Vols. Berlin, 1926.

Dahlgren de Jordan, B., *La Mixteca. Su cultura e historia prehispánicas*. Mexico, 1954.

Díaz del Castillo, Bernal, "Verdadera historia de los sucesos de la conquista de la Nueva-España." *Historiadores primitivos de Indias*. Vol. 2. Madrid, 1947.

Gage, Thomas, *A New Survey of the West Indies*. 1648. New York, 1929.

Gibson, C., "Tlaxcala in the sixteenth century." *Yale Historical Publications, Miscellany LVI*. New Haven, 1952.

Hendrichs, P. R., "Datos sobre la técnica minera prehispánica. Continuación." *El México Antiguo*, Vol. 5: 179–194. 1940–41.

Herrera y Tordesillas, Antonio de, *Historia general de los hechos de los castillanos en las islas y tierra-firme del mar oceano*. 10 Vols., recent re-issue of the 1726–30 edition. Editorial Guarania. Ascunción del Paraguay. [n.d.]

Ixtlilxochitl, Fernando del Alva, *Obras históricas de don Fernando del Alva Ixtlilxochitl*. Edited by Alfredo Chavero. 2 Vols. Mexico, 1891–92.

Jímenez Moreno, W., *Fray Bernardino de Sahagún y su obra*. Mexico, 1938.

Kelly, I. and A. Palerm, *The Tajin Totonac. Part I. History, subsistence, shelter and technology*. Smithsonian Institute, Institute of Social Anthropology, no. 13. Washington, 1950.

152   *Aztec-Maya; Dahomey; Berber; India*

Kirchhoff, P., "Meso-America." In *Heritage of Conquest.* Edited by S. Tax: 17–30. Glencoe, Illinois, 1952.

Landa, Diego de, *Landa's Relación de las cosas de Yucatán.* A translation edited with notes by A. M. Tozzer. Papers, Peabody Museum, Harvard University, Vol. 18. Cambridge, 1941.

Lothrop, S. K., "The Southeastern Frontier of the Maya." *American Anthropologist,* Vol. 41:42–45 (1939).

——, *Archaeology of Southern Veraguas, Panama.* Memoirs, Peabody Museum, Harvard University, Vol. 9, no. 3. Cambridge, 1950.

McBryde, F. W., *Sololá. A Guatemalan town and Cakchiquel market-center.* Middle American Research Series, no. 3 of pub. no. 5. Tulane University of Louisiana. New Orleans, 1933.

——, *Cultural and historical geography of southwest Guatemala.* Smithsonian Institute, Institute of Social Anthropology, no. 4. Washington, 1945.

Mendizábal, M. O. de, *Obras completas.* 6 Vols. Mexico, 1946–47.

Millon, R. F., *When money grew on trees. A study of cacao in ancient Mesoamerica.* Ph.D. dissertation, unpublished. Columbia University. New York, 1955.

Molina, Alonso de, *Vocabulario de la lengua castellana y mexicana.* Madrid, 1585.

Monzón, A., *El calpulli en la organización social de los Tenochca.* Mexico, 1949.

Moreno, M. M., *La organización política y social de los Aztecas.* Mexico, 1931.

Morison, S. E., *Admiral of the ocean sea. A life of Christopher Columbus.* 2 Vols. Boston, 1942.

Prescott, W. H., *History of the conquest of Mexico and history of the conquest of Peru.* The Modern Library. New York, n.d.

Polanyi, K., *Semantics of general economic history* (revised). Council for Research in the Social Sciences, Columbia University. New York, 1953.

Relaciones históricas y geográficas de América Central. Edited by V. Suárez. Madrid, 1908.

Relación de Soconusco. "(1574) Carta de D. Luis Ponce de León, gobernador de Soconusco. . . ." In Fuentes y Guzman, *Historia de Guatemala ó recordación florida.* Vol. I, 423–428. Madrid, 1882.

Roys, R. L., *The titles of Ebtun.* Carnegie Institute of Washington, Pub. 505. Washington, 1939.

——, *The Indian background of colonial Yucatan.* Carnegie Institute of Washington, Pub. 548. Washington, 1943.

——, See Scholes, F. V. and Roys, R. L. 1948.

Sahagún, Bernardino de, *Historia general de las cosas de Nueva Espana.* Notes by M. Acosta Saignes, 3 Vols. Mexico, 1946.

Saville, M. H., *The Goldsmith's art in ancient Mexico.* Indian Notes and Monographs. Museum of the American Indian, Heye Foundation. New York, 1920.

Scholes, F. V. and R. L. Roys, *The Maya Chontal Indians of Acalan-Tixchel: a contribution to the history and ethnography of the Yucatan Peninsula.* Carnegie Institute of Washington. Pub. 560. Washington, 1948.

Siméon, R., *Dictionnaire de la langue Nahuatl ou Mexicaine.* Paris, 1885.

Stone, D. Z., "The Ulua Valley and Lake Yojoa." In *The Maya and their Neighbors:* 386–94. New York, 1940.

——, *Archaeology of the north coast of Honduras.* Memoirs Peabody Museum, Harvard University, Vol. 9, no. 1. Cambridge, 1941.

——, "Los grupos Mexicanos en la América Central y su importancia." *Antropología e Historia de Guatemala,* Vol. 1, no. 1:43–46. Guatemala, 1949.

—, "Una definición de dos culturas distintas vistas en la antropología de la América Central." In *Homenaje al Dr. Alfonso Caso*: 353–61. Mexico, 1951.

Strong, W. D., "Anthropological problems in Central America." In *The Maya and their Neighbors*: 377–85. New York, 1940.

Suarez de Peralta, Juan, *Noticias históricas de la Nueva Espana*. Madrid, 1878.

Tax, S., And others, *Heritage of Conquest*, Glencoe, Ill., 1952.

Tezozomoc, Hernando Alvarado, *Crónica Mexicana*. Mexico, 1944.

Thompson, J. E. S., "Comunicaciones y Comercio de los Antiguos Mayas." *Anales de la Sociedad de Geografia e Historia de Guatemala*, Vol. 6, no. 1: 40–44 (1929).

—, "The Itza of Tayasal. Peten." In *Homenaje al Dr. Alfonso Caso*: 389–400. Mexico, 1951.

—, *The Rise and Fall of Maya Civilization*. Norman, Oklahoma, 1954.

Torquemada, Juan de, *Veintiún libros rituales y monarquía Indiana*. 3 Vols. Mexico, 1943.

Tozzer, A. M., See Landa, D. de. 1941.

Vaillant, G. C., *The Aztecs of Mexico*. Penguin Books. 1950.

Veytia, Mariano, *Tezcoco en los Ultimos tiempos de sus antiguos reyes ó sea relación tomada de los manuscritos inéditos de Boturini*. Edited by Mariano Veytia. Mexico, 1826.

Ximénez, Francisco, *Historia de la provincia de San Vicente de Chiapa y Guatemala de la orden predicadores*. 3 Vols. Guatemala, 1929–31.

Zavala, S. and J. Miranda, "Instituciones indígenas en la colonia." *Memorias del Instituto Nacional Indigenista*, Vol. VI: 29–112. Mexico, 1954.

Zurita, Alonso de, "Breve y sumaria relación de los senores . . . en la Nueva España." In *Relaciones de Texcoco y la Nueva España*: 65–206. Mexico, 1941.

VIII

A Port of Trade:
Whydah on the Guinea Coast

———•———

IT was in the course of inquiring into the commercial organization of eighteenth-century Whydah, historically known as the slave port of the Negro kingdom of Dahomey, that attention was first drawn to the subject of this chapter—the port of trade.[1] Whydah was an organ of administered trade, a way of trading which appears as general from antiquity almost to the threshold of modern times.* The capacity of the port of trade for outlasting the millennia reflected the positive role played by that institution in resolving some of the less obvious problems of statecraft under archaic conditions, such as military requirements and protection against undesirable culture contact.

In the institution of the port of trade, therefore, many strands meet, some deriving from the early state, some from even earlier primitive conditions. Apart from the military and cultural considerations which made the inland empires shun the coast, there was the position of the foreign trader, who refused to venture for the sake of commerce onto a strange and distant shore unless the safety of his person and goods was fairly assured. No one but the armed pirate could feel secure on a beach. Hence the combination of pirate and trader famed from the Odyssey. It was a long time before the neutrality of the trading place was ensured not by native weakness, as in silent trade, or around the mariners' altars on secluded beaches, but by the deliberate neutrality with which law and order enforced equal justice to all comers at the hand of port authorities. Fear would drive out traffic.

The international status of the port of trade thus ran the gamut from a free port "in weak hands," as Whydah originally was, to a mere port-town of an inland power administered from the distant capital as Whydah became under Dahoman rule after the conquest, in 1727.

Since the last quarter of the seventeenth century Whydah was famed in the Western world as the port of call of the African slave trade. In the beginning of the eighteenth century the small coastal kingdom that formed Whydah's immediate neighborhood was overrun by the powerful inland state of Dahomey, which thus appeared in the limelight of history. Whydah was incorporated in Dahomey, the capital of which, Abomey, was some 150 miles removed from the coast. While Whydah was frequented by the crews of the White slavers of many nations, Abomey, secluded in the Dark Continent, remained inaccessible to foreigners. Whydah, a flourishing· port town, renowned in distant countries, was never deemed worthy of the King of Dahomey's personal presence. Although a commercial emporium, no native class interested in trade was in evidence. European observers were sometimes baffled by the ambiguous status which this trading place held in Dahomey. An inquiry into the organization of trade in Whydah may then well start from the history of Dahomey, and the reasons which made it seize Whydah, and having done so, keep it at arm's length.

Dahomey was one of the great Negro states of West Africa, an inland kingdom of some 300,000 population, heir to a political tradition stemming from the empire-builders of the Western Sudan. For several hundred years, from the foundation of the kingdom, which legend places around 1625, until its conquest by the French in 1892, Dahomey was governed by the same dynasty of Negro kings and maintained its independence until borne down by overwhelming military forces.

Eighteenth-century Dahomey had produced a planned economy of an advanced type, using trade, money and markets with sophistication. Viewed in historical perspective, this planned economy was a method of coping with the massive pressures which the external situation, the danger of foreign conquest, brought to bear upon Dahomey. Planning was a technique for survival, and the monarchy, the central planning organ, performed functions without which the society could not have maintained its independent existence. Given Dahomey's situation, the organs of a tribal society would have been powerless. No loose tribal formation could have organized a sustained military effort on the scale required nor dealt effectively with the outside world through trade nor assured internal peace under the stresses and strains of permanent mobilization. A power transcending the tribal organs had to be called into being to meet the threat to the communal existence.

The kings of the Alladoxonou dynasty created such a power and succeeded in welding the Dahoman peoples into an empire. Out of disunity and impotence, a military organization was created which Dahomey's neighbors were compelled to respect. Despite the strain which an annual war placed upon the resources of the country and its institutions, the well-being of the population was assured by an unquestionably efficient administration of the economy. And out of diverse traditions, a common tradition was forged, so deeprooted that it lives on among the people of Dahomey even today despite military conquest and a couple of generations of foreign rule.[2]

Yet Dahomey under the monarchy retained its tribal base—it was an empire built on tribal foundations. The traditions of the clan were the core values of Dahoman life, constitutive of the political community as of the tribal community. Far from disintegrating under the pressure of the throne, the clans of Dahomey remained as the basic social units and exercised indispensable functions in economic and political life. Even the monarchy appeared in the guise of the clan. The royal house ranked as the highest of the clans and the ancestors of the royal house were regarded as the ancestors of all Dahomans. As mediator between the living and the dead, the king's relationship to his people was that of head of a clan to its members—he was the link with the ancestors, high priest and chief magistrate, first among warriors, and guardian of the people's livelihood. While the king embodied the aristocratic virtues of a tribal chief, the democratic traditions of the tribal society were likewise perpetuated in the rights enjoyed by the clans, the villages, the gilds, and the innumerable voluntary associations—a charter of freedoms which was the keystone of Dahoman society.

In adapting tribal institutions and traditions to the new circumstances created by political expansion, Dahomey produced that singular combination of centralization and decentralization, of authority and flexibility, of controls and freedoms, which characterized its redistributive economy.

War and Trade in Native Dahomey

If a military policy was forced upon Dahomey in self-defense, this was no less true of its trade policy. The Dahomans were anything but a trading people. Their geographical position isolated them from trade. A glance at the map reveals that Dahomey stood well below the 12th parallel which marks the southernmost extension of the great trade routes of Africa. These well-worn tracks link the west-east flow of the middle Niger exclusively with the Moorish north and the Haussa country in the east. No roads whatsoever lead from the middle Niger to the western or southern coast.[3]

Though sheltered from the main approaches of trade, the Niger to the north and Guinea coast to the south, Dahomey could not remain entirely aloof from trade. Like the other Negro peoples of the interior, Dahomey was accustomed to fight only with bow and arrow. But once the Moors from the north had introduced firearms into the Sudan, and once the Europeans on the Guinea Coast were arming the coastal natives of the south with European muskets, those who knew only the bow and arrow were doomed to extinction or unending flight. Dahomey was caught between two fires. Trade with the Europeans at Whydah had become essential since it was this trade, as the Dahomans themselves said, which "brings guns and powder to Dahomey." So crucial was the control of the trade that Dahomey permitted guns and powder to move inland only to those border peoples who had certified their friendship by alliance with Dahomey. "The Mahee," Duncan says of the northern neighbors of Dahomey, "use the bow and arrow, the King of Dahomey forbidding the transport of firearms through his kingdom from the coast."[4]

Yet trade with the Europeans at Whydah—literally a condition for survival—raised at the same time the gravest threat to Dahomey's security. Dahomey was a passive trader, maintaining, herself, no organization for active trade over long distances. While there are a few reports of trading parties sent into the interior, the meagerness of these reports suggests that active trade was the exception rather than the rule. As a passive trader, however, dependent upon supplies brought by others from afar, Dahomey would be exposed to all the dangers involved in letting down the gates to the foreigner. Without a counter-organization for trade, by which the movements of foreigners and their goods could be regulated in conformity with the requirements of state, Dahomey would stand defenseless before a dual enemy: her hostile neighbors, and the strangers come to trade.

Herein lies the explanation of Dahomey's policy toward Whydah. So long as Dahomey's access to the port was secure, Dahomey was content to leave Whydah in the hands of the Whydasians. Dahoman traders, it seems, had been accustomed to come freely to Whydah for some time before 1727 when Whydah passed to Dahomey.[5] Such a relationship permitted Dahomey to secure the essential trade goods and yet remain aloof from the foreigner in her inland retreat.

What, then, prompted Dahomey to change her policy and take Whydah by force in 1727?

This question was the subject of considerable controversy among the Europeans who witnessed the event. Norris, upholding the viewpoint that Dahomey's commercial interests were the motivating factor, commented as follows:

I knew many of the old Whydasians as well as Dahomans who were present when Trudo attacked that kingdom. They attributed his enterprize solely to the desire of extending his dominions, and of enjoying at first hand, those commodities which he had been used to purchase of the Whydasians. . . .[6]

Herskovits follows this interpretation, affirming

that the principal reason why Agadja was eager to conquer his way to the sea-coast was that . . . the transportation of goods through the kingdoms of Whydah and Ardra took from him a large proportion of his profits from slaving, and greatly increased the price of European goods which he received in exchange for the proceeds from slaves.[7]

And, further, that the conquest of Whydah

gained for Agadja the right to sell his slaves directly to the captains of the slave vessels who called at the port, and from them to get, without paying the duties imposed by an intervening power, the European goods he valued so highly.[8]

These views are hardly consistent with the facts. Whatever their varying interpretations of the event, contemporary witnesses agreed as to the facts, and the most significant fact was that the king of Whydah had closed the port to traders from Dahomey. Norris says that the Dahoman king, Trudo,

had solicited permission from the king of Whydah to enjoy free commercial passage through his country to the sea side, on condition of paying the usual custom upon slaves exported; this was peremptorily refused by the king of Whydah; and in consequence of this refusal, Trudo determined to obtain his purpose by force of arms. . . .[9]

Likewise, Snelgrave confirms that Dahomey

sent an Ambasasdor to the King of Whidaw, requesting to have an open Traffick to the Sea side, and offering to pay him his usual Customs on Negroes exported: which being refused, he from that time resolved to resent it, when Opportunity offered.

Furthermore, the king of Whydah, after refusing Dahomey's request, told Snelgrave that

if the King of Dahome should offer to invade him, he would not use him when taken according to their Custom, that is, cut off his Head, but would keep him for a Slave to do the vilest Offices.[10]

Atkins suggests that there were further provocations against Dahomey. "The king of Dahomey," he says,

was probably incited to the Conquest from the generous Motive of redeeming his own, and the neighbouring Country People from those cruel Wars, and Slavery that was continually imposed on them by these Snakes (Whydasians) and the King of Ardra; . . . against those in particular, his Resentments were fired: First, on account of their public Robberies, and Manstealing, even to his Dominions; and Secondly, That Contempt the King of Whydah had expressed towards him. . . .[11]

There is, then, no question of Dahomey's attempting to evade payment of the duties upon the trade since the king offers to pay Whydah "his usual Customs on Negroes exported." And indeed, the first step taken by Dahomey after its capture of Whydah was to reduce the customs to one half those fixed previously by the king of Whydah.[12] Instead, there was a security problem of the first order. Dahomey was being denied access to the Coast and the opportunity to secure firearms, while the public insult to Dahomey proffered by the king of Whydah could not be overlooked without grave damage to Dahomey's position. We may recall, moreover, that Dahomey was at this time under tremendous pressure from the Oyo, having suffered one invasion and standing in dread of another. Indeed, it seems likely that the taking of Whydah was regarded by Dahomey as a counter-move against the Oyo. During the first Oyo invasion, according to Snelgrave, the Daho-mans had "comforted themselves with this Thought," that, in the event of a second invasion

they might save their Persons, by flying to the Sea Coast, to which the J-oes durst not follow them. For as their national Fetiche was the Sea, they were prohibited by their Priests from ever seeing it, under no less a Penalty than Death.[13]

It may well be, then, that an outlet to the seaside was contemplated as an avenue of retreat from the Oyo. For the ultimate preserve of the "fugitive" peoples were the lagoons of the tropical coast.

Under these circumstances, it was only by placing Whydah in its own hands that Dahomey could secure access to the coast and guar-antee the neutrality of the place of trade. The compelling urgency of such a move is underlined by the subsequent difficulties which it en-countered in holding the port. The intrigues of the coastal peoples, spurred on intermittently by various European governors, were, for a time, a recurring threat to Dahomey's hold upon the trade—all the more since Oyo was also seeking to establish trade relationships with the coast. At any rate, by the end of the century, Oyo had succeeded in wresting control from Dahomey of the neighboring kingdom of Ardra and its port, Jaquin, or Porto Novo, so that the Oyo were in a position to close off the coast entirely unless Dahomey was securely in possession of its own port. The threat was a very real one. At one time, Dalzel says,

The King of Ardrah . . . stopped all communication with Whydah. The messengers from Porto Novo were no longer seen at the King of Dahomey's Customs; and the Dahoman traders, who had been accustomed to visit Ardrah, were no more allowed that liberty.[14]

When Dahomey protested this action, even sending an expedition against Porto Novo, the king of Oyo replied with the warning that Dahomey should undertake no further offensive actions against Ardra, since "Ardra was Eyeo's callabash, out of which nobody should be permitted to eat but himself.[15]

Far from looking upon Whydah as a source of commercial gain, then, Dahomey regarded the acquisition of Whydah as a security measure. The Dahoman attitude toward Whydah was that of an in-land people who abhor the foreigner-infected coast and its cosmopoli-tan activities, but who are forced to maintain contact because of imperative military considerations.[16] In short, the port of trade was a liability, not a source of profit.

Only this interpretation is consistent with the well attested massive fact that Dahomey, on more than one occasion, offered to cede Whydah to the British. The most complete account of such negotiations is that given by Duncan to whom the king

> expressed his earnest desire to give up Whydah to the English Government, with full powers to exercise our own laws and customs; . . . [and] to afford us every necessary assistance and protection, and to give us any . . . quantity of land in the vicinity of that settlement we might require for agricultural purposes.[17]

Nothing could more definitely indicate Dahomey's noncommercial interests in Whydah than this offer to turn it over to the English crown. Moreover, this offer explicitly commits the king to the abolition of the slave traffic as well. "When we (i.e., the English) should have obtained possession of Whydah," the king goes on to say to Duncan, "we should have power to use our own discretion respecting the Slave-trade; and that . . . we could with much more propriety exert our authority to prevent slave traffic than he himself." And again, "He said he should be ready and very glad to make any reasonable arrangement with the English Government for the abolition of slavery, and the establishment of another trade."[18]

The king is evidently concerned to place the port of trade in the hands of a superlatively strong power. "He had, he said, refused possession of Whydah to the Prince de Joinville, stating his determination to treat with none but the Queen of England, who was the greatest of all white sovereigns."[19] The port of trade must be in the hands of a power strong enough to guarantee its neutrality even against the other powers and itself a power that is friendly to Dahomey and committed by treaty to respect her interests. This would be a solution to the vexing problem of the port of trade. There can be no doubt that the king regarded such a solution as preferable to continued possession of the port by Dahomey herself.

This offer, surprising as it may seem, represents Dahoman policy at the highest level. When the discussion with Duncan is concluded, Duncan reports, the king himself "dictated to me a letter to the Secretary of State for the Colonies, in which he formally ceded Whydah to the English Government . . . and when he found it satisfactory, he held the upper end of the pen while I signed his name."[20]

Again, some twenty years later, Commander Wilmot, meeting with the king in 1863, remarks "the friendly disposition evinced by the King towards the English," and quotes the monarch as saying:

"From hence forth the King of Dahomey and the Queen of England are one; you shall hold the tail of the kingdom, and I will take the head": meaning that we should have possession of Whydah for trading purposes, and supply him with everything.[21]

For Dahomey, then, war and trade were not commercial activities but conditions for survival. It is only in these terms that the economy and the society become intelligible. To misread war and trade as commercial activities is to distort beyond recognition the organs and techniques which Dahomey developed to cope with the conditions of existence imposed by its environment.

Remote Control of Whydah

For Dahomey, the creation of the port of trade at Whydah was the solution to a problem that might well have seemed insoluble. Here was Aristotle's dilemma concerning the Piraeus aggravated by manifold complications.[22] If neutrality demanded the admittance of all comers to the port of trade, it also demanded the isolation of the port, else how were the foreigners, both European and African, to be prevented from intriguing against Dahomey and interfering in Dahoman affairs? At the same time isolation could not signify a hands-off policy. There was need for a strong hand at Whydah to keep the flotsam and jetsam population of a port town in check and to compel respect for life and property so that trade would be secure. Yet how was Dahomey, supremely indifferent as she was to maritime commerce and its concerns, to exercise a strong hand and achieve an efficient administration of the port without shifting the very axis of her existence?

The dilemma was all the more complex in that trade and war imposed incompatible conditions, yet both were essential to Dahomey's survival. A regular trade was impossible except under peaceful conditions, yet war was no less a necessary condition for trade, since it provided the captives without which Dahomey could not trade at all. One aspect of the matter is revealed in the comments of those experienced Guinea traders, Snelgrave and Barbot. Snelgrave observes that for some time after the capture of Whydah by Dahomey, "the Trade . . . is almost ruined; for the far Inland People having now no Markets to carry their Slaves to, as formerly, and the Dahomes using no Trade but that of War, few Negroes are now brought down to be sold to the Europeans." This war between Dahomey and Whydah had not only disorganized the ordinary channels of trade and closed off the trade routes, but there was as well a "great Destruction of the Inhabitants of the neighbouring Countries, who used to carry on a regular Trade with the far Inland People."[23] Obviously, trade could not operate under such disturbed conditions. On the other hand, peace might be equally disruptive of trade in so far as it cut off the supply of slaves. As Barbot complains: "In the year 1682, I could get but very few (slaves) because there was at that time almost a general peace among the Blacks along the coast."[24] Certainly Dahomey would have to find a way of separating war and trade so that the captives could be supplied to Whydah without embroiling the traders in military affairs and disrupting the peace of the port of trade.

Small wonder that Dahomey desired to avoid the problem of Whydah altogether. It was this attitude which explains, as we have seen, the repeated offers by the kings of Dahomey to cede Whydah to the English and thus to be relieved of the responsibility for its administration. Certainly it is striking that none of the kings of Dahomey was ever known to set foot in Whydah, even the conquest of Whydah being accomplished with the king remaining at a distance, in war encampment some miles outside of the town. Whydah was beyond the pale, and the Whydasians themselves an irritant in the body politic. On numerous occasions, the king displayed his contempt for these coastal people—a people of different stock, professing a strange religion, and worst of all, corrupted by trade with the foreigner.[25] To Norris, who pleaded with the king to spare the lives of the Whydasians taken by the Dahomans, in the assault upon Whydah, the king replied as follows:

. . . it would be setting a bad example, and keeping people in the country, who might hold seditious language; that his was a peculiar government, and that these strangers [my italics] might prejudice his people against it, and infect them with sentiments incompatible with it.[26]

And, Duncan, setting off for the Kong Mountains, found that his Whydah carriers were put under the Dahoman captain of the guard, to whom the king had given "strict orders to watch them narrowly, on account of their thievish propensities."

Yet the problem of Whydah could not be avoided. The trade was essential to Dahomey and the hostility of the Whydasians left no alternative but to take over the port. Dahomey's conflict of interests was reconciled by an indirect administration of the port, a system of remote control as it were, which protected the trade while keeping trade and traders at a safe distance.

Foreigners' Enclave

It was the distinctive characteristic of the port of trade that trade was open to all comers from the European side. It was an alien enclave. In contrast with the trading settlements of the European companies which sought to exclude the interlopers, Whydah ". . . was a free Port of all the Guinea Coast for the Slave Trade."[27] While the French, Portuguese, and English maintained permanent factories at Whydah, the king gave permission to trade to all ships: "Chaque navire qui arrive ici pour faire le commerce, ouvre une factorie et fait ses affaires lui-même. Pour ce privilege, il paie au roi. . . ."[28] Such a policy of "free trade" would seem to serve Dahomey's trade advantage, yet there was more than this involved. A grant of exclusive privileges to one European nation carried grave risks, as is hinted in Barbot's remarks about Bissos:

I took notice of a grant made by the Black king of Bissos to the Portuguese, to trade and settle there, exclusive of all other Europeans; but not long after, the natives observing, that the Portuguese had built a fort with eight guns, oppos'd their design of ingrossing the whole trade of their island, and laid it open to all strangers resorting to their ports; who may carry on their commerce there with all imaginable safety, and without apprehending any insult, if they offer none.[29]

Opening the port to all comers was thus the only way to keep the peace and void the disastrous trade rivalries among the Europeans which, at other points along the Coast where the Europeans were settled, had ruined the trade and involved the natives in sanguinary wars.[29] From the standpoint of Dahomey's strategic political interests, the neutrality of the port of trade had to be assured, and Dahomey sought safety in numbers.

The inland position of Whydah made it possible to regulate the trade more effectively than at other places on the Guinea Coast where trade was conducted in the coastal settlements of the chartered companies or on board ship.

With the first sighting of a vessel off Whydah, the port authorities went into action. As soon as ships were sighted in the road, porters were sent from the town to assist in the landing. No goods or men could be disembarked in that forbidding surf without assistance, and not a move could be made by the traders without the full glare of publicity. As each ship arrived, an official party from the town, consisting of the Viceroy of Whydah, the local lords, and their armed escort, greeted the traders at the famous place of reception outside the town, the "Captain's Tree." Since the town of Whydah was some two miles from the beach, goods were stored temporarily in buildings on the beach and porters were appointed by the authorities to haul the goods inland to the factories or to other places in town set aside for the foreigners. Carrying was completely in the hands of the natives and no goods moved inland until the terms of trade were negotiated with the authorities—"This regulation being agreed on by the king and the factors," as Barbot relates, "the goods are brought ashore, and carried on men's backs to the French house. . . ."[31] While residing in the town, the traders were provided with servants, carriers, and other attendants by the native "head men" who had the disposal over labor. Fresh provisions for ships' crews and the daily table were procured on the local market at Whydah; at other places along the Coast provisions might likewise be secured in the markets, or, as was often the case, supplied to the traders by the natives under treaty arrangements.

These physical facilities provided for the foreigners by the port authority served a dual purpose: they safeguarded the traders' person and property, while at the same time making any evasion of the regulations well-nigh impossible.

Whydah was administered as a "White Man's Town," sealed off from Dahomey proper, and under the jurisdiction of resident officials. The immediate administration of Whydah was left in the hands of the Viceroy of Whydah appointed by the king—the Yevogan or "White Man's Captain," a title stemming from the pre-Dahoman period. In accordance with the customary Dahoman policy toward territories incorporated into the kingdom, Whydah was permitted to retain many of its previous customs, including the indigenous snake worship, and the traditions of administration stemming from the days of Whydasian rule were carried over under the Dahoman regime. The administrative personnel was changed, however, since the Whydasians had resisted Dahoman authority, although in other cases where submission to Dahomey was voluntarily tendered, local rulers were permitted to continue in power. The affairs of Whydah were conducted by the Viceroy and his staff, with trade matters directly under the supervision of the Chacha and the other trade officials appointed by the king.

The Europeans at Whydah enjoyed certain extraterritorial privileges. Each of the European factories, with its surrounding native settlement, constituted a separate quarter of Whydah. Each quarter had its own governor, usually of European nationality, though under the general supervision of the Viceroy of Whydah, and the natives of the settlement were placed at the service of the Europeans. In Burton's time, there were four such European quarters: French Town; Brazilian Town; English Town; and Portuguese Town.[32]

The European traders at Whydah were the "King's Men" and their factories the "King's Houses" so that any offense against the person of the traders or their places of trade constituted an affront to the monarch himself. Any native caught stealing from them would be put to death. If the king "were requested to take cognizance of any case of robbery of a white man, the robber would certainly lose his head," Duncan comments, adding, however, that ". . . the King of Dahomey not wishing to interfere with white people's affairs, and the merchants being too humane to urge the King's interference," the law might not be strictly enforced.[33] While the Europeans enjoyed the rights to practice their own religion, their factories were protected by native fetishes, the English fort, as Burton observed, having two fetishes, called the "Defenders of White Men."[34] While Burton was scandalized that native fetish ceremonies were performed at the factory, it is obvious that the fetish put the peace of the place of trade under sacral sanctions. The purpose to be served was the same that made Alexander the Great enjoin Cleomenes to have two temples to deified Hephaistion erected in the confines of the future Alexandria, prospective port of trade of the Hellenic oecumene.*

Whydah enjoyed considerable autonomy so long as the law was observed. The king rarely interfered with the local administration, yet

* See above, pp. 60–1.

if any bad report should reach the capital, a royal messenger forthwith descended upon the town and the local authorities trembled. While the Viceroy was "judge and jury" in Whydah, only the king wielded the power of life and death, and all cases involving the death penalty were handled by the king's court at Abomey. The dual sets of officials, here as elsewhere throughout Dahomey, provided a check upon illegitimate extensions of power. The Chacha and the superintendents of trade "attended all conferences," Forbes says, "reporting directly to the king any infringement of the royal prerogative," and acting as "political spies" upon the Viceroy and the local administration.[35]

The Europeans were left to their own affairs so long as they did not violate the regulations, but the king's justice was swiftly visited upon those who infringed the law. Twice, the governors of the French forts were expelled from Whydah, in one case "upon the charge of having sold contraband articles to the enemies of Dahomey," and the governor of the English fort, in the days of Trudo, was put to death by the king for insults to Dahomey.[36]

The royal justice, severe as it might be, was effective in maintaining law and order in Whydah. In pre-Dahoman Whydah, the white traders had often complained of the "impositions of great Men" and the thievery of the natives, while the common people of Whydah, as elsewhere throughout the kingdom, might find the king their only succor against the oppression of their native lords or the Europeans. Upon first meeting with the king of Dahomey immediately after the conquest of Whydah, Snelgrave urged the king

That the best way to make Trade flourish, was to impose easy Customs, and to protect us from the Thievery of the Natives, and the impositions of great Men which the King of Whidaw not doing, greatly hurt the Trade. For the ill usage the Europeans had met with of late from him and his People, had caused them to send fewer Ships than formerly they did.

The king responded sympathetically, saying that

He designed to make Trade flourish; and I might depend upon it, he would prevent all Impositions, and Thievery, and protect the Europeans that came to his Country. . . .[37]

Duncan testifies to the king's justice when he remarks that

During my stay at Abomey, I was never asked by any individual for an article of even the most trifling value, nor ever lost anything, except what was stolen by my people from the coast. The Dahoman laws are certainly severe, but they have the desired effect.[38]

How necessary these safeguards were to the security of the realm, and how real the threat of oppression by upstart local lords is illustrated by the story of Tanga, Viceroy of Whydah, which is related by Norris.[39] Tanga, appointed by the king to his post, was an ambitious man and sought to make himself king of Whydah. He acquired a large body of retainers, "attached to his person by his liberality" and by the protection he afforded them "in their villainies" against the king's law. "His oppressions rendered him odious to the garrison at the fort" as well, Norris adds. The European governors at Whydah, on the way to Abomey to lodge a protest with the king against the exactions of the Viceroy, were intercepted by Tanga and imprisoned. Learning of Tanga's attempt to take the English fort by stratagem, the king declared him a traitor, set a price upon his head, and sent troops against him. Besieged in the house, which he had fortified against the king's troops, and surrounded by his hundreds of wives and the retainers whose loyalty he had secured by a reckless distribution of treasure, Tanga finally met his death.

Administered Trade

In pre-Dahoman Whydah, prices, as well as all other terms, had been negotiated with the king before any transactions could take place. The king "fixes the price of every sort of European goods, as also of slaves," Barbot tells us, "which is to stand betwixt his subjects and foreigners; and therefore no European must go there to trade, without waiting on him before he presumes to buy or sell." After the terms were agreed upon and the king's customs paid, Barbot goes on to say, "the factor has full liberty to trade, which is proclaimed throughout the country by the king's cryer."[40] Under Dahoman rule, the same principles applied but general administrative regulations replaced separate treaty negotiations. Equivalencies were fixed by law and administered by the king's officials resident at Whydah. "The cha-cha is the principal agent to the king in all matters of trade," Forbes says,

and to him must be subjected all commerce, whether in slaves or palm-oil, that he may have the refusal. The price is laid down by law, subject to his alteration if concurred in by the viceroy and six traders or superintendents of trade appointed by the king. . . . One or the other of these must be present at all sales to take the royal duty. . . .[41]

This indirect administration of Whydah provided the necessary safeguards for trade while at the same time serving to isolate Whydah and its affairs from Dahomey proper. The policy of isolation was carried further in a series of measures which barred foreigners and their trade from the interior of the country and placed the organization of internal trade exclusively in Dahoman hands.

In laying drastic restrictions upon the movements of the European traders, Dahoman policy was animated by considerations similar to those reported of the neighboring kingdom of Ardra: ". . . we commonly travel only by night," Barbot says of Ardra,

unless we be in company of the prince, or of some very notable men of the court, when we can travel by day; but the political Blacks carry us then along by-roads, and never through any town or village . . . and alledge, that it is a positive order from the government so to do, that no strangers may observe the disposition of the country, and the nature and situation of places.[42]

Traders, of course, were always regarded as spies, and it was standard procedure for a native kingdom, contemplating a military operation, to send spies into the territory of the enemy disguised as traders. Even without these policy deterrents, however, the Europeans could not get very far inland. Of the Gold Coast, Barbot says:

None of the Europeans dwelling along the coast [have] even ventured far up the land . . . what account can be given of it, is taken from the most intelligent Blacks, particularly as to the remotest countries, it being extraordinarily difficult and dangerous, if not altogether impossible, for Europeans to venture so far into such wild savage countries.[43]

As for Whydah, no movements outside the town could be made without the permission of the authorities. Along the lagoons which ring the town, ferrymen were stationed, as Duncan reports,

to inspect all passes or permits obtained from the [king's minister] of Whydah to persons leaving the port, specifying the number of people wishing to proceed by canoe for any other place on the lagoon.[44]

The efficiency of the system was remarkable; in one instance, a whole party was turned back because one person had been included for whom no authorization had been received from the Viceroy. Europeans might go inland only with the permission of the king—"I say permission," Forbes remarks, "for such it is, as travelling is not allowed in Dahomey without a passport, in the shape of his Majesty's stick." Such permission was usually granted on state occasions, as for example, when the invitations were issued to the Europeans to attend the Annual Customs at Abomey. All travelers moved under escorts provided by the king and under the protection of the "King's Stick."[45] As the "King's Strangers," they were isolated from the local population and hosteled in special way-stations provided for travelers along the road to Abomey. There was another reason, of course, for the safeguards surrounding the traveler. As a foreigner, he stood under the protection of the king, and any accident would be a fateful matter, as Burton suggests in the following comment:

The late king relaxed the usual Dahoman severity in matter of ingress, giving escorts to Dr. Dickson . . . and to Mr. Duncan. . . . His son, on the contrary, has shut up all the roads. . . . He promised that, on my return, I should penetrate into the mountain-land; pleaded want of time and troops, and consoled me by the suggestion that I was too important a personage to be risked in the bush. This was not wholly "blarney"; any accident to the "King's Stranger" would be looked upon as a dire and portentous occurrence.[46]

If the Europeans were barred from the interior as a security measure, similar considerations prompted restrictions on the movements of native traders from neighboring states. While the king of Whydah in pre-Dahoman times had admitted the Mahee, Nagoes, Oyo, and other traders from inland countries to the port, Dahomey apparently reversed this policy. Under the Dahoman regime, these traders from inland were refused passage through Dahoman territory, the port of trade was closed to them, and the European traders at Whydah were permitted to deal directly only with the Dahomans themselves. Snelgrave visited Whydah immediately after its capture by Dahomey and observed that "the far Inland People [have] now no Markets to carry their Slaves to, as formerly."[47] And Norris remarks that the slaves offered for sale by the Mahee and other inland traders "are disposed of to the factors of Dahomey."[48] The reasons for such a policy are implied in the account given by Dalzel of the actions of Adahoonzou:

In consequence of the failure of some of his expeditions, the King took it into his head, that it was owing to the intrigues of aliens residing in his dominions. He therefore ordered the Gongong to be beat; giving warning to all strangers, Eyeos excepted, immediately to quit the kingdom; alledging, that whenever any expedition was on foot, his designs were by them communicated to the enemy. . . .

An additional reason for precautionary measures against foreigners of course was the danger of military supplies falling into their hands, "guns, powder, and iron [being] articles forbidden to be dealt in by strangers in Dahomey." As a result of the king's decree, Dalzel adds, "the Mahees, Nagoes, and other inland merchants . . . [came] no more through the Dahoman dominions."[48]

The interior was thus closed off, both to the native traders on Dahomey's borders and to the Europeans at Whydah. In contrast with the situation elsewhere along the Coast, Dahomey did not permit the Europeans settled on the Coast to send agents to inland places of trade, or even to meet face-to-face with caravans of traders from the interior coming to the Coast to trade, as was the case on the Gold Coast. The Europeans were completely excluded from trade within Dahomey proper and from any direct trade relations with the countries farther inland. They were permitted to meet face-to-face in trade only with the Dahoman traders and within the confines of the port of trade at Whydah.

By such measures, Dahomey was sealed off from the foreigner and the handling of trade goods within the country was kept entirely in Dahoman hands. Such a policy was clearly not dictated by considerations of "monopoly profit" but by vital political interests. If we take a look at the character of Dahomey's trade goods, we see clearly the political interest which motivated trade policy and made necessary the rigorous restrictions on the movement of goods in trade.

Dahomey's exports were slaves and palm-oil, the latter becoming of importance, however, only with the decline of the slave trade in the nineteenth century. Since slaves were enemies taken captive in war or criminals condemned by law, they constituted a menace to domestic security and it was inconceivable that they should be permitted to move throughout the country without adequate safeguards. As the king protested to Governor Abson, should these enemies be left free "to cut the throats of my subjects?" Slaves were elite goods, moreover, and their movements were restricted on this account as well. In principle, all slaves belonged to the king, as was the case with all property in Dahomey, and the king's subjects held slaves only by his leave. To own slaves was a privilege limited to persons of rank, and to trade in slaves was a prerogative of status, "licence to trade" being in effect contingent upon receiving an endowment in slaves from the hand of the king. As elite goods, slaves carried high political significance. Da-

homey paid tribute in slaves to the king of Oyo, and slaves were frequently presented by the king of Dahomey to visiting foreign emissaries as a matter of diplomatic etiquette, as well as to the nobles of his
own court.

From start to finish, then, the handling of slaves was an operation
subject to meticulous controls and one from which outsiders were
completely barred. Slaves were "collected" in war, obviously an operation at the highest levels of state in which strangers had no part. Or, if
slaves were "collected" by purchase from inland merchants, they passed
at once into Dahoman custody, as we have seen. All dispositions or
transfers of slaves were matters of public record. The captives taken in
war were ceremonially presented to the king at the Annual Customs, a
count being kept in cowries of the number of captives thus presented,
and thereafter the king might make a ceremonial award of some of the
captives to the nobles of his court or to soldiers who had distinguished
themselves in combat. Such awards were acts of state and immediately
publicized. A witness who was present when the Dahoman army returned from a campaign with prisoners of war reports that:

As soon as any person had a Slave presented to them, a proper Officer made
Proclamation of it, which was immediately echoed by the Populace, who
were waiting in great numbers at the King's Gate for the Sacrifices.[50]

The slaves received as gifts from the king's hand could be disposed of
thereafter by the owners only with the royal permission. While the
caboceers who led their own armies into the field were entitled to keep
the captives taken by their soldiers, "the caboceers always pay a nominal duty upon all slaves taken in war when sold."[51] Such a tax must
have served as a device for keeping record as well as a source of revenue
for the king.

When the slaves were turned over to the Europeans at Whydah,
the transfer was subject to rigorous supervision. The confinement of
the Europeans to Whydah made it easier to exercise control since all
transactions between natives and Europeans could take place only in
the authorized trading places in the European quarters where full publicity attended transactions and a close watch was kept on the handling
of goods. Here is how the slaves passed from native hands to European hands:

When these slaves come to Fida, they are put in Prison all together, and
when we treat concerning buying them, they are all brought out together

in a large Plain; . . . When we have agreed with the Owners of the Slaves, they are returned to their Prison; where from that time forwards they are kept at our charge. . . . So that to save Charges we send them on Board our Ships with the very first Opportunity.[52]

Procedures had changed somewhat a hundred years later but the safeguards were no less rigorous:

Les courtiers, vont tous les matins par toute la ville, demander à chaque negociant, s'il lui est arrivé des esclaves. Ils le font savoir au facteur qui va avec eux, la measure à la main, dans la maison de ces negocians noirs, voi les esclaves, & s'ils lui conviennent, il les achète, donne une specification des marchandises d'échange dont ils sont convenus, & imprime sa marque à feu sur le corps des esclaves. Ceux-ci, s'ils ne sont point esclaves du roi, sont transporté dès le soir même au fort ou dans la factorie; mais si ce sont des Nègres du roi, il doivent demeurer chez le marchand, jusqu'à ce qu'ils puissent être transportés de suite à bord.[53]

With trading carried on only at these specified places of trade and under official scrutiny, it is clear that any private "street-corner" dealings were out of the question.

As for imports, they were similarly affected with a public interest. Goods imported were for the most part war material or elite goods which circulated only among the dignitaries of the kingdom. Foreign cloth, umbrellas, shoes, and other imported goods were regarded as attributes of status; special safeguards surrounded dealings in such goods and sumptuary laws banned their possession by the common people. Guns, powder, iron, and coral could not be sold except to the king or his officials, and the king forbade the transit of firearms through his kingdom, in order to prevent war material from falling into the hands of his enemies. That coral should be included in this list seems at first glance strange, but coral was treasure, and clearly a "security" item since it was demanded of Dahomey as tribute by the neighboring kings of Oyo. Dalzel relates an incident involving a woman trader at Whydah, by the name of Paussie, who had sold coral illicitly to the French traders.[54] This action precipitated a diplomatic crisis. When word of this reached the king of Oyo, he lodged official protest with the king of Dahomey, accusing Dahomey of deception in withholding the customary tribute of coral on the false plea that no ships had brought coral to Whydah recently. The woman Paussie, was seized by the king's messengers and taken to Abomey for punishment as a traitor, her residence in Whydah leveled to the ground and all her possessions confiscated by the king.

As in collecting slaves for export, so in distributing imported goods, foreigners were completely excluded. Imported cloth, rum, and cowries were distributed to the people from the hand of the king himself at the Annual Customs, and high-ranking dignitaries of the kingdom made similar distributions to their retainers on ceremonial occasions. Small quantities of imported goods were also made available to the general population in local markets throughout the country. The right to dispose of European goods on local markets was awarded by the king as a monopoly privilege to certain of his officials. This interesting arrangement was observed at first hand by Duncan, who was the only European ever allowed to penetrate through Dahomey and to the border countries beyond. He has left us descriptions of the trading arrangements in the various villages at which he stopped. At each town, he observed there were customs houses "for collecting the duties upon all goods carried through it, from whatever part they come." Moreover:

These customs are bestowed by the king as rewards of conquest upon his caboceers . . . ; when a war takes place, and the Dahomans prove victorious, the town taken is considered as belonging to the minister or caboceer whose soldiers capture the town; or rather, his right of monopolizing the trade of the town is established, so far as to supply it himself with all goods of British manufacture or produce, with the exception of such traders as have obtained permits, as a proof of their having paid the duty. The trade is entrusted to the most confidential or head men belonging to the caboceer owning the trade. . . . The King also imposes on each caboceer a slight duty, according to the amount of their trade.[55]

Dahomey's vital interests were thus protected by an organization of internal and external trade which lodged control exclusively in Dahoman hands. In establishing an autonomous organization for trade, Dahomey made certain of isolating the foreign trader and securing the inviolability of the internal community. Without such an organization, surrender to the foreigner would have been inevitable.

The dilemma of war and trade was also resolved—at least to the degree permitted by the inherent limitations of the situation—by a drastic institutional separation of the trading organization and the military organization. By this administrative technique, Dahomey succeeded in severing trade affairs from military affairs and assuring the neutrality of the port of trade. The traders formed a separate class of officials, completely distinct in personnel and function from the military. The Akhi'sino, or "great traders," ranked fourth in the Dahoman hierarchy, just below the Ahwan-gan, or military officials, and thus set apart from them. Of these "great traders," Burton remarks, scornfully as usual, that they "certainly lead a more useful life than the Ahwan-gan, or military class, which will do nothing but eat and drink, dance, make war, and attend Customs."[56] Whatever one's opinion of the usefulness of the military—and the Dahomans certainly held a more balanced view than Burton's—it is evident from this account that the warriors of the kingdom washed their hands of trade, while the traders had nothing to do with military affairs. The Viceroy of Whydah never went to war, since he was expected to concern himself exclusively with the affairs of trade at Whydah, but the sub-Viceroy represented him at all military campaigns. Similarly at Benin, Barbot reports, the trade officials "are forbid under heavy mulots, or bodily punishment, to intermeddle in any manner of affairs relating to war."[57] Thus Whydah could live at peace, her trading organization intact, and her residents unmolested by the wars which took place at a safe distance inland, while Dahomey was free to manage her military affairs without intervention from the traders, whether European or Dahoman.

Rosemary Arnold

Notes to Chapter VIII*

1. This and the following chapter result from research carried on under the auspices of the Council for Research in the Social Sciences, Columbia University, 1948–1952.

2. Compare the intimate picture of Dahoman culture in Professor Herskovits' classic, on which we have been leaning heavily.

3. Bovill, p. 254.

4. Duncan, II, 11–12.

5. Snelgrave, granted an audience with the King of Dahomey immediately after his armies had taken Whydah, met with a royal official by the name of Zunglar, "a cunning Fellow, who had formerly been the King's Agent for several Years at Whidaw; where I had seen him in my former Voyages." (61)

6. Norris, XIII–XIV.

7. Herskovits, I, 109.

8. *Ibid.*, I, 17.

9. Norris, X.

10. Snelgrave, pp. 5–6.

11. Atkins, p. 120.

* Bibliography appears at end of chapter IX.

12. Snelgrave, p. 64.
13. *Ibid.*, pp. 58–9.
14. Dalzel, p. 207.
15. *Ibid.*, p. 196.
16. See chapter IV.
17. Duncan, II, 268–9.
18. *Ibid.*, 269–70.
19. *Ibid.*, 269–70.
20. *Ibid.*, 270–71.
21. Burton, II, 361.
22. The dominance of the import interest required such a practice (Arist. *Pol.*, Bk. VI).
23. Snelgrave, pp. 130 and 136.
24. Barbot, p. 261.
25. The Whydasians had, after the conquest by Dahomey the status of metics in the Dahoman empire. Cf. on this problem *Arist. Pol.*, 1327a 11.
26. Norris, p. 135.
27. Snelgrave, pp. 2–3.
28. Isert, pp. 134–5.
29. Barbot, p. 428.
30. Trading peoples' traditional policy is to be at peace with all.
31. Barbot, p. 326.
32. Burton, I, 64–5.
33. Duncan, I, 198.
34. Burton, I, 64.
35. Forbes, I, 111.
36. Dalzel, pp. 228–9, and 58.
37. Snelgrave, p. 60 ff.
38. Duncan, II, 276.
39. Norris, p. 40 ff.
40. Barbot, p. 326.
41. Forbes, I, 110–1.
42. Barbot, p. 351.
43. *Ibid.*, p. 186.
44. Duncan, I, 110–112.
45. Forbes, II, 3.
46. Burton, II, 265–6.
47. Snelgrave, p. 130.
48. Norris, p. 138.
49. Dalzel, p. 213 ff.
50. Snelgrave, p. 39.
51. Duncan II, 263–4.
52. Bosman, p. 363 ff.
53. Isert, p. 136.
54. Dalzel, p. 208 ff.
55. Duncan, I, 282–3.
56. Burton, I, 226.
57. Barbot, p. 360.

IX

Separation of Trade and Market: Great Market of Whydah

Zobeme, the Native Market

ONE of the showplaces of Whydah was the Zobeme or Great Market. "The lions of Whydah are the snake fetish house and the market," Forbes remarks. The market, he adds, is the finest he has seen in Africa.[1]

As the reader may have noted in the previous chapter, we had no need to refer to markets in order to explain the conduct of trade. From start to finish, the trading operation is an affair of state, administered from the palace, and conducted by the dignitaries of the land under terms of treaty. The presence or absence of markets makes no difference to the trading operations described there. That a market exists in the port of trade itself is, then, striking confirmation of the independence of trade from market.

But what needs does this market serve in the port of trade? What needs does it serve? And how is it set apart from trade?

A composite picture of the Great Market at Whydah can be drawn from several authors.

Southwest of the Boa temple is the Zobeme, or market place. It covers an area of about fourteen acres, and is divided into several principal sections by cross streets. Each section is exclusively appointed to the sale of one class of articles, such as pottery, hardware, fetish charms, oil, and so forth. The meat, fish, corn, flour, vegetable, fruit, and foreign goods all have separate markets.

The market shops are low booths, about ten feet by six, raised upon banks of clay, beaten hard, and are thatched with palm leaves, and the floor is usually smeared with cow dung. Each shop stands upon its own "islet," as they may be called, for in the rain the footpaths are not infrequently six inches deep in water. The vendor squats at the side of her booth, a black clay pipe stuck between her lips, sometimes a babe at her breast. The medium of exchange is the cowrie, although large purchases may be paid for in coin.

The market is held daily. It is well supplied with every article of native consumption and many articles of European manufacture.

Primarily it is a food market for the sale of cooked victuals. Half the shops contain either raw or cooked provisions, Burton says, and many a "working man" breakfasts and dines in the alley, or quenches his thirst at the "gin palace" where liquor is dispensed.

Numerous huts were devoted to the sale of cooked provisions, such as eggs, fried fish from the lagoons, smoked shrimps, baked ground nuts, yams, sweet potatoes. Others were vendors of ready-cooked meats. These generally affected a conical extinguisher shaped hut, and squatted on a low stool behind a circular table, with a broad rim and a depression in the centre. Set out to the best advantage on the rim were joints of roast and boiled pork, goat, fowls, ducks, etc. Of these for two cowries about a mouthful could be purchased, the butcher dexterously carving Vauxhall slices from the joint; slapping the morsel on a plantain leaf, he sprinkled some pounded chillies upon it, and handed it to the customer with all the airs of a London stall-keeper.

Marketing is in full sway about 4 P.M., when a scene that baffles description is to be witnessed. Swarms of people, especially women, meet to buy and sell. Here an old beldame, with shrivelled breasts hanging down to her waist, will be haggling with a child four years old for a farthing's-worth of fetish. It is a curious contrast, the placidity and impassiveness with which the seller, hardly taking the trouble to remove her pipe, drawls out the price of her two-cowrie lots, and the noisy excitement of the buyers, who know that they must purchase and pay the demand.

Such was the Great Market of Whydah. Certainly nothing could be more remote from the world of trade than this bustling market scene. Here is not a place of audience with kings, but a meeting place for the multitude. Not slaves, gold, ivory, and fine cloth are on display here, but the joints of meat smoking on the butcher's tables, the farthing's-worth of fetish, or the two-cowrie mouthfuls dished up on a plantain leaf. Not the careful etiquette of court, the studied exchange of gifts, the diplomatic negotiation, but the merry confusion of a crowd enjoying the sport of berating the wares of the old beldames.

Craft products are there too, but mostly utility wares—pottery and hardware, and the poorer sorts of cloth. For the fine cloth—the umbrellas with appliqué designs, the ornaments of brass, gold, and silver —these are not for sale. The makers of these products serve the great houses of king and lords.

Foreign goods are in evidence, though not in such plenty as those the natives produce. Duncan lists the articles exposed for sale, and among them we can identify those which appear to be foreign goods, cotton cloth, native and English, he says, thread, beads, gun flints, flints and steel. This is a scanty array and the articles are all of a utilitarian character, sold in small quantities.

Two smaller markets, subsidiary to the Great Market, are found in other parts of the town. One of them is described by Skertchly as a small accessory of the Zobeme established for the convenience of the residents in the northwest of the town. Here groups of vendors, chiefly women, squabble in full chorus. The stock in trade of each person is but small, and in this market there are no booths, but each seller squats on a diminutive stool behind her collection. The principal wares are "raw or cooked provisions," beads, a few pieces of the commonest cotton cloth, water, and firewood. Provisions are cheap enough so that "sufficient food for a native's meal can be procured ready cooked for about three pence."[2]

These are markets "for the convenience of the residents," reminding us, in modern terms, of the corner grocery or the all-night hamburger counter where one may pick up a late snack or the loaf of bread overlooked in the day's shopping. The foreign goods are missing here altogether. Foodstuffs, and the barest household necessities, water and firewood, are the stock in trade.

The market at Cape Corso affords much the same kind of picture. It is kept every day, except Tuesdays, Barbot says, in a large place at the end of the town, whither great numbers of all the neighboring people resort every morning very early, "with all sorts of goods and eatables the land affords: besides the European goods carried by us. They come

thither by break of day, from five or six leagues around about, loaded
like horses, with each of them, one, or more sorts of goods: as sugar-
cane, bananas, figs, yams, lemons, oranges, rice, millet, Indian wheat,
malaguette or Guinea pepper, bread, kankies, fowl, fish raw, boiled,
roasted, and fried, palm-oil, eggs, . . . earthen-ware, beer . . . , wood for
fuel, thatch for houses, tobacco of the growth of the country, etc. The
Blacks of the coast also carry thither several sorts of European goods."

Here, as at Whydah, the market is primarily a goods market, supplying the townsfolk with provisions from the countryside. The vendors
are mostly women, Barbot says, who are commonly employed to keep
market, "being looked upon as fitter for it than the men. . . ." Here also
there are "several sorts of European goods" brought to market by the
"Blacks of the Coast."[3] Though Barbot speaks earlier in this passage
of the European goods "carried by us," it is obvious from the context
that the goods are carried to market by the Blacks, and that he uses the
phrase to mean "carried by ship." But goods other than food seem to be
of lesser importance. Barbot refers to "bartering with the market
women, for garlick, pins, small looking-glasses, ribbands, flints and
steels, and such like trifles."

Nowhere in this inventory of market goods—this should be noted
—are the native export staples to be found. Slaves, gold, ivory, etc., are
not up for sale in the market place. Palm-oil, to be sure, is sold in the
market for household use, or ladled out to flavor a mouthful of cooked
meat, but this is a far cry from the export trade in large quantities. Nor
are there anywhere foreign goods exposed by white men (or, for that
matter, by Blacks) otherwise than in small quantities, in retail.

Neither in the collection nor in the disposition of export staples
does the market figure. Slaves are booty taken in war, or procured by
trade with the native peoples of the continent. They move from the
hands of the king and the war captains to the European traders without passing at any point through the market. It is inconceivable that a
war lord of Dahomey should set up stall in the market place to dispose
of his booty. Bosman reminds us of the safeguards observed in handling
slaves. Speaking of the trade at Whydah, he says, "most of the Slaves
that are offered to us are Prisoners of War, which are sold by the Victors as their Booty. When these Slaves come to Fida, they are put in
Prison all together, and when we treat concerning buying them, they
are all brought out together in a large Plain,* where, by our Chirur-

* See above, pp. 172–3.

geons, . . . they are thoroughly examined. . . . The Invalides and the Maimed being thrown out, . . . the remainder are numbered, and it is entred who delivered them. In the mean while a burn-in Iron, with the Arms or Name of the Companies, lyes in the Fire; with which ours are marked on the Breast. This done that we may distinguish them from the Slaves of the English, French, or others; (which are also marked with their Mark) and to prevent the Negroes exchanging them for worse; at which they have a good Hand. . . . When we have agreed with the Owners of the Slaves, they are returned to their Prison; where from that time forwards they are kept at our charge. . . . So that to save Charges we send them on Board our Ships with the very first Opportunity. . . ."[4]

Nor does the European trader sit in the market place shouting his wares. Bosman, writing to his correspondent at home, takes care to disabuse him of any such notion. "I would not have you conceive," he says, "that we set up a Market with our Wares, or send any of them to be sold without our Forts: No, that is not our Business; but the Negroes come daily to our Castle, or Fort, with their Gold; for which, after it is weighed, essayed and purified, they receive our Commodities; none of which ever go out of our Ware-houses before they are paid for. . . ."[5] This passage refers to the gold trade at Elmina, the major settlement on the Gold Coast.

Export-import transactions, then, are conducted in separate places of trade completely removed from the market place. Trade negotiations with the authorities take place at court, in formal conversation, or in special places of audience. Disposition of goods is made at the European forts, and for those traders not attached to the chartered companies, in lodges appointed for their use by the authorities, or on board ship.

How, then, do European goods reach the local market? Here, surely, is a crucial point of contact between trade and market. But nothing could more sharply emphasize the segregation of trade from market than the manner of appearance of trade goods on the local market in the port of trade itself. Since trade dealings between European and native are confined to the places of trade, and the European has access to the local market only as a purchaser of provisions and other necessaries, the distribution of imported goods within the country, whether through markets or otherwise, is entirely in native hands. At every point in the movement of goods throughout the interior, as likewise in the port of trade, the institutional separation of trade from market is safeguarded by administrative regulations and operational devices of an all-embracing character.

Administered Trade and Local Food Distribution

At Whydah, the isolation of places of trade from market place is the basis for the administrative divisions of the town. Each of the European forts, with its surrounding native settlement, constitutes a separate town under administration. In Burton's time, there were four such European quarters: French Town, Brazilian Town, English Town, and Portuguese Town. The fifth section of Whydah, Zobeme or Market Town, taking its name from the Great Market, comprised the market and its environs. All of these separate quarters have their own governors, under the jurisdiction of the Viceroy of Whydah. While the governors of the European towns are usually of the respective European nationality, the caboceer of the Market Town is a native official.

These administrative divisions facilitate the regulation of trade. Access to trade at the European forts is permitted only to those natives authorized to trade. Since exports must be licensed, and an export duty paid by the seller, the royal officials who "exercise the refusal of all commerce" have the means to control dealings between natives and Europeans. Any indiscriminate traffic with the Europeans is out of the question. Infractions of the regulations by the Europeans brought immediate reprisal by the "closing of the roads" to the European fort, that is, the cutting off of trade with the fort in question.

This physical separation of trade and market emphasizes the difference in function. Trade stocks the palace, the army, and the houses of the great. The market caters to the common wants of the population. The great ones of the lands have no need to resort to the market place for their provisions. Their tables are supplied from their own plantations, and their cloth and military stores from the warehouses of the Europeans in return for slaves.

The market is for the common folk and, in the port of trade, also for the foreigner. It is the "working man" taking his breakfast and dinner "in the alley," or the women selling in the market place, who have need of the piece of firewood or the two-cowrie mouthful of cooked meat. The resident native population of Whydah, belonging to one or the other of the European forts and subject to labor service for their masters, are "hired out" in menial capacities to the traders and receive "subsistence," partly in kind and partly in cowries, with which they can feed themselves in the market.

There is also the large floating population of a port town to be supplied with food and necessaries, men with no hearth or kin to care for them in Whydah: canoemen and carriers from other points on the coast, temporarily beached in Whydah; fishermen from the rivers and lagoons; and, after Britain's abolition of the slave trade, the liberated slaves dumped in Sierra Leone and finding their way back by stages to their native countries.

The Europeans may also rely upon the market. Barbot says of the market at Cape Corso that "not only the neighboring inhabitants, but also the crews of European ships riding in the road are plentifully supplied with many necessaries and refreshments." Ships captains whose provisions are running low may stock up for the return voyage by purchasing grain, fresh vegetables, and casava for the slave cargo taken on board at the coast. In principle, provisions in wholesale quantities are provided by treaty arrangement, as is seen, for instance, at Great Bandy, and watering and wooding privileges for ships are almost always a matter of treaty. Anyway, the resident European traders have less need to resort to the market since their forts are provisioned from overseas, and gifts for their table from the Viceroy of Whydah are liberal, or were in earlier times. Fresh foods, however, are purchased in the market, and the lower ranks of the garrisons receive "board wages" with which they purchase food and necessaries in the local market, or from the warehouses of the company.

The social distance between trade and market can be measured by the difference in status between those who engage in trade and those who go to market. The vendors in the market place are women. But trade, like war, is the affair of men, and more particularly "the business of kings, rich men, and prime merchants, exclusive of the inferior sort of Blacks," as Barbot says. Only women go to market "loaded like horses" with the produce of the countryside, or the makers of common wares such as hoes and iron utensils, or slaves who traffic for their masters.

Trade and market are administered by separate bodies of officials. Among the officials appointed by the king of Whydah, Bosman records, there were the Captains, "of which there are a great number; and each of these hath a particular Character: He to whom the care of the Market is entrusted, is Captain of the Market; by the same rule another is Captain of the Slaves, a third of the Tronks or Prisons, another of the Shoar." And yet another is "the Captain to whom the European Affairs were all entrusted." There was no break with this tradition under Dahoman rule. Snelgrave, upon his first meeting with the king of Dahomey, reports that the king had in his entourage one "Allegee, the English Cabocier . . . that is, the Person appointed to trade with them in particular," as well as other "great men" for each of the "different Nations." In a later period, according to Forbes, "The cha-cha is the principal agent to the king in all matters of trade; and to him must be subjected all commerce, whether in *slaves* or *palm-oil*, that he may have the refusal. The price is laid down by law, subject to his alteration if concurred in by the viceroy and six traders or superintendents of trade appointed by the king. . . . One or the other of these must be present at all sales to take the royal duty. . . ."

Slaves—or palm-oil! This, and nothing else, is trade. All other produce of the country goes through the market.

The market, on the other hand, is under the watchful eye of its own officials. "The market is presided over by an officer," Skertchly reports of the Great Market at Whydah, "who expects a toll from every vendor, and the safety of the articles exposed for sale, is guarded by the native police."[6] For every market throughout the country, the king appoints a market chief and a corps of assistants to keep order in the market and enforce the regulations. In addition, associations of vendors and craftsmen exercise jurisdiction over each separate quarter of the market. Skertchly tells us of the Whydah market that "each section is exclusively appointed for the sale of one class of articles"; and Forbes reports that "The meat, fish, corn, flour, vegetable, fruit, and foreign goods have all separate markets." Thus the sale of foreign goods, as well as native produce, is allocated a definite place in the market and becomes subject to the supervision of the association of vendors and of the market officials. These physical arrangements in the market place obviously assure full publicity for all transactions and facilitate the enforcement of regulations.

There is no unregulated buying and selling. There are no shops in Whydah, Forbes says, so that all such transactions must take place in the market. This is undoubtedly a normative regulation. By restricting sales to the market place, the legality of transactions is assured.

Similar arrangements obtain in the market at Cape Corso, according to Barbot. "It is rare to hear of any quarrels or disorder committed," he says, "by reason of the good government of the Caboceiros, or magistrates, during the market." And, as at Whydah, "This place is so disposed, and the rules prescrib'd for the more orderly keeping of the market so religiously observ'd, that all who are of one trade, or sell the same sort of things, sit in good order together."[7]

Access to the market is no less strictly controlled. Toll-houses are located at the entrances to Whydah, as to every market town throughout the kingdom. The collection of tolls on all persons carrying goods serves not only as a revenue measure but as a device to ensure control of entry into the market.

Most remarkable of all the devices and regulations which maintain the separation of trade and market is the dual market, one outside the town and one inside the town. These inner and outer markets are the usual arrangement throughout the interior of Dahomey.

The segregation of trade and market is a general feature of the port of trade organization. Measures similar to those at Whydah are reported for the kingdom of Benin. "There are four principal places where the Europeans trade," Barbot says of Benin. These "places of trade," though located inland, are ports of trade in the institutional sense. They are isolated from the capital of the kingdom which is out of bounds to foreigners. Barbot says that the inhabitants of the capital "must be all natives of the country, for no foreigners are allow'd to settle there."

In the ports of trade, lodges are set aside for the use of the European traders. At all these places, the merchants and brokers, called mercadors and veadors, are appointed by the government of Benin to deal with the Europeans. "None but the Veadors or brokers can deal with us, and even the greatest person of the nation dare not enter the European factories or lodges, under severe fines." The Europeans, then, have no contact with the native population except through the brokers appointed by the king. The markets at which European goods are sold to the native population are out of bounds to the European traders. Barbot makes this situation quite clear. "Besides the above-mentioned trading places," he says, "which are properly for dealing with Europeans, the king of Benin has appointed publick markets in many provinces of his kingdom, for the subjects to trade together, every three days in the week; they have one at Gotton, to which they bring . . . abundance of Benin cloths, . . . with all the various species of European goods, usually imported into this country, bought of the Whites at Arebo, by the Veadors and brokers." Arebo and Gotton are two of the "above-mentioned trading places which are properly for dealing with Europeans." At Gotton, a port of trade, there is also a "publick market," a situation closely analogous to Whydah. But these markets are only for "the subjects to trade together," and European imports reach these markets only through the hands of the brokers appointed to deal with European traders.

Trade with the native peoples further inland is not permitted to the Europeans but is reserved to the subjects of Benin. "They have also at certain times of the year," Barbot explains, "publick markets or fairs appointed, and kept in large open plains . . . near the high-way; to which a great number of people resort from all the neighbouring places, to buy and sell goods." These fairs are not for the Benin people only, as were the markets mentioned above, but for the peoples of "all the neighbouring places," and these fairs are held only at certain times of the year instead of every three days in the week. These fairs have other special features. "It is a custom there," Barbot continues, "for the king to send his proper officers to the said markets to keep the peace and good order amongst the people that come to it, appointing every merchant a proper place, according to the nature of the goods he deals in, etc., for the reason, during the market-time, the ordinary justices of the place have no manner of authority; but it is vested for that time only in the court-officers."

These inland fairs resemble, therefore, the port of trade. As in the port of trade, safeguards are set up in dealing with strangers and guarantees of neutrality are provided by political authority. The intent is clearly to regulate transactions with foreigners, whether these be Europeans from overseas, or native peoples from inland countries.

The separation of trade and market is the transcending principle in regard to either.

Rosemary Arnold

Notes to Chapter IX

1. Forbes, I, 108.
2. Skertchly, p. 27.
3. Barbot, pp. 268–9.

4. Bosman, pp. 363 ff.
5. *Ibid.*, p. 91.
6. Skertchly, p. 59.
7. Barbot, p. 269.

Bibliography to Chapter IX

Atkins, John, A Voyage to Guinea, London, 1735.
Barbot, John A., A Description of the Coasts of North and South Guinea, London, 1732.
Bosman, William, A New and Accurate Description of the Coast of Guinea, London, 1705.
Bovill, E. W., Caravans of the Old Sahara, Oxford, 1933.
Burton, Richard F., A Mission to Gelele, King of Dahomey, London, 1864.
Dalzel, Archibald, The History of Dahomey, London, 1793.
Duncan, John, Travels in Western Africa, London, 1847.
Forbes, Frederick E., Dahomey and the Dahomans, London, 1851.
Herskovits, Melville J., Dahomey, an Ancient West African Kingdom, New York, 1938.
Isert, Paul E., Voyages en Guinée et dans les îles Caraibes en Amerique, Paris, 1793.
McLeod, John, A Voyage to Africa, London, 1820.
Nadel, S. F., A Black Byzantium, Oxford, 1942.
Norris, Robert, Memoirs of the Reign of Bossa Ahadee, King of Dahomey, London, 1789.
Skertchly, J. A., Dahomey As It Is, London, 1874.
Snelgrave, William, A New Account of Some Parts of Guinea, London, 1734.

NOTES ON SOURCES

The works listed above are the major sources for the internal economy.

We have relied heavily upon Herskovits. While Herskovits' direct observations were made in the modern period, his account of economic administration under the kings (including accounts of the Census, Taxation, Operational Devices) was obtained from informants who had lived under the monarchy. Wherever possible, this information has been checked against earlier observations.

X

Explosive Markets:
The Berber Highlands

---•---

THE place occupied by the market in society has usually been investigated in regard to societies characterized by a normal functioning of government. It has become almost an obsession to associate the development of markets with peaceable communities.* At the back of such a preconception there lurk unrealistic ideologies concerning the institutional character of what we are wont to call the peace of the market. The fact that in noncentralized societies, where no power structure links the segments, especially where blood feud and tribal clashes are prevalent, markets do exist, but in the absence of government they must rely for the peace of the market on the political device of intergroup truces. With nomadic desert dwellers these truces are usually made to coincide with the seasonal periods so as to make the most of the chances offered for trading. But this would, of course, by no means suffice for the needs of sedentary highland tribes. Regular markets for fresh food are to them a matter of life and death. Where they have to fall back for their provisions on mutual exchanges these have to be continuous, not merely occasional.

This throws into relief the sociological paradox of everyday markets under conditions of near-anarchy. Such markets are bedevilled by the ambiguities of neutral jurisdictions in the midst of the complexities of

* The author is indebted to Professor Arensberg for suggesting the possibilities inherent in the Berber material.

intertribal relations. Yet the peace of the market must rely on the balance of forces between the hostile groups.

The sociologist of economic institutions has cause to explore societies such as these for the enlightenment they offer on the functioning of markets in a labile societal context. Offhand, he will find these societies only in the regions of the world where we meet with highland peoples whose general attitude is one of militant refusal to accept the rule of the governments of the plains below. The political institutions of these peoples reflect a spirit of utter independence. The groups which compose these societies, though they may not altogether fail to fuse are scattered in mosaic fashion. Each group stands to the other very nearly in the same relation of a hostile sovereignty, in which the highland society as a whole relates to the society of the plain. These societies are composed of a mere juxtaposition of segments each of which possesses an acute consciousness of its own singularity and solidarity.

The salient feature is, of course, the complete absence of centralizing institutions. Unified government is exceptional. Only occasionally is it brought about through the ire of all the groups against "interference" by the government of the plains. The ambition of outstanding individuals may for a while break the strait-jacket of clan or tribal affiliations and set up its iron rule. But when the self-made chieftain fails, things once more lapse into their previous state of a segmented anarchy.

The signal success of such societies in resisting imposition of the forms of government of the plains springs from the endurance of sturdy patterns of decentralization. Within a mountain ecology isolation is traditional and a thin scattering of groups living in widly separated valleys keeps the centralizing forces at low ebb, be they acting from within or the outside.

In our inquiry the economic process is best discussed in terms of integration. It may then be found that in a society lacking political centralization the economy would be without redistributive forms of integration; that the political tension that is permanent between the segments of such a society would prevent economic reciprocity to develop between the villages, clans or tribes; that in absence of redistributive relations as well as of out-group reciprocity market exchanges usually gain great significance and, indeed, play an integrative role that may transcend the economic sphere itself.

Siba and Makhzen

The conditions described above are nowhere found with more striking clarity than in the highland societies of North West Africa. The Berbers of the Atlas exist politically as a loose aggregate of social segments without reference to a common center. The reluctance of these societies to accept the patterns of the world below has resulted in a complete severance of ties between the society of the plains and that of the mountains.

C. S. Coon pointedly uses the Moroccan name *Bled el Makhzen*— literally, "The Land of Government"—to denote the area of the lowland urban centers and those villages which recognize the authority of a central government. The word *Makhzen* comes from the Arabic *khazana*, "to lock up," "to hoard."[1] The word was synonymous with "government" and, more especially, with the treasury department. The word is certainly expressive of a government based on the redistribution of staples.[2] From the word *makhzen* comes the French *magasin*, the German *Magazin*, and the Spanish *almacén*. It is a graphic term for what might be described as a polity based on a storage and tax-levying economy in kind.

In opposition to it, the independent mountain societies are known as the *Bled es Siba*, the Land of Independence (literally "insolence"). We shall use these two terms abridged as *Siba* and *Makhzen* to denote the two different societies.[3]

The Siba is untouched by forcible centralization, and may be compared with the manner of existence of annulated worms consisting of rings and capable of easy fission. Even the tribes are but an aggregate of a few of the cells which are the units of society. These segments are the cantons (*taqbilt*), expanses of some 8 or 10 kms. across, inhabited by a few hundred families in a dozen or so of scattered hamlets or three or four bigger villages, and forming for all practical purposes minute independent states. Beyond the cantons the feeling of attachment fades, so that the tribes—a group of cantons, from three to twelve—are hardly more than a name, a definite territory and some commonly shared traditions. Their unity appears only in times of danger and, in between, it dissolves into a vague sentiment of brotherhood between tribesmen which may be rationalized in terms of an assumed common descent.

Not so the cantons. These are vital organisms. Small though they be they have to be considered for all practical purposes as true states. The feeling of attachment to the canton is narrowly territorial and is enhanced by the fact that in a mountain area there inevitably must be, if only for military reasons, some adjustment of the size of each social unit to the natural dimensions of hills and valleys. Nevertheless, as Robert Montagne discovered, the cantonal territories proper tend to be of fairly equal size throughout the Berber lands. For the limits of the canton do not, quite coincide with the natural boundaries of these mountain habitats, but may fall short of them, a canton occupying only the space it actually requires, ignoring the more generous expanse offered by nature.[4] This standard size of the cantons is due to organizational reasons. The cantons are ruled by assemblies (*djema'a*) of notables (*inflas*) or heads of the extended families, who are supposed to meet regularly. A day's walk over hilly terrain is therefore the canton's natural radius.

Rule by representative assemblies (*djema'a*) is, as this feature strikingly shows, typical of Berber society. It is a form of republican democracy suitable to a society of equals. There is a *djema'a* of the village, of the canton (composed of the notables of all the villages of the canton), of the tribe (composed of the notables of the diverse cantons of the tribe). In certain regions the chiefs of powerful families may overthrow the democratic process and start out on an authoritarian rule. Such personalities are called *amghar*, chiefs of war, and as the term indicates, their origin may lie in the custom of appointing chiefs to rule the cantons when war was declared. The local regulations of the codes of village law are called *qanun*—from the Greek *canon*. Within the village regulations are enforced and the *djema'a* sees to it that fines are imposed on infractors. A harsher punishment is exile, applied when feuds between families threaten the existence of the township or canton.

Internal dissensions might mean that neighboring cantons would take advantage of a weak moment and make war. This danger was parried in an unusual, but most effective way. The cantons of a whole region were affiliated to either the one or the other of two political parties which formed in this way intercantonal alliances. Of these "political parties" there were, as we said, but two, so that if we plot on the map the territories of the cantons and color them according to the party (*leff*) they belong to, the result is something like a checkerboard. The fractions which compose a tribe are exactly divided among the *leffs*, so that an equilibrium is achieved inside the tribe. When a canton was attacked by another canton of the opposite hue, it could call to its aid its *leff* allies. A war involving a vast range of mountains would thus be provoked over night, a possibility which alone would be enough to make the two original contenders come to their senses. In this way the division of the cantons of a tribe between two opposite parties becomes a guarantee for the survival of the cantons. Equilibrium is maintained in spite of the wars; permanently balanced opposite parties (*leff*) contribute to this result as much as either common markets or common shrines. Local wars remain innocuous even inside the smaller tribes, so neatly are the hostile forces balanced within.[5] In Kabylia, a region of large villages, the townships are divided into two parties called *soffs*. The village is here the equivalent of the canton, and the *soff* plays a part comparable to the *leff* of the mountain regions.

We have here, in effect, the very reverse of a system of centralized authority. Instead of a pinnacle of power at the center there is balance of power where opposite forces check one another and conflicts are resolved not by decision from summit but by agreement, or, if no agreement is reached, the efforts to limit warfare to local bounds.

Under these singular conditions the market or *suq* is a preeminent organ of the formation of public (larger than canton) opinion, directing common effort and integrating otherwise disparate forces.

The usual and, indeed, obvious rendering of the Arabic term *suq* as market leaves much unsaid. Both the bazaar and the *suq* are markets, yet they differ very much, not only from one another but also from the Western concept of market. Nowhere perhaps is this truer than in the Berber mountain region, where the market forms also locationally a counterpart to the village. In effect in the *suq* we are confronted with a complex legal, social, political and often even religious institution which serves primarily economic ends. Important *suqs* are of historical origin. In no case does the mere frequency of random exchanges taking place in it make an open space a *suq*. Only under the auspices of authority, after proclamation has been made and a table of fines posted in a customary or appointed spot, does a gathering over a definite stretch of time assume the character of a *suq*. The complex criteria that make for a *suq* raise even the most modest *suq* onto the institutional level of the Champagne fairs of the thirteenth century. It is not the externalities that matter. A *suq* may be installed in an elaborately fitted walled area, furnished with important public buildings; other *suqs*—and these are the great majority—are held at a desert site with hardly a trace to indicate their whereabouts when the *suq* is over. Just as a Parliament building should not be confused with the political institution known as Parliament, a market place does not amount to a *suq*. Though market place and *suq* may be here used interchangeably, it is always the specific, *sui generis* institution that is meant.

Certain Kabyle laws fine those who, under the pretext of having nothing to buy or sell, do not attend the market.[6] To attend the market of the tribe is at least in certain cases an obligation even though otherwise the villager may also attend other markets. When a tribe in Kabylia establishes a new market the tribesmen are compelled to frequent it to the exclusion of any other.[7]

Observers are unanimous in their insistence on the unique significance of the *suq* for the existence of the Berber polity. Earlier and later writers are equally emphatic on this point. Robin, in 1874, wrote: "The markets are the forums of the tribe. Ideas and business affairs are dealt with here once a week between individuals who live at a considerable distance. It is here that collective sentiments form and manifest themselves. Villages and families fuse their emotions into that often entirely different product which grows from mass contacts. The market creates that external individuality of the group often so dissimilar from the feelings of the individuals composing it. The egotism of the tribe or the *douar* [village] takes the place of the egotism of the individuals."[8] E. Doutts, a generation later, could still confirm his statement. "The market," he attests, "is a factor of highest importance in Arab [read Berber] life; it is no exaggeration to say that the life of the tribe almost in its entirety happens in the market. It is the place where the natives meet; not only do they provide for their daily needs through sales in the market but it is also the spot where ideas are exchanged, political information is passed on, the announcements of the authorities are made and the reaction to these are formed, where decisions about peace and war are taken, political conspiracies started, public outcries raised, broadminded proposals mooted and crimes hatched."[9] De Segonzac sums up its political function with brevity and precision. "Markets," he writes, "have here a dual significance, which is not less political than economic, for they are the source of news, the place where people assemble, discussion takes place and decisions fall."[10]

The Market in the Siba

The market could, of course, never have attained to the political importance it is universally credited with but for the part that fell to it in the everyday life of the highland Berber. The economic organization of the Makhzen and the Siba is of interest in this order of things.

The heart of the Makhzen is the level country with its urban agglomerations. The storage economy of a central government forms the material backbone of the army and civil service, maintained by a taxation system comprising all classes of the population. The Siba is the hill country which, though lacking towns, has nevertheless a sedentary population of farmers, living in settled fortified villages. They tend their flocks in the temperate season around the scattered crude shelters right in the middle of the individual holdings, and on the hillocks in winter. Each hilltop is crested by an *agadir*, as the squat stone quadrangles are called, solid structures of military value, along the four walls of which small storage rooms are located within. Under lock and key the grain of the householders is hoarded in these cells. The *agadir* is the mainstay of the political and military independence of the village or perhaps of a whole canton. Yet in spite of the common defence based on the *agadir*, the householders keep their grain in the *agadir* stored in strictly separate cells—a remarkable demonstration of economic individualism.

Within this economic frame the market played an essential part in sustaining the livelihood of the people of the Siba. Their isolated villages had no shops or inns; no regular trade reached them; there were no grocers' shops where meat, butter, eggs, fowl, vegetables or other fresh food could be procured. Apart from some spices there was a lack of imported household goods like coffee, tea, sugar, or salt. The highland markets which provided these were a vital necessity.

The mountain markets are primarily places for the purchase of fresh foodstuffs. They offer the possibility of buying cuts of meat which are certainly the most important item in these transactions. ". . . Early in the afternoon the men begin the trek back to their villages. . . . Most of them will be carrying some meat on a string or have it tied to the saddle of the donkey. Market day is often the only time the Kabyle has meat. . . ."[11]

Butter may well come next in importance. In retail markets it is sold in small jars "and it is up to the buyer to judge whether the price demanded corresponds to the weight offered."[12] However in markets that specialize in the wholesaling of butter—as, e.g., in the Suq el-had of the Ulad Jellul, it is sold by weight.

Thus, the markets of the Siba amounted to externally located grocery stores and butcher shops where foodstuffs were retailed and taken home. Indeed, the waste incurred in killing a sheep for each day the family wants meat at their meals would be prohibitive. These markets have come to supersede the collective customs by facilitating individual isolated consumption.

This does not mean that the Berber markets are places where cooked food can be purchased, in contrast to the Makhzen where such markets are the rule. To give an example, in the small Makhzen town of Agadir the market is sure to offer fresh meat at every hour of the day and bread fresh from the oven.[15] Very little meat is bought at the butcher's. Instead it is purchased cooked, seasoned and prepared to be eaten.

The feeding of the poorer subjects, clients or followers of a chief or sovereign is an unavoidable necessity which is sometimes resolved in the cooked-food markets. A chief, *qaid* or *sayyid* keeps "maison et table ouvertes,"[17] especially when on the rise to power. At other times he may try to ensure a cheap supply of staples which may be directly distributed, e.g., at the "gates."

Generally speaking the Bled es Siba has no such proletariat because it has not suffered detribalization, and division of labor remains primitive. The need to feed the poor is absent in a society over which no sovereign rules and where everyone is the equal of everyone else. The appearance of an internal proletariat in the Siba is a sure sign that it is developing an oligarchic tyranny of local character and a Makhzen of its own.

Reciprocity produces an important form of assistance in the *muna*,[19] a dole of food given to a needy stranger or neighbor, taking place in a public reunion, usually at night so that the occasion is called "the night of succor (*laila el muna*). In its ancient Arabic form the *muna* was simply a gift of food to the hungry or, rather, a first-fruit of alms owed to the needy or to God. A Berber who desires the benefit of a *muna* appeals to the chief of the notables of the group in the bustle of a market day. The following night, as soon as the group has returned

home, food is collected from the households and served to the needy
person and his family. The muna obliges the other villagers to do likewise.

The village itself is devoid of shops. Everything that is not domestically produced has, therefore, to be obtained from the market, through
market transactions, and no exchanges or commercial activities of any
kind are attempted outside of these times and places. The market
place has a monopoly of exchange transactions.

Itinerant traders, again, do not visit the villages, but only the markets. This does not, of course, apply to travelling craftsmen who repair
saddles, ploughs, or other bulky objects which cannot be taken to the
distant market, nor to the doctor (tubíb al-muslimín) who pays irregu-
lar visits and carries and sells his own drugs and medicines. Nor does it
apply, by a remarkable exception, to a class of peddlers who visit the
villages when the men are away, for the women are their only clients.
In return for the foodstuffs, spices, small manufactured articles, jewelry, cosmetics, charms or whatever their all-purpose bags may contain,
they receive eggs, wool rags or fleeces or small quantities of oil filched
by the housewives from home supplies. This uncommercial form of
trade is undisputed women's prerogative; no money is used, barter is
the governing principle. In the face of such an exception, restriction of
all other commerce to the suq is all the more striking.

The physical equipment of the market may be simple enough. It
is held on a flat surface, sandy where possible, so as to avoid dust in
summer and mud in winter. Essential to a market site is a good source
of water, often connected with a shrine, so that at least in the big places
of pilgrimage (mussem) marketing is combined with religious practices and ritual bathing. At the shrine oaths are taken in litigation
cases. The shrines possess a holy perimeter (haran), serving as a refuge
in case of need, and where people in danger (blood-feud, etc.) may take
shelter. All this contributes to the security conferred on this turbulent
area by the covenant of the market. The correlation between shrines
and markets is too close to be of very recent origin. If the shrine of the
spring or of the mosque is a famed one (siyyid) the yearly pilgrimage
will most likely coincide with an increase of the merchandise offered in
the market.[21]

According to the volume of business transacted in the markets and
the number of persons who attend, we may divide suqs into two classes.

The first kind are small and held in the territory of a mountain canton or at the boundary limits of two or three cantons; some crude removable shelters forming shops (*tahanout*) provide room for the few dozen persons who visit the market (a hundred at the most). The notables of the place will run such a market without receiving any remuneration. The large kind of *suq* occurs at crossroads or strategic locations, or other important points of communication, as at the foot of mountains, on the borderline between ecological regions. In some instances such markets may be surrounded by a wall, especially if market dues are collected. They may contain hundreds of shops, like cells in a beehive, made of mud and stone, each the stall of a merchant. Within the enclosure we find permanent buildings (storehouses, coffee shops, a mosque, etc.). Such markets may be frequented by all the tribes of the region and several thousand persons may gather in them every week.

Suqs as just described are typical of rural North Africa, whether Arab or Berber. With the single exception of the desert areas they form a system of weekly markets held alternately within walking distance of the villages. This method is not only advantageous for the farmer who gets a larger choice of products, but also necessary in nonpoliced countries where no towns are in reach. It is made possible by the villages being close together, not in a line, but rather radially. Indeed, the system is at home throughout the Middle East, for the products of the countryside appear in the city bazaars on appointed days. But nowhere is the system as elaborately perfected as in North Africa.[22] The markets are there named for the day of the week in which they are held followed by the name of the tribe to which they belong, and the market days are so allotted between neighboring market places that it is always possible to make weekly rounds of markets, returning home for the night. The whole area could be plotted in this way: as clusters of markets of which it is possible to make weekly rounds, their clustering offering pointers to the student of the geography of economic units. Each village school has its free day on the allotted market day.[23]

Such a distribution of markets must have been reached in each region by a method of trial and error. Rivalries were bound to arise if two neighboring markets were held on the same day. In Kabylia, when a tribe wanted to establish a new market it had to obtain the consent of the neighboring tribes and select a day which would not infringe their rights.[25]

Thus, decision by decision, always with the general interest in

mind—the nearer and more frequent the markets, the better—the mesh
came to be knit. Eventually, on appointed days persons protected by
their particular day's safe conducts, flowed from all directions into the
paths leading to definite markets. Such a piecemeal method of evolution did not favor a national development. While in pre-Muhammedan
nomadic Arabia the time allotted to trading was a specific season of
the year (the *maswin* or monsoon months), when blood feuds and
tribal feuds would be dropped, the sedentary population of North
Africa seemed to have been prevented by its own devices for continuous trading from achieving a common period of truce which could
have acted as an amalgamating factor on a national scale.

More often than not the market places are located in the valleys
halfway between opposite *leffs* occupying parallel mountain ranges.
They are thus fully exposed to the consequences of that peculiar system of power vacua which is at the heart of the Berber polity.

In these nonpoliced and politically split areas, attendance at the
markets as well as travel between territories is achieved under agreements providing for neutrality. The Berber *ánaia* or safe conduct is
granted either by the tribes themselves or by individual tribesmen who
are, of course, supposedly backed by the full force of the tribe to which
they belong. Anyone can grant his *anaia* on his own responsibility and
expect his tribesmen to respect it. Thus a person going to the market
finds himself the balanced focus of opposite forces and entrusts life
and limb to the recognized guarantees that protect the market place.

Safe Conduct

To secure this peace of the market is one of the supreme aims of
the highland polity. This is indeed a dominant theme of Berber life.
The markets are the places for "external" contacts, where the narrow
in-group solidarity of village life gives way to a "freer" behavior that
results from the intercourse with individuals who belong to other
groups. Cantonal isolation thus finds its counterpoise and its outlet in
the market habit.

Psychologically as well as physically market places stand on the
"fringes" of the in-groups. Here the world of the villager comes into
contact with similar outside groups. The *villages*, centers of life and
habitation of the in-groups, and the *markets*, centers of commerce of

the out-groups, are completely dissociated in the physical sense. The *suq* stands locationally apart from and in contrast to the village. It is situated well outside of the settled centers, in low-lying and deserted spots, far from the plowed fields. After the market ends, the merchants and shop keepers pack their stands away and the market place remains deserted, unmarked—almost indistinguishable in the landscape. These places resemble in fact no man's lands assigned to the weekly truces of commerce.

There are important exceptions. In all regions travelling traders may be stopped and asked to sell the merchandise they carry—compulsory trade—in the villages or in the middle of the road.[26] In certain areas, indeed, the markets stand just on the outskirts of the village. Finally, in the specialized towns of the oases (*qsar*) the market place is in the middle of the town itself which is in fact to be considered as a "market-town" servicing both the visiting nomads and the cultivators of the place. Yet though these last "markets" are "towns" they also carry the imprint of the neutrality that goes with the noninhabited market place. The *qsars* are generally under the protection of nomadic groups that rent buildings in the town as storehouses. If the *qsar* is central to different nomadic tribes, its independence may be even more complete. Indeed, the situation of the *qsar* of the oases seems in many respects to approach that of the "port of trade." Desert and sea are akin.

The physical separation of village and market makes possible the co-existence of two well-developed forms of integration in the same society—market exchange and in-group reciprocity. Though at certain times of the year a full tenth of the Kabyle population is engaged in itinerant commerce (mostly of the peddling and barter type described above), in the villages themselves there is a striking absence of professional merchants.[27] Nevertheless, apart from some transactions on real estate, sale of trees, or the crops, etc., which may be prepared at the villages and concluded in the market, the extent of the transactions made in the villages is very limited, probably no more than a fraction of the volume of business done in the market. Further, payment in kind, services, barter, etc., prevail in the villages whereas cash payment is the invariable rule at the market.

Over and above the *anaias* and related conventions which made a safe access to markets possible, the groups which "owned" a market delegated authority to certain individuals or certain bodies. The regime of the market which resulted might vary from district to district, but, as we shall see, there were only a few methods available for delegating the administration and the policing of the markets.

When the market was truly intertribal, "owned" by different groups, their representatives would obviously sit together and deal with all cases either by common decision or separately, i.e., each representative settling the disputes of his own tribesmen. There is a limit to this method. In the Rif, for instance, the markets are occasions for the concluding of tribal alliances (*ribat*). In such reunions the chiefs may have to decide litigations that arise in assemblies composed of crowds of armed warriors.[28] The market of Tarqist, for instance, situated at a crossroads of the High-Ghis region, was under the control of three *amghars* appointed by the three interested tribes, the Beni Mesdwi, Tarqist and Zerquet.[29] Thus the system of intertribal markets is prevalent in districts belonging to the Makhzen, where the tribes tend to be at peace with one another, and stand moreover under the jurisdiction of the central government.

When, on the contrary, a single tribe or village owned the market, the *djema'a* of one tribe alone could not very well exercise control over the market, for this would have been equivalent to applying local jurisdiction to an interlocal affair. Also, it might not be convenient for a single *djema'a* to handle the administration of a market place where great distances were involved. Authority over the market would therefore have to be delegated.

Now, the simplest solution in the areas where religious personages played an important role in the Berber parts of Kabylia and Northern Morocco consisted in turning control over to a holy man (*murabit*) or a family of *murabits*. Such markets under murabitic authority, we are told, while exempt of all specific regulations, offer a picture of general harmony.

To the same type belong in the tribal areas of the Makhzen the markets of religious teachers (*tolba*). Their origin is ancient; in olden times in these places of reunion young men or students would get together to discuss professional questions. Merchants, attracted by the periodic congregations, put up shops and stalls and started a market. Examples are the Kjouma'a Tolba, the Thenin Tolba, where the religious teachers themselves sell all kinds of foodstuffs. The *tolba* rule and police these markets which have no master, neither *qaid* nor *khalifa*. Only to watch over judicial matters does a judge (*qadi*) turn up from a nearby center.[30] These *tolba* markets seem very independent of

Makhzen authority. Towards 1898 the market of Thenin de Smid el-Ma was suppressed at the demand of the lease-holders of the tolls in the neighboring town of El-Ksar. They had complained of unfair competition exerted by the unofficial *tolba* market which diverted many goods. But the inhabitants of the countryside continued to visit the market in spite of prohibition by the Makhzen, and the religious men managed without any representatives of authority.[31]

The *murabits* to whom the market had been entrusted could be long dead. The market place then would continue as a shrine and there remained only the malediction (*tagat*) of the saint venerated in the sanctuary to punish troublemakers. Since oaths were taken at the shrine, the notables were spared the trouble of intervening in litigations. In particular the great autumn fairs were of this type. "Such fairs," we learn, "attract the populations of whole countrysides of several days distance. The crowds that meet here are rent by lifelong feuds and no chief, no committee of notables can be expected to overawe them. Nothing less than a formidable saint and the awful penalties dispensed by him will suffice."[32]

In the regions where these religious institutions could not insure neutrality, private individuals were entrusted with the policing of the market. Offhand, it would seem as if this was only a secular variant of murabitic control. But the purpose of this method was rather the opposite, namely, to hand the police of the market not to a superauthority, but to a nonauthority, so as to make it more palatable to visiting aliens by offering the chance of a neutral jurisdiction. Nevertheless the person had to be rich and well connected, able to depend on his *soff* or *leff* for allegiance. These persons, a sort of *custodes nundinarum*, were known as "masters of the market." Actually their semi-official status was only the result of the abstention of the group from applying its territorial jurisdiction over the market. Hanoteau and Letourneux rightly affirmed that the "masters of the market" were, in Kabylia, the only office-holders comparable to our magistrates.[33] The practice was an old one. Robert Montagne has traced it, perhaps stretching it too fine, to Roman Africa, where rich gentlemen farmers would establish native markets to their great profit.[34]

An alternative to the appointment of some local notable was the procedure of farming out the market to individuals by auction. Markets were auctioned for a fixed period of time, generally one year, to the highest bidder, who recouped himself through the collection of market dues. Since the taxes were to be paid over to the Makhzen in full, the tax farmer had to increase their amount, in order to pay the taxes to the government and still retain a profit for himself. It became an open invitation to abuse, sparing only the European and other influential persons who should not be antagonized.

Such farmed markets seem in general to run smoothly. The collectors are regarded as individuals who make an investment and therefore can expect a return. Moreover, the policing functions are also auctioned, so that fines are imposed with alacrity by the market constables. In auctioned markets, furthermore, there is a virtual separation of the administrative from the judiciary apparatus, resulting in a better functioning of the whole.

The method of farming out the markets, widespread in the Makhzen tribal areas, is almost absent from the Siba. It was a useful method for collecting central government taxes from outlying areas by auctioning them out to local persons. We cannot expect to find such a feature in the Siba regions. Payment of taxes to the Makhzen or the qaids is here not known and, in general, there is a disinclination to tax the goods which enter the market. Nevertheless the men of the Siba accepted this innovation like many other economic or social practices reaching them from the Makhzen.

By and large, command of the market is a stepping stone to power. The mere growth of the market entrusted or farmed to the authority of an individual seems to help in the development of his personal power. In the regions of rampant chieftainship, it is in "commanding over the market" that an amghar shows best his prestige and ability.[36] This may open the door to a Makhzen development. A very close dependence upon markets, especially in the High Atlas, follows in the wake of the destruction of the old democratic and co-operative ways, the true home of in-group reciprocity. Sociologically, we have here a set of interacting factors where markets can hardly function without successful oligarchs or prominent chiefs, and the development of chieftainship leads to a further growth in the size of the market. The process may be cumulative and become overwhelming: the amghars or chiefs (later qaids) come to be more and more dependent on Jewish moneylenders, and complicated financial operations begin to take place; the old tribal law is replaced by the religious shari'a, and the local market regulations traditional to the Siba are absorbed by those of the Makhzen.

But this is only the latest stage of a line of evolution. In the regions where the oligarchy did not rise to the status of a social class, representative assemblymen (*inflas*) continued to administer the markets. In Kabylia, where chieftainship has not made any strides at all though an oligarchy did establish itself as a class, markets are administered by prominent members of the oligarchy appointed as masters of the market. The dangerous combination of expanding market exchanges and self-aggrandizing personal authority was averted by increasing the number of the markets while keeping their size as small as before. This, in conjunction with the *soff* or *leff* mechanisms, themselves the greatest obstacle to the emergence of despotism, kept the traditional social structure intact, and chieftainship did not develop.

Explosive Markets

The different types of control—whether of the supernatural, conventional or administrative order—would normally appear sufficient to ensure the peace of the market place. But not under the extreme conditions obtaining in these traditionally feuding party-ridden areas. Here markets are powder kegs which may go off at the slightest shock. There is a customary name for the sudden, panicky "snapping" which breaks the peace of the *suq*: the *nefra'a*.

These markets, it must be remembered, are supposedly[37] neutral ground, and tribesmen of hostile groups are able to meet each other, even if a merciless intertribal war is raging during the other days of the week. The situation is overloaded with latent conflict and the precarious truce may dissolve in mutual violence.

The *nefra'a* is naturally more common in large intertribal markets, and rather rare in the small markets of the mountain cantons, for these gather too few people to give rise to such a phenomenon of mass psychology as is the *nefra'a*. The larger intertribal markets are the place where members of opposite tribes, *leffs*, or *soffs* meet squarely with each other. Where blood feud is the immemorial right of the families even the best controls emanating from neutrality, *anaias* and covenants cannot replace a common positive authority. The *nefra'as* thus are not exceptional phenomena; a *nefra'a* can be intentionally provoked by rogues out for pillage, but generally it is a spillover from a simple dissension between two individuals, ending in a brawl in which all take sides. In 1880, in the Sunday *suq* of El Had Berriada, one Ait Boudvar tribesman and one Ait Wasif tribesman argued about a kidskin worth no more than thirty cents. Two factions took part in the dispute and came to fight each other for the whole day, using small stones, hatchets and knives. Firearms were prohibited in this *suq*; everyone was carrying his own dagger. At the end of the day 300 men were lying dead or wounded.[38] In the *suq* of the Ak'bil a man of the Ait el Arba (Ait Yenne) argued with a debtor of his of the Ait Hikhem (Ait Yahyia). The debt was in the amount of forty-five cents. A tribal war ensued.[39]

Most of these market battles, and the bloodiest ones, are fought in Kabylia. This is a region of large villages, as we saw, divided into *soffs* which readily organize into *leff*-type alliances. Also, Kabylia is a country of important markets where the tribesmen act as tradesmen and itinerant merchants, mixing freely in the territories of foreign tribes. If the chiefs and constables of the market, as so often happens, are unable to separate the contenders, only exhaustion puts an end to the fray.

The very tenseness of the crowd in the market place sometimes acts as a mechanism of control. The people in a market may take terrifyingly swift measures to stop an imminent *nefra'a* through a sort of lynch-law. The lightning action of the crowd and the ferocity of the punishment inflicted is the true measure of the instability of these meetings.

Often the prohibition of arms was observed in so far as long arms were concerned, but the practice of carrying concealed guns was widespread. In the Sunday *suq* of the Ait Iraten, Said Naid Ahmed of the village of Ait el Arba (Ait Yenne tribe) was in blood-feud with the clan of Kassi-ou Mrad, an old headman of the Taguemiont Ihedden (*soff* of the Ait Irsten). Said wanted to kill Kassi, and following the old man to a corner of the market, he cocked the gun he was carrying under his burnous. The noise betrayed him; someone uttered a cry, and only minutes later he lay dead under the pile of stones with which he had been lapidated. Such piles covering a dead body may be left untouched to serve as a reminder.

Nothing but brutal preventive behavior can ensure the neutrality of the market place. The Berber social structure permits a chain-reaction of ever larger conflicts. In this politically cleft society it is more important to isolate trouble spots than to punish merely because there was breach of the law. The *qanuns* chastise threats as heavily as completed acts. To unsheath a yatagan in the *suq* is as bad as to stab someone. And no meddler in a dispute not his own can get away without a fine. He who fires a gun at the *suq* of Massat, though nobody is injured, pays as much as the murderer of a man on nonmarket days. To our ears: "Be bold and quick. Give to your act all the marks of the inevitable. Don't fumble."

It is not surprising that the *nefra'a* breeds xenophobia. Strangers and foreigners are sometimes inclined to take the law in their own hands;[40] they have no part in the policing of the market and do not suffer from the long-range consequences of a *nefra'a*. *Nefra'as* will discredit a *suq* and people will stop coming to it. Besides, if a murder has been committed in the *suq* the market is closed for a period of purification, generally one year.[41]

Lynch law and draconic legislation is thus an outstanding feature of the Berber highland market. Under conditions of anarchy only extreme rigor of the law and its ruthless application can ensure an area of peace and freedom such as these markets broadly represent.

Incidentally, women play an important part in maintaining the peace of the market. This sociologically well-grounded fact may also account for the tradition that all through history the Moghreb women were conciliators and messengers of peace in wars and private quarrels. Among the Arabs this mediating function of women derives from the marriage alliance (*çihr*) which acts to unite two social groups. In many tribes the woman who marries a foreigner becomes a citizen of both tribes. The Ait Mesruh and their neighbors admit also that foreign women married in the tribes become automatically Mesruiah. The Talsint only grant citizenship, however, when the woman gives birth to a male child.[42] The *anaia* of women is the strongest kind of *anaia*, a cloak of immunity and protection that involves a group's honor. Moreover, as housewives, women are eager for their market supplies and market earnings. Their presence in the market place is a matter of course. To the women belong exclusively two fields of economic activity, namely, poultry and eggs, pottery, as well as within limits, the sale of wool, charcoal and henna. They keep their gains for themselves so that the market is a source of feminine private income. The cash they obtain in these exchanges they keep as ornament money, or convert it into jewels, perfumes, dresses, etc. Many breaches of market peace are avoided by their presence and others are restored by their intervention.

Rigor of Market Law

Islam itself has never developed special codes for commerce, since religious law encompasses all activities. Subject to this limitation, the Berbers have tables of fines for villages and tables of fines for markets.

Characteristically, the market, as such, is little mentioned in the qanuns of the villages; out of the 25 complete qanuns and 29 incomplete ones examined, the author has been able to collect only a dozen references to the market (though some qanuns count up to 50 and even up to 150 articles). Almost none exist in regard to the regulation of the markets themselves. In the few cases when the village qanun mentions a specific market it does so to enact penalties that are harsher in the market than elsewhere.

The market is the danger spot in the social structure. The full rigor of the law is applied there with intent. Of this we have a confirmation in the qanun of Massat. This tribe of recent constitution in the Moroccan south was studied by Robert Montagne.[45] The physical center which held together the newly formed Massat confederation was the market. We can follow step by step its body of laws as it developed, for in the qanuns the regulations appear as added year by year.

The climax of this progression is provided by the penalties for thieving in the market. In the final articles—180 and 181—enacted a few years after 1880, we read:

The Suq et Tetla being transferred to its old site to the N. of Touba, the Tribe of the Ida u Mont has decided that all adults in full possession of their faculties guilty of stealing in the aforementioned market, will pay 110 mitqals. If one such refuses to pay, or if his means of fortune do not permit him to do so, he will be blinded by gouging out his two eyes, if he cannot manage to obtain the pardon of the inflas. Such is the debt to society of the transgressors of the law.

And article 182:

The ancient custom by virtue of which fines could be paid for the culprit by the seven nearest kinsmen's houses is hereby abolished, for it was an arbitrary measure which was not according to the Shar'ia [Moslem religious law] nor the orf [Berber customary law]. Only the wife of the thief, or his father, or both together, can help in the payment of the fine, if there has been between them no separation of their property. Otherwise, the transgressor alone is responsible for his act.

These two articles reinforced each other. The abrogation of the customary principle of extended family responsibility stands here alongside of the till then harshest law against thievery.

What was especially meant by the "neutrality" of the markets was their insulation from all conflicts arising out of other contexts. In the qanun of Massat (article 113) it is forbidden to bring into the market place any litigation of cases except the local commercial ones. Conversely, local commercial transactions have to be executed and completed on one and the same market day, and incompleted ones cannot be left over for the next market day. In Kabylia, for instance,

Anyone quitting the market and leaving behind him a debt of more than 1 real is fined ½ real.[47]

Such provisions would necessarily prevent the emergence of a system of markets, i.e., a linking of markets with one another. No credit system can develop; no price arbitrage can be practiced. The road leading to market trade is blocked. Even finance and business evolve outside of these markets. Not markets, but trade and government are their founts.

The Berbers never fully accepted the usury laws of orthodox Islam. It was traditional of the earlier French writers of the conquest to contrast Berbers and Arabs in this respect.

In a typical year during the second half of the nineteenth century the French issued 8,000 to 10,000 passports to traders in the circle of Fort National. Considering that the population there numbered only 76,616 inhabitants, at least one-eighth of the total population was, off and on, actively engaged in trade. Three-fourths of these passports were issued to itinerant peddlers, or "perfumers." In payment for their cosmetics, ribbons, charms, kerchiefs and other trifles of female attire, they took some handfuls of flour, or raisins, some wool rags, or oil, whatever the household could dispense with. If these peddlers never asked for money, neither did they spend any. Successful begging was one of the marks of a thriving peddler. When he had gathered enough by barter and begging, he went to town to sell. An Ait Yenne who started with a capital of 25 fr. allegedly made 1,000 by the end of the season. Another Ait Yenne who invested all his capital, amounting to 10 frs. in cheap wares netted 500 frs. These peddlers carry their cheap merchandise in bags, and they are called "traders of the bag" to distinguish them from "traders of the tent," who have pack animals, tents and servants. The bags weigh sometimes 35 or 40 kgs., and when the poorer Kabyle comes home after one of these ventures, he has deep scars on his back.[51-52]

Segmental Anarchy and "Free" Prices

We have to take up finally the question of price formation in these markets.[53] Very broadly we may say that Makhzen and Siba markets were organized along different lines. Markets in the Makhzen were strictly controlled; prices were fixed by authority and publicly announced; such control permitted fluctuations from month to month, week to week, or even day to day, according to proclamations. In the Siba, on the contrary, evidence points to a much greater freedom of transactions with prices at least to some extent the result of the bargaining of the parties.[54]

Unfortunately, the evidence is one-sided. The Makhzen is fully documented; price lists are available over long periods of time and even the organization of trade is fairly well known. In regard to the Siba we are almost completely in the dark. Our authors offer merely vague statements; not a single detailed description of activities in a typical Siba market is in evidence.

In the Makhzen cities the prices of goods—especially foodstuffs, necessities, textiles, etc.—are set by proclamation of an official delegated by the central authority, the *muhtasib*. His rates are decided upon after consultation with wholesalers and taking into account the prices paid by these to the producers. Once the official rates are proclaimed, nobody is allowed to sell at a higher price although underselling is allowed. The Makhzen prices remain therefore partly a function of the prices paid in the wholesale markets. In these markets, rural and regional, the prices were arrived at by free transactions and by auctioning. Lower prices were obtained whenever wholesale transactions were concluded through long-term operations, the brokers buying up the crops in advance.

The Siba markets resented the presence of such rural wholesale markets in the making, since they themselves were often supply markets for the towns. Further, the complicated organization which in the

Makhzen was responsible for the setting of prices, and which involved consultations with wholesalers, examinations of the merchandise, punishments for the infractors, and a minute policing of the market places, could hardly be expected from the fickle and transitory political equilibrium of the Siba markets, which moreover lacked the specific administrative machineries of control.[55] Thus, if some of the Siba markets served, as we have said, as supply markets for the towns, yet wholesaling of crops by the Berber peasants to the town brokers did not set the latter's prices, for the wholesale operations and the urban retail sales belonged to two different orders of things. It happened often, then, that although the rural markets supplied the towns, their own subsequent retail prices rose higher than in the Makhzen cities.

Speculation by manipulating the supply was not an unknown phenomenon in the Morocca of pre-Protectorate days. Its effects were, however, not much felt. In the cities and towns of the Makhzen, the organization was based on a policy of protecting the consumers by fixing the retail price of foodstuffs and other necessities. Wherever such organization was lacking, as in the Siba, speculation could not be controlled to the same extent; but there the consequences of hoarding and of manipulating the supplies of necessities were, in the nature of things, much less grave for most consumers were also producers of the same necessities. However, even in the Siba the possibility of speculation appeared in some cases as potentially dangerous. The Kabyles, for one, were ready to cope with this problem, and there is no reason why we should exclude similar restrictive measures in many other of the socially compact tribes or districts of North Africa. Temporary scarcity was met by rationing. As Hanoteau and Letourneux put it, "Trade is almost always free. In wartime when communications are interrupted or inadequate, the *djema'a* fixes the ration of grain that any person may buy at any one time. Similar measures are taken if the roads are blocked by snowfall or there is a failure of crops; in this latter case able-bodied adults must wait their turn until the sick, expectant or recently confined women have been provided for."[56]

The implications of such *ad hoc* rationing are far-reaching. It presupposes a high measure of market discipline on the part of the general public; also it establishes a strong presumption in favor of a practice of set prices for the staple and interchangeable necessities of life.

Abuses of the freedom of transactions were punished. To dissuade competitors from buying, either by gifts or promises, is not an offense in itself among the Kabyles, but "he who runs down the merchandise out of malice, or with intent of purchasing himself at a cheaper rate, is fined 5 duros if it turns out that the merchandise did not suffer from the shortcomings he had asserted."[57] From this interesting provision it is further evident that norms of fair bargaining were obtained.

In the matter of prices, then, we cannot say that the evidence is very satisfactory. We do not possess any exact details of the bargained prices and of the specific price-mechanisms which functioned in the Siba. Yet there are sufficient indications which point to the fact that these were mostly of the "free" type, and that spontaneous price fluctuations were a widespread feature. Nevertheless the limitation of business ventures to those of the peddler-trade type carried on through barter indicates that profit was taken more on the side of trade, i.e., carrying, than on price differentials in the market itself. The Berber mountain markets, however, remain in economic anthropology one of the rare cases which may approach to bargained market prices for daily necessities. The extent to which they do this may well be related to the fact that attitudes in markets were formed in an implicit system of cultural and social conventions wherein freedom could manifest itself in a pattern of action.

Conclusions

In-group reciprocity and out-group market exchanges are the two most obvious forms of integration which obtain in this society.[58] Their co-existence seems to go hand in hand with the communal, individualistic and segmented traits of a culture of which Hanoteau and Letourneux said that "nowhere else could we find such a combination which is nearer equality and farther from communism."[59] The reciprocal exchanges, to be sure, bolster the communal feelings of interdependency in a community.[60] Planting or harvesting are often done communally, especially if a family is short of hands for the occasion. The solicited help received is returned in kind; also he who receives help is host to all who worked for him. The resulting scheme of reciprocally co-operative interaction comprises the whole community. Such work-bees do not exhaust the forms of interpersonal relations of Berber society. The individual is by no means submerged in the group and occasionally he can be the sole beneficiary of reciprocative communal behavior.[61] Nevertheless the large field of Berber market exchanges is the ground for the expression of individualistic tendencies.

The Berber combination of in-group reciprocity and individualism is made possible because the society is "free" in the sense that the groups which compose it are not related except "freely" to one another. No higher center enforces the unity of the whole—this most basic feature of Berber society, its absence of any political, urban or social center and its lack of any centralization, is so fraught with consequences that we have to stop for a moment in their analysis. The idea of centralization has penetrated our thought to the point that whenever we find a society where it is absent, we are prone to interpret that society incorrectly and to misjudge it for living in a chaos. As E. Masqueray said of the Berbers: ". . . des populations qui n'ont aucune idée, aucun sentiment, qui ne soit l'inverse des nôtres, ne doivent pas être étudiés avec des idée préconçues."[62]

The only comparison which comes to mind for Berber society is one of the utopian anarchist schemes of a Proudhon, Bakunin or Kropotkin. Even there, given the relationships of which the social philosopher is aware, the utopian, like the modern social scientist, is always inclined to confuse organization with central authority. He is likely to assume, for instance, that a change in population density or numbers necessarily means a complete change in the constitution or structure of society. Bakunin himself—even if it was in the temporary need of launching the revolution—thought it necessary to combine a system of federations of workingmen forming, in the language of the time, free pacts with one another, with a central executive revolutionary body which controlled them. This has been the traditional set-up of the anarchist movements down to the present, deeply affecting the doctrine.

Nevertheless, empirically, when centralization is truly absent or only exists in embryo, as is the case here, a change in numbers, for instance, will not readily change the quality of social organization. Society may also develop—as the ethnographic record best shows—along the lines which this very lack of centrality permits. This is the case of

Berber society which, like the phoenix, is reborn. The absence of a center makes for a system of balances which can regenerate, and in fact has often done so. Sporadically centralization has taken on importance among the Berbers. Nevertheless, every time these new sovereignties were destroyed, decentralized and locally autonomous institutions regained their force as if nothing had happened. They emerged once again, as before, into a wide cultural integration through their inherent system of out-group balances and in-group reciprocities. And alongside them, the economic constitution which fitted that decentralization and balanced integration reappeared. Market exchanges revived and eventually the closed fabric of village and cantonal life was counterbalanced. If markets were wiped out, maybe as a result of warfare, the balance would tip over to the other side, and in-group reciprocities in village, kinship and canton would be strengthened.

All this, in the last resort, is possible because, due to the lack of centrality, there is an interplay of two types of behavior which can alternate and find a natural setting in the in-group vs. out-group dichotomy. This society has a double *facies*, an alternance of reciprocative forms and of free individualizing forms. The social anthropologist may be at pains to work out the two faces presented in village and market. To the economist this duality appears in a greatly simplified form: whenever the first *facies*, that of the village, comes to the fore, economic behavior is reciprocative; when the second *facies* comes up, in out-group customs of pilgrimages, safe-conducts, travel and trade, exchange and market dominate the economic scene. If the individual ventures out of the district, he is safeguarded only by the customs which govern markets and market places and he himself acts individually—an economic man of market mentality. His personality is limited by the nature of his "free" pacts with the other members of his group in this society and by the contexts, the one reciprocative and bound, the other individualizing and free, which his society and culture provide. Note that no allowance is made at the villages for a disrupting bargaining behavior. It is only at the markets that legislation favors individual action. That both these contexts of Berber life are institutionalized into physically separate places of action, village and markets, is important indeed. If they were not, these contraries would come to a head-on collision.

If we look again at the market as we saw it, this situation has curious consequences. First, there was the lack of specific administrative stipulations of internal control of price, motive, or marketing action. It was the context itself, the market peace, which had to be safeguarded and explicitly rigged. Secondly, in the absence of such internal controls, the markets, one would assume, may be on the way to becoming free markets with free and fluctuating prices. This happens, however, only to a point, for essentially they are still merely places where supplies are in fact exchanged by producers against supplies fitted for consumption. They are, in other words, transformation centers which do not acquire an acting power of their own, and where therefore marketing continues to be limited. Thus the markets may threaten the communal fabric of the society, but only within bounds, which again ensures the permanence of the duality of village and market. With this crucial reservation, markets are here external places for exchanges between individuals who are shedding the corporate personality of which they were a part within township and village. One may wonder if this combination of individual behavior and marginal intergroup location is not, where it occurs, a compound which tends to result out of the working of the market institution.

Francisco Benet

Notes to Chapter X

1. The word is believed to have been first used in North Africa as an official term in the 2nd century A.H., applied to an iron chest in which Ibrahim i. al Aghlab, emir of Ifriqiya, kept the collected taxes.

2. Cf. E. Michaux-Bellaire, article "Makhzen," *Encyclopedia of Islam*.

3. For a discussion of the typicalities of these two worlds cf. C. S. Coon, *Caravan*, pp. 263 ff.

4. B. Montagne, *Berbères et Makhzen*, p. 153.

5. *Ibid.*, p. 162–163.

6. Cf. Robin, "Fetna Meriem," *Revue Africaine*, XVIII, no. 105 (mai-juin 1874) 173; cf. E. Doutté, *Merrakech*, p. 141; also, H. Basset, *Literature des Berbères*, p. 94, where he says: "En Kabylie plus souvent qu'ailleurs il arrive que la coûtume reconnaisse, á côté des individus, l'ensemble en tant qu'état. . . . Un citoyen n'a pas le droit de ne pas assister au marché, n'eût-il rien à scheter ni à vendre."

7. Hanoteau et Letourneux, *Kabylie*, III, 65.

8. Robin, loc. cit.

9. E. Doutte, Merrakech, p. 144.

10. De Segonzac, Au coeur de l'Atlas, p. 162.

11. G. Wysner, The Kabyle People, p. 131–132.

12. E. Michaux-Bellaire, Le Gharb, p. 229.

13. Abridged from a Berber text translated by E. Laoust, Mots et choses Berbères, p. 102–104.

14. Ibid., p. 308, note 25.

15. Ch. de Foucauld, Reconnaissance au Maroc, p. 126.

16. W. Marçais, Tanger, p. 129.

17. This applies both to organized political states and to tribal societies.

18. Hanoteau et Letourneux, op. cit., II, 57; cf. G. Wysner, p. 144.

19. For the muna cf. R. Maunier, Coûtumes Algeriennes, pp. 65–66; also E. Daumas, La vie arabe et la société musulmane, pp. 449–457.

20. R. Naunier, "Les groups d'interêt en Afrique du Nord," p. 45. Probably Naunier mistakes here an uza between friends for a muna.

21. W. Fogg, "A Moroccan Tribal Shrine and its relation to a near-by Tribal Market." Also Folklore, Vol. 51 (June, 1940). In the market of Sidi el Yemani (Djebala) after the wheat harvest there is every year an important mussem at this shrine. The grain is disposed of.

22. This cyclic organization has been studied by E. Michaux-Bellaire, "Le Gharb"; L. Massignon for Fez, Ênquête sur les corporations musulmanes, pp. 97–98, and the Dukkala, Le Maroc au XVIe siècle d'aprés Léon l'Africaine, p. 116; for the Djebala and Anjera regions of Spanish Morocco by Walter Fogg, "Tribal markets in Spanish Morocco," Journal of the Royal Asiatic Society (July, 1939) pp. 322–26 and "The importance of tribal markets in the commercial life of the countryside of Northwestern Morocco," Africa, XI, 4 (1938).

23. G. Wysner, op. cit., p. 130.

24. I. Biarnay, "Un cas de regression vers la coûtume Berbère dans une tribu arabisée," fasc. 4, p. 221, note 1.

25. Hanoteau et Letourneux, op. cit., II, 65.

26. Cf. for instance de Segonzac, Au coeur de l'Atlas, pp. 68–69.

27. Hanoteau et Letourneux, op. cit., II, 77.

28. R. Montagne, op. cit., p. 252.

29. Ibid., p. 253.

30. Michaux-Bellaire et G. Salmon, "Les tribus arabas de la vallée du Lekkous," Archives Marocaines, VI (1906), 257–258.

31. Ibid., pp. 261–262.

32. R. Montagne, op. cit., p. 261.

33. Hanoteau et Letourneux, op. cit., III, 47.

34. Boissier, Afrique Romaine, p. 149; quoted by Montagne, Berbères et Makhzen, p. 231.

35. Ubach and Rackow, Sitte und Recht in Nordafrika, pp. 130–132. The money of the grand auction feeds the treasury of the village (Dorfgeldkiste).

36. R. Montagne, op. cit., p. 253.

37. To a lesser extent the cults and pilgrimages of religion function likewise, of course.

38. Hanoteau et Letourneux, op. cit., III, 303.

39. Ibid.

40. Ibid., p. 79.

41. I. Biarnay, op. cit., p. 221.

42. M. Morand, *Études de droit Musulman et de droit coutumier Berbère,* pp. 314–315.

43. Hanoteau et Letourneux, *op. cit.,* II, 80.

44. A. Hanoteau, *Essai de Grammaire Kabyle, Règlement du Village de Thaslent,* pp. 321–328.

45. R. Montagne, "Une tribu berbère su Sud-Marocain, Massat"; also, M. Ben Daoud, "Recueil du droit coûtumier de Massat." Montagne et Ben Daoud, "Documents pour servier a l'histoire due droit coûtumier du Sud-Marocain."

46. Cf. R. Maunier, *Coûtumes Algeriennes,* p. 44 ff. The Post Office at Fort National, in the middle of Kabyle country, receives the largest number of money remittances from France in North Africa.

47. Qanun of the tribe of the Ait b. Youcef (village of Taourirt Amran), Hanoteau et Letourneux, *op. cit.,* III, 429, art. 8.

48. Qanun of the villages of Taourirt Abdallah and Adrar Amellal, Hanoteau et Letourneux, *op. cit.,* III, 342, art. 20.

49. E. Daumas, *Moeurs et coûtumes de l'Algérie,* pp. 183–184.

50. Hanoteau et Letourneux, *op. cit.,* I, 564 ff. Not all the tribes were equally bent on commerce. Those of the left bank of the Sebaau (Illiten, Ait Itswar, Ait Yahyia, Ait Frawcen, Igawawen, Ait Iraten, Ait Sedka, Ait Aissai, Maakha) seem to be so much more than those of the right bank (Ait Djennat, Ait Waguennun, Izerfawen, Iflissen, etc.).

51. *Ibid.,* I, 564, ff.

52. Ch. de Segonzac, *Voyages au Maroc,* p. 221.

53. Market exchanges at set rates (equivalencies) were also known in North Africa, but only in the desert regions. It seems to be proper only with the Arab nomadic tribes. The equivalency of barley against dates, for instance, would alter progressively travelling from North to South.

54. R. Maunier, *Loi Francaise etûtume indigène en Algérie,* pp. 137–138; *Kabylie, op. cit.,* III, 397.

55. It is a pity that most travellers have not given more attention to prices. It is understandable that they were unable to record the index of fluctuation of the market prices from market day to market day, for their weekly nature made it difficult for travelers to attend these markets more than once.

56. Hanoteau et Letourneux, *op. cit.,* III, p. 268.

57. Qanun of the Ait Frawsen, art. 94, Hanoteau et Letourneux, *op. cit.,* III, 393.

58. It can be argued that householding is the most important form of integration in this society, but as it always applies to a group smaller than society, it does not encompass all the systems of relationship found there.

59. Hanoteau et Letourneux, *op. cit.,* II, 468.

60. We have briefly described customs such as the *muna* and *usa.* The *twiza* is bee-work and it is so fundamental that it almost makes unnecessary the existence of a labor market. For the *twiza* cf. E. Laoust, *Mots et choses Berbères,* p. 322 ff.; J. Bourrilly, *Éléments d'ethnographie Marocaine,* p. 153 ff.; E. Richardot, *Notes sur la touiza: essay d'utilisation de la touiza dans un but mutualiste;* R. Richardot, *La mutualité agricole des indigènes de l'Algérie;* R. Maunier, *La construction collective de la maison en Kablie,* etc.

61. Cf. the *tawsa* rituals, a sort of gift-exchange by which the individual obtains cash at certain specific occasions (weddings, births, etc.) at high interest and in mutualistic fashion.

62. E. Masqueray, *Comparaison des dialectes,* Introduction, p. 5.

Bibliography to Chapter X

Basset, H., *Essai sur la littérature des Berbères*. Alger, bonel, 1920.

Ben Daoud, M., "Recueil du droit coûtumier de Massat." *Hesperis*, 1924.

Ben Daoud, M. and Montagne, R., "Documents pour servir a l'étude du droit coûtumier du Sud-Marocain." *Hesperis*, 1927.

Biarnay, I., "Un cas de regression vers la coûtume Berbère chez une tribu arabisée." *Archives Berbères*, I, 1916.

Boulifa, "Le Kanoun d'Adni," *Travaux et Memoires publiés en l'honneur du XIVe Congrès des Orientalistes par l'École Supérieure des Lettres d'Alger*, 1905.

Bourrilly, J., *Éléments d'Ethnographie Marocaine*. Paris, 1932.

Coon, C. S., *Caravan: the Story of the Middle East*. New York, 1953.

Daumas, E., *Moeurs et coûtumes de l'Algérie*. Paris, 1853.

——, *La vie arabe et la société musulmane*. Paris, 1869.

Doutte, E., *Merrakech, Comité du Maroc*. 1905.

Dresch, J., *Commentaries des cartes sur les genres de vie de montagne dans le massif central du Grand-Atlas*. Tours, 1941.

Fogg, W., "A Tribal Market in Spanish Morocco," *Africa*, XII, n. 4, 1939.

——, "A Moroccan Tribal Shrine and its relation to a near-by Tribal Market," *Man*, 1940, n. 124.

Foucauld, Ch. de, *Reconnaissance au Maroc*, 1883–1884. Paris, 1888.

Hanoteau, A., "Essai de Grammaire Kabyle." Alar, n.d.

Hanoteau, A. and Letourneux, *La Kabylie et les coûtumes Kabyles*. 3 vols. Paris, 1872–73.

Laoust, E., *Mots et choses Berbères*. Paris, 1920.

Luc, B., *Le droit Kabyle*. Toulouse, 1911.

Marçais, W., *Textes Arabes de Tanger*. Bibliothèque de l'École des Langues Orientales Vivantes. Paris, 1911.

Maunier, R., *La Construction collective de la maison en Kabylie*. Institut d'ethnographie de l'Université de Paris, n. 3, 1926.

——, "Recherches sur les échanges rituels en Afrique du Nord," *Année Sociologique*, nouvelle série, 1924/25. Paris, 1927.

——, *Loi Française et Coûtume indigène en Algérie*. Paris, Domat-Montchrestien, 1932.

——, *Coûtumes Algériennes*. Paris, Domat-Montchrestien, 1935.

——, "Les groups d'interêt en Afrique du Nord," in *Annals Sociologiques*, coll. de *L'Année Sociologique*, fasc. 2. Paris, 1937.

Michaux-Bellaire, E. and Salmon, G., "El Qcar el Kabir: Une ville de province au Maroc septentrional," *Archives Marocaines*, II, 1905.

——, "Les tribus arabes de la vallée du Lekkous," *Archives Marocaines*, VI, 1906.

Michaux-Bellaire, "Le Gharb," *Archives Marocaines*, XX, 1913.

——, "Makhzen," in *Encyclopedia of Islam*.

Montagne, R., "Le regime juridique des tribus de Sud-Marocain." *Hesperis*, 1924.

——, "Une tribu berbère du Sud-Marocain: Massat." *Hesperis*, 1924.

——, *Les Berbères et le Makhzen dans le Sud du Maroc*. Paris, 1930.

Morand, M., *Études de droit Musulman et de droit coûtumier Berbère*. Alger, 1931.

Richardot, E., *Notes sur la touiza*. Alger, 1909.

——, *La mutualité agricole des indigènes de l'Algérie*. Paris, 1935.

Robin, "Fetna Meriem," *Revue Africaine*, XVIII, n. 105, 1874.
de Segonzac, Marquis, *Voyages au Maroc, 1899–1901*. Paris.
——, *Au Coeur de l'Atlas, Mission au Maroc, 1904–1905*. Paris, 1905.
Ubach, E. and Rackow, E., *Sitte und Recht in Nordafrika*. Stuttgart, 1923.
Wysner, G., *The Kabyle People*. New York, 1945.

XI

Reciprocity and Redistribution in the Indian Village: Sequel to Some Notable Discussions

THE discipline of economic history has to deal with many areas and many periods in which productive and distributive activities do not depend on buying and selling or the concept of economic efficiency. The economic activities of such nonmarket societies can present themselves in bewildering complexity unless we possess some broad exploratory approach as an alternative to the market theorem. In the case of the Indian village the need for such nonmarket alternatives has been recognized by a succession of students, but a satisfactory solution requires positive patterns of a nonmarket type. This chapter will show how some of the intractable aspects of the village economy yield to the concepts of reciprocity and redistribution.

The Indian village has been described as precapitalistic, as having a barter economy, a subsistence economy, or as being communistic or collectivistic. However, "precapitalistic" tells us only that it is not capitalistic, and implies a sequence with teleological overtones. A "barter economy" refers to the absence of money, and is, as we shall see, misleading. A "subsistence economy" means only that the main occupation is agriculture, and usually implies poverty. As for "communistic," the term is vague. It is not used in the sense of modern variants of

Marxism, but refers to a state of affairs in which both none and all are owners. While the term "collectivistic" recognizes this difficulty by implying that public property requires some definite organization in order to function, it still does not tell us much about specific economic operations. In any case no explanations or descriptions starting from such concepts can develop a set of formal principles showing how the production of goods is organized and how the goods are distributed. All these terms serve merely to stress the absence of certain market institutions in the village system, and while the denial of the existence of the market is correct, no frame of reference for positive description or analysis is offered by them.

The problem of describing the Indian village economy was attacked chiefly by a succession of British administrators of India who had practical purposes in mind, and then by Sir Henry Maine.

From the beginning of the nineteenth century the village community and its economic structure has been a subject of serious consideration. In 1819 Holt Mackenzie, a revenue officer of the East India Company's Bengal administration, submitted a minute on the various forms of land tenure to be found in the newly acquired districts to the northwest of Bengal. His analysis was inspired by the practical desire for a simple, sure, and yet just way of assessing and collecting revenue. The administrators were faced with the task of raising the revenue and had to work out the technical means to that end. In order to develop an affective revenue system they had to place responsibility for payment on particular persons or groups, and a knowledge of the village structure was necessary in order to decide who these persons or groups should be.

There were two considerations. First, the Company had but few officers to administer a very large territory. Responsibility had to be placed where assessment and collection required the least direct supervision and framed in such a way that enforcement would be easy, if not automatic. This consideration reinforced a natural bent to model India after the system existing in the English countryside. Second, equity required that those who enjoyed rights in the land and its produce should be protected in those rights. Further, it required that those who were made responsible for payment of the revenue should have a chance to profit from their responsibilities so long as they did not do so at the expense of the customary privileges of those placed

under them in the revenue hierarchy. This second consideration reinforced the tendency to regard Indian rural areas as counterparts to the
hierarchical system in the English countryside, where it could be fairly
said that the squirearchy did protect its tenants while profiting from
their own position. In order to accomplish these aims the officers of
the Company had to be certain that they knew who controlled the produce of the village, and thus would be able to meet the demands of
the revenue administration, and they also had to know what rights and
obligations attached to other members of the community.

The scope of the problem was but slowly realized. In the latter part
of the eighteenth and the first decade of the nineteenth century the
Company had simply contracted with local personages of power, or
revenue farmers, but unrest and dissatisfaction soon showed that stability of the revenue and economy of administration could only be
achieved in the long run if the officers of the Company understood the
true relationships obtaining among the native villagers. It was for these
reasons that Holt Mackenzie set forth the traditional rights and duties
of those living on the land in north western Provinces.

In addition to the considerations governing the administration of
the revenue, the British were faced with a policy decision of how to
divide between the Company and other claimants the economic return attributable to land. Until this matter of principle was settled, a
permanent system could not be devised. The problem was phrased in
terms of ownership. It was accepted as axiomatic that some person or
group of persons "owned" the land, and, equally, that whoever owned
the land had a right to the economic rent, or, as it was then called, the
"net assets" resulting from the productivity of the land. Thus a decision on a matter of policy—how high the land revenue assessment
should be—came largely to rest on the answer to a question of law:
whether the ruler and his heirs, the Company, or certain private persons or groups of persons owned the land.

The decision did not, however, rest on the legal question alone. It
was no less important to keep consistently to some practical ideal of
rural organization. A persistent aim of the British was to create a native
landed gentry. That the Company's servants thought in terms of the
English system of landlord, farmer, and agricultural laborer is shown
by the Permanent Settlement of Bengal. The Permanent Settlement
was a fixing in perpetuity of the amount of land revenue due from those
whom the British recognized as owners. The belief was that these

owners would use the profits of their privileged position to develop the countryside and bring prosperity to agriculture.

The ideas which the British brought to India were out of tune with the actual relationships of Indian cultivators and artisans. The British found themselves committing one error after another and thereby compounding their difficulties in administering a foreign land. Instead of finding landlords and tenants operating through a system of prices, bargaining, and contracts, the British found a maze of caste and custom regulating inter-family relationships. Where the British expected to find an owner they found a profusion of overlapping claims.

These questions came to the attention of scholars with the publication of Sir Henry Maine's work.[1] His original interest lay in the history of Roman legal institutions. In examining the laws and customs of ancient Hindu society he wanted at first merely to illustrate the structure of early Roman law. He found support for his interpretation of Roman law as primarily interfamilial by analogy with Hindu law and custom, and argued that the Hindu village was the prototype of the family system of ancient Rome and early Europe. Reaching out from Roman law to Hindu law, Maine found his interests leading him into a comparative jurisprudence encompassing not only Roman and Hindu law, but also early Germanic law and the Brehon Code of ancient Ireland.

As Maine's interests spread over a wider geographical area, so also did they spread over a wider area of social thought. From an interest in the development of Western personal and property law the pursuit of origins brought him insights into the structure of the Eastern village community. The invaluable contribution to economic history came with his proof that the Indian village economy did not center on the market; that in fact some new frame of reference was needed in which to discuss its characteristics. Maine himself made the fundamental differentiation between status society and contract society—a distinction which proved extraordinarily fruitful, yet still failed to indicate the variety of institutions of a status nature or to spell out the formal arrangements that status economies may use.

Maine recognized that the Hindu village was a closed unit with rights and obligations of its own. It was made up of extended or joint family groups and castes whose legal and economic relationships were interfamilial rather than interpersonal. Our conception of property rights, and consequently of alienability, sale, and market relationships was not applicable to a system organized on principles of a religio-legal nature.

The Hindu village as pictured by Maine has since been criticized as inaccurate in detail,[2] but the general direction of his argument is not open to question. The importance of his discoveries lay in their emphasis upon the corporate unity of the village economy, upon its system of collective responsibility, and above all on status as a rationale of motivation, and as the principle on which the village economy was organized and integrated. The problem of the structure of the village community thus centered on the question of how precisely status was used to organize its economy.

While the range of interests encompassed by the work of Sir Henry Maine and the work of British administrators extended from practical questions of establishing responsibility for the payment of revenue to comparative jurisprudence, they never engaged in a formal analysis of the principles of economic integration of the village economy. Maine and his successors were interested in law and rights, while the administrators did not feel called upon to move beyond solutions to their immediate concern with finding a workable system for collecting the revenue and dividing the return from land between the ruler and the ruled. Once the impact of British administration itself had altered original native conditions the problems of administration were so deeply affected by past British actions that an analysis of the "native state of affairs" must have appeared to the practical administrator as of academic interest only.

The intention of this paper is to show that the structure of the village economy and the nature of land revenue can be far better explained by the concepts of reciprocity and redistribution* than they can by the more usual terms of economic theory or by the vaguer terms of pre-capitalistic, barter, or subsistence economy.

Reciprocity means that members of one group act towards members of another group as members of that group or a third or fourth group act toward them. There is no implication of equality, justice, or the golden rule. Rather, reciprocity implies only that there is a two-way or round-the-circle flow of goods as exemplified in the Melanesian Kula ring or the Trobriand Islanders' fish and yams transfer between coastal and inland villages. The groups are mutually self-supporting in regard to the articles involved in the reciprocative relationship.

* See Ch. XIII.

Redistribution means that the produce of the group is brought together, either physically or by appropriation, and then parcelled out again among the members. Again there is no implication of equality of treatment, fair shares, or payment for value. The social pattern is characterized by centricity—peripheral points all connected with the central point.

The symmetrical patterns of reciprocative relationships may merge with the centralized pattern of redistributive relationships, as with the Trobriand Islanders, where the king is the redistributive center of a large number of reciprocative relationships with the brothers of his many wives.

In putting these concepts to use in the patterning of empirical economies it must be understood that reciprocity and redistribution do not provide classifications for economies as a whole, for both kinds of relationships may be found in the same economy, either in regard to different goods or in regard to different groups of people. The different relationships of the various groups can be patterned on one or the other, or sometimes both principles. The strength of these concepts lies in their ability to reduce complex relationships to simple patterns. As shall appear, the maze of relationships in the Indian village economy can be set out in terms of reciprocity and redistribution applied to the groups that make up the village as well as to the main goods and services.

Two focal points in the workings of the village economy have so far resisted analysis. The one concerns the economic structure of the village; the other refers to the nature of land revenue, its source and its position in the village economy.

The Village Economy

The three main bodies of Indian social organization were the *joint family*, made up of related members, numbering up to a hundred or more; the *village*, essentially a grouping of such families; and the *castes*. The family generally was a self-sufficient unit under the direction of its head or its senior members. Where special skills or certain specific services were required, it could call on the village artisans, servants, or priests. The basic political and social unit was the village. Within its confines almost all economic needs were satisfied. The caste system was much wider than the village and its lines cut across village lines. It was founded upon religious sanction. Over these basic units ebbed and flowed the surf of political life. Sometimes it was the life of empires such as the Gupta and Mughal Empires. More often it was organized in petty kingdoms varying in size from the area of a New England township to a very few square miles.

In eighteenth-century Oudh[3] we find a society in which the cultivators are "independent of each other, but connected through village heads, and the villages also independent among themselves, but joined in allegiance to a common Raja; the basis of the whole society being the grain heap, in which each constituent rank had its definite interest."[4] The village did not hold its lands in common but it did have common officials and servants: watchman, headman, clerk, blacksmith, carpenter, herdsman, washerman, barber, priest, and potter. These officials and servants received their remuneration in a share of the cultivators' grain heaps.

Production of food, the main material item in Indian life, was the business of the joint agricultural family. The officials and servants saw to their jobs, doing the appropriate work as and where it was needed. Throughout the year there was no exchange or payment for services rendered. The herdsman watched the cows and the blacksmith made the implements and repaired any ploughs that broke. Each activity was carried on according to the custom and tradition of the village and within the joint family according to its traditions, station in life, and the judgment of its head.

At harvest time the means of subsistence for the rest of the year were distributed. The system of allotting shares in the gross produce of the village was highly complex, yet it did not require any previous knowledge of total gross produce to be divided among the members of the community. While the exact arrangements in the division and distribution of the produce varied from place to place, we may take as a typical example the system recorded by W. C. Bennett.[5]

Distribution in Gonda took place in three stages: From the standing crop; from the undivided grain heap of each cultivator; and from the heaps after the cultivator had contributed to the Raja's heap.

From the standing crop of each cultivator the watchman, the blacksmith, the carpenter, the herdsman, the priest, and often the cultivator himself cut a twentieth of a bigha.[6] Next, the crop was harvested and threshed by the whole community, the grain from the fields of each cultivator being heaped in a separate pile on the community threshing floor. The "slave-ploughman"[7] took a share varying from a fifth to a seventh of the heap of the cultivating family to which he was attached. To this share he added a *panseri*.[8] From each pile each person who had cut or threshed the crop (and this meant everyone) took a sixteenth of the rice and the "fattest sheaf in thirty" of the other crops. Then the carpenter, blacksmith, barber, washerman, and watchman each took twelve *panseris* of threshed grain from each cultivator for each four-bullock plough he owned, and six *panseris* for each two-bullock plough. When these shares had been passed out the grain heaps were divided in half, the cultivator retaining one half and the other going to the Raja, subject however to further distributions. One *sir*[9] in every maund of the Raja's heap was returned to the cultivator, another *sir* was given to the scribe, a "double handful" to the priest, and a tenth of the remainder was given to the village headman. From the cultivator's remaining heap the blacksmith and carpenter each received three more *panseris*, the herdsman one more, and a *sir* or two went to the scribe.

The matter is certainly intricate. Given all the data it would still be possible, of course, to compute the fraction of the total going to any cultivator or servant or to the Raja, but it is not possible to express it in any formula shorter than several pages in length and utterly unmanageable in practice. The proportions vary with the number, size, and distribution of cultivators' holdings, the number, size and distribution of ploughs, the number of bullocks, the number and distribution of slave-ploughmen, as well as the amount of gross produce. Not only do the deductions depend upon variations among these factors but some of the deductions are stated in proportional and some in absolute terms. Besides the inordinate length and cumbersomeness of the formula, there is the fact that the fraction could still not be converted into actual figures since the total was unknown. But again, here lies the true strength of the system employed.

Despite the numerous factors involved and the unknown total, the system was not confusing to the participants. It was simple to operate precisely because no aggregate data were required. The operational device took care of the problem, and the device is described by the phrases used, such as: "One *sir* in every maund," "one seventh of the heap." Each step in the distribution was carried out separately. If the slave-ploughman was to get a seventh of the heap, six measures were ladled out to the cultivator, and a seventh to the slave until the heap disappeared. With each proportional division the same process was followed, so that at no point was it necessary to know how much grain there was in the heap. The only accurate measures needed were a container for a *panseri* of grain and one for a *sir* of grain.[10] Any measure could be used for the other sharing processes, for all they did was to dispose of the heap, so many measures to this pile, so many to that. By such a simple device a great many claimants were served in a great many different ways without need for accounting. Furthermore, honesty was assured because the distribution was public, taking place under the eyes of the villagers and of the Raja or his representative.

There were built-in devices which assured each villager a minimum income, and which also tended to equalize the incomes of all the villagers. The fixed quantities going to the village servants gave them a basic minimum even if the harvest was so small that their proportional shares would not support them. When the cultivator "pre-harvested" a twentieth of a *bigha* of his own land the proportion of the revenue the small-holder was expected to carry was reduced in the same way that the personal exemption reduces the relative burden of the income tax on the man with a small income. The contribution of a sixteenth of the rice heap and a thirtieth of other crops to the common heap and then dividing the heap equally among all the villagers also tended to equalize incomes since the wealthier contributed more than the poor, while each shared equally.

There was scant regard for economic rationality in the distribution. Some rough approximation to work rendered is indicated in the carpenters' and blacksmiths' shares based upon number and size of ploughs, which were also related to the area protected by the watchmen, but this cannot be said of basing the washerman's and barber's shares on the same criteria. The only approach to payment based on service was that to the herdsman per bullock cared for.

Each villager participated in the division of the grain heap. There was no bargaining, and no payment for specific services rendered. There was no accounting, yet each contributor to the life of the village had a claim on its produce, and the whole produce was easily and successfully divided among the villagers. It was a redistributive system.[11]

Below and above the village level the redistributive pattern continued to prevail. Below, the share remaining to the cultivator's joint family was managed by the head of the family and parcelled out to the members of the family. The handling of the family's share was a matter of administration on a small scale, the principle being redistributive, for the grain was held in common and its consumption was regulated by handing out from the family store.

Above the village level there might be only one or there might be a multiplicity of political authorities, depending on the size of the kingdom and the degree of central control which the king was able to exercise. Whether any economic function was or was not performed by the authorities, the division of the grain heap at the village level was *the* foundation upon which political authority rested. As the size of the kingdom grew the number of intermediate authorities multiplied, although strong kings attempted to eliminate some of them. The ruler's share was distributed among the competing levels of the military and political bureaucracy according to their relative strengths. In a large kingdom with a moderately powerful center, such as the Mughal Empire was at times, there was a hierarchy of redistributive centers with the village grain heap at the bottom and the king's storehouses at the top. In between, the local powers and provincial governors maintained their own storehouses, retaining a share and passing on the remainder to the level above. In regard to grain, the whole political and social structure was founded on redistribution.

Intertwined with the redistributive system of family-village-kingdom was the caste system through which crafts and their services were organized. No contract, no bargaining will account for its structure. It was founded on reciprocity. Every member of each caste contributed his services and skills to the support of every member of the other castes. Its sanction was religious, while its function was largely economic. Rather than a simple dual symmetry, a multiple symmetry underlay the caste system: a large number of groups were sharing out their services among each other although they acted independently. Each caste was economically entirely dependent upon the performance of their duties by the other groups. The members of the society could survive only if each caste did its job for the others, yet each caste remained a "self-governing community" and "set up its own standards of life and conduct."[12] Territorially the castes cut across village and political boundaries and functioned whatever course political life was taking.

Briefly, it can be said that relationships were reciprocative in regard to services, and redistributive in regard to agricultural produce.

But the reciprocative caste system as a whole was itself an element within the redistributive system of the village. The functions of priest, watchman, barber and carpenter were caste functions and it was by virtue of each member of each caste within the village fulfilling his or her religiously sanctioned duties that the grain heap was there to be divided at harvest time. Cultivator-artisan relations might therefore be said to be both reciprocative and redistributive. The artisan was supplying the cultivator with his skills, and the cultivator in turn, and regardless of the specific services the artisan had performed for him, supplied the artisan with agricultural products. At the same time the artisan and the cultivator jointly contributed to the production of a village grain heap which was in turn redistributed to all the residents of the village.

This analysis of the pre-British Indian village shows that formal principles are available to us which are capable of describing a non-market economy. There is no reason why such an economy should be described with negative references or irrelevant ones. An economy is not analyzed by placing it before capitalism in an evolutionary sequence; nor by the mere statement that money is not used. Barter, as a classification, is, if anything, inaccurate, for neither interfamily nor intercaste bargaining was practiced. While there is no disputing the poverty of the Indian villager, the system under which he worked did not depend on the fact that he was at a subsistence level. The same principles were as applicable to the well-to-do village as to the poorer ones, and as applicable to the wealthy rulers as to the peasant cultivators. To call the village economy communistic puts the problem in the wrong light, for our present-day concepts of ownership are here inapplicable. Things were not held in common in the Indian village. Rather, different families as well as other groups had different kinds of rights.

To say that the services in the village economy were patterned out by reciprocity and the grain by redistribution still leaves open for detailed description the particular procedures used and shares received by the participants. However, it does acquaint us with the structure of the manifold village activities so that we perceive how it came about that these activities were made to mesh. More than that, we may also, within reasonable limits, compare the organization of the Indian village economy with the organization of other economies—group by group, product by product and service by service.

The Nature of Land Revenue

The concepts of reciprocity and redistribution will also help to clarify the old problem of where and how land revenue fitted into the structure of the Indian economy. This was, and is, a problem of great practical importance, for the British Raj drew its resources from the land revenue, and today the Indian states still depend upon the same revenue for their development programs. Both ease of, and justice in, administration of the revenue depended upon an accurate appraisal of the nature and function of land revenue.

The question whether to regard land revenue as a rent or as a tax exercised the minds of British administrators for a century.[13] When the East India Company began to govern India in the last half of the eighteenth century land revenue was the major source of revenue for the native rulers. The Company perforce adopted their fiscal system, and set out to rationalize it. Having succeeded to the political position of the native rulers, the Company had also succeeded to their rights to land revenue. It naturally wished to determine the origin, source, and nature of land revenue so as to adjust the assessment and collection of the revenue correctly.

The officers of the East India Company, thinking in European terms, saw only two possibilities, and took the view that their administration of the revenue must depend upon the answer. Land revenue was either a tax on land or it was the rent of the land. If land revenue were in the nature of a tax, then it should be administered according to the canons of taxation, which required that the tax should be as low as possible after allowing for legitimate expenses of government. Any surplus from the land over the costs of management, cultivation, and taxation would then be the property of the owner of the land and should go to him. Assessment of the revenue would then present the problem of an equitable allotment of the gross revenue burden among the owners who were made responsible for payment of the revenue. On the other hand, if land revenue were the rent of the land, then there would be no limit to what the government could claim other than what the traffic would bear. As the owner of the land, the government could claim any surplus over the costs of production, and the rent of land would be a legitimate source of profit to the East India Company. Assessment would in principle be a problem of competitive renting of land holdings, and the government would not have to worry about the equity of each assessment.

While this was the underlying issue of principle in the discussion, three other considerations weighed heavily with the British. Until 1790 the first two of these had shaped policy. One was the absence of a staff of trustworthy civil servants. The other was the great need for revenue.

The absence of a staff made it impossible to attempt a just settlement of the revenue in individual cases, so that the Company had to settle for a rough and ready system requiring neither knowledge nor honesty on the part of those responsible for seeing that the revenue flowed into the Company's coffers.

The great need for revenue meant that the Company felt it had to charge as much as the traffic would bear, no matter what principle was applicable to the revenue. This amounted to the view that the legitimate expenses of government would absorb the whole of the economic rent, and more if that were possible.

Both considerations were met by the system adopted in the early years: the right to collect the revenue was sold by auction, the native tax-farmer being allowed a ten percent allowance for his labor and, in practice, whatever else he could extract from the cultivator. Thus the Company achieved a maximum extraction rate[14] and needed few administrators. However, the system could be justified neither on grounds of equity nor on those of efficiency, and certainly led to widespread dissatisfaction and disaffection.

The third consideration to modify a Company policy based on the solution to the rent *v.* revenue controversy was the belief that a stable landowning class could be created to govern the country-side; that this class would build up the agricultural and natural resources of the area; and that the stability and prosperity so achieved would lead to large trading profits for the Company. This meant taking a long view, anticipating ample future gains at the price of a somewhat reduced tax revenue for the present. It was this consideration, combined with the simplicity of the arrangement and the guarantee of a minimum revenue, that led to the introduction of "permanent settlement" in 1790. Permanent settlement meant that the revenue assessment was fixed in perpetuity, the landowner retaining any future increase of income accruing to the land so long as he paid the assessment.

The policy of permanent settlement was dropped after 1795, but until the late 1860's it was constantly upheld by a sizeable number of Company officials and, later, government officials. Temporary settlements, in which the revenue was fixed for periods up to thirty years were made in the areas west of Bengal as they came under Company government, and the question whether land revenue was a rent or a tax came to the fore.

The specific issue of fact on which the debate over the nature of land revenue turned was whether the Emperor at Delhi was or was not the owner of the land at the time the Company succeeded to his powers. Such a question of absolute property, being one which can only be asked in a market economy, was in the nature of things insoluble. In dividing the grain heap between the Raja, the cultivators, and the artisans there was no need to differentiate between rent and tax—one only needed to know the operational devices by which the Raja's share was determined. Nevertheless, the debate continued for years. In practice, victory went to those who supported the view that land revenue was a tax. Certainly the permanent assessment of Bengal implied that answer, as did the progressive reductions in the share of rents taken as revenue in the districts to the northwest of Bengal.

Did choosing "tax" instead of "rent" make a difference? It is doubtful whether it did. Whatever it deemed to be the correct position, the Company had good reason to reduce the burden of revenue so as to keep the population moderately happy. What did make a difference was the attitude that prompted the question to be put in terms of rent v. tax.

The alternative of rent v. tax stemmed from a deep misunderstanding of the nature of the land revenue. The British administrators were treating land revenue as if it were part and parcel of a market system. Once that assumption is made land revenue must be either rent or tax. If it is rent, land revenue is a return to the inherent productive capacity of the soil and must be measured by the difference between the value of the product and the costs of production, for rent implies that the market evaluates the contribution of land to the productive process. But while in an abstract sense there is always a rent for land because land contributes to the productive process, it is impossible to determine its amount unless there is a market on which people express their judgment of that contribution by offering to pay for its use. They do so by paying a rent. When it became apparent to the British administrators that there was no market for the use of land they made efforts to calculate the amount of rent which would be paid if there were such a market. This is called "imputing economic rent." The effort of course proved unavailing. How can the value of a product be computed when so much of it is consumed by the producer and never reaches the market? What meaning can be attached to computations based on prices that vary widely within an area? How can one compute costs when virtually all the costs are implicit and there is no such thing as a standard wage for agricultural labor? Economic rent is a quantity that requires a market system, and could not therefore have meaning in the context of the Indian village economy.

A decision to regard land revenue as a tax also implied a market. Since government services must employ economic resources and since it may be impossible or undesirable to sell these services on a market, the government must extract a sum from the current income stream, either directly by a tax on payments made, or indirectly on values created by the market. These taxes are generally levied on income, on property, or on transactions. Taxes on income and property are levied as proportions of the value which is arrived at by the "bid and ask" process of the market. Taxes on transactions are either a proportion of the price at which the goods change hands or a flat rate depending on the quantity of goods which change hands. While it is true that the government can raise money by a charge on transactions that are free of market elements, such as a poll-tax, or upon the mere existence of an item, such as "windows in walls," it is generally true that the British had market values and market transfers in mind when they considered taxes.

That the market was implicit in the concept of a tax is shown by the first attempts at assessing the land revenue. Assiduous efforts were made to compute the "net assets" of estate in land. These were to be computed by deducting from the gross value of the produce the costs of production including wages of labor and profits on capital. Now, the remainder, the net assets, is by definition economic rent. For the reasons outlined above the attempts to compute net assets were never successful. Eventually, the British administration fell back on going by rule of thumb, and simply tried to find out how much the owner responsible for the payment of land revenue was collecting from his tenants, and then charging him with part of the rent.

That land revenue was not a straightforward tax was further illustrated by the problems associated with the various proposed methods of levying it. The main proposals were that land revenue be regarded as a share in the gross produce of the land, either in kind or in money value; a money share in the net produce of the land (i.e., the economic rent); or, finally, a money share in the rents actually collected by the proprietor.[15] All three met difficulties in administration and in a just application of the principle invoked.

A share in kind is difficult to collect, and for a modern government there is the added problem of converting the produce into money. These were not problems for the earlier rulers. In the first place, the taking of a share in kind fitted neatly into the common village harvest and distribution. Secondly, it was evidence of the prerogatives and power of the ruler. Thirdly, the ruler did not need or wish to convert his share into money until well into the Mughal period. The British, on the other hand, did not desire to fit into the village distribution in the personal way in which the Raja did, and furthermore were simultaneously engaged in market trading activities and did not want a share in kind. Eventually, as the concepts of British law and the produce of British industry entered the village, the redistributive system lost much of its relevance. The share of the grainheap, whether in kind or in money, did not accurately reflect ability to pay, and the British did not wish to be affected by the fluctuations in income which such a sharing system involved. If the share of gross produce were to be taken in money there would be the trouble of estimating the produce and arriving at a price for conversion into money values, in the absence of a market.

A tax based on economic rent could only prove impossible to assess. It is noteworthy that after nine years of effort in the north western Provinces, the Company's officers observed that it might take another half century to compute the economic rents for the rest of the province.

Land revenue based on the rents actually paid, which was the compromise the British finally adopted, was obviously inequitable. In addition, its computation was so burdensome that the assessments were revised only every thirty years. At best, the rents reflected values as of the time the leases were made, but as a rule the actual amounts charged in rent were affected by caste, local custom, and to no small degree, by favoritism. Unless these extraneous considerations were eliminated, the actual rents would not reflect the ability of the various holdings to pay revenue. A complex set of rules therefore came into being to guide the officers in their attempts to adjust the recorded rents. These rules boiled down to a general rule that the officer assessing the revenue should try to adjust recorded rents to the rents at which a genuinely competitive market would arrive. However, a tax on economic rent or actual rents paid is not the same as in income tax, and the British system has been criticized on the grounds that taxes on rent are not taxes based on ability to pay, nor can it be shown that they are equitable according to any other generally accepted standard.

The fact of the matter is that land revenue cannot be levied in such a way as to satisfy the canons of taxation as understood in the modern world. It is not a tax on values created by the market nor is it a tax on transactions. The incidence of a tax should be foreseeable if it is to be just. Yet the incidence of land revenue is not foreseeable. Even under the original native system the revenue share of the Raja lacked this characteristic. One could alter the shares in the grain heap so as to give certain participants more, but the ultimate effect of merely changing the Raja's share was anything but obvious. Consequently the efforts to adapt the native system to British conceptions of taxation was fraught with difficulties.

These perpetual difficulties which beset the British had their roots in their misconception that land revenue was a tax like any other tax commonly levied where a market system obtains. The picture of the village economy as presented in the preceding section shows the correct answer to be that land revenue formed part of a nonmarket system. Taxes are affected by, and in turn affect, the working of the price mechanism, but land revenue under the Mughals and before left unaffected the cultivator's choice of crops, his methods of cultivation, and his reciprocative and redistributive relationships with the village artisans. The cultivator's decisions were made prior to, and independently of, the assessment of land revenue. The solution was, then, that land revenue was the ruler's share in the produce of the land under a redistributive system. It is not a phenomenon of the market order and cannot be translated into market terms. To ask whether land revenue was a rent or a tax was to misconstrue the economic organization of pre-British India. It falsely assumed that the use of market terminology would prove revealing; actually employment of such terminology clouded the issue. To understand the nature of land revenue one must understand the original native system: here the patterning of the economy in terms of reciprocity and redistribution can alone provide a clear picture.

Sir Henry Maine first presented to Western scholars a picture of the village economy. He characterized it as a "status" as opposed to a "contract" economy. While there can be nothing but admiration for this seminal insight, it left unanswered the question of the principles upon which some seemingly intractable problems of status economies rested. Yet once a pattern of these status relationships is drawn, the concepts of reciprocity and redistribution reveal the comparatively simple devices for distributing services and their products.

These concepts also throw light on the underlying difficulties which have dogged the efforts of modern administrations to adopt and adapt the devices of a redistributive economy to the market system. The land revenue which was the raja's share in the village grain heap became the foundation stone of British fiscal resources in India, and is still today a major source of government revenue. Even in our time no generally satisfactory system for assessing and collecting this tax has been found.

A scheme for patterning nonmarket economic activities such as is suggested here is needed, if we are to understand institutions and devices which have their origin in nonmarket economies.

Walter C. Neale

Notes to Chapter XI

1. Sir Henry Sumner Maine, *Ancient Law* (New York, 1906), especially chapters I, V, and VIII; *Village Communities in the East and West* (London, 1861); *Dissertations on Early Law and Custom* (New York, 1886) especially chapters I through IV.
2. See B. H. Baden-Powell, *The Origin and Growth of Village Communities in India* (London, 1899), especially in regard to geographical variations in the village hierarchy, and the impossibility of establishing an original or "pure" village type.
3. Now part of Uttar Pradesh, in north-central India.
4. W. C. Bennet, *Final Settlement Report on District Gonda* (Allahabad, 1878), pp. 48–9.
5. *Op. cit.*, pp. 43–8.
6. A *bigha* is a measure of land which varied from place to place, from a quarter of an acre in Bengal to two-thirds of an acre in U.P., with other variants both

elsewhere and within these provinces. The right to the standing crop was called *biswa*.

7. Apparently a typical "debt-slave."

8. One twenty-second of a *maund* of eighty-two pounds.

9. A fortieth of a *maund*.

10. In addition, the exact size of a *panseri*, or *seer* varied from village to village, and for that matter still does.

11. It may be of interest to mention that distributions in kind at the time of harvest are still widespread in India. In the Deccan they are known as "*balvta*" payments; in the Punjam as payments to "*kamins*." These are still customary rather than bargained shares, but the figures this writer has seen for individual holdings indicate that such payments are now a small proportion of artisans' and servants' income.

12. L. S. S. O'Malley, *Modern India and the West* (London, New York, 1941), p. 5.

13. By the last quarter of the nineteenth century the problem had become, so far as the British officials were concerned, academic. The methods of assessing and collecting the revenue had been established and no new insight into the original state of affairs would have induced the British to alter their procedures. When Baden-Powell (op. cit.), writing in the 1890's, mentioned the history of the dispute over the nature of land revenue, but insisted most strongly that it was a matter of no importance because it was by then clear that land revenue was de facto and de jure a prior charge on the land, its produce being "hypothecated" to the land revenue by virtue of British legislation.

14. There is evidence that optimistic tax farmers actually overrated their capacity to collect, and that the revenue may have exceeded the maximum the Company should legitimately have expected.

15. By the nineteenth century something which we might as well call rents were paid. They grew out of the Mughal conversions of revenue shares into money payments in some districts, but mostly out of the legal concepts imposed by the British. The amounts paid and here called rents were a mixture of traditional payments of various sorts and of the market forces introduced by the British.

PART III

Institutional Analysis

XII

The Place of Economies in Societies

FEW social scientists today accept in the whole the Enlightenment's ingenuous view of pristine man contracting for his freedoms and bartering his goods in bush and jungle to form his society and economy. The discoveries of Comte, Quetelet, Marx, Maine, Weber, Malinowski, Durkheim and Freud figure predominantly in the accretion of our current knowledge that the social process is a tissue of relationships between man as biological entity and the unique structure of symbols and techniques that results in maintaining his existence. But while in this sense we have discovered the reality of society, the new knowledge has not produced a vision of society comparable in popularity to the traditional picture of an atomistic individualism. At important junctures we fall back on the earlier rationalizations of man as a utilitarian atom. And nowhere is this lapse more apparent than in our ideas concerning the economy. Approaching the economy in any of its widely varied aspects, the social scientist is still hampered by an intellectual heritage of man as an entity with an innate propensity to truck, barter and exchange one thing for another. This remains so in spite of all the protestations against "economic man" and the intermittent attempts to provide a social framework for the economy.

The economic rationalism to which we are heir posits a type of action as *sui generis* economic. In this perspective an actor—a single man, a family, a whole society—is seen facing a natural environment that is slow to yield its life-giving elements. Economic action—or, more precisely, economizing action, the essence of rationality—is, then, re-

239

garded as a manner of disposing of time and energy so that a maximum of goals are achieved out of this man-nature relationship. And the economy becomes the locus of such action. It is, of course, admitted that, in reality, the operation of this economy may be influenced in any number of ways by other factors of a noneconomic character, be they political, military, artistic, or religious. But the essential core of utilitarian rationality remains as the model of the economy.

This view of the economy as the locus of units allocating, saving up, marketing surpluses, forming prices, grew out of the Western milieu of the eighteenth century and it is admittedly relevant under the institutional arrangements of a market system, since actual conditions here roughly satisfy the requirements set by the economistic postulate. But does this postulate allow us to infer the generality of a market system in the realm of empirical fact? The claim of formal economics to an historically universal applicability answers in the affirmative. In effect this argues the virtual presence of a market system in every society, whether such a system is empirically present or not. All human economy might then be regarded as a potential supply-demand-price mechanism, and the actual processes, whatever they are, explained in terms of this hypostatization.

If empirical research is ever to enhance our understanding of the basic operation and the position of various forms of the economy in different societies, we must put the test of relevance to this economistic postulate. Approaching the economic process from the vantage point of the new knowledge we have gained of the reality of society, we must say that there is no necessary relationship between economizing action and the empirical economy. The institutional structure of the economy need not compel, as with the market system, economizing actions. The implications of such an insight for all the social sciences which must deal with the economy could hardly be more far-reaching. Nothing less than a fundamentally different starting point for the analysis of the human economy as a social process is required.

In search for a new beginning, we turn from the economizing to the substantive meaning of the term "economic," unfashionable though it is. This is not to ignore the popular use of "economic" which compounds economizing with materiality: it is merely to urge the limited applicability of that common-sense compound. Unless a man has food to eat, he must starve, be he rational or not: but his safety, indeed his education, art and religion also require material means, weapons, schools, temples of wood, stone or steel. This fact was, of course, never overlooked. Time and again it was urged that "economics" should be based upon the whole range of man's material want satisfaction—his material wants, on the one hand, the means of satisfying his wants, be these material or not, on the other.

As experts are unanimous to recognize, all strivings for such a naturalistic economics remained unsuccessful. The reason is simple. No merely naturalistic concept of the economy can even approximately compete with economic analysis in explaining the mechanics of livelihood under a market system. And since the economy in general was equated with the market system those naïve attempts to replace economic analysis by a naturalistic scheme stood justly discredited.

But was this a conclusive argument against the use of the substantive concept of the economy in the social sciences? By no means. It was overlooked that economic theory, economic analysis, or plain economics is only *one* of several disciplines that busy themselves with the livelihood of man from the material angle, that is, the economy. Practically, it is no more than a study of market phenomena; apart from mere generalities its relevance to other than market systems, e.g., a planned economy, is negligible. What can it do, for instance, for the anthropologist to disentangle the economy from the general tissues of society under a kinship system? In the absence of markets and market prices, the economist cannot be of help to the student of primitive economies; indeed, he may hinder him. Or take the sociologist faced with the question of the changing place occupied by economies in societies as a whole. Unless we keep to times and regions where price-making markets are extant, economics cannot supply him with orientation of any value. This is even more true of the economic historian outside of that slim strip of a few centuries in which the price-making markets and consequently money as a means of exchange have become general. Prehistory, early history, and indeed, as Karl Bücher was the first to proclaim, the whole of history apart from those last centuries, had economies the organization of which differed from anything assumed by the economist. And the difference, we now begin to infer, can be reduced to one single point—they possessed no system of price-making markets. In the whole range of economic disciplines, the point of common interest is set by the process through which material want satisfaction is provided. Locating this process and examining its operation can only be achieved by shifting the emphasis from a type of rational action to the configuration of goods and person movements which actually make up the economy.

To shift in natural science from one conceptual framework to another is one thing; to do so in the social sciences is quite another. It is like rebuilding a house, foundation, walls, fittings and all, while continuing to live in it. We must rid ourselves of the ingrained notion that the economy is a field of experience of which human beings have necessarily always been conscious. To employ a metaphor, the facts of the economy were originally embedded in situations that were not in themselves of an economic nature, neither the ends nor the means being primarily material. The crystallization of the concept of the economy was a matter of time and history. But neither time nor history have provided us with those conceptual tools required to penetrate the maze of social relationships in which the economy was embedded. This is the task of what we will here call institutional analysis.

Karl Polanyi, Conrad M. Arensberg, and Harry W. Pearson

XIII

The Economy as Instituted Process

———————•—•———————

OUR main purpose in this chapter is to determine the meaning that can be attached with consistency to the term "economic" in all the social sciences.

The simple recognition from which all such attempts must start is the fact that in referring to human activities the term economic is a compound of two meanings that have independent roots. We will call them the substantive and the formal meaning.

The substantive meaning of economic derives from man's dependence for his living upon nature and his fellows. It refers to the interchange with his natural and social environment, in so far as this results in supplying him with the means of material want satisfaction.

The formal meaning of economic derives from the logical character of the means-ends relationship, as apparent in such words as "economical" or "economizing." It refers to a definite situation of choice, namely, that between the different uses of means induced by an insufficiency of those means. If we call the rules governing choice of means the logic of rational action, then we may denote this variant of logic, with an improvised term, as formal economics.

The two root meanings of "economic," the substantive and the formal, have nothing in common. The latter derives from logic, the former from fact. The formal meaning implies a set of rules referring to choice between the alternative uses of insufficient means. The substantive meaning implies neither choice nor insufficiency of means; man's livelihood may or may not involve the necessity of choice and, if choice there be, it need not be induced by the limiting effect of a "scarcity" of the means; indeed, some of the most important physical and social conditions of livelihood such as the availability of air and water or a loving mother's devotion to her infant are not, as a rule, so limiting. The cogency that is in play in the one case and in the other differs as the power of syllogism differs from the force of gravitation. The laws of the one are those of the mind; the laws of the other are those of nature. The two meanings could not be further apart; semantically they lie in opposite directions of the compass.

It is our proposition that only the substantive meaning of "economic" is capable of yielding the concepts that are required by the social sciences for an investigation of all the empirical economies of the past and present. The general frame of reference that we endeavor to construct requires, therefore, treatment of the subject matter in substantive terms. The immediate obstacle in our path lies, as indicated, in that concept of "economic" in which the two meanings, the substantive and the formal, are naively compounded. Such a merger of meanings is, of course, unexceptionable as long as we remain conscious of its restrictive effects. But the current concept of economic fuses the "subsistence" and the "scarcity" meanings of economic without a sufficient awareness of the dangers to clear thinking inherent in that merger.

This combination of terms sprang from logically adventitious circumstances. The last two centuries produced in Western Europe and North America an organization of man's livelihood to which the rules of choice happened to be singularly applicable. This form of the economy consisted in a system of price-making markets. Since acts of exchange, as practiced under such a system, involve the participants in choices induced by an insufficiency of means, the system could be reduced to a pattern that lent itself to the application of methods based on the formal meaning of "economic." As long as the economy was controlled by such a system, the formal and the substantive meanings would in practice coincide. Laymen accepted this compound concept as a matter of course; a Marshall, Pareto or Durkheim equally adhered to it. Menger alone in his posthumous work criticized the term, but neither he nor Max Weber, nor Talcott Parsons after him, apprehended the significance of the distinction for sociological analysis. Indeed, there seemed to be no valid reason for distinguishing between two root meanings of a term which, as we said, were bound to coincide in practice.

While it would have been therefore sheer pedantry to differentiate in common parlance between the two meanings of "economic," their merging in one concept nevertheless proved a bane to a precise methodology in the social sciences. Economics naturally formed an exception, since under the market system its terms were bound to be fairly realistic. But the anthropologist, the sociologist or the historian, each in his study of the place occupied by the economy in human society, was faced with a great variety of institutions other than markets, in which man's livelihood was embedded. Its problems could not be attacked with the help of an analytical method devised for a special form of the economy, which was dependent upon the presence of specific market elements.[1]

This lays down the rough sequence of the argument.

We will begin with a closer examination of the concepts derived from the two meanings of "economic," starting with the formal and thence proceeding to the substantive meaning. It should then prove possible to describe the empirical economies—whether primitive or archaic—according to the manner in which the economic process is instituted. The three institutions of trade, money and market will provide a test case. They have previously been defined in formal terms only; thus any other than a marketing approach was barred. Their treatment in substantive terms should then bring us nearer to the desired universal frame of reference.

The Formal and the Substantive Meanings of "Economic"

Let us examine the formal concepts starting from the manner in which the logic of rational action produces formal economics, and the latter, in turn, gives rise to economic analysis.

Rational action is here defined as choice of means in relation to ends. Means are anything appropriate to serve the end, whether by virtue of the laws of nature or by virtue of the laws of the game. Thus "rational" does not refer either to ends or to means, but rather to the relating of means to ends. It is not assumed, for instance, that it is more rational to wish to live than to wish to die, or that, in the first case, it is more rational to seek a long life through the means of science than through those of superstition. For whatever the end, it is rational to choose one's means accordingly; and as to the means, it would not be rational to act upon any other test than that which one happens to believe in. Thus it is rational for the suicide to select means that will accomplish his death; and if he be an adept of black magic, to pay a witch doctor to contrive that end.

The logic of rational action applies, then, to all conceivable means and ends covering an almost infinite variety of human interests. In chess or technology, in religious life or philosophy ends may range from commonplace issues to the most recondite and complex ones. Similarly, in the field of the economy, where ends may range from the momentary assuaging of thirst to the attaining of a sturdy old age, while the corresponding means comprise a glass of water and a combined reliance on filial solicitude and open air life, respectively.

Assuming that the choice is induced by an insufficiency of the means, the logic of rational action turns into that variant of the theory of choice which we have called formal economics. It is still logically unrelated to the concept of the human economy, but it is closer to it by one step. Formal economics refers, as we said, to a situation of choice that arises out of an insufficiency of means. This is the so-called scarcity postulate. It requires, first, insufficiency of means; second, that choice be induced by that insufficiency. Insufficiency of means in relation to ends is determined with the help of the simple operation of "earmarking," which demonstrates whether there is or is not enough to go round. For the insufficiency to induce choice there must be given more than one use to the means, as well as graded ends, i.e., at least two ends ordered in sequence of preference. Both conditions are factual. It is irrelevant whether the reason for which means can be used in one way only happens to be conventional or technological; the same is true of the grading of ends.

Having thus defined choice, insufficiency and scarcity in operational terms, it is easy to see that as there is choice of means without insufficiency, so there is insufficiency of means without choice. Choice may be induced by a preference for right against wrong (moral choice) or, at a crossroads, where two or more paths happen to lead to our destination, possessing identical advantages and disadvantages (operationally induced choice). In either case an abundance of means, far from diminishing the difficulties of choice, would rather increase them. Of course, scarcity may or may not be present in almost all fields of rational action. Not all philosophy is sheer imaginative creativity, it may also be a matter of economizing with assumptions. Or, to get back to the sphere of man's livelihood, in some civilizations scarcity situations seem to be almost exceptional, in others they appear to be painfully general. In either case the presence or absence of scarcity is a question of fact, whether the insufficiency is due to Nature or to Law.

Last but not least, economic analysis. This discipline results from the application of formal economics to an economy of a definite type, namely, a market system. The economy is here embodied in institutions that cause individual choices to give rise to interdependent movements that constitute the economic process. This is achieved by generalizing the use of price-making markets. All goods and services, including the use of labor, land and capital are available for purchase in markets and have, therefore, a price; all forms of income derive from the sale of goods and services—wages, rent and interest, respectively, appearing only as different instances of price according to the items sold. The general introduction of purchasing power as the means of acquisition converts the process of meeting requirements into an allocation of insufficient means with alternative uses, namely, money. It follows that both the conditions of choice and its consequences are quantifiable in the form of prices. It can be asserted that by concentrating on price as the economic fact *par excellence*, the formal method of approach offers a total description of the economy as determined by choices induced by an insufficiency of means. The conceptual tools by which this is performed make up the discipline of economic analysis.

From this follow the limits within which economic analysis can prove effective as a method. The use of the formal meaning denotes the economy as a sequence of acts of economizing, i.e., of choices induced by scarcity situations. While the rules governing such acts are universal, the extent to which the rules are applicable to a definite economy depends upon whether or not that economy is, in actual fact, a sequence of such acts. To produce quantitative results, the locational and appropriational movements, of which the economic process consists, must here present themselves as functions of social actions in regard to insufficient means and oriented on resulting prices. Such a situation obtains only under a market system.

The relation between formal economics and the human economy is, in effect, contingent. Outside of a system of price-making markets economic analysis loses most of its relevance as a method of inquiry into the working of the economy. A centrally planned economy, relying on nonmarket prices is a well-known instance.

The fount of the substantive concept is the empirical economy. It can be briefly (if not engagingly) defined as an instituted process of interaction between man and his environment, which results in a continuous supply of want satisfying material means. Want satisfaction is "material," if it involves the use of material means to satisfy ends; in the case of a definite type of physiological wants, such as food or shelter, this includes the use of so-called services only.

The economy, then, is an instituted process. Two concepts stand out, that of "process" and its "institutedness." Let us see what they contribute to our frame of reference.

Process suggests analysis in terms of motion. The movements refer either to changes in location, or in appropriation, or both. In other words, the material elements may alter their position either by changing place or by changing "hands"; again, these otherwise very different shifts of position may go together or not. Between them, these two kinds of movements may be said to exhaust the possibilities comprised in the economic process as a natural and social phenomenon.

Locational movements include production, alongside of transportation, to which the spatial shifting of objects is equally essential. Goods are of a lower order or of a higher order, according to the manner of their usefulness from the consumer's point of view. This famous "order of goods" sets consumers' goods against producers' goods, according to whether they satisfy wants directly, or only indirectly, through a combination with other goods. This type of movement of the elements represents an essential of the economy in the substantive sense of the term, namely, production.

The appropriative movement governs both what is usually referred to as the circulation of goods and their administration. In the first case, the appropriative movement results from transactions, in the second case, from dispositions. Accordingly, a transaction is an appropriative movement as between hands; a disposition is a one-sided act of the hand, to which by force of custom or of law definite appropriative effects are attached. The term "hand" here serves to denote public bodies and offices as well as private persons or firms, the difference between them being mainly a matter of internal organization. It should be noted, however, that in the nineteenth century private hands were commonly associated with transactions, while public hands were usually credited with dispositions.

In this choice of terms a number of further definitions are implied.

Social activities, insofar as they form part of the process, may be called economic; institutions are so called to the extent to which they contain a concentration of such activities; any components of the process may be regarded as economic elements. These elements can be conveniently grouped as ecological, technological or societal according to whether they belong primarily to the natural environment, the mechanical equipment, or the human setting. Thus a series of concepts, old and new, accrue to our frame of reference by virtue of the process aspect of the economy.

Nevertheless, reduced to a mechanical, biological and psychological interaction of elements that economic process would possess no all-round reality. It contains no more than the bare bones of the processes of production and transportation, as well as of the appropriative changes. In the absence of any indication of societal conditions from which the motives of the individuals spring, there would be little, if anything, to sustain the interdependence of the movements and their recurrence on which the unity and the stability of the process depends. The interacting elements of nature and humanity would form no coherent unit, in effect, no structural entity that could be said to have a function in society or to possess a history. The process would lack the very qualities which cause everyday thought as well as scholarship to turn towards matters of human livelihood as a field of eminent practical interest as well as theoretical and moral dignity.

Hence the transcending importance of the institutional aspect of the economy. What occurs on the process level between man and soil in hoeing a plot or what on the conveyor belt in the constructing of an automobile is, *prima facie* a mere jig-sawing of human and nonhuman movements. From the institutional point of view it is a mere referent of terms like labor and capital, craft and union, slacking and speeding, the spreading of risks and the other semantic units of the social context. The choice between capitalism and socialism, for instance, refers to two different ways of instituting modern technology in the process of production. On the policy level, again, the industrialization of under-developed countries involves, on the one hand, alternative techniques; on the other, alternative methods of instituting them. Our conceptual distinction is vital for any understanding of the interdependence of technology and institutions as well as their relative independence.

The instituting of the economic process vests that process with unity and stability; it produces a structure with a definite function in society; it shifts the place of the process in society, thus adding significance to its history; it centers interest on values, motives and policy. Unity and stability, structure and function, history and policy spell out operationally the content of our assertion that the human economy is an instituted process.

The human economy, then, is embedded and enmeshed in institutions, economic and noneconomic. The inclusion of the noneconomic is vital. For religion or government may be as important for the structure and functioning of the economy as monetary institutions or the availability of tools and machines themselves that lighten the toil of labor.

The study of the shifting place occupied by the economy in society is therefore no other than the study of the manner in which the economic process is instituted at different times and places.

This requires a special tool box.

Reciprocity, Redistribution, and Exchange

A study of how empirical economies are instituted should start from the way in which the economy acquires unity and stability, that is the interdependence and recurrence of its parts. This is achieved through a combination of a very few patterns which may be called forms of integration. Since they occur side by side on different levels and in different sectors of the economy it may often be impossible to select one of them as dominant so that they could be employed for a classification of empirical economies as a whole. Yet by differentiating between sectors and levels of the economy those forms offer a means of describing the economic process in comparatively simple terms, thereby introducing a measure of order into its endless variations.

Empirically, we find the main patterns to be reciprocity, redistribution and exchange. Reciprocity denotes movements between correlative points of symmetrical groupings; redistribution designates appropriational movements toward a center and out of it again; exchange refers here to vice-versa movements taking place as between "hands" under a market system. Reciprocity, then, assumes for a background symmetrically arranged groupings; redistribution is dependent upon the presence of some measure of centricity in the group; exchange in order to produce integration requires a system of price-making markets. It is apparent that the different patterns of integration assume definite institutional supports.

At this point some clarification may be welcome. The terms reciprocity, redistribution and exchange, by which we refer to our forms of integration, are often employed to denote personal interrelations. Superficially then it might seem as if the forms of integration merely reflected aggregates of the respective forms of individual behavior: If mutuality between individuals were frequent, a reciprocative integration would emerge; where sharing among individuals were common, redistributive integration would be present; similarly, frequent acts of barter between individuals would result in exchange as a form of integration. If this were so, our patterns of integration would be indeed no more than simple aggregates of corresponding forms of behavior on the personal level. To be sure, we insisted that the integrative effect was conditioned by the presence of definite institutional arrangements, such as symmetrical organizations, central points and market systems, respectively. But such arrangements seem to represent a mere aggregate of the same personal patterns the eventual effects of which they are supposed to condition. The significant fact is that mere aggregates of the personal behaviors in question do not by themselves produce such structures. Reciprocity behavior between individuals integrates the economy only if symmetrically organized structures, such as a symmetrical system of kinship groups, are given. But a kinship system never arises as the result of mere reciprocating behavior on the personal level. Similarly, in regard to redistribution. It presupposes the presence of an allocative center in the community, yet the organization and validation of such a center does not come about merely as a consequence of frequent acts of sharing as between individuals. Finally, the same is true of the market system. Acts of exchange on the personal level produce prices only if they occur under a system of price-making markets, an institutional setup which is nowhere created by mere random acts of exchange. We do not wish to imply, of course, that those supporting patterns are the outcome of some mysterious forces acting outside the range of personal or individual behavior. We merely insist that if, in any given case, the societal effects of individual behavior depend on the presence of definite institutional conditions, these conditions do not for that reason result from the personal behavior in question. Superficially, the supporting pattern may *seem* to result from a cumulation of a corresponding kind of personal behavior, but the vital elements of organization and validation are necessarily contributed by an altogether different type of behavior.

The first writer to our knowledge to have hit upon the factual connection between reciprocative behavior on the interpersonal level, on the one hand, and given symmetrical groupings, on the other, was the anthropologist Richard Thurnwald, in 1915, in an empirical study on the marriage system of the Bánaro of New Guinea. Bronislaw Malinowski, some ten years later, referring to Thurnwald, predicted that socially relevant reciprocation would regularly be found to rest on symmetrical forms of basic social organization. His own description of the Trobriand kinship system as well as of the Kula trade bore out the point. This lead was followed up by this writer, in regarding symmetry as merely one of several supporting patterns. He then added redistribution and exchange to reciprocity, as further forms of integration; similarly, he added centricity and market to symmetry, as other instances of institutional support. Hence our forms of integration and supporting structure patterns.

This should help to explain why in the economic sphere interpersonal behavior so often fails to have the expected societal effects in the absence of definite institutional preconditions. Only in a symmetrically organized environment will reciprocative behavior result in economic institutions of any importance; only where allocative centers have been set up can individual acts of sharing produce a redistributive economy; and only in the presence of a system of price-making markets will exchange acts of individuals result in fluctuating prices that integrate the economy. Otherwise such acts of barter will remain ineffective and therefore tend not to occur. Should they nevertheless happen, in a random fashion, a violent emotional reaction would set in, as against acts of indecency or acts of treason, since trading behavior is never emotionally indifferent behavior and is not, therefore, tolerated by opinion outside of the approved channels.

Let us now return to our forms of integration.

A group which deliberately undertook to organize its economic relationships on a reciprocative footing would, to effect its purpose, have to split up into sub-groups the corresponding members of which could identify one another as such. Members of Group A would then be able to establish relationships of reciprocity with their counterparts in Group B and vice versa. But symmetry is not restricted to duality. Three, four, or more groups may be symmetrical in regard to two or more axes; also members of the groups need not reciprocate with one another but may do so with the corresponding members of third groups toward which they stand in analogous relations. A Trobriand man's responsibility is toward his sister's family. But he himself is not on that account assisted by his sister's husband, but, if he is married, by his own wife's brother—a member of a third, correspondingly placed family.

Aristotle taught that to every kind of community (*koinōnia*) there corresponded a kind of good-will (*philia*) amongst its members which expressed itself in reciprocity (*antipeponthos*). This was true both of the more permanent communities such as families, tribes or city states as of those less permanent ones that may be comprised in, and subordinate to, the former. In our terms this implies a tendency in the larger communities to develop a multiple symmetry in regard to which reciprocative behavior may develop in the subordinate communities. The closer the members of the encompassing community feel drawn to one another, the more general will be the tendency among them to develop reciprocative attitudes in regard to specific relationships limited in space, time or otherwise. Kinship, neighborhood, or totem belong to the more permanent and comprehensive groupings; within their compass voluntary and semi-voluntary associations of a military, vocational, religious or social character create situations in which, at least transitorily or in regard to a given locality or a typical situation, there would form symmetrical groupings the members of which practice some sort of mutuality.

Reciprocity as a form of integration gains greatly in power through its capacity of employing both redistribution and exchange as subordinate methods. Reciprocity may be attained through a sharing of the burden of labor according to definite rules of redistribution as when taking things "in turn." Similarly, reciprocity is sometimes attained through exchange at set equivalencies for the benefit of the partner who happens to be short of some kind of necessities—a fundamental institution in ancient Oriental societies. In nonmarket economies these two forms of integration—reciprocity and redistribution—occur in effect usually together.

Redistribution obtains within a group to the extent to which the allocation of goods is collected in one hand and takes place by virtue of custom, law or *ad hoc* central decision. Sometimes it amounts to a physical collecting accompanied by storage-cum-redistribution, at other times the "collecting" is not physical, but merely appropriational, i.e., rights of disposal in the physical location of the goods. Redistribution occurs for many reasons, on all civilizational levels, from the primitive hunting tribe to the vast storage systems of ancient Egypt, Sumeria, Babylonia or Peru. In large countries differences of soil and climate may make redistribution necessary; in other cases it is caused by discrepancy in point of time, as between harvest and consumption. With a hunt, any other method of distribution would lead to disintegration of the horde or band, since only "division of labor" can here ensure results; a redistribution of purchasing power may be valued for its own sake, i.e., for the purposes demanded by social ideals as in the modern welfare state. The principle remains the same—collecting into, and distributing from, a center. Redistribution may also apply to a group smaller than society, such as the household or manor irrespective of the way in which the economy as a whole is integrated. The best known instances are the Central African *kraal*, the Hebrew patriarchal household, the Greek estate of Aristotle's time, the Roman *familia*, the medieval manor, or the typical large peasant household before the general marketing of grain. However, only under a comparatively advanced form of agricultural society is householding practicable, and then, fairly general. Before that, the widely spread "small family" is not economically instituted, except for some cooking of food; the use of pasture, land or cattle is still dominated by redistributive or reciprocative methods on a wider than family scale.

Redistribution, too, is apt to integrate groups at all levels and all degrees of permanence from the state itself to units of a transitory character. Here, again, as with reciprocity, the more closely knit the encompassing unit, the more varied will the subdivisions be in which redistribution can effectively operate. Plato taught that the number of citizens in the state should be 5040. This figure was divisible in 59 different ways, including division by the first ten numerals. For the assessment of taxes, the forming of groups for business transactions, the carrying of military and other burdens "in turn," etc., it would allow the widest scope, he explained.

Exchange in order to serve as a form of integration requires the support of a system of price-making markets. Three kinds of exchange should therefore be distinguished: The merely locational movement of a "changing of places" between the hands (operational exchange); the appropriational movements of exchange, either at a set rate (decisional exchange) or at a bargained rate (integrative exchange). In so far as exchange at a set rate is in question, the economy is integrated by the factors which fix that rate, not by the market mechanism. Even price-making markets are integrative only if they are linked up in a system which tends to spread the effect of prices to markets other than those directly affected.

Higgling-haggling has been rightly recognized as being of the essence of bargaining behavior. In order for exchange to be integrative the behavior of the partners must be oriented on producing a price that is as favorable to each partner as he can make it. Such a behavior contrasts sharply with that of exchange at a set price. The ambiguity of the term "gain" tends to cover up the difference. Exchange at set prices involves no more than the gain to either party implied in the decision of exchanging; exchange at fluctuating prices aims at a gain that can be attained only by an attitude involving a distinctive antagonistic relationship between the partners. The element of antagonism, however diluted, that accompanies this variant of exchange is ineradicable. No community intent on protecting the fount of solidarity between its members can allow latent hostility to develop around a matter as vital to animal existence and, therefore, capable of arousing as tense anxieties as food. Hence the universal banning of transactions of a gainful nature in regard to food and foodstuffs in primitive and archaic society. The very widely spread ban on higgling-haggling over victuals automatically removes price-making markets from the realm of early institutions.

Traditional groupings of economies which roughly approximate a classification according to the dominant forms of integration are illuminating. What historians are wont to call "economic systems" seem to fall fairly into this pattern. Dominance of a form of integration is here identified with the degree to which it comprises land and labor in society. So-called savage society, is characterized by the integration of land and labor into the economy by way of the ties of kinship. In feudal society the ties of fealty determine the fate of land and the labor that goes with it. In the floodwater empires land was largely distributed and sometimes redistributed by temple or palace, and so was labor, at least in its dependent form. The rise of the market to a ruling force in the economy can be traced by noting the extent to which land and food were mobilized through exchange, and labor was turned into a commodity free to be purchased in the market. This may help to explain the relevance of the historically untenable stages theory of slavery, serfdom and wage labor that is traditional with Marxism—a grouping which flowed from the conviction that the character of the economy was set by the status of labor. However, the integration of the soil into the economy should be regarded as hardly less vital.

In any case, forms of integration do not represent "stages" of development. No sequence in time is implied. Several subordinate forms may be present alongside of the dominant one, which may itself recur after a temporary eclipse. Tribal societies practice reciprocity and redistribution, while archaic societies are predominantly redistributive, though to some extent they may allow room for exchange. Reciprocity, which plays a dominant part in some Melanesian communities, occurs as a not unimportant although subordinate trait in the redistributive archaic empires, where foreign trade (carried on by gift and countergift) is still largely organized on the principle of reciprocity. Indeed, during a war emergency it was reintroduced on a large scale in the twentieth century, under the name of lend-lease, with societies where otherwise marketing and exchange were dominant. Redistribution, the ruling method in tribal and archaic society beside which exchange plays only a minor part, grew to great importance in the later Roman Empire and is actually gaining ground today in some modern industrial states. The Soviet Union is an extreme instance. Conversely, more than once before in the course of human history markets have played a part in the economy, although never on a territorial scale, or with an institutional comprehensiveness comparable to that of the nineteenth century. However, here again a change is noticeable. In our century, with the lapse of the gold standard, a recession of the world role of markets from their nineteenth century peak set in—a turn of the trend which, incidentally, takes us back to our starting point, namely, the increasing inadequacy of our limited marketing definitions for the purposes of the social scientist's study of the economic field.

Forms of Trade, Money Uses, and Market Elements

The restrictive influence of the marketing approach on the interpretation of trade and money institutions is incisive: inevitably, the market appears as the locus of exchange, trade as the actual exchange, and money as the means of exchange. Since trade is directed by prices and prices are a function of the market, all trade is market trade, just as all money is exchange money. The market is the generating institution of which trade and money are the functions.

Such notions are not true to the facts of anthropology and history. Trade, as well as some money uses, are as old as mankind; while markets, although meetings of an economic character may have existed as early as the neolithic, did not gain importance until comparatively late in history. Price-making markets, which alone are constitutive of a market system, were to all accounts non-existent before the first millennium of antiquity, and then only to be eclipsed by other forms of integration. Not even these main facts however could be uncovered as long as trade and money were thought to be limited to the exchange form of integration, as its specifically "economic" form. The long periods of history when reciprocity and redistribution integrated the economy and the considerable ranges within which, even in modern times, they continued to do so, were put out of bounds by a restrictive terminology.

Viewed as an exchange system, or, in brief, catallactically, trade, money and market form an indivisible whole. Their common conceptual framework is the market. Trade appears as a two-way movement of goods through the market, and money as quantifiable goods used for indirect exchange in order to facilitate that movement. Such an approach must induce a more or less tacit acceptance of the heuristic principle according to which, where trade is in evidence, markets should be assumed, and where money is in evidence trade, and therefore markets, should be assumed. Naturally, this leads to seeing markets where there are none and ignoring trade and money where they are present, because markets happen to be absent. The cumulative effect must be to create a stereotype of the economies of less familiar times and places, something in the way of an artificial landscape with only little or no resemblance to the original.

A separate analysis of trade, money and markets is therefore in order.

1. FORMS OF TRADE

From the substantive point of view, trade is a relatively peaceful method of acquiring goods which are not available on the spot. It is external to the group, similar to activities which we are used to associating with hunts, slaving expeditions, or piratic raids. In either case the point is acquisition and carrying of goods from a distance. What distinguishes trade from the questing for game, booty, plunder, rare woods or exotic animals, is the two-sidedness of the movement, which also ensures its broadly peaceful and fairly regular character.

From the catallactic viewpoint, trade is the movement of goods on their way through the market. All commodities—goods produced for sale—are potential objects of trade; one commodity is moving in one direction, the other in the opposite direction; the movement is controlled by prices: trade and market are co-terminous. All trade is market trade.

Again, like hunt, raid or expedition under native conditions, trade is not so much an individual as rather a group activity, in this respect closely akin to the organization of wooing and mating, which is often concerned with the acquisition of wives from a distance by more or less peaceful means. Trade thus centers in the meeting of different communities, one of its purposes being the exchange of goods. Such meetings do not, like price-making markets, produce rates of exchange, but on the contrary they rather presuppose such rates. Neither the persons of individual traders nor motives of individual gain are involved. Whether a chief or king is acting for the community after having collected the "export" goods from its members, or whether the group meets bodily their counterparts on the beach for the purpose of exchange—in either case the proceedings are essentially collective. Exchange between "partners in trade" is frequent, but so is, of course, partnership in wooing and mating. Individual and collective activities are intertwined.

Emphasis on "acquisition of goods from a distance" as a constitutive element in trade should bring out the dominant role played by the import interest in the early history of trade. In the nineteenth century export interests loomed large—a typically catallactic phenomenon.

Since something must be carried over a distance and that in two opposite directions, trade, in the nature of things, has a number of constituents such as personnel, goods, carrying, and two-sidedness, each of which can be broken down according to sociologically or technologically significant criteria. In following up those four factors we may hope to learn something about the changing place of trade in society.

First, the persons engaged in trade.

"Acquisition of goods from a distance" may be practiced either from motives attaching to the trader's standing in society, and as a rule comprising elements of duty or public service (status motive); or it may be done for the sake of the material gain accruing to him personally from the buying and selling transaction in hand (profit motive).

In spite of many possible combinations of those incentives, honor and duty on the one hand, profit on the other, stand out as sharply distinct primary motivations. If the "status motive," as is quite often the case, is reinforced by material benefits, the latter do not as a rule take the form of gain made on exchange, but rather of treasure or endowment with landed revenue bestowed on the trader by king or temple or lord, by way of recompense. Things being what they are, gains made on exchange do not usually add up to more than paltry sums that bear no comparison with the wealth bestowed by his lord upon the resourceful and successfully venturing trader. Thus he who trades for the sake of duty and honor grows rich, while he who trades for filthy lucre remains poor—an added reason why gainful motives are under a shadow in archaic society.

Another way of approaching the question of personnel is from the angle of the standard of life deemed appropriate to their status by the community to which they belong.

Archaic society in general knows, as a rule, no other figure of a trader than that which belongs either to the top or to the bottom rung of the social ladder. The first is connected with rulership and government, as required by the political and military conditions of trading, the other depends for his livelihood on the coarse labor of carrying. This fact is of great importance for the understanding of the organization of trade in ancient times. There can be no middle-class trader, at least among the citizenry. Apart from the Far East which we must disregard here, only three significant instances of a broad commercial middle class in premodern times are on record: the Hellenistic merchant of largely metic ancestry in the Eastern Mediterranean city states; the ubiquitous Islamitic merchant who grafted Hellenistic maritime traditions on to the ways of the bazaar; lastly, the descendants of Pirenne's "floating scum" in Western Europe, a sort of continental metic of the second third of the Middle Ages. The classical Greek middle class preconized by Aristotle was a landed class, not a commercial class at all.

A third manner of approach is more closely historical. The trader types of antiquity were the *tamkarum*, the metic or resident alien, and the "foreigner."

The *tamkarum* dominated the Mesopotamian scene from the Sumerian beginnings to the rise of Islam, i.e., over some 3000 years. Egypt, China, India, Palestine, pre-conquest Mesoamerica, or native West Africa knew no other type of trader. The *metic* became first historically conspicuous in Athens and some other Greek cities as a lower-class merchant, and rose with Hellenism to become the prototype of a Greek-speaking or Levantine commercial middle class from the Indus Valley to the Pillars of Hercules. The *foreigner* is of course ubiquitous. He carries on trade with foreign crews and in foreign bottoms; he neither "belongs" to the community, nor enjoys the semi-status of resident alien, but is a member of an altogether different community.

A fourth distinction is anthropological. It provides the key to that peculiar figure, the trading foreigner. Although the number of "trading peoples" to which these "foreigners" belonged was comparatively small, they accounted for the widely spread institution of "passive trade." Amongst themselves, trading peoples differed again in an important respect: trading peoples proper, as we may call them, were exclusively dependent for their subsistence on trade in which, directly or indirectly, the whole population was engaged, as with the Phoenicians, the Rhodians, the inhabitants of Gades (the modern Cadix), or at some periods Armenians and Jews; in the case of others—a more numerous group—trade was only one of the occupations in which from time to time a considerable part of the population engaged, travelling abroad, sometimes with their families, over shorter or longer periods. The Haussa and the Mandingo in the Western Sudan are instances. The latter are also known as Duala, but, as recently turned out, only when trading abroad. Formerly they were taken to be a separate people by those whom they visited when trading.

Second, the organization of trade in early times must differ according to the goods carried, the distance to be travelled, the obstacles to be overcome by the carriers, the political and the ecological conditions of the venture. For this, if for no other reason, all trade is originally specific. The goods and their carriage make it so. There can be, under these conditions, no such thing as trading "in general."

Unless full weight is given to this fact, no understanding of the early development of trading institutions is possible. The decision to acquire some kinds of goods from a definite distance and place of origin will be taken under circumstances different from those under which other kinds of goods would have to be acquired from somewhere else. Trading ventures are, for this reason, a discontinuous affair. They are restricted to concrete undertakings, which are liquidated one by one and do not tend to develop into a continuous enterprise. The Roman *societas*, like the later *commenda*, was a trade partnership limited to one undertaking. Only the *societas publicanorum*, for tax farming and contracting, was incorporated—it was the one great exception. Not before modern times were permanent trade associations known.

The specificity of trade is enhanced in the natural course of things by the necessity of acquiring the imported goods with exported ones. For under nonmarket conditions imports and exports tend to fall under different regimes. The process through which goods are collected for export is mostly separate from, and relatively independent of, that by which the imported goods are repartitioned. The first may be a matter of tribute or taxation or feudal gifts or under whatever other designation the goods flow to the center, while the repartitioned imports may cascade along different lines. Hammurabi's "Seisachtheia" appears to make an exception of *simu* goods, which may have sometimes been imports passed on by the king via the *tamkarum* to such tenants who wished to exchange them for their own produce. Some of the preconquest long-distance trading of the *pochteca* of the Aztec of Mesoamerica appears to carry similar features.

What nature made distinct, the market makes homogeneous. Even the difference between goods and their transportation may be obliterated, since in the market both can be bought and sold—the one in the commodity market, the other in the freight and insurance market. In either case there is supply and demand, and prices are formed in the same fashion. Carrying and goods, these constituents of trade, acquire a common denominator in terms of cost. Preoccupation with the market and its artificial homogeneity thus makes for good economic theory rather than for good economic history. Eventually, we will find that trade routes, too, as well as means of transportation may be of no less incisive importance for the institutional forms of trade than the types of goods carried. For in all these cases the geographical and technological conditions interpenetrate with the social structure.

According to the rationale of two-sidedness we meet with three main types of trade: gift trade, administered trade, and market trade.

Gift trade links the partners in relationships of reciprocity, such as: guest friends; Kula partners; visiting parties. Over millennia trade between empires was carried on as gift trade—no other rationale of two-sidedness would have met quite as well the needs of the situation. The organization of trading is here usually ceremonial, involving mutual presentation; embassies; political dealings between chiefs or kings. The goods are treasure, objects of élite circulation; in the border case of visiting parties they may be of a more "democratic" character. But contacts are tenuous and exchanges few and far between.

Administered trade has its firm foundation in treaty relationships that are more or less formal. Since on both sides the import interest is as a rule determinative, trading runs through government-controlled channels. The export trade is usually organized in a similar way. Consequently, the whole of trade is carried on by administrative methods. This extends to the manner in which business is transacted, including arrangements concerning "rates" or proportions of the units exchanged; port facilities; weighing; checking of quality; the physical exchange of the goods; storage; safekeeping; the control of the trading personnel; regulation of "payments"; credits; price differentials. Some of these matters would naturally be linked with the collection of the export goods and the repartition of the imported ones, both belonging to the redistributive sphere of the domestic economy. The goods that are mutually imported are standardized in regard to quality and package, weight, and other easily ascertainable criteria. Only such "trade goods" can be traded. Equivalencies are set out in simple unit relations; in principle, trade is one-to-one.

Higgling and haggling is not part of the proceedings; equivalencies are set once and for all. But since to meet changing circumstances adjustments cannot be avoided, higgling-haggling is practiced only on other items than price, such as measures, quality, or means of payment. Endless arguments are possible about the quality of the foodstuffs, the capacity and weight of the units employed, the proportions of the currencies if different ones are jointly used. Even "profits" are often "bargained." The rationale of the procedure is, of course, to keep prices unchanged; if they must adjust to actual supply situations, as in an emergency, this is phrased as trading two-to-one or two-and-a-half-to-one, or, as we would say, at 100 per cent or 150 per cent profit. This method of haggling on profits at stable prices, which may have been fairly general in archaic society, is well authenticated from the Central Sudan as late as the nineteenth century.

Administered trade presupposes relatively permanent trading bodies such as governments or at least companies chartered by them. The understanding with the natives may be tacit, as in the case of traditional or customary relationships. Between sovereign bodies, however, trade assumes formal treaties even in the relatively early times of the second millennium B.C.

Once established in a region, under solemn protection of the gods, administrative forms of trade may be practiced without any previous treaty. The main institution, as we now begin to realize, is the port of trade, as we here call this site of all administered foreign trade. The port of trade offers military security to the inland power; civil protection to the foreign trader; facilities of anchorage, debarkation and storage; the benefit of judicial authorities; agreement on the goods to be traded; agreement concerning the "proportions" of the different trade goods in the mixed packages or "sortings."

Market trade is the third typical form of trading. Here exchange is the form of integration that relates the partners to each other. This comparatively modern variant of trade released a torrent of material wealth over Western Europe and North America. Though presently in recession, it is still by far the most important of all. The range of tradable goods—the commodities—is practically unlimited and the organization of market trade follows the lines traced out by the supply-demand-price mechanism. The market mechanism shows its immense range of application by being adaptable to the handling not only of goods, but of every element of trade itself—storage, transportation, risk, credit, payments, etc.—through the forming of special markets for freight, insurance, short-term credit, capital, warehouse space, banking facilities, and so on.

The main interest of the economic historian today turns towards the questions: When and how did trade become linked with markets? At what time and place do we meet the general result known as market trade?

Strictly speaking, such questions are precluded under the sway of catallactic logic, which tends to fuse trade and market inseparably.

2. MONEY USES

The catallactic definition of money is that of means of indirect exchange. Modern money is used for payment and as a "standard" precisely because it is a means of exchange. Thus our money is "all-purpose" money. Other uses of money are merely unimportant variants of its exchange use, and all money uses are dependent upon the existence of markets.

The substantive definition of money, like that of trade, is independent of markets. It is derived from definite uses to which quantifiable objects are put. These uses are payment, standard and exchange. Money, therefore, is defined here as quantifiable objects employed in any one or several of these uses. The question is whether independent definitions of those uses are possible.

The definitions of the various money uses contain two criteria: the sociologically defined situation in which the use arises, and the operation performed with the money objects in that situation.

Payment is the discharge of obligations in which quantifiable objects change hands. The situation refers here not to one kind of obligation only, but to several of them, since only if an object is used to discharge more than one obligation can we speak of it as "means of payment" in the distinctive sense of the term (otherwise merely an obligation to be discharged in kind is so discharged).

The payment use of money belongs to its most common uses in early times. The obligations do not here commonly spring from transactions. In unstratified primitive society payments are regularly made in connection with the institutions of bride price, blood money, and fines. In archaic society such payments continue, but they are overshadowed by customary dues, taxes, rent and tribute that give rise to payments on the largest scale.

The standard, or accounting use of money is the equating of amounts of different kinds of goods for definite purposes. The "situation" is either barter or the storage and management of staples; the "operation" consists in the attaching of numerical tags to the various objects to facilitate the manipulation of those objects. Thus in the case of barter, the summation of objects on either side can eventually be equated; in the case of the management of staples a possibility of planning, balancing, budgeting, as well as general accounting is attained.

The standard use of money is essential to the elasticity of a redistributive system. The equating of such staples as barley, oil and wool in which taxes or rent have to be paid or alternatively rations or wages may be claimed is vital, since it ensures the possibility of choice between the different staples for payer and claimant alike. At the same time the precondition of large scale finance "in kind" is created, which presupposes the notion of funds and balances, in other words, the interchangeability of staples.

The exchange use of money arises out of a need for quantifiable objects for indirect exchange. The "operation" consists in acquiring units of such objects through direct exchange, in order to acquire the desired objects through a further act of exchange. Sometimes the money objects are available from the start, and the twofold exchange is merely designed to net an increased amount of the same objects. Such a use of quantifiable objects develops not from random acts of barter—a favored fancy of eighteenth century rationalism—but rather in connection with organized trade, especially in markets. In the absence of markets the exchange use of money is no more than a subordinate culture trait. The surprising reluctance of the great trading peoples of antiquity such as Tyre and Carthage to adopt coins, that new form of money eminently suited for exchange, may have been due to the fact that the trading ports of the commercial empires were not organized as markets, but as "ports of trade."

Two extensions of the meaning of money should be noted. The one extends the definition of money other than physical objects, namely, ideal units; the other comprises alongside of the three conventional money uses, also the use of money objects as operational devices.

Ideal units are mere verbalizations or written symbols employed as if they were quantifiable units, mainly for payment or as a standard. The "operation" consists in the manipulation of debt accounts according to the rules of the game. Such accounts are common facts of primitive life and not, as was often believed, peculiar to monetarized economies. The earliest temple economies of Mesopotamia as well as the early Assyrian traders practiced the clearing of accounts without the intervention of money objects.

At the other end it seemed advisable not to omit the mention of operational devices among money uses, exceptional though they be. Occasionally quantifiable objects are used in archaic society for arithmetical, statistical, taxational, administrative or other non-monetary

purposes connected with economic life. In eighteenth-century Whydah cowrie money was used for statistical ends, and *damba* beans
(never employed as money) served as a gold weight and, in that capacity, were cleverly used as a device for accountancy.

Early money is, as we saw, special-purpose money. Different kinds
of objects are employed in the different money uses; moreover, the
uses are instituted independently of one another. The implications are
of the most far-reaching nature. There is, for instance, no contradic-
tion involved in "paying" with a means with which one cannot buy,
nor in employing objects as a "standard" which are not used as a means
of exchange. In Hammurabi's Babylonia barley was the means of payment; silver was the universal standard; in exchange, of which there
was very little, both were used alongside of oil, wool, and some other
staples. It becomes apparent why money uses—like trade activities—
can reach an almost unlimited level of development, not only outside
of market-dominated economies, but in the very absence of markets.

3. MARKET ELEMENTS

Now, the market itself. Catallactically, the market is the *locus* of
exchange; market and exchange are co-extensive. For under the catallactic postulate economic life is both reducible to acts of exchange
effected through higgling-haggling and it is embodied in markets. Exchange is thus described as *the* economic relationship, with the market
as *the* economic institution. The definition of the market derives logically from the catallactic premises.

Under the substantive range of terms, market and exchange have
independent empirical characteristics. What then is here the meaning
of exchange and market? And to what extent are they necessarily connected?

Exchange, substantively defined, is the mutual appropriative movement of goods between hands. Such a movement as we saw may occur
either at set rates or at bargained rates. The latter only is the result of
higgling-haggling between the partners.

Whenever, then, there is exchange, there is a rate. This remains
true whether the rate be bargained or set. It will be noted that exchange
at bargained prices is identical with catallactic exchange or "exchange
as a form of integration." This kind of exchange alone is typically

limited to a definite type of market institution, namely price-making markets.

Market institutions shall be defined as institutions comprising a supply crowd or a demand crowd or both. Supply crowds and demand crowds, again, shall be defined as a multiplicity of hands desirous to acquire, or alternatively, to dispose of, goods in exchange. Although market institutions, therefore, are exchange institutions, market and exchange are *not* coterminous. Exchange at set rates occurs under reciprocative or redistributive forms of integration; exchange at bargained rates, as we said, is limited to price-making markets. It may seem paradoxical that exchange at set rates should be compatible with any form of integration except that of exchange: yet this follows logically since only bargained exchange represents exchange in the catallactic sense of the term, in which it is a form of integration.

The best way of approaching the world of market institutions appears to be in terms of "market elements." Eventually, this will not only serve as a guide through the variety of configurations subsumed under the name of markets and market type institutions, but also as a tool with which to dissect some of the conventional concepts that obstruct our understanding of those institutions.

Two market elements should be regarded as specific, namely, supply crowds and demand crowds; if either is present, we shall speak of a market institution (if both are present, we call it a market, if one of them only, a market-type institution). Next in importance is the element of equivalency, i.e., the rate of the exchange; according to the character of the equivalency, markets are set-price markets or price-making markets.

Competition is another characteristic of some market institutions, such as price-making markets and auctions, but in contrast to equivalencies, economic competition is restricted to markets. Finally, there are elements that can be designated as functional. Regularly they occur apart from market institutions, but if they make their appearance alongside of supply crowds or demand crowds, they pattern out those institutions in a manner that may be of great practical relevance. Amongst these functional elements are physical site, goods present, custom and law.

This diversity of market institutions was in recent times obscured in the name of the formal concept of a supply-demand-price mechanism. No wonder that it is in regard to the pivotal terms of supply, demand and price that the substantive approach leads to a significant widening of our outlook.

Supply crowds and demand crowds were referred to above as separate and distinct market elements. In regard to the modern market this would be, of course, inadmissible; here there is a price level at which bears turn bulls, and another price level at which the miracle is reversed. This has induced many to overlook the fact that buyers and sellers are separate in any other than the modern type of market. This again gave support to a twofold misconception. Firstly, "supply and demand" appeared as combined elemental forces while actually each consisted of two very different components, namely, an amount of *goods*, on the one hand, and a number of *persons*, related as buyers and sellers to those goods, on the other. Secondly, "supply and demand" seemed inseparable like Siamese twins, while actually forming distinct groups of persons, according to whether they disposed of the goods as of resources, or sought them as requirements. Supply crowds and demand crowds need not therefore be present together. When, for instance, booty is auctioned by the victorious general to the highest bidder only a demand crowd is in evidence; similarly, only a supply crowd is met with when contracts are assigned to the lowest submission. Yet auctions and submissions were widespread in archaic society, and in ancient Greece auctions ranked amongst the precursors of markets proper. This distinctness of "supply" and "demand" crowds shaped the organization of all premodern market institutions.

As to the market element commonly called "price," it was here subsumed under the category of equivalencies. The use of this general term should help avoid misunderstandings. Price suggests fluctuation, while equivalency lacks this association. The very phrase "set" or "fixed" price suggests that the price, before being fixed or set was apt to change. Thus language itself makes it difficult to convey the true state of affairs, namely, that "price" is originally a rigidly fixed quantity, in the absence of which trading cannot start. Changing or fluctuating prices of a competitive character are a comparatively recent development and their emergence forms one of the main interests of the economic history of antiquity. Traditionally, the sequence was supposed to be the reverse: price was conceived of as the result of trade and exchange, not as their precondition.

"Price" is the designation of quantitative ratios between goods of different kinds, effected through barter or higgling-haggling. It is that form of equivalency which is characteristic of economies that are integrated through exchange. But equivalencies are by no means restricted to exchange relations. Under a redistributive form of integration equivalencies are also common. They designate the quantitative relationship between goods of different kinds that are acceptable in payment of taxes, rents, dues, fines, or that denote qualifications for a civic status dependent on a property census. Also the equivalency may set the ratio at which wages or rations in kind can be claimed, at the beneficiary's choosing. The elasticity of a system of staple finance—the planning, balancing and accounting—hinges on this device. The equivalency here denotes not what should be given *for* another good, but what can be claimed *instead* of it. Under reciprocative forms of integration, again, equivalencies determine the amount that is "adequate" in relation to the symmetrically placed party. Clearly, this behavioral context is different from either exchange or redistribution.

Price systems, as they develop over time, may contain layers of equivalencies that historically originated under different forms of integration. Hellenistic market prices show ample evidence of having derived from redistributive equivalencies of the cuneiform civilizations that preceded them. The thirty pieces of silver received by Judas as the price of a man for betraying Jesus was a close variant of the equivalency of a slave as set out in Hammurabi's Code some 1700 years earlier. Soviet redistributive equivalencies, on the other hand, for a long time echoed nineteenth century world market prices. These, too, in their turn, had their predecessors. Max Weber remarked that for lack of a costing basis Western capitalism would not have been possible but for the medieval network of statuated and regulated prices, customary rents, etc., a legacy of gild and manor. Thus price systems may have an institutional history of their own in terms of the types of equivalencies that entered into their making.

It is with the help of noncatallactic concepts of trade, money and markets of this kind that such fundamental problems of economic and social history as the origin of fluctuating prices and the development of market trading can best be tackled and, as we hope, eventually resolved.

To conclude: A critical survey of the catallactic definitions of trade, money and market should make available a number of concepts which form the raw material of the social sciences in their economic aspect. The bearing of this recognition on questions of theory, policy and outlook should be viewed in the light of the gradual institutional transformation that has been in progress since the first World War. Even in regard to the market system itself, the market as the sole frame of reference is somewhat out of date. Yet, as should be more clearly realized than it sometimes has been in the past, the market cannot be superseded as a general frame of reference unless the social sciences succeed in developing a wider frame of reference to which the market itself is referable. This indeed is our main intellectual task today in the field of economic studies. As we have attempted to show, such a conceptual structure will have to be grounded on the substantive meaning of economic.

Karl Polanyi

Note to Chapter XIII

1. The uncritical employment of the compound concept fostered what may well be called the "economistic fallacy." It consisted in an artificial identification of the economy with its market form. From Hume and Spencer to Frank H. Knight and Northrop, social thought suffered from this limitation wherever it touched on the economy. Lionel Robbins' essay (1932), though useful to economists, fatefully distorted the problem. In the field of anthropology Melville Herskovits' recent work (1952) represents a relapse after his pioneering effort of 1940.

XIV

Sociology and the Substantive View of the Economy

————— •◦• —————

EVER since Comte first introduced "sociology" to designate the then new science of society, the term has denoted the discipline whose subject matter is the interrelations among the sundry social processes constituting society. One of the more important of these processes is the economy, for through it the members of society receive a continuous supply of want-satisfying material means. Yet, sociologists have shown rather little originality in developing basic conceptions of this fundamental process. Instead, they have taken economic theory for their point of departure and thereby made the uncritical assumption that rational action and the market are the source and form respectively of the economic process. As a result, economies diverging from the format of the market model are dismissed in advance from serious examination, being viewed instead either as merely curious illustrations of how archaic "traditionalism" curbs the expression of rationality or, among the more skeptical, as substantiating the belief that for a number of "economic" problems orthodox theory needs to be supplemented by sociological propositions.

Such easy renderings of the many "deviations" from the market model have for too long marked sociological discussions of the economy. A more critical perspective is now needed. For if in some instances it is not by economizing actions that empirical economies are identified, then what is it that serves to distinguish them from other societal processes? Or, more fundamentally, what is meant by the very term "economy" when it is applied to a set of activities in which economizing plays a minor role, if indeed it is present at all? As developed in chapter XIII the answer once given appears almost self-evident; the term is then used to denote the processes by which people secure a livelihood. In short, "economy" denotes two quite different concepts, one having the formal or "economizing" meaning, the other the substantive or "livelihood" meaning. Typically, both meanings are combined, so that "economy" designates the compound concept of securing a livelihood by economizing. Whether economic theory provides a suitable explanatory model depends directly, then, on whether this compound concept is an adequate description of actual economies.

The two concepts are not only logically disparate. The actual processes to which they refer also occur independently—just as generals may economize in the disposition of their troops, so may people secure a livelihood without economizing. Nevertheless, in what we call a market system the two processes not only appear jointly, but bring about the subject matter of economic analysis, the phenomena of fluctuating prices and of action oriented to them. It is our observations of these phenomena (of an essentially mathematical form) that economics attempts to order. The restriction deriving from this reasoning is of some moment for sociologists, for it implies that the "generality" of economic theory does not lie in the substantive direction, towards other than market-type economies. Rather, as recent applications of "game theory" to such diverse activities as air combat and administrative behavior suggest, the "generality" of economic theory lies in the formal direction, towards other than price-oriented rational actions.

Yet, to my knowledge, no sociologist has presented a systematic discussion of the economy in any but formal terms. The more sophisticated the theory, the more prominent is the "economizing" element, the point already having been reached in some theories at which the substantive meaning of the compound concept drops out altogether. And with it has gone such an elementary distinction as that between the processes by which want-satisfying material means are produced and distributed, and the "production" and "distribution" of political power or of social prestige.

The argument here is for a change in emphasis. Not the formal, but the substantive element of "livelihood," in all its apparent vagueness, should be at the center of *sociological* theories of the economic process, of those theories in which the economy is seen as one of several generic social processes.

No attempt is made in this chapter to review in detail the various versions of the operation and place of the human economy in society proposed by the score or so of sociologists who have dealt seriously with the problems. Instead, three of the more influential conceptions are examined for conceptual clarity, empirical scope, and logical adequacy. Following this abbreviated survey and concluding the chapter is a discussion of one way in which the economy conceived as a substantive process may be introduced into current sociological thinking.

To avoid misunderstandings at the outset, brief remarks on two topics not otherwise explicitly discussed are included in this introduction. One is the significance of economizing actions within a substantive approach. The other concerns the related question of the connections between the disciplines of economics and sociology.

One of the major attractions which the substantive view of the economy has for sociologists is its clear compatibility with functional theory. To say of the economic process that its operation in all societies results in the continuous supply of want-satisfying material means is to define that process through a particular set of consequences and to leave unspecified initially the characteristics of the social relations through which this supply is effected. However, this vacancy is one of definition not of knowledge, as other parts of this volume demonstrate. Several types of social arrangements, for example, have been repeatedly found to facilitate the supply of material means, such as the port of trade and gift exchange. But what we know of these devices is indeed little compared with our richer and better organized knowledge of the structures effecting the supply in market-organized economies. So long as the limitations of this knowledge in its present form are recognized, we are in virtue of it far along towards filling the space left open in the definition of the economic process. In so far as structures of economizing actions effect the supply of want-satisfying material means, they thus enter into the substantive conception of the economy on a par with any other type of facilitating structure.

With regard to the second topic, then, sociologists have much to gain from economic theory (which according to its postulates is concerned with economizing action) in the study of market-organized economies. But the correct use by sociologists of the theories and findings of economics presupposes on their part a clearer recognition of the differences between what is sociological and what is economic, in the sense of the theory, than is now sometimes in evidence. For the matter at hand, "sociological" refers not to events but to concepts, problems and propositions, and the same is true of "economic" (again, in the sense of theory).[2] Sociological problems cannot, then, be adequately treated merely by generalizing to the total society supply and demand propositions.[3] Rather, if such statements are to be used, their contents need recasting into sociological terms.

A recent attempt at such a recasting was made by Talcott Parsons in the Marshall Lectures for 1953,[4] but in such a way that the conceptual distinctions in fact dividing the problems and propositions of sociology from those of economies come perilously close to being defined away rather than bridged.* In brief, Professor Parsons sees the relations between economy and society as paralleling those between economics and his version of the theory of action: since, he argues, the economy is a sub-system of the wider society, and since the general theory applies to society as a whole, economics (which he seems here to accept as the theory of the economy) must be a special case of the general theory.

To include in this manner the corpus of economics within his general theory, not only must Professor Parsons limit the forms that the economic process can take to those found in market and modern planned economies; he must also carry out some strange operations on the concept "society" in order to make it compatible with the given premises of economic theory. Whatever the gain to economics from this incorporation, the net effect for sociology is of doubtful value. For, if the market becomes in this way a sociologically relevant phenomenon, it also becomes thereby the prototypical economic institution within the general theory, a result restricting considerably the theory's generality. In short, "economy" as a social process is confounded or intentionally identified with the subject matter of economics as a discipline. (And, as a result, that the place of the market economy in modern society is the actual problem in these lectures, and the one to which they seem to make a substantial contribution, is almost hidden from the reader.) Conversely, in order that the categories

* See below, Ch. XV.

of his theory may be congruent with those developed by economists, for describing the rather unusual social structures with which they are concerned, the processes making up Professor Parsons' "society" become little more than formal equivalents, metaphorical restatements, of the market economy's price-making process.

More generally, however, it would seem to be an open question whether the possibility of characterizing the relations between social structure and economic process depends on being able to describe the connections between sociology and economics. If the two activities are at all related, the order of dependence appears logically to be the reverse of what Professor Parsons assumes. For, to explicate the links between two disciplines one must first be able to show how they differ in their descriptions of similar events. But a sociological conception of how economies operate, developed independently of economic analysis, is precisely what at present is lacking. Professor Parsons has thus not joined two independent disciplines but instead has defined for sociology what it will mean by "economy" and for economics what it will mean by "society." However engaging to the sociologist in his more imperialistic moods the latter prospect may appear, he cannot but pause long and thoughtfully, and eventually reject, a definition of "economy" arrived at in this manner and having such limited content.

Despite, then, the partial similarity of the problems dealt with in this chapter and by Professor Parsons, the approach here differs from his considerably, especially in the matter of assumptions about connections between sociology and economics. To omit this topic is not to deny that such connections are a valid intellectual concern. But spelling out these interdisciplinary linkages is simply a markedly different activity from developing a specifically sociological concept of the economy.

Reciprocally, the following critical comments on current sociologies of the economy (and the concluding suggestions for a revision) are not assumed to have any implications for economic theory or to be of more than casual interest to economists. The discipline of economics may have its theoretical problems, and some of these may involve the concept of society, but they are not for that reason the immediate concern of sociologists. Rather, the sociologist, as such, must assume economic theory to be adequate for the solution of its own problems, just as he ought also to view with skepticism both its claims to universality and its imputed power to transform into a full grown shade tree the viable but yet slender sociological sapling.

Criticism of Current Sociological Views of the Economy

Because a sociologist views the economy as an elemental part or process of society, there exist, corresponding to two main conceptions of society, two main conceptions of the economy. In one, the economy is defined through "division-of-labor," in the other, it is the locus of rationality.[5] With the development and elaboration of functional analysis in sociology,[6] though, some theorists have come to stress less the content of the economy in their initial definitions and more its consequences for society, retaining however the presumption that "economy" denotes primarily "economizing." A third major conception of the economy can be distinguished, then, one which was developed from the rational action view in an attempt to give the latter a functional foundation. This is the "scarcity" conception where the economy is defined as the process through which society's presumed problem of "scarcity" is solved.

THE DIVISION-OF-LABOR CONCEPTION

The division-of-labor definition of the economy is part of a rather familiar theory of society—the one that holds it to be an aggregate of more or less freely moving individual atoms coming together, bouncing off, or avoiding one another in accordance with the laws of nature and rationality. Both the effects of nature and the expression of rationality may be modified, however, by custom, morality, and law, so that society becomes the resultant of three "orders of reality": the physical and chemical order of nature, the psychological and biological order of drives and rationality, and the social and cultural order of "conventions." Such inclusiveness, characteristic of theories purporting to explain uniformities "in their concrete totality" (in contrast to those attempting to explain selected aspects of uniformities through the abstract relations said to exist among inferred properties of behavior), coupled with elevating the classic distinction between society and individual from an heuristic device to a cardinal principle, marks the atomistic theory of society as a product of nineteenth century social thought.

Seen as the locus of a "division of labor" and a correlative network of "exchange" among these atomistically conceived individuals, the economy is held to evolve through a set sequence of "stages." Actual economies are classified as being in one stage of development or another on the basis of degree of specialization, dominant mode of production, and the scope of the exchange network. (The most familiar of these evolutionary sequences is, perhaps, that which runs from hunting and gathering economies, through pastoral and agricultural, to manufacturing.) Because the stages picture fairly concrete situations that result more from physical and biological factors than from social factors, cultural values and their socio-psychological counterparts (i.e., motives) occupy at best a secondary place in this conception. The agricultural stage is compatible, for example, with both a system of free peasants and one of serfs. In this sense, the economy is viewed in the "division of labor" approach as basically a "non-cultural" entity. Its structure, composed of the relations among individuals as psycho-biological entities, is grounded in a dependence on others for the satisfaction of organic needs, and its operation is mainly a matter of some kind of overt "exchanges" which occur among the specialized producers and which contribute to the "satisfactions" of each. Finally, the "reality" of the economy is attested by the observable physical "flow" of useful things and by the overt behavior of individuals in relation to this observable movement. Throughout, then, the elements on which interest is centered are more frequently non-social than specifically social.

The many attempts to define the economy through "division of labor," however, have generally involved two rather basic difficulties. One of these has to do with marking off the boundaries of the economy as a distinct part of society, the other, with integrating the different parts of the economy.

The trouble with using "division of labor" to mark off the boundaries of any social sphere is that the universality which is the concept's main virtue is also its prime defect, a point made by Durkheim over fifty years ago.[7] With respect to the problem of distinguishing the economy from the rest of society, "division of labor" provides no help at all, for what would seem to be distinctly economic matters cannot, by employing that concept as a starting point, be separated from non-economic matters. This becomes evident if one inquires into the empirical content of the "labor" which is divided.

When "labor" refers to all social activities, "economy" has no specific content but is coterminous with "society": if "labor" designates the same things as "human behavior," then it is no more able than that term to mark off the boundaries of the economy. Praying, playing, and producing are here all equally "economic" activities.

Generally, however, "labor" is intended to refer not to all social activities but to some delimited set of them. But then one necessarily, if implicitly, starts from the activities specified and not from the degree of "division of labor." *What is of initial conceptual importance is not that "labor" is divided to varying extents—which is true in some sense for activities in every sphere of social life—but that certain activities and not others are "labor," that is, constitute the economy.*

Such a specification of "labor" is not a minor point, to be made parenthetically, as it were, while one passes on to more important topics. It is, perhaps, the major point. The intelligibility of a discussion of the economy—under any label—is dependent upon the boundaries of the economy being marked out. At this point, though, it is enough simply to note that some references to the nature of the divided "labor" are in fact usually made, for such references, however ill-conceived, substantiate the claim raised here that "the division of labor" is, taken alone, an inadequate point of departure for conceptualizing the economy.

The second difficulty attending this view of the economy is connected with the problem of re-uniting "divided" labor. Within the "division-of-labor" theory this problem of integration is typically surmounted by invoking the concept of "exchange," so that "specialized" individuals form a unity through the multiplicity of imputed "exchange" relations among them.

Now, it is quite true that if an economy consisting of independent individuals is to have unity whatsoever these individuals must be in some way "related" to one another. And if one wants to use the term "exchange" to denote *all* the social relations which are found empirically to structure the continuous flow of want-satisfying material means this is certainly permissible, if somewhat misleading. But one cannot then proceed to equate "exchange" in this inclusive operational sense of a mere change of place of material objects, for example, as between places occupied by different individuals, with "exchange" in the market sense. In particular such a concept is neither the prototype of "market exchange" nor even implies anything about "exchange" as a transaction within an instituted system of market relations.[8] *Movements of things* may very well occur through other than market arrangements and a market system, on the other hand, may operate without any changes in the physical places of the objects being in evidence. But of course, once these two meanings of "exchange" are equated, the entire value structure of the market-organized economy can be introduced without further difficulty—and the method of history can thereby be reduced to developing the several phases which mark the gradual distention of the market economy.

Thus, on the one hand, this conception provides no systematic way to distinguish what parts of a society comprise its economy while, on the other hand, it is all too specific about the ways in which these parts are related within an economy, if it could be distinguished.[9]

THE RATIONAL ACTION POSITION

The introductory summary here of the modern action view of society will be somewhat more extensive than that accorded the more familiar atomistic view, it being both the lesser known of the two and the basis of the discussion in the final section of this chapter.

Fundamental differences clearly distinguish the two points of view: (1) in action theory the units of society are not individuals but patterns of interaction; (2) the society formed from these units is not a concrete aggregation but an abstract system. Each of these foci, "interaction patterns" and "society as a system," which are the reference points for the concepts in the action frame of reference, will be taken up in turn.[10]

First, the idea of a complex of "*interaction patterns.*" The main idea here can be likened to a play: just as Shakespeare's lines in their totality are the fundamental source of unity in any performance of *Hamlet*, whatever the physical conditions of the staging or the psychological states of the actors may be, so interaction patterns are viewed as the fundamental source for the coherence which characterizes human societies. In the simplest model, that of a fully integrated system, what people "want" to do is no more and no less than what they are "required" or "expected" to do. This identity of personal preferences and social role requirements is asserted by "the postulate of institutionalization," one of the most basic premises of contemporary sociology. In marked contrast to the atomistic conception, cultural values are of prime importance, for they are instituted in the two systems of society and personality.[11] In the action system formed by society, values state in general what is expected of persons in different situations and what will be the consequences of conformity or deviance. They are thus the main content of social role definitions. In the personality system, through the socialization processes, values become *integral* parts of personality, in the sense that such "internalized" values are no less essential to individuals as humans than are lungs to individuals as organisms. Any fully instituted "role," then, is a part of two systems—society and personality—so that from the standpoint of the social system as a whole the mature adult's motivation to conform to role requirements is not generally in doubt.

No actual groups are, of course, "fully integrated," few if any roles are "fully institutionalized," and the previously asserted "identity of personal preference and social role requirements" is seldom an empirically accurate statement. However, in most groups the "fit" is sufficiently close so that the picture given by the postulate of institutionalization is usually a much closer approximation to the actual state of affairs than is its negation. In addition to empirical discrepancies, there are, however, various theoretical reasons why deviance from social role requirements is usually to be found in all groups. Such behavior is said to call into play the "mechanisms of social control" which, ranging from the informal opinions of others to formal enforcement agencies, operate to maintain or to increase the degree to which the relevant system of cultural values is institutionalized.

Compared with the other conception of society, then, here we find cultural elements of primary importance and "individuals" of secondary importance. The latter, in fact, do not even enter sociological theory except to play roles and thus to be "points" at which several roles are conjoined. No assumption is made of course that such a conjunction-of-roles conception of the individual exhausts even his socially relevant characteristics. To sociologists, however, whose concern is with the typical and recurrent social situations rather than with the idiosyncratic and unique, what is common to divers performances of Hamlet's role is of greater moment than what distinguishes Gieglud's playing from that of Olivier or Evans.

Second, the idea of "*society as a system*." For our purposes here this can be taken to mean that a certain set of processes, those "in" the system, operate in *relative* independence from other processes, those "external" to the system. But society is generally conceived to be a "self-maintaining" type of system, and this means that the internal processes constituting the system do not vary greatly in their operation even though the external processes to which they are causally linked show considerable variation.[12] Thus two primary aspects of society exist to which its constituent social processes may be functionally related. They can be evaluated for their contributions to the internal interrelations among the parts of the system, to "integration," or to the external relations between the system as a whole and its environment, to "adaptation." Primary social processes, such as the economy, make major contributions to the maintenance of the system in both the adaptive and the integrative respects.

As was mentioned previously, two formulations of the economy can be distinguished within this general view of society as a system of inter-action patterns, since the way in which the economy is defined has changed from an emphasis on interaction patterns to an emphasis on the economy's functional relevance for the total system. Initially, the economy was held to consist of rational actions—or of contractual relations in which such actions occurred—the economist's model of the market being introduced explicitly as the functional and structural prototype of all economies. Subsequently, the emphasis in the defini-tion of the economy was shifted from the economy's content to its consequences for society. As a result, the economy is at present defined functionally but in terms of the functions for society of a sub-system of rational actions, namely, the solution of the alleged problem of "scarcity." The initial conception and its development may perhaps best be presented by singling out from a host of representative views the perspective advanced by Max Weber.[13]

An antithesis to the rather non-social evolutionary view of the economy represented by the division-of-labor school would be an "idealistic" view (e.g., Sombart's) in which the uniqueness of empirical cultures and of their derivative social and economic structures is empha-sized.[14] While such an extreme cultural determinism has found little favor among American sociologists, the action view of the economy does, as has been said, include cultural values as a fundamental concept, and Weber was one of two or three important figures in the introduc-tion of cultural values into the definitions of the economy. Weber's approach to social institutions was generally to ignore the traditional facades, and to enter instead by a side door from where he drew up "ideal" versions of the several types of social action occurring in the religious, political, and economic spheres. These types he distinguished according to (1) various psychological dispositions—which, generalized, are cultural values—and (2) the social relational contexts of the actions in which these dispositions are appropriate motivational forces. Society is thus seen, basically if implicitly, as several structures of social relationships in which various types of action occur. The economy is that part of society which consists of rational actions in the context of impersonal relationships.

Weber developed his views on the economy not as a formulation in a general theory—he considered such a theory impossible or at least fruitless—but as an aid in working through a particular historical problem, the social conditions necessary for the development and persistence of modern capitalism. While his analyses and conceptions became gradually a part of American sociology, his opinion on the usefulness of a general theory was by and large rejected, and with it, the limited role he had intended his conception of the economy to play. The result was a confounding of two fundamentally different questions. A concern with the conditions for rational action was not clearly distinguished from a concern with the divers types of structures occurring in various economies. This confusion of the history and functioning of one type of economy with the problem of comparing economies led to the presumption, held here to be unwarranted, that the market economy is the structural and functional prototype of the economy in general.

This failure to distinguish clearly between these sets of problems would probably not have persisted were it not for the singularly important orientation to economic matters which fell to Americans in their package inheritance of European sociology and which continues today to permeate sociological thinking about the economy. In essence, this orientation is that insofar as economies consist of rational action, economic theory is adequate as a kind of sociology. However, some economies do not manifest primarily rational action, and the institutional contexts of the rest are characterized predominantly by values other than rationality. Therefore, this view holds, certain economic problems—those which are peripheral in the study of rational action, though perhaps of some importance in the study of society—cannot be fully analyzed within the discipline of economics. Instead they are fit subject matter for sociological analysis, and the study of such problems is to constitute the sociology of the economy.

The result of this orientation, and of the eventual generalization of

Weber's conception, is the widespread use of the economist's model of the economy as a roughly accurate formulation of the economy, so that non-market economies become mere appendages composed of deviant forms of essentially market economy parts. Such an approach, however, seems very like using as the guide to how all types of houses are built the principles by which, say, wooden houses are constructed. While brick, mud, and wooden houses are put together in quite different ways, one could never find it out by employing this procedure. Nevertheless, in this manner have the two action versions of the economy been formulated. The criticisms of these two will be presented separately, but those lodged against the direct rational action approach apply also to the "scarcity" approach, since the latter is actually little more than a functionally formulated justification for equating the economic process in general with its market form. For this very reason, though, the "scarcity" view has more serious theoretical implications.

1. The market model view

The values used to characterize "economic action" may be summed up by the terms "rationality" and "utilitarianism." In its formal sense the first denotes allocating means in order to maximize returns, while the second refers to viewing all objects, persons as well as things, as means and never as ends in themselves.[15] Of course, as far as introducing the market model is concerned, whether the economy is defined as consisting of actions guided by these values or of social relations in which the role definitions permit if they do not enjoin such actions makes no difference. In the latter type of definition, impersonal "contractual" relations are usually contrasted with the gemeinschaft character of "familistic" relations and with the unilateral, if also gesellschaft character, of "compulsory" relations.[16]

That no empirical economy is wholly constituted either by "economic actions" or by "contractual relations" is of course recognized. These are "pure" or "ideal" types. But the operation of just such an "ideal" version of the economy is what the market model explains. By working with such a view sociologists can therefore include almost without modification the economist's model as a detailed description of how economies are supposed to work. Moreover, because any actual economy only more or less conforms to the economist's description, adjustments in his basic model are called for in specific instances. All in all, a generalized economic theory together with its largely ad hoc empirical qualifications are taken to constitute the beginnings of a sociology of the economy. It must be emphasized that those who proceed in this fashion towards a sociological theory of the economy do not deny the extremely limited role played by a self-interested rationality in what are called "traditional economies." But they presume that, whether or not rationality is in fact present, they can draw conclusions about the extent to which actions are "economic"—which they can do, of course, only in the formal sense of the term—and that such conclusions are steps towards a general sociological theory of the economy.

From the fundamental assumptions that economizing is, or should be, central in all substantively economic activities and that the market pattern offers an explanatory paradigm, there follow for theory several types of consequences, only two of which are discussed in any detail here, a third being but briefly mentioned.

First is the consequence that the concepts used in analysis are initially concepts of economics, not of sociology. In conjunction with the view that economic theory describes the activities within the "pure" form of contractual relations,[17] this results in the derivative sociological "theory" being little more than a series of metaphorical constructions faulty at both ends. The data which support the assertions are taken from their meaningful context in society and the terms used to interpret them are lifted from their context in economic theory.[18] The different meanings of the term "choice" may illustrate this point.

In economic theory, roles and social relationships are just two more objects of choice: whether to enter or to leave social relations, in terms of the net satisfactions expected, is merely one of the several alternatives among which "individuals" are seen to choose. The "satisfactions" from being a member of a particular work crew, for example, are treated as theoretically commensurable with the "satisfactions" of an additional dollar a day income. Sociologically, however, "choice" denotes a behavioral relating of means to ends that is carried out by the acting person in accordance with a generally held norm which, by virtue of his roles and the corresponding internalized values, he also presumably holds. Thus, in sociology one's "choice" has no meaning except where explicit reference is made to the values defining current role obligations or to those internalized in his personality. In economics it is not only meaningful independently of such references, but values and obligations are among the very objects to be chosen. To treat these as equal concepts is to relativize "choice" beyond the point where it carries any significant meaning.

The very different way individuals enter into economic compared with sociological analyses may serve as an example of the contextual differences which distinguish the two disciplines. Economists can strip individuals of their beliefs and divorce them from their social relations because such specters are all that are needed to enact the processes in which, as economists, they are interested. This is not a "mistake" on the part of economists; on the contrary, by simplifying the situation they are able to center their attention on economizing action and its results and to ignore by and large the many "complicating factors" which from most other perspectives cannot be overlooked. Nevertheless almost every major contribution to sociological thinking in the past half century constitutes in some measure a challenge to the adequacy of this view. The current conception of society as a system of interaction patterns is one result. True, in studying contemporary societies, the degree of rationality in the patterned interactions is a strategic concern. But it has no intrinsic preeminence over other instituted values. Individuals, although entering mainly as centers at which diverse roles are conjoined, are enmeshed in social relations and must hold dear at least those beliefs corresponding to the values defining their major role obligations. The presuppositions of modern sociology are thus markedly different from the "individualistic" grounding of economics.

A second set of consequences of the market view of the economy concerns the reading of the interrelations between the economy and the several other institutional spheres of society. In short, in the construction of general sociological theories as well as in the largely *ad hoc* interpretations of empirical cases, these relations are frequently grossly misread. Questions concerning social structures alternative to market arrangements are seldom raised, while the functional implications of the market system are generalized into propositions about *the* economy. For example, that "natives" do not respond with more work when they are offered more pay is not usually because they have "fixed" wants— whatever this may mean in a situation as unstable as one where a wage system impinges on a village economy—but is because in most "native" economies wants are met through distributive arrangements other than market exchange. Such arrangements are not, it is true, *structural* equivalents of market patterns, but they are *functional equivalents*.[19] Through them as well as through market arrangements the economic process is in part carried on. Thus the ubiquitous activity of gift-giving need not be viewed as an anomaly. Although its content is marked usually neither by rational calculation nor by underlying elements of a competitive antagonism, its consequences for the economic process are similar to those of market exchange.

In the same way, what contributions other social structures make to the economy are overlooked unless equivalent to those they make to the market economy. Rules of kinship obligation or of political obedience become "primitive" forms of contractual law, while socialization processes can always be alleged to foster in personalities the "economic" attitude par excellence, self-interest, since in all societies some scope is in fact allowed for individually oriented decisions.

That many economic activities are organized through non-market structures obscures not only the contributions of such activities to the actual economy, if it is viewed as if it were a market system. Their significance for other institutional spheres is also overlooked. Reciprocity activities that are organized through kinship relations constitute in most instances reaffirmations of these ties. In this way they contribute directly to the stability of the kinship system, a result entirely foreign to the market system. On the contrary, the historical consequences of the market economy for the family structure have not infrequently led to the mistaken assumption of an intrinsic incompatibility between economic and kinship activities.

It is just such an unwarranted generalization, in another institutional sphere, that characterizes Professor MacIver's resurrection of the Spencerian antithesis between state and economy:

> The political system is . . . an organization of means for the control of means, an authoritative ordainment for the socal regulation of the basic technology. The economic system is also an organization of means for the control of means, directing under conditions laid down by the state, the production, exchange, and distribution of commodities and services. This function the economic system fulfills not by authoritative regulation but by the interadjustment of divers and conflicting interests that bargain and compete in terms of their respective command of money and credit. The political and the economic systems together form a co-ordinate institutional complex, the character of which is always changing according as more or fewer regulative functions are performed by one or the other system.[20]

What is implied here is that the state and the economy are functionally alternative structures for securing order in society. It is of somewhat more than passing interest that though his basic orientation is so alien to the action viewpoint, Herbert Spencer was perhaps the first to give this contrast a fundamental place in sociology. If for Comte the state was needed to counteract the disintegrating effects of occupational specialization, for Spencer—much more than for Engels—it could indeed wither away since free enterprise would in the fullness of time organize the whole of the "sustaining system." In any case, the nice phrasing of the contrast drawn in the excerpt should not obscure that it is a generalization from the relations observed to hold between the liberal state and the market economy.

Let us be clear on the basic point at issue here and in the immediately preceding paragraphs. All societies, viewed as self-maintaining social systems, have certain fundamental requirements which must be met if they are to continue in operation.[21] One of these requirements is that the members of a society be provided with a continuous supply of want-satisfying material means. Furthermore, all societies in fact have structures of social relations through which this supply is maintained, and in any given case that structure (or structures) *is* its economy. But, on the one hand, many different combinations on the structural theme can maintain *some* supply; on the other, the structure in any given case will perform for its society some functions which its counterpart in a different society does not perform. If, as in the instance recorded above, "the state" is identified as a certain type of structure, and if in some actual societies it plays a minor role in effecting the supply of material means, this fact says nothing about its role in this respect in other societies. Similarly, that in some societies a certain type of structure is observed to effect this supply cannot be taken to mean that this supply is invariably secured through such a structure.

A third consequence of the market model view of the economy need be only briefly mentioned. This is the ideological bias built into sociological theory through taking uncritically the economist's path as a shortcut to a sociology of the economy. For, as the MacIver excerpt indicates, integrating consequences are thereby ascribed by definition to the market form of the economy. Admittedly, many have agreed both before and after Adam Smith that frequent commerce increases trust. But the occasional integrating contributions of a type of economy are not sufficient to assert integration as a function universally performed by that type. To make such an assertion is to invite the criticism raised by Merton against picturing "religion as integrative, without limiting the range of social structures in which this is indeed the case." If, when this is done to religion, "the entire history of religious wars, of the Inquisition (which drove a wedge into society after society), of internecine conflicts among religious groups" is blotted out,[22] then, when it is done to commerce, the wars of conquest, class conflict, and agrarian uprisings are also struck from the historical record—and the sociology of the economy takes on the character of an inadvertent apologia for exploitation.

2. The "scarcity" defined economy

With the development of functional formulations attention has ostensibly turned from the structural content of the economy to its contributions to society as a system of interaction patterns. I say "ostensibly" because it is the functions of the market system that have been generalized and made to account for all economies. Given the prominence of the formal element in the compound concept of "economy," such a generalization amounts to little more than the provision of a functional explanation of economizing actions. It is, then, on the basis of a revised version of economic theory's "scarcity postulate" that this explanation is developed.

As has recently been emphasized, however, the so-called "scarcity postulate" is not one postulate at all but a carefully constructed set of premises defining a situation from which the act of choosing logically follows (and dubious motivational assumptions are thereby avoided).[23]* Briefly, a "scarcity-situation" should be defined as one where means have alternative uses and are insufficient to achieve all of a set of goals; since the goals must be ranked in the order preferred, and some action is presumed, a choice between the uses of the means is logically implied. When this "postulate" is carried into sociology, however, the specifying premises are left behind, so that "scarcity" comes to denote no more than insufficiency:

By virtue of the primordial fact that objects—social and non-social—which are instrumentally useful or intrinsically valuable are scarce in relation to the amount required for the full gratification of the need-dispositions of every actor, there arises the problem of allocation: the problem of who is

* See above, pp. 245–7.

to get what, who is to do what, and the manner and conditions under which it is to be done.[24]

But shorn of its specifying premises—that the means have alternative uses and that the goals are arranged in a priority scale—"the postulate of scarcity" merely denotes a condition of "not enough." This is an important change in meaning, for from the sheer "fact of scarcity," which after all is only the minor premise of a syllogism, nothing at all logically follows, much less the act of choosing. Thus certain assumptions must be made in order for the existential condition of "scarcity" to give any result. These assumptions vary, depending on whether "scarcity" is held to characterize the situation of the individual or that of society as a whole. In either case, however, a statement about how the individual or society will behave when faced with "scarcity" must be asserted or assumed.

As to the first, the individual, the two quotations below state, and with equal clarity despite three centuries of intervening thought, the naturalistic premise usually associated with "the scarcity postulate" when it is used to characterize the individual's situation:

If any two men desire the same thing, which neverthelesse they cannot both enjoy, they become enemies; and in the way to their End, (which is principally their owne conservation, and sometimes their delectation only) endeavour to destroy, or subdue one an other. (Hobbes)

Both the facilities necessary to perform functions and the rewards which are important to the motivation of individual actors are inherently scarce. Hence their allocation cannot be left to an unregulated competitive process without great frustration and conflict ensuing. (Parsons, et al.)[25]

Stated in the form of a syllogism this naturalistic argument reads: if there is not enough, there will be war; there is not enough (i.e., the "scarcity postulate"); and therefore, there is war—or, in Hobbes' version, would be except that government restrains men's impulsive behavior.

Underlying this argument is the assumption that what men strive for is given in nature, independently of their existence in society. Therefore, since men must live "in society," societies must provide solutions to this conflict of natural interests. But, in company with Rousseau, modern sociological theory flatly denies Hobbes' "solution" —the fundamental social controls are "not graven on tablets of marble or brass, but on the hearts of the citizens"[26]—and thereby it denies also the major premise. Instead, the sociological premise reads, "If there is not enough, men will act in accordance with the instituted values"— which is of course how they will act whether or not there is enough. This sweeping assertion must be understood in the spirit in which it is written. There is no intention of denying that scarcity, under certain social conditions and used in the technical sense, may not be of relevance for sociological theory. But the concept of "society" has meaning for action-theory sociologists only insofar as it refers to a system of interaction *patterns*. Both the patterning of interaction and the integration of the patterns into a system result from a coherent set of cultural values being present. Furthermore, they are present in a definite way, as basic parts both of the role definitions and of the personalities of the persons playing the roles. *Independently of values instituted in this double sense, there can be no conception of a system of interaction patterns and hence none of society either.* It cannot be "scarcity as a fact of nature" which is relevant, then, but only "scarcity" either as a critical shortage or as a generally acted upon *cultural definition of situations*. In neither case is "scarcity" universal, since neither famines and floods nor money as a generalized means of exchange are recurrent characteristics of all societies.

As to the second—when "scarcity" is held to characterize the situation of society as a whole—we confront a type of formulation which is unfortunately all too frequent in the social sciences. For, to propose the question of how "society will act" under conditions of chronic shortage—or under any others—and to give a literal answer is to commit the sin of reification. The concept of "society" refers to a system of varied modes of behavior, but the concept of "action" requires a substantial agent, and one to which subjective states such as "end" or "attitude" can be attributed. "Society" cannot, then, in the literal sense, perform an "action."

But if a literal reading of the question of how society responds to "scarcity" is logically fallacious, a metaphorical reading results in the elimination of "scarcity." The alleged response of society to the condition of "scarcity" is "allocation," a term referring either to the process of distributing things or to the state of affairs consequent upon such a distributing. In either case, "allocation" denotes what we already know, that members of society are continually being supplied with material means or that at any given time they have a supply. The process of supplying them consists, in the part denoted by the summary concept of "allocation," of a multiplicity of "allocating" actions that are performed by individuals in their respective social roles and in accordance with the instituted values. "Scarcity" can be said to cause this process only if it is said to cause the actions by individuals through which it is carried on. And this argument, except for rather special cases, we have already seen to be sociologically untenable.

To deny the universal relevance of "scarcity" for the operation of the economy is of course not to deny the relevance of *scarcity-situations* under specific social conditions.* Correspondingly, while the compound concept of "economy" is certainly unsatisfactory as a conception of the generic economic process, it just as certainly is of great importance in certain types of cases. The actual conditions under which scarcity-situations occur and the compound concept applies remain in large part still a problem for research. But two conditions seem of obvious importance: one is the presence of money as a generalized means of exchange, the other, the extent to which cultural definitions and social control permit "free choices" to occur. In the absence of the first, the uses to which material means may be put are considerably restricted—at least to the objects' culturally recognized technical characteristics. Because "generalized" refers to a means' usefulness in very many ways, a generalized means can be said to be invariably "scarce." But because wheat, for example, has a distinctly limited range of uses, there can be too much of it as well as too little. Moreover, whatever the listed range of uses to which an object is at some time or another put, individuals may not be free at any one time to choose among these technical alternatives. If, in particular, automatic rules govern an object's use for all times and places, and if most objects are covered by such rules, then no one exercises "choice" about how the objects are to be used, no matter what the amount available. (A variation on this point is where choice in the use of material objects is a prerogative of authority positions, so that again the bulk of the population make no choices.)

Thus the presence of scarcity-situations would seem to be a matter of degree. And the actual extent to which such situations affect the supply of material means would seem to be a result in part of the

* See above, pp. 246–7.

"generality" of money, assuming of course it is present as a means of exchange at all, and of the scope permitted to individuals to choose among the uses to which the means may be put. But both the exchange use of money and the frequence and scope of choosing stand within the sphere of culturally defined and socially sanctioned activities. Neither is present in all societies, and so scarcity-situations cannot be used to define what is present in all societies, the economic process. At the same time, both are present in some societies, and in these the social activities contributing to the economic process are typically organized by market-type arrangements, for which "economy" in the compound sense is the appropriate initial conception.

The basic point remains, however, that "economy" defined functionally in terms of certain requirements of the system is a different process, sub-system or institution from "economy" defined in terms of constituent actions. To presume that one can use "scarcity" as a system-problem and thereby introduce the economizing process is either to strip the concept of its meaning and substitute instead naturalistic assumptions or to retain the formal economic assumptions and make all economies variations on the market theme, thereby negating the very purpose of a functional formulation. The functional and the rational action formulations of "economy" may coincide in fact—under those specific conditions when scarcity-situations are instituted. But this is only one type of economy.

CONCLUSION OF PART I

The description of the economy as a generalized version of the theory of the market is simply one more instance of an indiscriminate eclecticism which has occasionally marked the development to modern sociological theory. In this instance, the lens of the borrowed looking glass was too powerful and sociologists, failing to make the necessary adjustments, have ignored economic phenomena where they exist, postulated market phenomena where they do not in fact exist, and confused questions about the historical and functional conditions of structures of rational action with questions about the types of social structure which make up different kinds of economies. More concerned in theory with the relations between economics and sociology than with the relations between economy and society, and their researches limited to areas bordering on economic analysis, they have neglected the basic problem of comparing economies, namely the conceptualization of a generic economic process. In effect, sociological problems within the sphere of the economy have been defined by economists, and one result is that today we are largely ignorant of economies other than our own. And, lacking a sociology of the market, we understand even that only partially.

The Substantive View of the Economy

Despite the popularity of the *gemeinschaft-gesellschaft* theme, the assumption has persisted in sociological circles that the only "real" economic process is the one observed to operate in market-type economies. Some years ago, the usefulness was demonstrated of taking the distinction literally and of not presuming that the economies of communally or centrally ordered societies are organized through legally limited and contractually specified relations entered into by what Max Weber called "formally free" individuals. In the years since *The Great Transformation*[27] was written much effort has gone into developing what is in this book called the substantive conception of the economy. The problem in this second part of this chapter will be to develop in sociological terms the high points of this conception. The discussion will proceed in two steps, focusing first on the manner in which the economic process is instituted in all societies and then on the various ways in which it may be organized in different societies. Addressing the discussion to this pair of questions would seem to be doubly useful. Answers to them not only may constitute a step in the direction of a sociological theory of the economy, but will also give the sociological import of the recurrent assertions that the economic process is an instituted process and that it may be instituted in significantly different ways. Whether the ideas presented are useful depends, however, less on the stated points of convergence between them and contemporary sociological theory than on the extent to which they jibe with present knowledge of current and historical economies. This test, however, cannot in the limited scope of this chapter be carried out, so that the conceptions advanced here are done so very tentatively.

THE ECONOMIC PROCESS AND SOCIETY

The economic process—that which results in the continuous supply of want-satisfying material means—*is not only, nor even mainly, an object of sociological concern.* Physical, chemical, biological, and psychological factors, as well as social factors, contribute to the actual livelihood of men, so that the total process is a complex network of causality effecting this supply. However, the causal web is not all of a piece. Rather, it is chain-like, each link having distinctive properties. It is, so to speak, broken up into several segments, each of which forms a part of the subject matter of a special discipline. But each segment can be such subject matter only because its activities operate in relative independence of the activities in the other segments; or, the properties of no one segment determine the properties of either any other segment or the total process. For our purposes here, it is sufficient to distinguish three segments or levels, the strictly social, the psychological, and the naturalistic.

From an outright naturalistic position, the social and psychological aspects of the total economic process appear as mere epiphenomena in the fundamental relation between the human organism as a biological system and the biological, physical, and chemical processes in the environment which satisfy the organism's requirements. The other two enter, if they enter at all, as no more than complicating links in a chain which otherwise consists of phenomena like breathing, processes which directly involve an interchange between organic requirements and the satisfying objects in the environment.

Fortunately for our concern, however, the biological relation is basically the same within an enormously variable range of human activities. This relative independence of the biological and the specifically human aspects of the economic process means that those primarily interested in the latter can abstract them from the total economic process. For the causally related biological aspects cannot account for any of the *differences* which are in fact observed in the patterning of the social activities. From a social standpoint, then, the non-social aspects of the economic process appear largely as constant processes which in no wise determine the variations in human activities although they just as certainly are present in all concrete actions.

These relatively independent social aspects of the economic process are usually introduced by saying that the organic needs and what in the environment satisfies them are "socially defined," but in the sense that the needs become "wants" (or "felt needs") and the objects must be "perceived." This casting of a psychological light on the whole subject has been a constant source of trouble for the sociologist, since he has had to deal with what is from the standpoint of substantive economies the pseudo-problem of a specific type of "economic motivation." That there is a psychological level to the economic process which is intermediate to the sociological and sub-social and links them, is of course true. But the specifically psychological processes (e.g., memory, perception, etc.) are also, like the naturalistic processes, fairly constant over a wide range of human activities. For this reason, we can go one step further here. "Socially defined" can be interpreted to refer to the conception that role definitions—what from the perspective of the person playing the role are role-expectations—state the socially acceptable or required goals that are to be pursued and the similarly acceptable or required meanings which are to be imputed to material objects.

Thus while *the economic process* includes much more than the socially defined activities of men that contribute to the supply of material means, this set of activities is what in the total process primarily interests the sociologist. This social aspect, denoted here by the usual term "economy," is relatively independent of the non-social and psychological aspects of the total economic process, in the sense that the latter remain fairly constant over a wide range of variations in the character of the specifically social aspect. To explain these variations in men's economic activities, then, one must turn to the wider system of social actions, the society, of which the economy as a social process is a part. For these economic activities, while attuned to the environing conditions, are the product not primarily of these conditions but of the ordered ways of group living, of the patterns of interaction; and the coherence that the activities clearly manifest results primarily from being a part of this system of interaction patterns.

The economic process is an "instituted process," then, in the obvious sense that an essential part of it is also a part of a social system—that part composed of the activities of men contributing to the supply of material means. The patterning manifested by these "economic activities" derives from the same source that the patterning of any set of social actions derives, namely, the process of institutionalization. Thus what goals are pursued, either in regard to the economic process or otherwise, and how material objects are defined (i.e., the meanings imputed to them) can be viewed as patterned by social role definitions. It is not, then, the economic process in its totality that is instituted, but only that part consisting of men's actions. The other parts of the economic process, specifically, the "natural" or non-social parts, while they can in varying extents be "controlled" by men, can never be instituted in the strict sense of the concept. Thus so long as men cannot live by moral convictions alone there will be a constant source of instability in their action systems, no matter how well integrated these convictions are. For, some of the properties of the situation on which the stability of the action systems causally depends are in turn causally dependent on natural processes external to social systems, and in this way are a source of instability.

This formulation of the social aspects of the economic process suggests the basis for developing a functional conception of the economy, for the economy is evidently one of the mechanisms through which this potential instability is kept to a minimum. If it is true that the meanings of material objects are given by role definitions, then it is also true that the stability of the system of role definitions, and hence of the actions carried out in accordance with them, depends upon the objects being present in the situation of action in order to be defined. A shoemaker must "have" leather in order to make shoes, but his "having" the leather is only partly a resultant of processes internal to the system of roles. The calf's maturation and the action of the acid on the hide are just as important as the feeding of the calf and the application of the acid. But these causally relevant processes external to the social system continually vary in ways which would upset the equilibrium of expectations if the economy, a part of both the economic process and the social system, did not operate as a reduction gear, transforming the large fluctuations in the non-social part of the economic process into smaller rhythmic variations to which role expectations can be attuned. This function is, logically, a necessary one if the social system is to be viewed as a relatively independent focus of investigation. If every fluctuation in nature produced a corresponding fluctuation in society, the hypothesis that social processes constitute a system sufficiently independent to be the subject of a scientific discipline would be invalid.

Thus a tentative way of viewing the economy functionally is as a process operating within the "boundary sphere" between the "purely" social and the "purely" natural. In this capacity as a boundary-process, it functions to maintain the line separating the social processes which are internal to society and compose it, from the natural processes which, while external to society, are causally related to the social processes. It performs this function by keeping the fluctuations in the natural environment from impinging on social processes in forms, or to degrees, not taken into account by the instituted set of role expectations.

THE INSTITUTING OF THE ECONOMIC PROCESS

In the preceding analysis it was suggested that the economy consists of all those social actions which contribute to the supply of material means, and that the defining function for society of this aggregate of actions is to maintain the boundary between processes internal to society and the external processes of the natural environment. The next question to take up is how this functionally identified aggregate of actions comes to manifest the stability and recurrence which characterizes in varying degrees all economies. By using the market model, sociologists have had to assume in fact, if not explicitly, that the immediate and most important source has been the price system. As the following paragraphs will suggest in more detail, the problem is substantially more complicated. The stability and recurrence of economic activities derive from sources so various that even a simple formulation of the question leads directly to fundamental sociological problems.

The assumption which underlies any explanation of the stability and recurrence of the set of functionally defined economic actions is that they are not only an aggregate of actions, a logical class, but are also an "economy," a natural grouping. It is assumed that the actions occur in ordered sequences and that these bear definite relations to one another and to sequences of non-economic actions. The problem is thus to locate in various societies the patterned social arrangements of which economic actions are a part and from which their orderly occurrence derives.

This is, however, a complicated problem. These social arrangements, that give to sets of economic actions their stability and recurrence, are social units of more or less inclusiveness, existing at different "levels" within society. They may be, for example, the roles of which economic action patterns are a part; or the organizations of which economic roles are a part; or the broader structures of which economic organizations themselves are a part.[28] One result of this complication is that we must expect to see considerable variation from society to society in the "level" at which economic action patterns are integrated with non-economic action patterns. In what follows, mention will be made only of the four most evident levels.

At the first level, economic actions are carried out in roles that are constituted predominantly by actions having negligible effects on the economic process. The basic values defining activity in such roles and thus ordering the action sequences are not likely to be oriented primarily to the economic process, so that economic actions are closely integrated and guided by non-economic considerations. An example of integration at this level is the distribution of foodstuffs (economic action) to the poor by a priest (non-economic role context). Second, economic actions may be the major elements in roles, but these economic roles themselves may be units of structures consisting mainly of non-economic roles. The *tamkarum*, a specifically economic role found throughout the societies of the ancient Near East, is almost always a unit of a structure political in overall organization and basic policy.* The purchasing agent of a modern university is, similarly, an economic role in an organizational context that is primarily non-economic. Predominantly economic roles may however be grouped or organized to form continuous economic organizations, such as plantations, factories, guilds, etc. The third level at which economic and non-economic action patterns are integrated is where such organizations operate in non-economic structural contexts, as in an Israeli commune. Finally, the structure of relations among economic organizations may itself be economic, as in a market system or in the planned economy of a modern complex society. In so far as the set of economic actions are all elements within this inclusive structure, the economy is a relatively independent sub-system of society and is integrated with non-economic sub-systems *primarily* through that set of instituted values common to all roles (secondary means being the structural modes of interdependence, e.g., multiple roles).

To use the market model as the theory explaining how all economies operate, then, is to assume that the coherence undoubtedly manifested by the economic activities in all societies results mainly from

* See above, Ch. II. and p. 260.

the integration of economic actions at the fourth system-level and thus in *relative independence* from the organization of action patterns in other institutional spheres. Generally, this means assuming coherence to occur because actions are oriented to the conditions of a price-making market system; but, with certain adjustments in the model, it can also mean assuming coherence to result from actions being oriented to the conditions of a modern "nationalized" economy. In any case, the implied assumption is the basic reason why, where such markets or planning are absent, no understanding of the structuring of economic activities is possible by using this model.

Here lies also the significance of the distinction between "embedded" and "unembedded" economies.[29] As the above description of system-levels suggests, "embeddedness" is a matter of more or less, at one end being economies whose constituent actions are patterned through their occurrence in non-economic roles, at the other end, those economies organized through such economic institutions as fluctuating prices and centralized planning. While the market model may explain the coherence of actions in economies near the zero end of the "embeddedness" dimension, it can never explain this property of the economic actions carried out either as secondary aspects of non-economic roles (such as the priests) or within economic roles which are secondary elements in non-economic organizations (such as the university or state).

Strictly speaking, then, there are no "different ways" of instituting the economic process, since all actions are instituted in basically only one way. What is meant by the phrase is that the economic process is instituted at different social *levels*, in the sense that the explanation for its degrees of unity and stability in one society may be a matter of the integration of actions in roles, while in another, of the integration of roles in organizations, and in yet another, of the integration of organizations into systems.

Yet another way of phrasing the limitations of the market model, then, is to say that a necessary condition of its application is the organization of almost all economic activities into a coherent and relatively independent sub-system of society. In so far as the economy, defined as the aggregate of actions contributing to the supply of material means, is not organized as a structurally distinctive sub-system of society, then the market model is not merely useless, it is positively misleading.

LOCATIONAL AND APPROPRIATIONAL TYPES OF ECONOMIC ACTION

However, the substantive analysis of economies is complex not only because the economic process may be instituted at different levels in different societies. It is complex also because this may be true within any one society. Since any empirical economy consists in its social aspects of an aggregate of actions, some of these may be organized in non-economic roles while others are parts of roles occurring within economic organizations. (This is the main difference between the economic actions of the housewife in our society and those of her husband.) This very general assertion suggests that economic actions may not be merely an undifferentiated aggregate but may be classifiable into types which are frequently found to be instituted at different levels within any one society. While a list of the dimensions useful for distinguishing types of economic actions which vary in this respect is yet to be drawn up, it is possible to indicate a seemingly basic distinction. The two types of economic action so derived appear likely to vary in the level, or at least in the concrete social arrangements, in which they are instituted. To develop this dichotomy, we must turn to a distinction between two kinds of changes which occur in the economic process.

While so far we have treated the economic process as divisible mainly in terms of social and non-social aspects, this has been a simplification which must now be given up, for from another perspective the material objects in the continuous flow are characterized by two basic types of movements. One type consists of changes in an object's relations to other objects, and is called "locational movements." The other consists of changes in an object's relations to social roles, is called "appropriational movements," and usually but not always involves "rights" (but in the broad sociological, not the legal sense).*

Corresponding to these two types of movements of objects are two types of economic actions, that is, of social actions contributing to the supply of material means. One consists of appropriational actions, which comprise almost all appropriational movements, whether these consist of one-sided dispositions, or two-sided transactions, whether of things, rights, or what Max Weber called "opportunities." The other consists of those actions which directly cause locational changes. In

* See above, pp. 248–9.

moving particles or masses of matter, in Locke's phrase, "men mix their labour with their produce." In company with natural processes, these locational actions account for all locational movements. In contrast to the redefinition of the social situation involved in appropriational actions, these imply "effort."

Before discussing these types of economic action in relation to levels of instituting, we should note that they correspond to the usual distinction between "production" and "distribution" (or "circulation" or "allocation"). However, they are more precise. "Distribution" in particular tends to be used in two quite different ways, one referring to locational movements, as in transporting, the other, to appropriational movements, as in retailing. From the substantive economic standpoint, "distribution" consists only of appropriational movements. Locational movements, on the other hand, include both transporting and what is usually understood by "production," the difference between the two being mainly a difference in the scale of the spatial frame of reference in which the locational operations are carried out.

That these two types of action may be instituted at different levels is exemplified in Walter Neale's analysis of the traditional Indian village.* There "labour" or, more strictly, locational actions (excepting tillage), is instituted through the caste system. What contributions (apart from grain) a person makes to the supply of material means are organized through his more inclusive caste role. On the other hand, the appropriational movements—who appropriates how much from what piles of produce—do not appear to follow caste lines. Within the total community they are organized through the different community roles, such as cultivator, priest, herdsman, etc., while within the joint family they are organized through the patriarchal structure of that social unit, the head of the family parcelling out shares to the family's members.

The distinction between the two types of economic action, empirically useful in describing the structure of an economy, is however not only based on the substantive conception of the economic process as consisting of two types of movements. It also relates to the previously formulated sociological conception of the economy as a boundary sphere, one which keeps the operation of natural processes from impinging on the total system of social processes. For the locational economic actions constitute the specific interchanges linking the social and non-social aspects of the total economic process. The appropria-

* See above, pp. 226-7.

tional actions, on the other hand, are the specific interchanges linking the economy as a social process to the other social processes—and to other economies, though this problem of inter-society "trade" will not be discussed here.

Those two dimensions, the degree of "embeddedness" and the types of movements, are basic to a substantive conception of the economy in its sociological aspects. Yet a third, the patterns which integrated sets of economic movements manifest, might also be mentioned. To date, these have been described by the "forms of integration" as "reciprocity," "redistribution," and "exchange." Whether there are other patterns as fundamental, or whether these three exhaust the principal "pure" types, must remain problems for research. That a similar threefold distinction characterizes both the mechanisms regulating the "allocative flow," in the monograph by Parsons, Shils, and Olds, and Pitirim Sorokin's types of social relations argues that the forms of integration are more than merely *ad hoc* principles.[30] The "allocative mechanisms" are in fact very close parallels, consisting of allocation through selective decisions by people in authority, automatic application of cultural rules, and impersonal competition among "free" individuals. Nevertheless, the theoretical underpinnings of the "forms of integration" have not been clearly stated—so that at times the "forms" are used to refer to locational changes of objects, at other times, to appropriational changes and occasionally to both—and need to be developed if the concepts are to be basic tools as well as pragmatically useful designations.

So far then it has been suggested that the economic process is instituted through the integration of men's patterned economic actions, which make up its social aspect, with their non-economic actions; that even within the same society the process may be instituted at different system levels, in the sense that the stability and recurrence of the economic actions may derive from their integration at any one of a number of these levels; and that "productive" and "distributive" actions, as these were defined above, are particularly subject to being instituted at different levels or at least through different sets of social arrangement. I have, perhaps too rigidly, attempted in this conceptual presentation to avoid identifying any *particular* subjective or psychological dispositions as appropriate by definition to economic actions. This by no means should be taken to mean that such dispositions are irrelevant (i.e., random) or even constant: not only can we presume variations, but we can expect *patterned* variations. However, since most contemporary writers have stressed a particular type of subjective element (i.e., rationality), I have wanted to indicate that many types are potentially compatible. While further conceptual elaborations easily suggest themselves, for example, the various motivational components of the types of actions when they are included in different kinds of social structure, such conjecturing would take us well beyond present knowledge. Indeed, the supply lines to this knowledge may already have become too long.

CONCLUSION

In this essay an attempt has been made to show that present sociological views of the economy are inadequate formulations of a generic economic process, and are thus unsuitable as basic conceptions within a general theory of social systems, and that what is needed is a conception based on the substantive meaning of "economy." In both the "division-of-labor" view and that of the economy as a sphere of rational actions (or of contractual relations), the economist's model of the market was seen to be the guiding image. In the first, "exchange" was assumed to be the only way in which the allegedly divided labor was united; in the second, it is the only mode of distribution. Where a functional definition of the economy has been introduced, the presumption has been that the economy consists of economizing, so that the relevant system problem, in terms of which the economy is functionally defined, is "scarcity." It was argued that this concept is ambiguous in meaning, has irrelevant naturalistic implications, and at best serves only to define the market system. Present functional formulations, being little more than devices to introduce a market economy, are also subject to the same criticisms made against viewing the economy as composed of rational actions, namely, conceptual confusions, parochialism, and a tacit ideological bias.

Starting from the fact that "economy" is usually used in its compound sense, of a process supplying material means through economizing actions, I suggested that a functional formulation of the economy, based on the substantive element of the supply of material means, would be more fruitful. From this fundamental idea, which included stating in what sense the total economic process is instituted, two basic dimensions of the economy were developed. One is the system level at which economic actions are integrated, the other is the distinction of these actions into two types, locational and appropriational.

As with most conceptions in the contemporary social sciences, the validity of those presented here depends perhaps more upon their usefulness in helping to pose theoretically important but researchable questions than upon their logical coherence—though it is hoped that that quality is not entirely lacking. The basic set of ideas in the substantive approach to the economy has already demonstrated its usefulness in economic history and anthropology, a fact to which other parts of this book bear witness. Perhaps it can similarly assist in the development of a sociological theory of the economy, one with relevance for a broader set of problems than those bounded by the Western economy of the nineteenth century.

Terence K. Hopkins

Notes to Chapter XIV

1. See esp. pp. 243 ff.
2. See, e.g., Wilbert Moore's *Economy and Society* (Garden City, N.Y., 1955), esp. 5.
3. For an instance of such a generalization, see Kingsley Davis and Wilbert Moore, "Some principles of stratification," *American Sociological Review*, 10 (1945): 242–9; reprinted in Logan Wilson and William L. Kolb, eds., *Sociological Analysis* (New York, 1949) 434–443.
4. *The Integration of Economic and Social Theory* (1953, mimeographed) on file at the Social Relations Library, Harvard University.
5. The concept of rationality may be introduced initially in several ways, for example, as a type of action, as a preferred norm in certain kinds of social relations, or as a general cultural value.
6. The most systematic presentation of functional concepts in sociology is in "Manifest and latent functions," ch. I of Robert K. Merton's collected essays, *Social Theory and Social Structure* (Glencoe, Ill.: 1949), esp. 49–81.
7. *The Division of Labor*, Introduction and ch. 1.
8. "Exchange" in this latter case denotes a concept that not only is operationally independent of observable vice-versa movements of useful things between people, but is instead theoretically dependent on a conception excluded from the basic schema of atomistic sociologies, namely, shared reciprocal expectations. For it is in the context of such expectations that rational calculations take place, as Adam Smith intuitively perceived when he writes of a "certainty of being able to exchange" (*The Wealth of Nations*, Bk. I, ch. 2). It is of course no solution to the complex problem of what socio-cultural phenomena are indicated by the various overt forms which men's activities take to assume simply that discrete movements of

material, whether organic or inorganic, stand in a one-to-one correlation with a particular type of normatively defined social relation.

9. At the root of both difficulties—marking off the economy and integrating its parts—is the conversion of a methodological problem, which resides in the fact that cultural values are not "observable" in the same way as overt forms of activity are, into the theoretic orientation that the forms of activity are to be understood without reference to values. While this radical disjunction between outer and inner forms of behavior is in fact maintained neither in specific concepts nor in drawing the social implications of the asocial premises, it nevertheless constitutes a fundamental tenet of atomistic sociology. That the dichotomy results in significant oversights was explicitly noted by Karl Marx (Capital, I, Pt. IV, ch. 14, Sec. 4) when he took Adam Smith to task for equating the division of labor in factories with its division in society: the social and psychological consequences of divided labor differ substantially when the way in which such labor is integrated differs. The distinction between the two forms cannot be one of basic sociological theory but at the most only of procedure: one can leave open the question of specific values and motivations associated with otherwise identifiable kinds of economic activity, but one cannot dismiss as irrelevant the categories of value and motivation.

10. As the discussion is necessarily brief, and to that extent imperfect and perhaps involuntarily misleading, the interested reader is advised to examine the following works which present in some detail the general action frame of reference: Talcott Parsons and Edward A. Shils, eds., *Toward a General Theory of Action* (Cambridge, Mass., 1952); Talcott Parsons, *The Social System* (Glencoe, Ill., 1951); Pitirim A. Sorokin, *Social and Cultural Dynamics* (New York, 1937–41, 4 vols); Pitirim A. Sorokin, *Society, Culture and Personality: Their Structure and Dynamics* (New York, 1947); Florian Znaniecki, *Cultural Sciences* (Urbana, Ill., 1952); and Robert M. MacIver, *Social Causation* (Boston, 1942).

11. These three spheres of culture, personality, and society are viewed as relatively independent systems of action patterns, representing not distinct entities, for men's activities are the common concrete points of reference, but distinctly different ways of perceiving such activities and of organizing the uniformities the activities manifest.

12. See Ernest Nagel, *A Formalization of Functionalism* (mimeographed, 1953) on file in Burgess Library, Columbia University. The logic of functional analysis in sociology is not yet well developed. In addition to Nagel, who should be read in conjunction with Merton, "Manifest and latent functions," and to several scattered comments in the works of Parsons, see the brief "axiomatic" statement by Morris Zelditch, Jr., "A Note on the Analysis of Equilibrium Systems," Appendix B, in Talcott Parsons and Robert F. Bales, *Family, Socialization and Interaction Process* (Glencoe, Ill., 1955). See also, Talcott Parsons, Robert F. Bales, and Edward A. Shils, *Working Papers in the Theory of Action* (Glencoe, Ill., 1953), chs. III–V.

13. Of the several works by Weber that are translated, the most relevant to cite here is *The Theory of Social and Economic Organization*, trans. by A. M. Henderson and Talcott Parsons (New York, 1947).

14. See the discussion in Talcott Parsons, *The Structure of Social Action* (Glencoe, Ill., 1949), ch. X, "The Idealistic Tradition."

15. See "The Motivation of Economic Activities" in Parsons' collected essays, *Essays in Sociological Theory* (Glencoe, Ill., 1949), esp. 202.

16. See, for example, Sorokin, *Social and Cultural Dynamics*, III, ch. 1; Hans Speier's review in *American Sociological Review*, 2 (1937), 924–929; and Sorokin's revision of these three types in *Society, Culture and Personality . . .* , 99–110.

17. For example, Znaniecki, *Cultural Sciences*, 322–323.

18. Evidence for this claim is to be found in several of the peripheral studies which Wilbert Moore has included in "The Sociology of Economic Organization," in Gurvitch and Moore, eds., *Twentieth Century Sociology*. However, Moore himself mentions explicitly that such terms as "demand," "labor," and "price" lose almost all of their precision in being transferred from economics to sociology.

19. See Merton, *Social Theory*, ch. 1, esp. 35–38.

20. *Social Causation*, 284–285.

21. For discussions of the concept "functional requirements" see the previously cited references on the logic of functional analysis. See also, Parsons, *The Social System*, chs. II and V; Kingsley Davis, *Human Society* (New York, 1949) 29–50; and David Aberle, et al., "The functional prerequisites of a society," *Ethics*, 60 (1950) 100–111. It is outside the scope of this paper to assay whether the statement, that those "requirements must be met," rests on the logical ground that the requirements are part of what is meant by "society as a system," on the theoretic ground that meeting them follows from some more basic postulates, or on the empirical ground that all known societies do in fact meet certain requirements.

22. *Social Theory* . . . , 81.

23. See Ch. XIII, pp. 245–247.

24. Talcott Parsons, Edward A. Shils, and James Olds, "Values, motives, and systems of action," in Parsons and Shils, eds., *Toward* . . . , 197.

25. Pt. 1, ch. 13 of *Leviathan*; Talcott Parsons, et al., "Some fundamental categories of the theory of action," in Parsons and Shils, eds., *Toward* . . . , 25.

26. *The Social Contract*, Bk. II, ch. 12.

27. Karl Polanyi, *The Great Transformation* (New York, 1944) esp. ch. 4.

28. Readers versed in "Columbia sociology" will recognize here the formulations of Professor Merton, from whose lectures on "The Functional Analysis of Social Structure," given at Columbia University, I have taken the idea.

29. See Polanyi, *The Great Transformation*, ch. IV. The distinction is comparable to, though not quite the equivalent of, the sociologist's distinction between "differentiated" and "undifferentiated."

30. "Values, motives and systems of action," 207; *Social and Cultural Dynamics*, III, ch. 1; see also, Margaret Mead, "Public Opinion Mechanisms Among Primitive Peoples," *Public Opinion Quarterly*, 1 (1937), 5–16, for a surprisingly similar trichotomy in this somewhat different field of "public opinion."

XV

Parsons and Smelser on the Economy

———•———

THE publication of a greatly enlarged and revised version of Professor Talcott Parsons' "Marshall Lectures"[1] lends impressive support to our conviction that a discipline which may be called "economic sociology" is being newly established in the United States. The impetus for the widely current efforts in the direction of an economic sociology comes from the increasing array of empirical problems met by all social scientists who must face up to economies as social systems. The problems arise in two different areas of interest; those involving premarket economies, both literate and nonliterate, and those where contemporary departures from the pattern of a self-regulating system of markets pose the problem. Attempts to deal systematically with these distinctly separate empirical problems converge on a common interest: the establishment of a generally relevant theory of economic organization and development.

It is this interest that we have in mind in attempting to appraise the accomplishments of Talcott Parsons and Neil Smelser in their new book, *Economy and Society*, for, although the empirical problems with which this book deals are derived from a market-ordered economy, it represents a theoretical *tour de force* aimed in the direction of a general theory. Starting at the opposite pole, the book in which this chapter appears is concerned with the problems of primitive, early historical and nonwestern economies, but it too is regarded as a modest offering in the same direction. The opportunity to discuss the position now taken by Professor Parsons is therefore welcomed on general grounds.

Our purpose is to clarify points held in common, differences in approach and fundamental disagreements in so far as both efforts come to grips with the problem of determining the shifting place of the economy in human society.

It is encouraging to find that there are important areas of agreement between these two books. A "functional" approach is common to both. Professor Parsons' sociology views society in terms of certain functional requirements all of which must be satisfied if that society is to continue and prosper. All of the specific units of the society—the "collectivities," institutions and roles—are seen as necessarily contributing to the fullfillment of these functional prerequisites; although they may, of course, be differentiated in terms of primary functions. The central analytical problem is that all the units of the whole society "*participate* in the economy," but, because every concrete unit is multifunctional, none is "purely economic" (p. 14). Thus, although we feel that the authors' analysis is based on a mistaken quasi-identification of economic theory and sociology, *in principle* the Parsons-Smelser book conceives the problem of economy and society in the same way as it is here conceived. The fruitfulness of employing the basic conceptual tools of modern sociology in approaching the economy—especially the conception of cultural values embedded in institutions, roles and personalities (i.e., the "reality" of society)—is clearly demonstrated in the ease with which this new book is able to dispose of some hoary problems of economic theory which arise from that theory's "psychological and sociological atomism" (p. 23). A functionally defined economy is seen as performing *within* the structural context of society. Thus, "the goal of the economy is not simply the production of income for the utility of an aggregate of individuals. It is the maximization of production relative to the whole complex of institutionalized value-systems and functions of the society and its subsystems" (p. 22). We believe that the maximization principle introduces a bias into the definition of the economy's function, but again in principle there is agreement with many of the basic ideas in the present book.

While we thus find important areas of fundamental agreement and the underlying concepts for the articulation of an economic sociology are clearly presented, the two efforts part company in their separate attempts to deal systematically with the problems. In fact they seem to move in almost opposite directions. This divergence may be due in large measure to the different location of the empirical problems which the two books set out to examine. But in so far as both make some claim to generality this reason cannot be accepted as decisive. More significant, is the fact that in the manner of attacking the problem, once it is stated, we are at opposite poles.

In the history of the attempt to locate the place of the economy in society—or, as we should prefer, of economies in societies—two distinct lines of approach can be discerned. Both take their cue from the entrance of the market system onto the scene of history.

One approach proceeds through what might be called "institutional" analysis. The economy in its concrete manifestations is here the subject of interest. Aristotle, Marx, the German "Historical School," Menger in his posthumous work, the American "Institutionalists," to name but a few, resorted to this approach with varying degrees of success. It is also the method of the book in which this chapter appears. It was the appearance of the market system with its inherent tendency to separate the economic process from its societal integument which urgently raised the question of the different ways in which the organization of livelihood affects the community. And this is the parent interest of all those who followed this line of attack. The first essential of this method (here most attempts have foundered) is a definition of the economy that allows an analytical distinction between what is economic and what is not. This requires a statement of the economy's function and of the operations necessary to that function. The analysis of any particular economy, its development over time, or the comparison of different economies hinges here upon observation of the manner in which the economic operations are institutionalized. And this is an empirical problem. The ability to generalize and predict depends, with this method, upon the emergence of common patterns in the institutionalized operations. The forms of integration—reciprocity, redistribution and exchange as they are employed in the present book, for example—are typical of such empirically derived patterns.*

There is another tradition of social thought which was brought to the consideration of our problem through an interest in, to use Weber's term, the *Zweckrational* orientation of modern western society, i.e., its heightened concern with the rational way of doing things whatever the ultimate ends. Represented most prominently by Weber, Marshall, Pareto, and Parsons, this strain of thought has therefore been concerned primarily with a certain "aspect" of social behavior, its develop-

* See above, Ch. XIII.

ment and organizational consequences. The link between this interest and the location of empirical economies in societies was provided by the advent of the market system which institutionalized economizing action so that the goods and person movements of the empirical economy tended to be ordered by individuals rationally choosing among alternative uses of scarce means. The interest of the scholars in this tradition thus turned very largely around the economy in its market form.

If this approach is consistently followed, it will become obvious, as Parsons has clearly shown, that economizing does not exhaust rational human experience, but is inevitably overlaid with other attitudes and orientations toward the just, the kind, the temperate, the politic, or otherwise "right" way of doing things.[2] In logic, the ultimate step in the development of this approach would be the proper identification of *all* the "aspects" of social action. If this were possible—an attempt Weber himself declined to make—it might then seem feasible to employ the universal "aspects" in the analysis of operating social systems, economic as well as noneconomic. Crucial to the fruitfulness of this approach in the analysis of empirical problems would be the ability to relate in a meaningful way the universals to the actual social structure under consideration. If, for example, the economizing "aspect" of behavior is under scrutiny, then it must first be located in some structure or other—the family, the government, the economy.

Economy and Society represents the logically ultimate step in the tradition of this latter attempt to locate economizing action in its social setting. Professor Parsons long ago rejected the "institutional" approach. His decision grew out of the "dilemma," as he saw it, presented by the American "institutionalist" school of economics, especially in the work of Veblen (pp. 5–6). Parsons viewed the "institutionalists" as rejecting economic theory (i.e., the theory of economizing behavior) on the grounds of its failure to explain the concrete facts of economic life, and as attempting, in its stead, to propound "a complete theory of social development." He felt strongly that in such a theory the "economic aspect" of social action "loses its theoretical specificity altogether," hence his own rejection of "institutionalism" (p. 6). Unfortunately, his new statement of the problem does not resolve so much as raise to another level precisely the "dilemma" which is presented not only by the American "institutionalist" movement, but by the whole tradition of western social thought in its attempts to deal with the economy.

The aim of the Parsons-Smelser work is stated as the formulation of "economic theory's relation to the non-economic aspects of social life" (p. 5), and this is equated with "the relation of the economy to the total society" (p. 16). It thus continues in the direction established by Parsons in *The Structure of Social Action*. Yet, in another sense, as we are told, the position here is "distinctly different" (p. 6). The alternative to the institutional approach which Professor Parsons took in his earlier work was to follow Pareto,[3] maintaining the general validity of economic theory, but admitting that it dealt only with "some of the *variables* which determine concrete social behavior in the 'economic' as in other spheres" (p. 6). The formal advance beyond Pareto in the new statement lies in the identification of *all* the "aspects" of social action ["on a cognate level" of abstraction] (pp. 5–6), and their inclusion in a general theory of action, applicable to *all* systems and subsystems of social interaction. Thus there are no special variables unique to economies as social systems, only "the general variables" of social theory, which are the universal "aspects." The economic case of the general theory is distinctive only in the sense that here "the concrete structures of different societies" are "most favorable empirically to 'purely economic' analysis." That is, economizing action tends to be located in the economy. The authors are aware that there are empirical economies where the social structure does not enforce economizing rationality to any important degree, and further that, "most so-called 'economic' processes must be regarded as resultants of economic and non-economic factors." The former condition, however, is that of the "completely routinized," "undifferentiated" economy with which they are not primarily concerned; the latter, i.e., the interplay of "economic" and "noneconomic" factors, is really the subject of the book (p. 6, n. 4; p. 42).

In developing their subject the authors identify four properties of social action as representing the universal functional requirements of social systems and subsystems. The "economic" aspect is said to arise out of the requirement of "adaptation" to an external environment in order that the goals of the system may be achieved. The function of this aspect is said to be, "the generalization of facilities for a variety of system and subsystem goals." The "facilities" are specified as "wealth" or "income" (pp. 18 ff). Their important feature is "their adaptability to . . . various uses" (p. 48). Thus the "economy" becomes a kind of value-neutral sphere of action devoted exclusively to making means available. Of the "noneconomic factors" with which "economic" processes are compounded, one is said to be "goal attainment," a requirement also growing out of the relationship between system and environment. It is distinguished from "adaptation," however, by its special function: "the *mobilization* of the necessary prerequisites for the *attainment* of given system goals of the society" (p. 48). Thus the attempt is made to distinguish between means and ends by making each a distinctive category of social action. In addition, the fact that these categories necessarily operate in a larger social environment is made the subject of two other system requirements. The process of attaining specific goals and making means generally available must be consistent with the values of the total social system, and it must be coordinated with other processes so as to avoid undue internal conflict among the parts. These two additional requirements are given the names "pattern maintenance" and "integration," respectively.

The means-ends distinction has, of course, long been basic to Professor Parsons' analysis of social action. And he has always identified "economic" action with "an intermediate position in the great chain of means and ends."[4] That is, economic action was held to be directed toward maximizing the supply of generally available means.[5] But Professor Parsons has, in the past, been careful to point out that economizing is a *norm* of action; its empirical relevance resting on the "circumstance that men do in fact try (not merely 'tend') to 'economize.' "[6] And economizing has been distinguished from other types of action in terms of the different norms involved in each case. Thus political action, for example, has been identified as "a rational process of the attainment of ends through the acquisition and exercise of coercive power over other individuals and groups."[7] It is important, therefore, to emphasize (a point we shall return to) that in this new elaboration of his position, Professor Parsons has, with Mr. Smelser, taken an important step beyond his previous stand. For while economic ("adaptive") and political ("goal attainment") action are defined in essentially the same way as before, they now assume an entirely new significance by being classed not merely as types of action, but as *functional* prerequisites of any and all social systems.

The "most general proposition" of the authors regarding these categories is that "total societies *tend* to differentiate into subsystems (social structures) which are specialized in each of the four primary functions" (p. 47). Thus they argue that the empirical economy tends to be specialized according to the "adaptive" requirement of the society as a whole, maximizing the flow of "fluidly disposable means," or "utility," to the total social system (pp. 20–1). In other words, although, like every other "concrete" social system, the empirical economy is a composite of all the "aspects" of social action, it tends to be structurally differentiated according to its primary function the definition of which corresponds to economizing with scarce means.

This leaves us in the following position: Economizing rationality has been identified as one of the universal aspects of human social behavior. The actual appearance of such behavior, however, is said to depend upon the prior existence of social structures which favor action so oriented. If we are primarily interested in locating the types of social structure in which economizing is found, all of this seems unexceptionable. But if the method is to enhance our understanding of that system whereby men secure the means of their livelihood, then a bridge must be provided between economizing and the economy. Parsons and Smelser do indeed fashion such a bridge, but it is constructed out of conjecture, not the empiry of comparative analysis. Apparently by virtue of a familiar developmental law involving the tendency toward greater division of labor and its assumed correlative, exchange* (p. 104, p. 141), the human economy is said to exhibit a tendency to differentiate according to the society's "adaptive" requirement, which is defined in terms of economizing with scarce means. It is a process consisting of instrumental activity designed to maximize the "economic value" of inherently scarce means.[8] By thus joining a formal category of action, economizing, with an empirical entity, the economy, the authors have committed a fateful error. Inevitably, the economy tends to be identified with its market form. The source of the error appears to lie in their having *confused the functional requirement of adaptation* to environment in the process of achieving system goals *with one of the modes of adaptation, namely, economizing.*

This leads us to suggest that the economic sociology of this new book is founded upon a confusion of two quite different methods of approach. The "Columbian map" by means of which the authors attempt to locate the universal aspects of social systems is capable of being read in two distinctly different ways, and these different interpretations are not adequately distinguished.

* For criticism of this view, see above, pp. 276 ff.

One reading implies a separation, for purposes of analysis, between goal states and the means of attaining them. It is a generalization of the means-ends distinction. The primary "function" of any particular system is, in this interpretation, defined in terms of specific "goals" of the subsystem. For example, at one point we are told, "the goal of the economy is to provide goods and services for consumption" (p. 42). Here we find no assumption regarding how the goal is to be achieved. Since every social structure must somehow reflect the requirement that it "adapt" to its environment, natural and social, there can be no objection to this reading of the "map." And the "exigencies" of that environment will necessarily shape the social structure. Thus societal values will leave their imprint and the necessity of integration with other structural units will be reflected. These are requirements of the social situation. The important feature of this interpretation is that it requires no unwarranted assumptions. Specific system goals and the mode of their attainment are here open to investigation. A social system is identified in terms of its goals, while its actual societal form is determined through study of the situation in which it functions.

Another interpretation, however, views the same "Columbian" classification in terms of certain types of social action. Here "adaptation" and "goal attainment" are defined as the locus of economizing and power, respectively, acquiring the names "economy" and "polity" (pp. 47–8). The analytical isolation of such spheres may be useful for some purposes, but they are, for that reason, not mere phantoms; *their actual appearance presupposes definite social structures.* That is, the social structure for economizing action can be clearly defined; it has definite requirements. A perfect market system is the embodiment, although certainly not the only one, of these requirements. The same may be said regarding the exercise of power, although here, of course, the typical social structure would be different. In any case, the correspondence between these types and actual social structures, the economy or government, for example, is problematical. It is precisely the problem for investigation, given this method of approach. To say that the empirical economy inevitably becomes more and more specialized in economizing is to posit a relationship between the livelihood process and a type of rationality which we must insist is not inherent.

The above criticism is relevant only in so far as the authors tend to generalize economic rationality as the typical economic process. A fatal blow to a general economic sociology, this false equation might be less serious given the principal subject of the book itself. For the authors are chiefly concerned with the "noneconomic" aspects of the market economy, and here, it is true, their analytical subsystem, "economy," and the empirical economy do in fact tend to coincide.

It seems to us, however, that a fallacy of misplaced concreteness ramifies throughout the whole presentation. The "Columbian map" according to which all of the aspects of the total social system are identified is employed to "locate" specifically the noneconomic social environment with which the "economy" (read, "economizing" action) must somehow come to terms in its functioning. As a social system the economy itself is said to have pattern maintenance, integrative, adaptive and goal-attainment exigencies of its own to meet (pp. 40–3). It too is thus composed of analytical subsystems, which, it must be remembered, may not be identified with the firms, unions, banks, etc., of the empirical economy. The economy thus differentiated is bounded by the remaining three subsystems of the total society. In order for the economy to perform its total function all of its system members must somehow come to terms with the apposite member of the societal subsystem at that boundary. This "coming to terms" with the counterpart in a bordering subsystem is viewed as a series of "inputs" and "outputs" and their "exchange" between system members. In these terms each subsystem is regarded as "producing" an output and exchanging it for the output of its bordering system to their mutual advantage, and contributing, incidentally, to the equilibrium of the total system (Cf. Ch. III). The subsystems of society thus behave toward one another like persons in a price-making market.

The details of this scheme of analysis are much too elaborate to describe here, but it clearly represents a highly formalized attempt to illustrate the subordination of the economy to the functional requirements of the whole society. While every social scientist must applaud the basic objective, and even agree that important insights may be gained from such schematic outlines, the same basic criticism must be levelled against the details of this sociology of the market economy as against the general scheme itself. The temptation to reify the purely analytical categories is apparently too great to be resisted. Thus the authors insist that there must be "some correspondence between these economic differentiations and those of social structure . . . though the concrete social structures vary from one society to another" (p. 52). But this is precisely what cannot be concluded from their scheme. It is said, for example, that the "polity" is that sphere where power is employed to achieve collective system goals (p. 48). The importance of the "polity" vis-à-vis the "economy" lies in its making available credit facilities for purposes of capital investment. In other words, money is a "political" instrument. Formally, this is stated in terms of the exchange between the "economy" and the "polity" across their "adaptive" boundaries, "rights to intervene" being exchanged for the polity's "decision" to provide credit facilities for capital investment (Cf. Ch. III). Putting aside the difficulty of distinguishing between analytical categories and concrete structures here, what is primarily objectionable is the identification of the *general* interest of the "polity" in the economic process with only *one* of the markets in the total system, i.e., the money market. At this point of the analysis, where it is argued that "each of the four [societal subsystems] has one boundary which interchanges primarily with *one* of the other three cognate subsystems" (p. 297), the "Columbian map" is in danger of becoming a Procrustean bed. Does not the "polity," for example, *necessarily* have a similar "interest" in regulating the employment of labor and land in the productive process, i.e., in the economy's "goal attainment" sphere?

Perhaps the most important achievement of this new statement by Professor Parsons and Mr. Smelser lies in their emphasizing the priority of a state of equilibrium for the society as a whole over that of the economy considered in isolation. In this way the problem of an economic sociology finds its proper statement. We feel however that, in their analysis of the problem, they have maintained the "theoretical specificity" of economics at what may well be the inevitable cost of confusing economizing with the economy. But what is more, their interpretation of the mode of interrelationship between the "economic" and "noneconomic" aspects of social life, i.e., the economic sociology itself, is imbued with a bias which appears to have been derived from formal economic theory. Basic to their analysis is the contention that in all social interaction, "The amount of performance contribution is a function of the expectation (and in the long run, receipt) of sanction. . . . Conversely, amount of sanction or reward is a function of amount of performance contribution" (p. 10). It is then suggested, however, that the "conceptual structure in economics which defines the elements involved in an exchange transaction can be generalized to all cases of performance-sanction balancing" (p. 13). It is a daring theoretical move to apply the concept of inputs and outputs in equilibrium to the whole of society, but whatever the ultimate verdict of scholarship regarding this move, it is surely premature to apply the terminology of the supply-demand scheme of economic theory to the general balancing of performances and sanctions in social interaction.

The "economistic" character of the sociology here is perhaps most apparent in Chapter III, where an attempt is made to develop a sociology of markets. The economics of imperfect competition is shown to be limited by the narrow range of the imperfections considered. It is suggested that the degrees of "imperfection" of markets can be more fully understood if their qualitative differences are analyzed. And such differences are sociological in character. The sellers in the money market, for example, are located at a different point on the sociological compass than the sellers in the labor market. These suggestions, while not new, are presented with a clarity that excites anticipation of what is to come. But in the analysis built upon these insights a penchant for the formalisms of economic theory mars the whole scheme. The concepts of property, contract, and market are expanded to include "properties" in the "possession" of noneconomic subsystems, the "noncontractual" elements of contract, and the noneconomic modifications of market behavior, respectively. Persistent imperfections in the "economic" market are then explained by the allusion to a broader hypothetical market which must always be in equilibrium if the economic market is not.

This is certainly an ingenious scheme, and no one will read the book without receiving important insights into the sociology of a market economy. But what have we learned about the actual mechanisms through which different markets are modified by the social situations in which they operate? Here, instead of maintaining the specificity of economic theory, the authors have so diffused it in application to phantom subsystems without shape or form that even the economist must object. A market is not a self-sufficing social system, but at least it presents us with a concrete mechanism which validates the abstractions of economic theory. It would seem that Professor Parsons and Mr. Smelser have indeed provided some relief from the one-sided rationalism of the economic theorist, but have they not conjured empty sociological boxes to replace their misnamed economic counterparts?

Weaknesses such as these which we find in the book, *Economy and Society*, lead us to suggest that Parsons and Smelser have not resolved the so-called "institutionalist dilemma," but only raised it to another level. Like the most sophisticated of the economic theorists, the authors do not set out to detail the operation of concrete economic systems. Several times they are at pains to point out the lack of correspondence between their categories and the real flesh and blood units of the economic system. Nevertheless, again like many economic theorists, they exhibit a persistent tendency to assume that there *must* be such a correspondence, and this assumption, when it is made, confuses the analysis, and bars the door to the understanding of how in fact social interaction in the economy is patterned.

Having in mind again the two traditions according to which western social scientists have attempted to place the economy in society, we suggest that the "dilemma" consists primarily of the question, What is it that we wish to know? If it is the problem, which occupied Weber and Pareto, of the degree to which the rationality of economizing with scarce means can be present in society, that is one thing. If we wish to generalize our understanding of the way in which substantive economic processes are institutionalized, that is another. Each will have its appropriate method. The two interests have been greatly confused because of their convergence on the presumed super-rational market economy of the eighteenth and nineteenth centuries. The market system in its ideal form is the very embodiment of that rationality of which economizing with scarce means is the essence. Economic analysis, as that discipline developed in the late nineteenth century, is the perfect theoretical statement of such action, *wherever it may actually be located in society*. But the unique convergence of substantive economic process, economizing rationality and economic theory is an event of history which cannot justify their being equated everywhere and always. And the attempt to locate the place of economies in societies which begins with the question of the relationship between economic theory and theory of other "aspects" of social action is doomed to failure unless the significance of this special case is clearly recognized.

Harry W. Pearson

Notes to Chapter XV

1. Talcott Parsons and Neil Smelser, *Economy and Society* (Glencoe, Ill., 1956). (The author wishes to express his sincere thanks to Professor Parsons and Mr. Smelser for providing the manuscript of *Economy and Society* so that this review

might appear in the present book. Page proof was also kindly provided so that references to *Economy and Society* might be identified by the page on which they appear.)

2. Cf. Talcott Parsons, *The Structure of Social Action* (Glencoe, Ill., 1949). See also, Paul Diesing, "The Nature and Limitations of Economic Rationality," *Ethics*, Vol. 61 (October, 1950); A. L. Macfie, "What Kind of Experience is Economizing?" *Ethics*, Vol. 60 (October, 1949); Paul Streeten, "Programs and Prognosis," *Quarterly Journal of Economics*, Vol. 68 (August, 1954).

3. Cf. *Structure of Social Action*, p. 757 ff.

4. Parsons, "Sociological Elements in Economic Thought," *Quarterly Journal of Economics*, Vol. 49 (May, 1935), p. 421. See also, Parsons, "Some Reflections on 'The Nature and Significance of Economics,' " *Quarterly Journal of Economics*, Vol. 47 (May, 1934), 522–529.

5. Parsons, "Some Reflections," p. 526.

6. *Ibid.*, p. 520.

7. *Ibid.*, p. 528.

8. On the inherent scarcity of the means involved in the adaptive process, see also, T. Parsons, Robert F. Bales and Edward Shils, *Working Papers in the Theory of Action* (Glencoe, Ill., 1953), p. 210; and T. Parsons and Edward Shils, eds., *Toward a General Theory of Action* (Cambridge, Mass., 1954), pp. 25, 197. See also Hopkins, this book, pp. 289 ff. There are exceptions to this interpretation of adaptation. When the authors discuss the "adaptive exigencies" of "concrete economic structures," for example, they say that the economy must "adapt" to its ecological-technological and socio-cultural environment. And the nature of that natural-social environment then will explain the differentiation of the economy into its structural elements (industries, etc.) (Ch. II). Here, in other words, the mode of adaptation is left open to research.

XVI

The Economy has no Surplus:
Critique of a Theory of Development

———•———

IN THE preceding chapters it has been shown that the concept of scarcity applied to the economy is a derivative of the market system, and of the Enlightenment's atomistic conception of society. Here, indeed, the conditions, institutional and ideal, are satisfied for the scarcity postulate to have operational significance. But the common assumption that the fact of scarce natural means sets off, everywhere and always, a series of economizing actions, skips over the vital step of introducing the social condition of man into consideration of his acting upon nature to produce his livelihood. The concept of scarcity will be fruitful only if the natural fact of limited means leads to a sequence of choices regarding the use of these means, and this situation is possible only if there is alternativity to the uses of means and there are preferentially graded ends. But these latter conditions are socially determined; they do not depend in any simple way upon the facts of nature. To postulate scarcity as an absolute condition from which all economic institutions derive is therefore to employ an abstraction which serves only to obscure the question of how economic activity is organized.

There is no formal theory of the development of economic institutions which has reached anything like the generality of formal economic theory. Nevertheless there is a concept of widely current use in anthropology, prehistory, and economic history which bears a relationship to the analysis of economic development similar to that between the scarcity postulate and economic analysis. This is the concept of surplus employed in a way which makes the appearance of a "surplus" over bare subsistence needs the critical determinant in the evolution of complex social and economic institutions from simple beginnings. Thus an oversufficiency of means is said to bring on the development of economic institutions just as an insufficiency of means is said to enforce the utilitarian management of resources, which is the economy in the formal sense.

The argument of this chapter is that when the surplus concept is employed in this way it too represents an inadmissable abstraction from the social conditions which surround the daily business of securing the material means of want satisfaction. Like the concept of scarcity, the surplus theorem is useful only where the conditions of a specific surplus are institutionally defined. Again, like the scarcity postulate, the concept of a general surplus arises out of that ideal and institutional complex which views man as economizing atom with "propensity to truck, barter and exchange,"[1] and then provides the system of markets to make it so. It has been said that under a market system the economic process is organized through scarcity situations. It might be added that of necessity market behavior is directed towards the creation of surpluses. A mistake is made, however, when it is assumed that these institutional characteristics of a market economy are a natural feature of economic life.

Invested as it is with a common sense plausibility, the popular surplus theorem has hitherto aroused little suspicion of its rationalistic bias. Let us examine its content.

When employed as the key to evolutionary change, the surplus theorem has two essential parts. There is first the very concept of such a surplus. It is taken to represent that quantity of material resources which exists over and above the subsistence requirements of the society in question. Such surpluses are supposed to appear with advancing technology and productivity, and serve to distinguish one level of social and economic organization from another. The second part of the surplus theorem is the expectation that the surplus has an enabling effect which allows typical social and economic developments of prime importance to take place. Trade and markets, money, cities, differentiation into social classes, indeed civilization itself, are thus said to follow upon the emergence of a surplus.[2]

"Surplus," as defined by Melville Herskovits, for example, is "an excess of goods over the minimum demands of necessity."[3] Following the lead of Thorstein Veblen,[4] he feels that surplus opens an important avenue for the investigation of economic change in primitive societies; although, "Just why the surplus is produced remains obscure."[5] Comparing the Bushmen of South Africa with the Hottentot, Herskovits notes that the Hottentot have developed a greater specialization of ruling function. He finds, "The reason [for this difference] is simple: the Bushmen produce no surplus."[6]

Gordon Childe defines "social surplus" as, "food above domestic requirements."[7] And, for him, the development of neolithic trade and the emergence of civilization hinge upon the appearance of such a surplus.[8]

The meaning of the concept is thus clear enough. There is a level of subsistence which once reached provides a measure—so to speak the dam over which the surplus flows. This surplus which is beyond needs however these happen to be defined, is then in some sense available: it may be traded abroad, or used to support the existence of craftsmen, a leisure class, or other nonproductive members of the society. In other words, it becomes the key variable in the emergence of more complex social and economic institutions.

In the argument which follows we shall discuss (1) The implications of the surplus concept when it is introduced as the enabling factor in the process of social and economic change; (2) The doctrinal origins and developments of the concept in order to shed light on its inherent rationalistic bias; (3) Briefly, the way in which an institutional concept of specific surpluses—their creation and employment—may be fruitfully applied to the analysis of economic development.

A Rationalistic Construct

Let us first reexamine the meaning of the term surplus itself. It is applied to that which is over and above subsistence needs. Therefore the first requirement of its usefulness as a concept is that subsistence needs be defined.

There are, logically, only two ways of defining these needs. They may be determined by reference to a biologically fixed requirement of food essentials for human existence. Or, on the other hand, it may be held that subsistence needs are socially derived, in which case biological necessity cannot be used as a measuring rod.

If subsistence needs are allowed to be biologically determined, then the surplus which is said to arise after these needs are met would be an absolute surplus. That is, it would be a quantity appearing with no socially defined purpose over and above that which is biologically necessary, thus available and in a distinctive sense having a causal effect of its own. The sequence moves from the availability of a quantity of goods or services to the decision that these may now be used to support the emergence of new economic or social institutions such as trade, markets, or a leisure class. Sometimes it is implied that the surplus is the causal factor; more often it seems to be regarded as a necessary, if not sufficient cause of development. Both uses, we shall argue, are inadmissible.

If it is held that subsistence needs are not biologically but socially defined, there is no room for the concept of absolute surplus, for then the distribution of economic resources between subsistence and other requirements is determined only within the *total* context of needs thus defined. There is no disentangling bare subsistence needs from the total functional demands which the society makes on the economy.

If the concept of surplus is to be employed here at all, it must be in a relative or constructive sense. In brief: A given quantity of goods or services would be surplus only if the society in some manner set these quantities aside and declared them to be available for a specific purpose. Into this category might then fall such things as food set aside for ceremonial feasts or in anticipation of future dearth, war chests, budgetary surpluses, or savings for whatever purpose. The essential point is that relative surpluses are initiated by the society in question. It is true that such surpluses may be made to appear along with a wind-fall increase of material means, or a more permanent rise in productive capacity; but they may also be created with no change whatever in the quantity of subsistence means by re-allocating goods or services from one use to another. The Biblical story of the grain storage by Joseph in Egypt is one illustration of the latter. More important than the natural conditions associated with the creation of relative surpluses is thus an attitude towards resources, and the institutional means of counting out, setting aside, and making available.

In the actual use of the surplus concept as a key to economic and social development there is much confusion which results from the failure to distinguish between these two possible meanings. The confusion results in attributing to relative surpluses the causal effects which only the absolute surplus would have if its existence and relevance could be established. Since the relative surplus is a mere construction, it must be apparent that only the absolute meaning can be employed to explain economic and social change. It is this meaning, therefore, the implications of which must be further examined.

If the subsistence level is the measure of what is to be deemed surplus, one must be able to determine, in any specific instance, just where that level is. Logically, it may seem as if there must be a biologically fixed minimum requirement of food for a man's existence. An individual man will surely perish in a short time if he has no food at all. But how long can a man exist on a deficient diet? And if it is difficult to establish the subsistence minimum for one individual, it is impossible to determine it for a society. There is no historical evidence of a whole human society ever having lived at this level. In fact, what would we accept as evidence? We know that large or small sections of the population of every society live at a level of subsistence which science has established as inadequate. As a consequence infant mortality will be high, and life expectancy low as disease takes its devastating toll, but does this mean that every member of these groups is therefore engaged in producing food during all his waking hours? There is no support for this assumption from contemporary primitive societies, even the poorest, for they too dance and sing, and fight wars, thus using their small resources in non-utilitarian ways. Nor does the mute evidence of archaeology help us. What appears to be an objective fact of nature disintegrates upon closer examination. The fact is that "Man does not live by bread alone," no matter how meager the bread.

The supposition that there is a biological minimum level of subsistence for a society fails to allow for the flexibility of a culturally determined subsistence level and thus the power of a society to employ physical resources in ways which may be regarded as even more important than a given level of subsistence. Modern India, for example,

is one of the countries of relatively rapid population growth, at least since 1921. Poor as the diet of the Indian people has been, and extremely low as their customary level of living has been, the country has fed, after a fashion, a population that has risen from 306 million in 1921 to about 438 million in 1951 (India and Pakistan). . . . Even the experts do not fully understand how this has been possible, and the evidence is conflicting as to how far the level of living of the people has changed for better or worse. In other words, no one can estimate with assurance how many more people India can feed at some level of diet, or how much the prevailing diet might deteriorate below current low levels without forcing deaths into balance with births.[9]

It may be argued, however, that the idea of a subsistence level is, after all, only an heuristic device. Whether or not it can be determined objectively, it is there in principle and can be used to establish the emergence of a surplus. Because of the obvious impossibility of determining the biological subsistence minimum for a whole society, it is in this heuristic sense that the surplus concept has most often been employed.

But this heuristic employ raises even more serious difficulties. It is based upon the a *priori* assumption that absolute economic surpluses are the generating force in social change. The very fact that the particular society under examination does not spend all of its time and resources in the pursuit of bare subsistence is then called in as proof that a surplus must have been produced.

The very fact that means of effectuating the circulation of goods within and between tribes do exist signifies that something more than just enough to feed, clothe, and shelter a people is available, while such phenomena as the delayed exchange of goods on a ceremonial basis, or the extension of credit by one tribesman to another prove that not only entire groups, but individuals within these groups possess a surplus over immediate need.[10]

The heuristic postulate then proves the existence of surplus. And it then follows that the more complex the society, the greater must have been the surplus. Clearly it is important to inquire into the legitimacy of such a postulate.

At the base of the surplus theorem thus employed is the assumed primacy both in time and urgency, of eating over thinking, socializing, governing, crafting, trading, playing. As expressed by Engels, it is "the simple fact . . . that human beings must have food and drink, clothing and shelter, first of all, before they can interest themselves in politics, science, art, religion, and the like."[11] Here is a crude kind of economic determinism which bases social and economic development upon "the narrow capacity of the human stomach."[12] Into the sphere of the hulogical and social requirements, the latter following only after the former are satisfied. It is sufficient, perhaps, to point out that such is the view of subsistence and society which, at bottom, supports this idea of surplus, for very few, even of those who employ it, would subscribe to this position.[13] In any case, the preponderant weight of modern evidence bearing on the social psychology and sociology of economic activity stands in opposition to this view of economy and society. We need point out only that the economy at all levels of material existence is a *social* process of interaction between man and his environment in the course of which goods and service change form, are moved about and change hands. They are produced and distributed. The shape of this process, i.e., its institutional form and the motives which make it run are determined not by any single factor either in nature or man, but are the resultants of several interdependent levels of human existence, ecological, technological, social and cultural. And questions such as what things and how much a given society produces, who is responsible for production, how much is consumed and in what proportion by the various groups in the society, how much is saved or diverted from immediate consumption and for what purposes, are resolved only through the complex interaction of these variables. Man, living in society, does not produce a surplus unless he names it such, and then its effect is given by the manner in which it is institutionalized.

To emphasize the complexity of the causal nexus in any given situation is not to deny that there may be important social consequences of increases in subsistence means. Changing technology and productivity play their role in the course of institutional development. The argument here is simply that they do not create generally available surpluses, for this implies a separation of technological development from the institutional complex of which it is but a part. To apply the concept of surplus to new economic means which result from improvement in productivity is to imply that they are outside the social forces which integrate and control the economic process. These means thus become a kind of "free-wheeling" entity which may then be called upon to explain any development from trade to shamanism[14] according to the predilections of the investigator.

It is this invitation to rationalize complex economic problems of development and change which is the most disturbing aspect of this widely used idea of an enabling surplus. A catalogue of the economic institutions which have been attributed to the appearance of a surplus at critical steps in the development of human society would include private property, barter, trade, division of labor, markets, money, commercial classes and exploitation.[15] But there is not a shred of evidence to support these constructions. The only conceivable justification for these claims is the postulate that the logical course of economic development, once there are sufficient means available, is toward the market system of nineteenth century western Europe. This assumed train of events is based upon a crude confusion of the economy with the state of technology. The economy, to repeat, is a social process which means that the production, movement and transfer of economic goods may be variously organized. Precisely how these elements of early economies were organized and integrated is the problem for investigation. Unless we can prove man to possess an "inherent propensity to truck, barter and exchange" there is no justification for assuming that his economy must follow the market pattern. In fact, as many contributions to this book have indicated, the evidence for the economies of primitive and archaic societies proves exactly the opposite. Neale has shown, for example, that the distribution of the grain heap in the Indian village follows the pattern of mutual sharing which is institutionalized in the system of reciprocative social relationships typical of the village community.* What a distortion of the actual situation it would be to regard this grain heap as an absolute surplus, and to expect it to leave commercial exchange, money, and the rest in its wake!

Reifying the Profit Concept

In the course of the argument so far we have tried to indicate the basic weaknesses of the surplus concept and to point out some of the rationalizations of institutional development following upon its use. We will now touch upon the doctrinal origins and development of the surplus construct, for only in this way can we learn how the figment of an absolute surplus arises.

There is little doubt that the surplus theorem in current usage is the result of the convergence of two distinct lines of inquiry. One is Lewis H. Morgan's general theory of social and economic evolution.[16] The other is Karl Marx's investigations of capitalism, the analytical heart of which was a theory of "surplus value." But Marx's theory was derived from the earlier economic theories of the Physiocratic and Classical schools, and it is thus to the substantive value theory of these

* See above, Ch. XI.

earlier economists that we must look for the origins of the concept of surplus value. The point of convergence was Friedrich Engels' adaptation of Morgan's work in *The Evolution of Private Property, the Family and the State*, first published in 1884. The theory of family and state development originally put forward by Morgan and by Engels' interpretation of Morgan have received wide critical review, and the relatively facile and dogmatic scheme of lineal evolution of those institutions implied therein is held by almost no one today. Implied in the Morgan-Engels theory, however, there is a scheme of economic evolution, especially of exchange institutions, which has not received the same critical attention as those more explicit theories regarding the family, state and private property.

Morgan had made "enlargement of the sources of subsistence" the independent variable in an evolutionary sequence.[17] Thus arose, according to him, the monogamous family, private property and territorial government out of the aboriginal gens and tribal property. As real wealth increased with the appearance of pastoralism, the "passion for its possession" also increased, and private property became a significant reality.[18] This emergence of private property in the stage of "barbarism" encouraged individual motives of accumulation and gain, economic inequality and, in general, the "principles which now govern society."[19] Thus, although Morgan was concerned more with establishing the emergence of private property than with the full range of economic institutions, the implication is clear that growth in means of subsistence led to the accumulation of "exchangeable" wealth, and that once this appeared the exchange institutions of civilized society were assumed to be not qualitatively different from those of modern Western society.

Engels superimposed upon this theory of Morgan's the concept of surplus which was, of course, derived from Marx's surplus value. Engels said that as the "productivity of labor increasingly develops" in kin-organized "savage" society, there comes a time when "human labor power" is able to produce a "surplus over and above its maintenance costs."[20] The crucial role of this surplus is explained by Engels as follows:

In the middle stages of barbarism we already find among the pastoral peoples a possession in the form of cattle which, once the herd has attained a certain size, regularly produces a surplus over and above the tribe's own requirements, leading to a division of labor between pastoral peoples and backward tribes without herds, and hence to the existence of two different levels of production side by side with one another and the conditions necessary for regular exchange. The upper stages of barbarism bring us the further division of labor between agriculture and handicrafts, hence the production of a continually increasing portion of the products of labor directly for exchange, so that exchange between individual producers assumes the importance of a vital social function.[21]

As the size of the surplus increases there is further division of labor, towns develop which brings a merchant class, money and even land becomes a commodity.[22] And since the surplus "grow[s] above the heads of the producers . . . [it will] raise up incorporeal alien powers against them, as in civilization is always and inevitably the case."[23] Thus the surplus also provides the basis for class division and exploitation.

This application of the surplus theorem to the evolution of economic institutions reflects a confusion between two entirely different concepts of surplus: a naturalistic absolute surplus which is an illusion, and a socially derived relative surplus. This same confusion lay at the heart of the value theory of the English Classical school and their immediate precursors, the French Physiocrats. It is, therefore, to the work of these early economists that we must turn to find the origin of the notion that economic activity besides being useful is somehow surplus-producing.

One prerequisite of an absolute surplus, as pointed out in Part I, is that there be an objectively ascertainable level of subsistence needs over and above which the surplus appears. We suggested there that while logically a minimum level of biological need may seem to satisfy this requirement, it can only be employed in an heuristic sense. In Engels' definition of surplus, however, the objective standard is provided by the key phrase, "maintenance costs." When "costs" of production are measurable it is indeed possible to think of that which is produced over and above these costs as constituting a general surplus. But there is one other prerequisite. There can be no other socially sanctioned claim on any product above maintenance costs. Again, in Part I, it was argued that such an assumption is contrary to fact, for the economic process provides the material means necessary for all societal roles to be played, whether of consumer or totemic destroyer of worldly goods. The surplus theorem gained currency because both of these prerequisites were satisfied by the institutional and philosophical framework of early economics. Measurable costs of production appear on the scene with the advent of the market system which affixed money prices to land and labor. These are the "costs." And since the first rule of the market game is the maintenance of a differential between these costs and selling price, the market system may seem to create a surplus as a matter of course. This, at any rate, was necessarily the case given the philosophical position which allowed of no legitimate non-cost claims on the product.

The increasing importance in the eighteenth and nineteenth centuries of the market as a relatively independent arbiter of production and distribution called forth the new discipline of economics. For under the market new mysteries had to be explained. Resources now moved into the productive process, and finished goods moved from producer to consumer under the aegis of price. The mystery was what does eventually determine the price, or value, of a day's work, a hogshead of wine, a woolen coat? It was this interest that absorbed the early economists, and since they believed that value must have a natural origin, traceable either to land or labor, they were convinced that whatever product appeared over and above these costs of production must be a surplus.

This idea of production as a surplus producing activity appears first in the works of the French Physiocrats of the eighteenth century, the so-called *economistes*.[24] Their orientation was far from being purely academic. The Physiocratic school represented the aspirations of the newly market-oriented class of French landowners. The first prerequisite of the surplus concept was fulfilled by the growing commercialization of French agriculture and the consequent interest in costs of production. The fortunes of commercial agriculture rested upon a *bon prix* for grain and a low price for manufactured articles. The Physiocrats therefore were opposed to the mercantile system of Colbert which, on the contrary, favored cheap grain to maintain low wages and to demand, in export, a good price for protected manufactures. In consonance with the Enlightenment's belief in the natural order of things, they reasoned that the original source of all economic value was Nature, and that the division of labor between agriculture and manufacturing, and the circulation of commodities through the economy in support of the non-productive or "sterile" classes, was made possible by the unique faculty of the land to produce a surplus over the costs of agricultural production. This gift of nature they called the *produit net*. Turgot, perhaps the most influential member of this school, explained the *produit net* most clearly.

The produce of the land divides into two parts. The one comprehends the subsistence and the profits of the husbandman, which are the rewards for his labor, and the conditions on which he agrees to cultivate the field of the proprietor; the other which remains is that independent and *disposable* part, which the earth produces as a free gift to the proprietor over and above what he had disbursed.[25]

Upon their analysis of surplus in circulation rested the Physiocrats' specific policy suggestions: *laissez faire, laissez aller* to allow the free export of grain and thereby achieve the *bon prix*, and the single tax to be levied on the *produit net*. What concerns us here, however, is the fact that the *produit net* was an illusion. The mysterious power of producing a surplus which the Physiocrats attributed to Nature was nothing more than the market measurement of the difference between production cost and selling price. If, through the normal operation of market forces the price of grain should fall to the level of the labor cost of production, the *produit net* would disappear. Because of their interest in finding the natural law of the circulation of commodities, they did not see that the production of economic value is a social phenomenon, and that in this case the surplus grew out of the institutional features of the market.[26]

Crossing the Channel, the surplus concept figured importantly in the work of Adam Smith, the first of the Classical economists. Smith disputed the Physiocratic claim that land was the progenitor of surplus, substituting labor instead as the original source of economic value.

The chain of reasoning is almost too familiar to bear repeating. The kernel is found in Locke's dissertation on property in the *Second Treatise on Civil Government*, and similarly in the first two books of Smith's *The Wealth of Nations*. The earth is given to all mankind in common, but man is an individual. Among other things he must eat. He therefore must work, and the mixing of the individual's energy with nature's common gift extracts from the common and stamps the subtracted part as private property. Hence the natural right of private property. But the individual soon finds that he can pick more acorns or kill more deer than his own subsistence requires, and since he is a rational utilitarian, he exchanges his surplus for that of another individual to the mutual advantage of both. Here is the naturalistic, or what we have called absolute surplus, an inevitable construction here, given the starting point of man as utilitarian atom. If man is viewed as atom, then once his biological needs are satisfied any remaining material goods must be regarded as surplus. The atomistic conception allows the existence of no socially derived claims on the product. And the utilitarian assumption directs the surplus into the uses of exchange.

But this is not the end of the surplus story, for classical economics went on to confuse this mistaken idea of an absolute surplus with the cost-price differential of the market. The economic problem was to determine the terms of exchange between individuals exchanging their surplus. The obvious answer, since these were regarded as free and equal individuals outside the integument of social valuation, was the quantity of labor that went into the production of the goods exchanged. But while the labor theory of value may have been the obvious construction for Locke's individualistic savages, it created problems logical as well as moral for Classical economics when applied to the complex economy of the eighteenth and nineteenth centuries.[27]

Smith reasoned logically that once the process is started, the exchange of surplus will lead to specialization and thus wider exchange relationships which finally call for the use of money to facilitate complex division of labor and ever expanding exchange. As society advances ". . . beyond that early and rude state which precedes both the accumulation of stock and the appropriation of land" some individuals "naturally" will use their accumulated surplus.

. . . in setting to work industrious people, whom they will supply with materials and subsistence, in order to make a profit by the sale of their work, or by what their labor adds to the value of the materials.[28]

The logical dilemma was how to explain the market price and still retain this substantive theory of value, for now price was clearly a composite of more than one factor of production, thus not reflecting the quantity of labor alone. The moral problem was to square the facts of a very real return to land (rent) and to capital (interest or "profits") with the conviction that capitalism represented the system of natural justice where each individual was free to receive only the rewards to which his own labor entitled him. Even the brilliant mind of David Ricardo could not resolve these contradictions.

At the heart of the difficulty was a massive confusion between a naturalistic concept of surplus and a socially determined difference between labor cost and price dictated by the requirements of the market. The "subsistence" which the capitalist pays the laborer is the wage, but the wage rate is determined by the forces of supply and demand operating in the market. There is no objective measure of subsistence which determines the wage and no absolute surplus appears. Other factors of production playing their respective roles (of which one may morally approve or disapprove) also receive market sanctioned returns. To the functioning of the market system, one is as important as the other. The idea that the economy produces an absolute surplus as a matter of course was due to the application of an atomistic philosophical position to the functional problems of the market system. As soon as economic theory recognized, in the second half of the 19th century, that a commodity is worth what it will fetch on the market, the logical, if not the moral, problem of surplus ceased to plague economic theory.[29]

For those who were morally opposed to the distribution of wealth under capitalism, however, the classical surplus dilemma was too obvious a tool to miss. It was left for Karl Marx to turn the contradictions of "this very Eden of the rights of man"[30] into a theory of exploitation. But Marx pulled the classical labor theory of value out of its original naturalistic setting and placed it into a definite social setting: that of capitalistic production. No more than Ricardo was Marx able successfully to resolve the logical contradictions involved in the labor theory of value. But the important point to be made here is that Marx made it perfectly clear that a surplus is not something that arises as a natural consequence of the labor process itself.

> Favorable natural conditions alone, gave us only the possibility, never the reality, of surplus-labour, nor, consequently, of surplus-value and a surplus-product. . . . In the midst of our West European society, where the labourer purchases the right to work for his own livelihood only by paying for it in surplus-labour, the idea easily takes root that it is an inherent quality of human labour to furnish a surplus-product. . . . The productiveness of labour that serves as its foundation and starting point, is a gift, not of nature, but of a history embracing thousands of centuries.[31]

The so-called "primitive accumulation" of capital that provides the starting point for capitalism and surplus value is not the gradual appearance of surpluses born of technological progress; it is "nothing else than the historical process of divorcing the producer from the means of production."[32] Marx scoffed at the idea of a naturalistic surplus and spoke only of "surplus *value*" which he attributed to the institutional features of capitalism alone. It is all the more ironic then that the facile rationalization of the development of economic institutions set in motion by the surplus concept should have been derived from Marx's surplus value.

Surplus—the Economic Aspect of Institutional Change

The argument thus far has necessarily taken a negative tack. A critical appraisal of the surplus concept has been undertaken in an effort to dispel the long-standing confusion between absolute and relative surpluses. Hardly anyone anymore accepts in the whole the atomistic philosophical position upon which the surplus theorem rested. But enforced as this position was by a misunderstanding of the market system with its numerous relative surpluses, and a misrendering of Marx's theorem of surplus value, the two meanings of surplus have been confused, with the result that important matters of institutional change are rationalized in alarming fashion.

We have argued against the idea of any absolute standard which automatically determines the availability of material resources for institutional development. The question rather is one of the relative uses to which resources are put under definite social arrangements, and whether or not it is useful to distinguish one use from another with the term surplus. We think it is, for, although such a distinction may be entirely arbitrary on the part of the investigator, it focuses attention upon a phenomenon of basic importance. It might be called the economic aspect of institutional growth. In these terms relative surpluses are simply material means and human services that are in some sense set aside or mobilized apart from the existing functional demands which a given social unit—a family—a firm—a society—makes upon its economy. Since we are not searching for absolute consumption levels after which surpluses automatically appear, research interest is directed toward the positive factor of the institutional means by which the course of the ongoing economic process is altered to support the material requirements of new or expanded societal roles, whether of consumer, producer, general or priest.

Viewing the problem from this angle it is clear that there are definite institutional requirements for the creation of relative surpluses. Briefly, the operational facilities, as well as the motivation for separating out, counting up, storing, mobilizing material means and human services must be provided by the institutional framework of the economy if surpluses are to be made available for specific purposes.

The institutional medium of money and market provide, of course, a set of conditions highly conducive to the manufacture of surpluses. Where money is used as a generalized means of exchange the infinite variety of substantive economic qualities are quantifiable in terms of a single measure; thus they are freely interchangeable and substitutable. Here the facilities for separating, counting, budgeting are fully provided. In addition, the institutional separation of the economic from other aspects of social existence in a market system provides a "self-conscious" economic process, as it were, directing the attention of all participants to the economic significance of all decisions. Outputs are measured against inputs. And the individuation-cum-contract feature of a market ordered economy attaches inevitable uncertainties to the roles of producer and consumer, uncertainties which can be hedged only by the creation of surpluses.[34] Families as well as business firms save, and entrepreneurs drive for profits. It is these features of the system which necessarily direct market behavior toward the creation of surpluses.

The apparently favorable milieu of market and money for the creation of specific surpluses should not, however, lead us to infer the absence of institutional means for making surpluses available in non-market economies. Nor, on the other hand, should the market way be taken as the paradigm for the production of surpluses. Raymond Firth has pointed out that primitive man does not live simply "by a day-to-day satisfaction of his needs but shows foresight and engages in forms of abstinence."[35] The difficulty, he goes on to emphasize, lies in finding out just how such decisions regarding the use of economic means are in fact carried out. Finding the economic process embedded in essentially noneconomic institutions as we do in the vast number of nonmarket economies, it would seem obvious to suggest that both the motives and the institutional means for accumulating surpluses would also be of a noneconomic character. The question, then, is what institutional provisions for the exceptional employment of material means do we find in economies where the basic continuity of the process is insured through the patterns of reciprocity and redistribution.

In the case where the goods and person movements of the economic process are channelled through redistributive institutions, the means for the creation of surpluses seem to be fairly direct and obvious. Since, under this form of integration, it is power located in a central institution which sanctions the locational and appropriational movements, the same power may demand tribute, levy assessments, mobilize labor, decree consumption standards, etc. And, in a similar vein, one of the most common of all means of surplus accumulation has been the power of arms to plunder and secure booty. Corvée, boon days, tithes, censuses, tax farming, auctions, markets by decree—these are some of the paraphernalia of surplus mobilization in redistributive economies. Interest here centers also on these operational devices by means of which the facility to count out, compare, and balance accounts is enhanced in the absence of a general medium of exchange. One example is the use of "money" as a standard of account, greatly facilitating thereby the planning and budgeting operations of staple finance in the redistributive economies of the ancient Near East.[36]

But if the means of establishing surpluses under redistributive forms of organization are straightforward, what of those economies, or those economic operations, held firmly in the reciprocities of kinship, neighborhood, community? The practice of mutually obligatory sharing typical of reciprocity is certainly not conducive to the individual building of surpluses since it insures against the very personal uncertainties which induce saving. Among the Bantu Bemba people of Africa, for example, one finds little attempt made to overcome the recurrent food shortage by saving up and marketing surpluses. The economic process is located in kinship units here; thus "they are unaccustomed to commerce of this kind."[37] This lack of saving and individual foresight is disastrous only where, in the neighborhood of the white man's towns, the kinship unit has broken down. The same Bemba tribe, however, keeps chickens, but they "do not use these for food, except for ceremonial occasions, or as presents of respect; nor do they ever eat the eggs. Pigeons are kept but very rarely eaten even in times of hunger. 'We like to see them flying about the village,' says the native, 'it is a sign of a man of rank.' "[38] Here we may have the clue to one of the most important of the means for the creation of surpluses in the absence of market methods or those centers of power able to enforce the production of surpluses. We refer, of course, to that omni-present catalytic agent in human society usually called the prestige factor.

The persistence and the power of the prestige factor in primitive and archaic societies is universally attested, but the complexity of its function and, especially, its economic significance is, to say the least, still an enigma. Viewing this phenomenon from the vantage point of a market ordered universe we may be hampered in our understanding of the economic relevance of prestige institutions in early societies. Prestige in a market system is very largely a by-product of successful market activity. Wealth is the exclusive symbol of prestige, and wealth is the product of successful selling. That such a state of affairs leads to "conspicuous consumption" and even distorts the substantive economy in the direction of "conspicuous waste" is now, thanks to the trenchant criticism of Veblen, a part of our common understanding. Nevertheless prestige is no more than an epiphenomenon to the functioning of the ideal market economy.

In primitive and archaic societies the function of prestige seems rather the reverse of that found in our economy. For there it appears as a culture pattern *sui generis* with a rationale and institutional fittings of its own, and capable, vis-à-vis the economy, of stimulating feverish goods and person movements, the goal of which may be the fierce destruction of wealth in Kwakiutl potlatch ceremonies, or the comely reciprocities of the Trobrianders' "trade game."[39] Prestige wealth whether the red sulawa necklaces and white umwala armbands of the Trobrianders, the copper plates of the Kwakiutl, or the iron, bronze, gold goblets, tripods and caldrons of Homeric Greece, circulates only among the gods, kings, and chiefs.[40] It may move against other prestige objects or against items of honor, power or safety, but always it adds up to an elite circulation of prestige wealth. Pointing to the frequency of money payments, calculation, interest, profit, business partnership, accountancy, and shrewd bargaining in this sphere of activity, Cora DuBois has employed the apt term, "prestige economy" to describe it.[41] But while the elite circulation of prestige wealth involves a certain amount of material means, sometimes absorbing a disproportionate amount of time and resources, it is not this feature which is of primary interest in the mobilization of surpluses. Strange though it may seem to the modern mind prestige wealth represented a regular claim upon the services and material resources of communities even on a very low level of subsistence.

Prestige is the prize of all this activity which may itself involve the accumulation of symbolic wealth, but it also functions indirectly as a mobilizer of relatively large quantities of material means as well as human services to be employed in a variety of ways, utilitarian and not, but which, in any case, make them available to the community at large, as they otherwise would not be. It is here that we see the surplus creating function of the prestige factor in early society. For with the prestige gained in the prestige economy go honorific duties and public trustee functions which result in making available to the community services and material means which would not otherwise be put to use. Food must be mobilized for the largesse which accompanies the potlatch ceremonies, or the feast of the Pomo prestige trade. The Tolowa-Tututni "rich man" must act as a state surrogate, negotiating in disputes, settling torts by the payments of fines for any of his village kinsmen. And probably the clearest example comes from classical Athens where it was the onerous privilege of the wealthy to provide the state with services at their own cost, the so-called *leiturgies*. Among these were the maintenance, command, and manning of the naval craft provided by the state (*trierarchy*); the training of personnel for the annual religious performances (*choregy*); the providing of physical training for the young (*gymnasiarchy* and *lampadarchy*); and the contributing of funds for the import of grain to be distributed freely or at low cost to the citizenry (*sitesis*).

So intricate is the interlacing of prestige and economy that our discussion offers little more than to suggest the lines along which investigation might move. So much is clear, however, prestige institutions are not simply a kind of societal afterthought appearing only upon the emergence of an imagined surplus above subsistence means. They are woven into the warp and weft of the social fabric, and, where the economic process is threaded into the same fabric, may shade into and even color over the economic threads.

Prestige institutions are not the result of surpluses appearing at certain stages of social development, but neither are cities, nor pyramids, nor markets, nor money, nor exploitation, nor civilization. The interrelationship between the material and the societal aspects of existence are such that they cannot be separated into "first," "then" sequences. And the market system with its institutional separation of economic and social is only an apparent exception. Here, too, those surpluses which seem to appear "above the heads of the producers" are explained only by the institutional features of the market economy. It is no good either to go half the distance in the surplus argument by admitting that surplus is a necessary but not sufficient cause of change, for this is to beg the question. There are always and everywhere potential surpluses available. What counts is the institutional means for bringing them to life. And these means for calling forth the special effort, setting aside the extra amount, devising the surplus, are as wide and varied as the organization of the economic process itself.

Harry W. Pearson

Notes to Chapter XVI

1. Adam Smith, *The Wealth of Nations*, Bk. I, ch. II.
2. Some examples: Melville J. Herskovits, *Economic Anthropology* (New York, 1952), esp. ch. XVIII; Gordon Childe, *What Happened in History* (New York, 1946); *Social Evolution* (1951); "The Birth of Civilization" in *Past and Present*, II (November, 1952), "Trade and Industry in Barbarian Europe till Roman Times," in *Cambridge Economic History of Europe*, II (Cambridge, 1952); Leslie White, *The Science of Culture* (New York, 1949); Melville Jacobs and Bernhard J. Stern, *Outline of Anthropology* (New York, 1947), esp. ch. VI; R. H. Hilton, "The Transformation from Feudalism to Capitalism," *Science and Society* (Fall, 1953); Shephard B. Clough, *The Rise and Fall of Civilization* (New York, 1951), pp. 6–7 ff.
3. Herskovits, *op. cit.*, p. 395.
4. *Ibid.*, pp. 396–7. For Veblen's employment of the surplus concept see *The Instinct of Workmanship and the State of the Industrial Arts* (New York, 1914), ch. IV.
5. *Ibid.*, p. 413.
6. *Ibid.*, p. 399.
7. Childe, *Past and Present*, p. 3.
8. *Ibid.*, p. 4, and *Cambridge Economic History of Europe*, II, 2 ff.
9. Joseph S. Davis, "Adam Smith and the Human Stomach," *Quarterly Journal of Economics*, Vol. 68, No. 3 (May, 1954), 283.
10. Herskovits, *op. cit.*, p. 395. Cf. G. Childe, *Cambridge Economic History of Europe*, II, 2.
11. Engels' funeral oration at the grave of Marx, March 17, 1883; quoted in Otto Ruhle, *Karl Marx, His Life and Work* (English translation, 1929), p. 366.
12. Adam Smith, *The Wealth of Nations*, Bk. I, ch. XI, Pt. II.
13. Cf. G. Childe, Introduction to *What Happened in History*, and Herskovits, *op. cit.*, ch. XXII and p. 294.
14. Cf. Paul Radin, *Primitive Religion* (New York, 1937), esp. pp. 40–58.
15. F. Engels, *The Origin of the Family, Private Property and the State* (New

York, 1942), pp. 6, 48, 146, 149, 160; Lewis H. Morgan, *Ancient Society* (New York, 1877), Part IV; Thorstein Veblen, *op. cit.*, pp. 150–1. Childe, *Cambridge Economic History of Europe*, II, 4–5; Herskovits, *op. cit.*, p. 395; Jacobs and Stern, *op. cit.*, p. 141; Hilton, *op. cit.*, p. 347.

16. *Ancient Society*.

17. *Ibid.*, p. 19.

18. *Ibid.*, p. 547.

19. *Ibid.*, p. 550.

20. *Op. cit.*, p. 6 (preface to first edition).

21. *Ibid.*, pp. 150–1.

22. *Ibid.*, p. 152.

23. *Ibid.*, p. 159.

24. Strictly, it is not true that the idea appears "first" with the Physiocrats. The idea was "in the air," so to speak; all of those who tackled the problem of exchange value came up with a surplus. The idea may be found in embryonic form in the work of Sir William Petty (1623–87) and, more fully developed in Richard Cantillon (1680–1734) *Essai sur la nature due commerce en general*. Cf. Joseph Schumpeter, *History of Economic Analysis* (New York, 1954), pp. 209–223; and J. J. Spengler, "Richard Cantillon: First of the Moderns," in *Journal of Political Economics*, Vol. 62, Nos. 4, 5 (August, October, 1954). For the Physiocrats, see Schumpeter, *op. cit.*, pp. 223–249; Norman J. Ware, "The Physiocrats," *American Economic Review*, XXI, No. 4 (December, 1931); and Marx's discussion in *Theories of Surplus Value* (Selections, translated from German by G. A. Bonner and Emile Burns (New York, 1952).

25. M. Turgot, *Reflections on the Formation and Distribution of Wealth* (Translated from French, London, 1793), p. 252.

26. Cf. K. Marx, *Theories of Surplus Value*, *op. cit.*, p. 56: "Their error flows from the fact that they confused the increase of *material substance* . . . with the increase of *exchange value*."

27. For the discussion of these difficulties see Talcott Parsons, *The Structure of Social Action* (Glencoe, Ill., 1947), Ch. III; Elie Halevy, *The Growth of Philosophic Radicalism* (Translated from French, New York, 1949); A. D. Lindsay, *Karl Marx's Capital* (London, 1925), esp. Ch. III.

28. *The Wealth of Nations* (1776), Book I, Part VI.

29. This is true of the objective surplus of classical economics but marginal utility economics invented subjective or "utility surpluses" to take their place. See, e.g., A. Marshall, *Principles of Economics* (8th ed., New York, 1920), pp. 124–133 and Appendix K. For criticism see F. H. Knight, *Risk, Uncertainty and Profit* (New York, 1921), pp. 69–73.

30. K. Marx, *Capital*, I (1867) Modern Library edition, p. 195.

31. *Ibid.*, pp. 562, 564–5.

32. *Ibid.*, p. 786.

33. Marx was perhaps the first to emphasize the institutional origin of relative surpluses in a market economy by focusing on the contractual relationship between worker and capitalist. Marginal utility economics imputed the surplus away by pointing to the functional significance of *all* contributors of "scarce" means to the productive process. J. Schumpeter (*The Theory of Economic Development*, English translation, Cambridge, Mass., 1934) and F. H. Knight (*Risk, Uncertainty and Profit*), showed that after values were imputed to all functional "cost" factors, there still remained "profit" and this "surplus" they explained in terms of specific institutional features of the market system. For an extension of these views see, Jean

Marchal, "The Construction of a New Theory of Profit," *American Economic Review*, Vol. 61, No. 4 (September, 1951); also Peter Drucker, *The New Society* (New York, 1950), ch. IV.

34. Cf. Joan Robinson, "Mr. Wiles' Rationality: a Comment," *Soviet Studies*, VII (January, 1956), 269: "The primary function of price, in both sorts of economy [capitalist and socialist], is to make accumulation possible."

35. *Primitive Polynesian Economy* (London, 1939), p. 9.

36. Cf. The use of cattle for "money" in Homeric Greece; M. I. Finley, *The World of Odysseus* (New York, 1954), p. 65.

37. A. I. Richards and E. M. Widdowson, "A dietary study in Northeastern Rhodesia," *Africa*, No. 9 (1936), p. 196.

38. *Ibid.*, p. 174.

39. R. T. Thurnwald, *Werden, Wandel und Gestaltung der Wirtschaft* (Berlin and Leipzig, 1932), p. 121.

40. See B. Malinowski, *Argonauts of the Western Pacific* (New York, 1922); Cora Du Bois, "The wealth concept as an integrative factor in Tolowa-Tututni culture," *Essays in Anthropology* (Berkeley, Calif., 1936); Herskovits, *op. cit.*, ch. XXI; Finley, *op. cit.*, pp. 58–9 ff.; A. P. Vayda, "Notes on trade among the Pomo Indians of California" (mimeographed) Columbia University Interdisciplinary Project (1954).

41. *Op. cit.*

XVII

Economic Theory Misplaced: Livelihood in Primitive Society

———•———

THIS chapter is an examination of some methodological problems that have developed in the study of primitive economics, with special reference to the application of economic theory to anthropological studies. The first section points out that the types of problems facing the anthropologist and the economic theorist have differed substantially and required different approaches; the second examines the contribution of leading writers on primitive economics who did not use formal economic theory as an analytical tool; the third is a critique of writers who have used formal economic theory in cross-cultural studies and points out the methodological problems that have been created; and the fourth summarizes the chief methodological problems and suggests that a broader approach to economic life than that offered by modern economic theory is necessary for the study of primitive economics if the results are to be meaningful.

Economic Anthropology

Although the study of the economic life of primitive peoples has not been a major concern of modern anthropologists, it is realized by most that no analysis of a culture is complete unless some attention is given to the production and distribution of goods and services. Not only must man feed, clothe and house himself, but the institutions he has developed to meet his material needs are an integral part of his social life. In understanding the nature of society it is essential to recognize that social institutions make up an integrated web of which the economic form a major part. And in understanding the nature of man it is essential to recognize that his motivations are all but determined by the web of social institutions within which he operates. The anthropologist has helped to make these ideas a part of the intellectual currency of our time, and in doing so has fostered the study of economic motivations within the broader context of society as a whole.

Modern economic theory, on the other hand, seeks to separate out the economic from other aspects of society. In doing so, two simplifying concepts have commonly been employed: the maximization principle and the allocation principle. The individual is conceived of as maximizing his satisfactions in the use of means to satisfy his wants, and is thereby given a set of motivations that can be thought of as purely economic, separated from other types of motivations that may be present at the same time. The whole individual operating in a web of social institutions is abstracted from in order to define a specialized aspect of behavior. While this simplifying technique may have resulted in important developments in economic theory, it has grave drawbacks if the investigator conceives of motivations as a pattern in which each part is influenced by the configuration as a whole. For the anthropologist, who works with the latter type of concept, the economic theorist's view of motivations seems narrow and tends to obscure rather than illuminate the questions he wants to ask.

Just as the maximization principle separates out economic motives, so that allocation principle abstracts from the institutional complex. Economics is conceived of as the rational allocation of scarce means to achieve given goals, and it is held that this type of activity must be carried on within any set of socio-economic institutions, at any time, and in any environment. It is argued that the logic of choice must therefore be applicable to any society. But the anthropologist has discovered that economic activity must be explained primarily in terms of a given society's social institutions. Even scarcity is present or absent in varying degrees as a result of the structure of society and social attitudes, and choice is often severely restricted by the social structure within which the individual functions. The very foundations of the theory of choice are socially conditioned, and to abstract those foundations from their social matrix obscures the essential problems.

Not only does economic theory seek to separate the economic from other facets of society, but it has developed a conceptual framework characteristic of the modern market economy that is difficult to apply to nonmarket economies. The concepts analyzed in economic theory—money, prices, supply and demand, capital, rent, interest, profit and the like—are characteristic of the institutional framework of the self-adjusting market system. Their theoretical analysis has a real basis in the actual structure of institutions. But in nonmarket economies those concepts have no institutional counterpart. Applying market concepts cross-culturally to an institutional framework in which they do not exist will result in a falsified picture of the actual structure and functioning of the social order.[1]

For practical purposes the economic theorist does not worry about the limitations of his discipline, because he applies it only to the market economy: for his purposes and problems it is a highly useful tool. But the social scientist who deals with cross-cultural problems is inevitably concerned with institutions and cannot use effectively a set of tools which deliberately abstracts from the institutional framework.

The problem is that the anthropologist asks a different type of question than that asked by the economic theorist: he wants to know about the interrelationships that exist within the societal complex and seeks to explain the functioning of society as a whole. The economic theorist has a different kind of problem: he is interested in the logical principles by which scarce resources can be allocated to maximize the attainment of desired goals—and in attacking this problem he has lifted his inquiry out of the institutional complex that is the center of interest of the anthropologist.

The Societal Approach

For many years anthropologists made little use of economic theory. When they first began investigating the economic life of primitive peoples they concentrated almost exclusively on ecology and technology. Economics was thought of narrowly in terms of the techniques employed in the production of useful things. There was some justification for this approach, for differences in technology are often associated with major differences in social structure based on hunting, herding, gardening, agriculture, handicrafts, and other means of gaining subsistence. And it has the advantage, at least, of centering attention on substantive problems of economics—production of material things—rather than the formal theoretical problems of maximization and allocation.

The narrowness of this early approach to economic life developed into a much broader one. In the period between 1910 and 1935 came pathbreaking work by Boas, Thurnwald and Malinowski. Economics was conceived by these writers as the process of satisfaction of material needs, and economic motivations and institutions were treated as integral parts of the total social process. Most significantly, it was shown that the acquisitive motivations characterstic of economic life in modern society were generally not to be found among primitive peoples, and that the market institutions of modern society were definitely not the rule in primitive society. The self-adjusting market economy of the western world was found to be unique in the history of mankind.

Perhaps the most important single work was Malinowski's multivolume study of the Trobriand Islanders.[2] He showed how thoroughly the production of goods and services was embedded in political, religious, social and kinship institutions. The economic activities of individuals were motivated by social and political obligations, by kinship, by friendship, and by magical rituals and beliefs. Exchange was carried on by gift-giving and ceremonial distribution of goods; barter existed only with persons outside the tribe; buying and selling were nonexistent. The Trobrianders were a typical nonmarket people, with an economic system and motivations that can hardly be understood by modern market-conditioned man.

Supplementing Malinowski's pathbreaking work were the studies made by the followers of Boas, particularly those of Benedict and Mead.[3] Proceeding from a different methodological base than Malinowski's, some of the conclusions are nevertheless startlingly similar. Especially important is confirmation of Malinowski's view that primitive economic institutions are so thoroughly entwined with other social institutions that one can hardly speak of economic motives in the modern sense of that term. Mead's description of the gift-giving Arapesh is a classic example of kinship and friendship obligations as motivations for economic activity. Indeed, the numerous descriptions of the *potlatch* of the Northwest Coast Indians illustrate a general principle; acquisitive motives are usually channeled into activities other than the provision of goods and services to meet material needs. Also of importance along these lines has been the work of DuBois, emphasizing the importance of prestige elements—a "noneconomic" factor—in channeling economic activity in primitive society.[4]

Of special relevance to the development of economic institutions is the work of Thurnwald.[5] From his ethnological studies in East Africa he developed a theory of the development of simple societies into stratified social systems, feudalisms and despotisms. He pointed out that a stratified society with clearly distinguishable social classes usually results from cultural contacts between gardening, artisan, or hunting-fishing peoples on the one hand and herding peoples on the other, with the herdsmen tending to form an aristocracy. Such a society may develop along feudal lines if the clan heads of the herdsmen remain relatively equal rivals, into a despotism if power can be centralized under a single dynasty, or into a tyrannis if someone outside the traditional aristocracy can seize power. The ancient despotic state, such as Egypt, is a development typical of this scheme.[6] Not only is the economy intimately connected with the social structure in Thurnwald's schema, but development of the two is pictured as a dynamic relationship.

The importance of Thurnwald's theory of economic development is twofold. In the first place, it directly connects modern anthropological studies of simple societies with the origins of ancient states, and whether his schema will be found by further studies to be right or wrong he has created a bridge between the anthropologist and the historian that must be explored further.

In the second place, Thurnwald's theory suggests that the present emphasis in historical research on gradual, evolutionary development of more advanced forms of society from simpler forms may be incorrect. It suggests that homogeneous societies do not develop into stratified societies without such exogenous forces as cultural contact, and his scheme of evolutionary development ends with feudalisms and despotisms. The market society of the modern world is not seen as a natural outgrowth of feudal forms of society. For the economic historian of the western world this means a re-evaluation of the neo-Darwinism that pervades much historical research. For example, did the modern market economy gradually evolve out of the commercial activities of the medieval bourgeoisie, as many historians believe, or did the whole fabric of feudal society have to be broken by new methods of warfare, the rise of national states, the discoveries and the Reformation before modern capitalism could emerge?[7]

Thurnwald also placed great stress on gift-giving, or reciprocity, as a pervasive element in primitive economic life, a pattern far removed from the acquisitive motives of the market economy and requiring a symmetrical pattern of social relationships for its operation. Indeed, Mauss has suggested that gift exchange is the fundamental principle underlying all primitive trade.[8]

Anthropologists such as Malinowski, Benedict, Mead and Thurnwald found little use for economic theory. In part this was because some of their chief targets were the postulates of man's acquisitive nature, his alleged dislike for work, and his economic rationality as they were described by economic theory. These scholars were engaged in building a concept of man's nature at odds with the "economic man" of economic theory. In part, also, they were concerned with the whole social structure and not just that part of it called the economic, realizing that the economic life of primitive man did not function through economic institutions separate from other social institutions. These writers recognized the methodological problem: their goals were different from those of the economic theorist and a different set of analytical tools had to be used.

The Use of Economic Theory[9]

In the last fifteen years the study of primitive economics has taken a different turn, making use of the concepts of modern economics to a much greater extent than did the earlier anthropologists. The results of this marriage of the two disciplines have not been happy.

The earlier studies had an important drawback. Since their major emphasis lay in the relationship of economic institutions to the total social structure there was a tendency to forego detailed study of economic processes themselves. In studying the distribution of goods from a chief to his tribesmen, for example, the earlier anthropologists emphasized the social setting of the distribution, the socio-political motives involved, and the submergence of economic life in the total life of the tribe. Economics was treated as only one facet of society, and although this position is methodologically unassailable it led to a slighting of the detailed facts of economic life. It is also important to know exactly what goods the chief distributed to his tribesmen, in what quantities, and under what circumstances, and in general terms that would permit comparison with other peoples. This would mean less attention being paid to the social matrix of economic life and more attention to the detailed facts themselves.

This weakness of the early studies of primitive economics has led to the appearance of a new "school" of anthropologists who have devoted themselves to studies of primitive economic life in great detail, using the terminology of economic theory in order to make comparisons between different societies. Less emphasis is placed upon the uniqueness of each society, and more is placed upon such things as incentives, exchange, trade and barter, money, use of capital, land tenure, and so on. The goal of this newer group of anthropologists is to derive some general principles of economic behavior among primitive peoples out of detailed studies of everyday economic affairs. Chief among them are Melville Herskovits, Sol Tax, Raymond Firth, and D. M. Goodfellow.[10]

Typical of this group of writers is Herskovits. His *Economic Anthropology* (1952) attempts to bring together all of the empirical knowledge of primitive economics and analyze it within the framework of orthodox economic theory. The major subjects treated are production, distribution, exchange, property and economic surplus—the outline might well have been taken from John Stuart Mill—and the goal is to understand the economics of primitive peoples in terms of the categories of modern economic theory so that general principles may be derived from the studies of individual peoples.

In pursuing the goal of understanding economic life in economic rather than social terms, Herskovits begins by accepting the definition of economics that most orthodox economists hold: economics is the study of the allocation of scarce means to achieve given ends. Every society, argues Herskovits, has this problem of choice, and has developed an economic system within which it is solved. Indeed, "it can also be taken as cross-culturally acceptable that, on the whole, the individual tends to maximize his satisfactions in terms of the choices he makes" (p. 18). Even though the choices may appear to us to be irrational or wasteful, in terms of a different social matrix and attitudes they will be seen to be rational.

This definition, of course, encompasess a universal principle that applies to many other areas of life in addition to the economic. But it can lead to valid analytical results in economics only when applied to a set of market institutions that permits a direct achievement of economic goals through the market. In the modern market economy allocation of resources is responsive to profits, and maximization of that calculable sum is the goal of business enterprise.[11] It is the complex of markets and prices, profits and acquisitiveness that provides an institutionalized means for the making of choices in our economy. In such an institutional setting the theory of choice has led to the development of modern economic theory.

But where economic life is embedded in an institutional matrix other than that of a system of markets the theory of the market tells us little. For example, when the economy of a tribe is based upon gift-giving the institutional framework of production and distribution is the prevailing system of kinship and friendship, and economic activities become entwined with motives of maintaining and promoting kinship and friendship ties. "Social motives" become more important than the "economic motives" of acquiring goods; resources are used to achieve "social goals." Under such circumstances the theory of choice leads only to the vague generalization that satisfactions have been maximized.

The most striking characteristic of Herskovits' work from the viewpoint of methodology is that his conceptual framework causes him to emphasize market phenomena and largely to ignore the remainder of primitive economic life. For example, he asserts that gift and ceremonial exchange are "noneconomic" because they are used to obtain "prestige," and devotes only a short chapter to them (Ch. VIII). This is in spite of his recognition that those forms of exchange are used to distribute goods "in many, perhaps a majority of instances" (p. 181). On the other hand, trade and barter are treated at great length (Ch. IX–XI), although Herskovits admits that trade "is usually *intertribal* and involves the acquisition of goods not available in one's own group" (p. 181; Herskovits' italics). This is strange economics indeed—practically to ignore institutions that channelize distribution within the economic system and center attention on intertribal economic relationships.

A similar methodological weakness is found in Herskovits' treatment of money. The modern economist defines money as anything generally acceptable in making payments, and adds that money also functions as a means of storing wealth, as a standard of value, and as a standard of deferred payments. In the modern market economy all of these functions have been institutionalized in a single object which we call money. But in primitive societies the various functions of money are institutionalized separately; that is, different things are used in making payments of different kinds, other objects are "valuables," other objects are used to validate the individual's social status, while still others are used to facilitate exchange where markets exist. It is to this last function of "money" that Herskovits limits his discussion; he defines money as "any kind of least common denominator of value— so long as it is regarded as part of a system of graded equivalents, and is used in payment for goods and services" (p. 245). Money, so defined, is currency, and that is how Herskovits treats it. But he ignores or treats only in passing all those monetary functions that are not performed by currency—storing of wealth in the form of cattle or "valuables," payments in kind or in services, and so on. In short, Herskovits has failed to realize that currency performs only a relatively insignificant role in primitive society, that the great bulk of payments are not made by currency, and that most wealth is not stored in the form of currency.[12]

Herskovits' faulty methodology stems from his use of the economist's conceptual framework. Such things as money, credit, value, business enterprise, capital formation, and the like are among the major subjects studied in modern economics, and he therefore concentrates on them. They are also separately institutionalized within a market economy. Needless to say, such a conceptual framework is inadequate in discussing economies in which market phenomena are relatively unimportant in channelizing production and distribution. Put bluntly, Herskovits seeks to cram the multifarious forms of non-market economic life into the pigeonholes of the market economy, ignoring what will not fit. The result is a distorted and inaccurate picture of primitive economic life.[13]

When Herskovits gets away from problems of exchange and distribution he gets away from his market-oriented terminology, and it is here that his work is most valuable. Modern economics takes for granted the institution of private property, and did not develop a specialized terminology for that aspect of economic life. Not being artificially restricted by a market terminology, Herskovits gives a very realistic description of land tenure and ownership of property among primitive peoples: private property in land, as we know it, does not exist, but land is held by the social unit and the individual has rights in it; the complex nature of rights in land make a market for land impossible; nevertheless, every primitive society recognizes some types of property as privately owned and capable of alienation—the wide prevalence of gift-giving and ceremonial exchange would be impossible without such property.

Suffering from similar methodological difficulties is Tax's work on the Guatemalan village of Panajachel.[14] Tax describes "a money economy organized in single households as both consumption and production units, with a strongly developed market (for commodities) which tends to be perfectly competitive" as "very strongly a market economy" (pp. 11–13). But as he describes it, the economy of Panajachel has only the most rudimentary of markets for factors of production: although land is freely transferable its sale is highly restricted by the attitude that land holdings must be preserved for the family; the absence of any large body of both free and landless workers precludes the development of a true labor market; and there hardly exists a capital market although loans are sometimes made for consumption purposes. The fundamental institutional bases of the market economy and the tremendous differences between market and non-market institutional patterns are not understood. The underlying difficulty is Tax's use of the conceptual framework of the economics of the market and analysis of the economy of Panajachel in terms of the maximization and allocation principles. Again a distorted picture and improper conclusions emerge.

Far more sophisticated than Herskovits or Tax in use of economic theory is D. M. Goodfellow. He has applied the basic concept of choice among alternatives in an analysis of the economic life of the Bantu peoples of south and east Africa, in an effort to show that individual choice is the universal phenomenon of economic activity and that it results in a scale of economic values by which material goods can be compared.[15] He argues that the concepts of economic theory have "universal validity" (p. 3) and that "there is no gulf between the civilized and the primitive; one cultural level shades imperceptibly into another" (p. 5). While arguing that "economic choice is constantly exercised by the individual" (p. 11) he recognizes that "resources are indeed disposed of according to the dictates of social values and rules of behavior, describable in terms of custom" (p. 15). On the basis of these principles the Bantu economy is examined; it is a society of patriarchal families in which kinship relations create reciprocal obligations, but in which each family manages its own household. Chief attention in Goodfellow's work is paid to the management of the household and practically no space is devoted to the economics of anything else in Bantu society. Among the aspects of Bantu economic life not adequately treated are reciprocal economic relationships based on kinship, redistribution through the chieftain, and economic relationships that transcend the household-kinship-chieftain complex. Here again is the methodological difficulty that emerged in Herskovits' work: the conceptual framework has limited the inquiry to only part of the subject. The saving feature of Goodfellow's work is that he chose for study an economy in which the principle of householding is the dominant feature of economic life, and it is obvious that economic management must take place in the household. Even within this type of economy, however, Goodfellow selected those aspects that involved choice, slighting those that did not involve choice, and came out with the conclusion that economics—the theory of choice—is applicable cross-culturally. The reader comes out with the conclusion that while choices may well be made within the Bantu economy, a full understanding of that economy requires a broader approach.

Much more useful than the work of Herskovits, Tax, or Goodfellow is that of Raymond Firth.[16] His study of the economy of the Polynesian island of Tikopia makes use of the concepts of modern economics, but Firth never allows those concepts to obscure the relationship between economic life and kinship, magic, ritual and chieftainship, nor to obscure reciprocal or redistributive forms of economic activity. While he shows that individual advantage is pursued, he emphasizes that such activity is closely limited and defined by traditional patterns of behavior and that the individual is not permitted by social sanctions to pursue his own interests to more than a very limited extent. Indeed, the concepts of economic theory are used primarily to show that the Polynesian is both realistic and rational in his economic life, rather than as a framework within which to analyze the economy.

Yet when economic theory and its concepts can be applied without distorting the picture, Firth does not hesitate to do so. In his book on the Malay fishing industry he describes a peasant fishing economy in which there are local, regional and export markets for dried fish, wholesalers and retailers, and a complex system of credit. The fish trade is market-oriented, and a meaningful analysis in terms of ownership and management of capital, credit, marketing organization, distribution, output and levels of income is possible. But Firth is frank in his recognition that the analysis does not explore the relationships between fishing activities and other aspects of social and economic life in the society. It is essentially a study of a single market-oriented industry in a peasant economy, and shows that modern economic theory can be successfully applied to market aspects of primitive economic life if its limitations are recognized.

While the weaknesses of Herskovits' and Goodfellow's work arise from a largely uncritical acceptance of economic theory, Firth's success is due in large part to his selective use of its concepts and principles. His awareness of the methodological pitfalls involved in economic theory is typified by the statement that "the anthropologist accepts as valid the body of economic doctrine" but "he can absorb only a very small part of it into his conceptual apparatus for the study of primitive society."[17]

A Cross-cultural Economics

To summarize, the use of modern economic theory as a tool of analysis in studying primitive economics has two principal drawbacks. First, the categories and definitions of modern economies are not applicable to cross-cultural studies. The basic reason for this lack of applicability is that the phenomena isolated for study—money, capital, profit, wages, rent, business enterprise, markets and the like—not only perform economic functions, but have an institutionalized reality in the modern economy that can be identified and usually measured. And they are the result of a unique historical development that has not been repeated in other cultures. Capital, for example, is not only the goods used for the production of other goods, but in the modern economy it can be identified and measured as part of business institutions, and enters into the calculations of businessmen through widely accepted accounting procedures. In the primitive economy the economic functions performed by capital can be analyzed and described, but there is no way of treating them as a separate and discrete part of the institutional structure of society. Rather, the economic functions of capital are generally found institutionalized as part of other social institutions —kinship, the family unit, religion and magic, tribal political structure, and the like—rather than separately, and an analysis of capital in the economy becomes analysis of the whole society. If the analysis were limited only to those cultural elements clearly identifiable as capital as a separately institutionalized element much of the relevant data would be missed.

Secondly, the formal economics of the maximization and allocation principles—the theory of choice—represents only a portion of the subject matter of economics.[18] Economics deals with the production and distribution of material goods and services. At one boundary of the subject it gets very close to the study of technology and processes of production. At the other limit it treats of attitudes and motivations, social classes and relationships, and the institutional framework within which production and distribution are carried on. Only a relatively small part of the subject matter of economics is the theory of choice among alternatives—and even choices are conditioned by technological possibilities and the social structure. If attention is centered narrowly on the logic of choice a large portion of economics will be ignored.

For the anthropologist a methodological difficulty of the utmost gravity is created. Use of the tools of economic theory offers only limited advantages in centering attention on individual choices, while it interferes with the institutional analysis that is at the heart of anthropological study. The anthropologist who studies primitive economics cannot go to another already developed discipline for his conceptual framework or his problems and questions. Instead, a broader theoretical schema must be developed—broad enough to encompass both the modern market economy and the economies of primitive peoples—in which the formal economics of the market is a special case. The task is no easy one. It requires not only empirical studies of production and distribution that center on economic institutions and their relationship to the larger social structure, but also a willingness to theorize about the place of the economic system in society and not merely about individual choices.[19] The leading ideas that have to be developed further are those of Malinowski, Thurnwald, Benedict, DuBois and Mead, and not those of the economic theorists. The real task is nothing less than the building of a cross-cultural economics based on the substantive problems of production and distribution rather than on formal problems of choice.

Daniel B. Fusfeld

Notes to Chapter XVII

1. See J. H. Boeke, *The Structure of Netherlands Indian Economy* (New York, 1942), pp. 3–6, for a discussion of the difficulty of applying modern economic theory to the Oriental peasant economy. For the opposite view see Raymond Firth, *Malay Fishermen: Their Peasant Economy* (London, 1946)—but note that Firth's discussion is limited to the Malay fishing industry, which operates within a market framework.

Simon Rottenberg has recently argued that failure of workers in primitive economies to respond to wage incentives does not mean that there is no effective labor market, but rather that the supply of labor is inelastic. See his "Discussion," *American Economic Review,* Vol. 65, No. 2 (May, 1955), 194. Such a conclusion is the inevitable result of the theoretician's method of abstracting from the institutional framework. What does it tell us about the functioning of the primitive economy? See also Simon Rottenberg, "Income and Leisure in an Underdeveloped Economy," *Journal of Political Economy,* Vol. 60, No. 2 (April, 1952).

2. Bronislaw Malinowski, "The Primitive Economics of the Trobriand Islanders," *Economic Journal,* XXXI, 1–16; *Argonauts of the Western Pacific* (New York, 1950); *Crime and Custom in Savage Society* (London, 1926); *Coral Gardens and Their Magic* (London, 1935).

3. The best introductions to this "configurational" school of anthropologists are Ruth Benedict, *Patterns of Culture* (New York, 1934) and Margaret Mead (ed.), *Cooperation and Competition Among Primitive Peoples* (New York, 1937).

4. Cora DuBois, "The Wealth Factor as an Integrative Factor in Tolowa-Tututui Culture" in *Essays in Anthropology Presented to A. L. Kroeber* (Berkeley, 1936), pp. 49–66.

5. Summarized in Richard Thurnwald, *Economics in Primitive Communities* (London, 1932).

6. Thurnwald's theory of the state has a close affinity with that of Franz Oppenheimer (*The State*, New York, 1914), but goes far beyond Oppenheimer's version.

7. The evolutionary approach to economic history is particularly prevalent among English and American scholars. German writers, on the other hand, have emphasized discontinuities and irregularities in economic development; this is especially true of Karl Marx, Gustav Schmoller, Werner Sombart, and Max Weber. Anthropologists since Thurnwald's day have eschewed consideration of problems of social change in a reaction against the earlier theories of "stages" of development. The whole range of problems explored by Thurnwald has unfortunately been dropped until very recently.

8. Marcel Mauss, *The Gift: Forms and Functions of Exchange in Archaic Societies* (Glencoe, Ill., 1954).

9. Parts of this section are reprinted from reviews in the *Journal of Economic History*, XIII, No. 2 (Spring 1953), 219–221 and *Explorations in Entrepreneurial History*, VI, No. 3 (February 1954), 190–191.

10. Melville Herskovits, *Economic Anthropology* (New York, 1952), originally published as *The Economic Life of Primitive Peoples* (New York, 1940); Sol Tax, *Penny Capitalism: A Guatemalan Indian Economy* (Washington, 1953); Raymond Firth, *Primitive Polynesian Economy* (London, 1939) and *Malay Fishermen: Their Peasant Economy* (London, 1946); D. M. Goodfellow, *Principles of Economic Sociology* (London, 1939; New York, 1950).

11. This is true, at least, of theoretical models of the market economy; it is less true of the actual world.

12. Firth recognizes this difficulty and points out that true money is not widely found among primitive peoples, but he also fails to consider adequately the wide diffusion of the functions of money and the problem of its institutionalization. He adopts the definition of money developed by the modern economist, and in so doing eliminates from consideration much of the reality of primitive economic life, and ignores the most important problem, namely, how the various functions of money come to be institutionalized in a single element of culture. See Raymond Firth, "Currency, Primitive," *Encyclopedia Brittanica*, 14th ed.

13. For the opposite view, praising Herskovits' use of the conceptual framework of modern economics, see K. F. Walker, "The Study of Primitive Economics," *Oceania*, XIII (1942–3), 131–42.

14. Sol Tax, *Penny Capitalism* (Washington, 1953).

15. D. M. Goodfellow, *Principles of Economic Sociology* (London, 1939; New York, 1950).

16. His two recent works in primitive economics are *Primitive Polynesian Economy* (London, 1939) and *Malay Fishermen: Their Peasant Economy* (London, 1946).

17. Raymond Firth, *Elements of Social Organization* (London, 1951) pp. 129–130.

18. See John R. Hicks, "Economic Theory and the Social Sciences," in *The Social Sciences: Their Relations in Theory and Teaching* (London, 1936), pp. 129–140.

19. A good recent example of this approach is Eleanor Leacock, "The Montagnais 'Hunting Territory' and the Fur Trade," *American Anthropologist*, Vol. 56, No. 5, Part 2 (Memoirs of the American Anthropological Association, No. 78). Other anthropologists who have been dealing with the problem of economic development have given similar emphasis to their work.

XVIII

The Market in Theory and History

THE existence of a market is often taken to establish the existence of a market system in the modern sense of price-making markets, and to imply the relevance of the body of economic theory to the analysis of the situation in which the market is found. As a result a modern, market economy is read into the social organizations of many historical and primitive societies where there is no other evidence to support the existence of a system similar to ours except the occurrence of some form of market. There would be no objection to such reasoning if the term market had only one, precise meaning, but this is not the case.

To the economist the market is a specific institution with rules of its own upon which he has built a very powerful analytic structure. To the historian and anthropologist the market is often the "market place," a meeting place for the transfer of goods from one set of hands to another, and such a market place is not necessarily the basis of the economic theory which economists have created. There is a great danger that in adopting the common terms of economics the less perfectly understood implications which economists attach to these terms may slip into the description of societies other than our own, and, in consequence, the inappropriate usage of the terms of economics will hide from the investigator the true institutional mechanisms of the society which he is analyzing.

In view, therefore, of the real differences between a market as it is conceived by economists and the market place as it is found by anthropologists and economic historians, it seems useful to make explicit the differences in meaning which may be attached to the term market, and so avoid serious mistakes in interpreting evidence of trade, money and market elements in societies without a market system.

Price-making Markets

To the economist the market is a mechanism which produces prices. The function of market prices is to regulate the supply of goods[1] in relation to the demand, and to channel the demand for goods in relation to the available supply. Hence the market may be called a supply-demand-price mechanism. As we shall see, all and everything that is comprised in a market economy can be subsumed under these terms.

(a) The *supply* is the amount of goods on the market at a given time, or flowing into the market over a given period of time. It is a characteristic of the market that the supply of a good offered for sale increases as the price rises, and this for two reasons:

(A) A higher price will bring higher cost producers into the market.
(B) At a higher price, holders of the good who had no intention of selling may change their minds because their command over other goods has thus increased.

Thus there is a definite relationship between the prevailing price and the goods made available by the suppliers. Prices regulate the movement of goods into the market.

(b) *Demand* means the quantity of goods which buyers will take at a particular price; e.g., so many pounds of butter per month if the price is, say, fifty cents. Given people's preferences, a market is expected to register a rise in the level of demand for a good if the prices of other goods rise relative to the price of that good, and a fall if the prices of other goods go down. Thus prices regulate the movement of goods out of the market.

Demand figures importantly at two junctures in the economist's market. There is demand for consumers' goods like butter, and demand for the various inputs needed to produce the butter. Relative prices play the decisive role in both cases. Consumers face an array of goods with limited purchasing power. Since they must, in order to get desired goods, cover prices with their limited purchasing power, their purchases will obviously depend on prices. Producers demand factors of production because they can make a profit by employing them as inputs. Within the limits set by technology producers demand more of the cheaper and less of the dearer inputs. If the price of labor rises producers will try to use more capital goods as substitutes for labor. Here again prices rule, for the producer will succeed only to the extent that he maximizes the spread between cost and price.

(c) The *mechanism* of the market refers to the systematic reactions of all prices and quantities to changes in any one of them. Prices move goods into the market (supply) and move them out of the market (demand). At the same time prices themselves are affected by supply and demand. As the conditions of supply—relative scarcity—or of demand —relative preferences—change, such changes will be reflected in prices. An increased preference for one good means that buyers will buy more of it than formerly at any given price. Suppliers will not sell more at the old price, so the price must rise until it has called forth an increased supply. At the same time the rise in price will eliminate a certain amount of the willingness to buy which existed at the lower price. This double action of fluctuating prices constantly moves supply and demand to a position of equilibrium. That is, relative prices are constantly moving toward the combination at which the quantity of each good which suppliers will sell at the market price is exactly matched by the quantity which buyers will purchase at that price, thus "clearing the market."

It is this self-equilibrating mechanism which the economist has in mind when he employs the term "market." Since all economic decisions will be based upon prices and all events of economic importance will become effective through prices, this concept of the market provides a simple, yet comprehensive, tool for explaining all the movements of goods and services involved in the complex process of production and distribution. The choice of what goods to produce and of what means to use to produce them, and thus the allocation of productive resources between uses, the distribution of income, the choice between present and future consumption (or how much to save and invest) and even the effects of social and political factors upon the economy—all these choices can be explained within the framework of the market concept.

To illustrate the scope of the economist's concept, and to give concreteness to the characteristics of the major subdivisions of the self-regulating market system, it may be helpful to present a bird's-eye view of the different types of markets.

Types of Markets: the Economist's View

Product markets are markets for goods which have been processed to some extent. The product markets which we, as consumers, are constantly influencing and being influenced by are the innumerable markets for the goods and services which we buy for ourselves and our families. These we may call Consumer Goods Markets. Another sub-classification can be made for the finished and semifinished goods which businesses buy to use in further production and distribution, for these product markets overlap with those of the consumer. These are the markets in which businesses buy buildings, machinery, processed raw materials, semifinished and finished goods.

Factor markets are the markets for land, labor, and capital. All basic inputs are classified under one of these three headings, being either a natural resource; human work of the manual or mental kinds; or buildings and equipment needed for production and distribution. Each of these markets has its special characteristics:

(a) *The Market for Land* is the market in which claims or title to land and all its natural characteristics can be bought and sold. The concept of "land" is broad, including not merely the surface area involved, but also the advantages of its climate, location, and mineral wealth. However, the concept of land is limited to the conditions and content which nature or chance put into the plot; the economist would say that all man-made changes are properly capital investments added to the land. While there is a purchase price for the paramount title—ownership—one generally takes Rent for the use of land over a period as the Price of land on the Land Market. The unique characteristic of this market is that the supply was fixed in Genesis and changes in rent cannot alter the amount on offer. If demand for land increases there is a rise in price, but the rise is incapable of calling forth a larger supply. Conversely the price can fall to zero and there will be no diminution of supply.[2]

(b) *The Market for Labor* is the market for the hiring of all humans used in the productive process. Unlike product and land markets, the buyer cannot buy the man, but only the use of his brain and brawn over a period. The price here is generally called the wage (per unit of time), and this term is taken to include salaries and the bonuses of top directors. The unique characteristic of this market is that it involves the buying and selling of the time and activities of the people who make up the society. On the demand side there is only one consideration involved in hiring the man: whether or not his labor will contribute to the productive process as much or more in value than the wage he is paid—exactly the same consideration that governs demand in any other factor market. But on the supply side, there are peculiarly human elements involved. A man must eat to live, and to eat he must work: i.e., hire out his labor. The more efficient or skilled a man is, the higher the wage he can command, but except for the small number of persons who can live on the proceeds of their titles to land and capital, everyone must succeed in getting a job at some wage. This means that the supply of labor has something in common with the supply of land. As wages vary old people, young people, wives, and such on-again-off-again laborers may add to or deduct from the labor supply, but the overwhelming part of the labor supply is determined by the size and age distribution of the population.

(c) *The Capital Market* refers not to the buildings and equipment which are in reality the capital used in the productive process, but to the market for the money (purchasing power) which can buy the capital equipment or the use of land and labor. Thus we have divided the capital market in two parts: the one a product market similar to the *Consumers Product Market* except that it is governed not by taste but by calculable profitability; and the other a market for the money which can buy these products. The Capital Market is subdivided into a number of *Financial Markets*: e.g., the *Stock Exchange* for the permanent borrowing of money in exchange for a share in the profits of the business using the money, the *Money Market* for the temporary borrowing of funds in exchange for a fixed return on the money until it is repaid. The price paid for the use of money on the Money Market is called interest, and since the Money Market and the Stock Exchange are alternative sources of money, economists generally treat only the interest rate when discussing the price of money. The Money Market is of course divided again into closely related parts, such as the *Mortgage Market* where funds are tied up for long periods, as they are in the *Long-Term Bond Market*; the *Short-Term Money Market* where money can be borrowed for as short a time as overnight, and various intermediate markets.

The distinguishing characteristics of the Money Markets, which constitute the central institution of the more general Capital Market, is again on the supply side. Demand for money and therefore the goods and factors which money controls depends, like the demand for land, labor and capital products, only on how much the business can pay for money and still increase, or at least maintain, its profits. The supply of money, like the supply of land and labor, is not primarily responsive to the price—the interest rate—offered for its use, although there is a tendency for owners of money to lend more when the interest rate rises because the alternative uses of money, such as the safety arising from hoarding, become relatively less attractive. However, we may distinguish two basic supply conditions for the money market:

(I) The supply of money is governed by the supply of precious metals, which meant gold in the late nineteenth century. Perhaps the purest example of this Gold Standard was the United States in the thirty-five years which preceded the Federal Reserve Bank Act (1879–1914). There was responsiveness to price changes, for the higher the price of money the more profitable it became to mine gold in high cost mines, but even this responsiveness (economists call it elasticity) was of small importance in comparison with the importance of fortuitous gold discoveries such as occurred in California (1849), in Australia (1850's) and in South Africa (1880's). Primarily the supply of money which is based upon precious metals is a matter of chance discoveries.

(II) The supply of money may be governed by the authority of the State, more or less directly through the issue of paper money by the treasury and the control of the Central Bank and the banking system. It is not necessary to describe the techniques of control. It is sufficient to recognize that the supply of money in this case depends on the decisions of the monetary authority as to whether the supply of money shall be increased or decreased. This is inevitably a control of the market, not a part of the formal market mechanism, for there cannot be a market determined money supply if the money supply is determined by an authority.

The supply of money can therefore be said to be relatively independent of the price offered.

These then are the markets with which the economist deals. Their characteristics may be briefly summarized:

(a) Prices on the Consumers Product Markets are set by equilibrating a demand based on tastes and relative prices with a supply based on prices and costs—i.e., profitability.

(b) Prices on Producers (Capital) Product Markets are set by equilibrating a demand based on prospective profitability (ultimate product price minus price of the input) and a supply based on the same consideration as under (a) just above.

(c) Prices on Factor Markets are set by equilibrating a demand again based upon prospective profitability with a supply resulting from considerations outside of the supply-demand mechanism of the market. This ultimate dependence of Factor Supply on nature, sex or government is the distinguishing characteristic of the Factor Markets.

The Self-Regulating Market is essentially the kind of market we have been discussing up to this point. It is a closed system. There is no need to go outside of the considerations already mentioned to understand the mechanism, nor to work out the theoretical implications of any added set of assumptions about demand or cost conditions. If one wants to determine the effects of government policy on this mechanism, it is not necessary to examine the political institutions, but only to make an assumption that a certain policy is put into effect, and then to examine its effects on the supply and demand sides and thus on the whole mechanism. To illustrate, questions about political constitution, religious ethics, or the structure of the family are irrelevant. All the economist need do is take the effects of these upon demand and costs and follow through the type of analysis indicated above.

A Market System is a group of such related markets. One can conceive of having a market for only one thing, perhaps a particular consumer good. Sitting isolated and alone there would not be much play for supply-demand-price interaction, but in fact the modern western economy is made up of a vast number of markets, each for one good or service. These markets are closely related, for every good has some substitute which will be chosen in greater or lesser quantity depending on their relative prices, and the particular allocation of expenditure between goods made at any time depends upon the relative prices existing in all product (goods and services) markets. All these product markets in turn may be related to the Factor Markets through the supply-demand-price mechanism, so that the market for milk affects other product markets (e.g., beer), producer goods markets (e.g., bottles), and factor markets (e.g., for farm land, for labor, and for the money to build barns and buy feed).

A *Self-Regulating Market System* is such a system as that outlined in the two preceding paragraphs. Each change in demand or supply conditions reacts through the whole system until each and every market has achieved a new equilibrium, where suppliers bring forward exactly the amount which buyers will take at the existing price, with no further pressures on either side to change the price.[3]

It is to be noted that it is the very strength of economic analysis in the market context which sets its limits in the analysis of non-market economies. It is the precision of the market concept which allows the economist to analyze our market system in such detail as he does, and it is this precision which sets the limit to his analysis when the economy involved is not based upon a price-making market.

All this amounts to saying that economic analysis is based upon the institutions of the markets: independent decision makers buying and selling and producing for sale with inputs bought on the market, protected by law in their contractual rights, and making their decisions with the objective of a monetary profit or gain. When these conditions and the specific institutions which embody them (such as business firms, corporations, banks, free wage labor, alienable land) are absent, economic analysis cannot be effective.

For the moment we will leave aside the possibilities of combining markets for some goods and factors into a System, while leaving other goods and factors out of the System. We will assume that everything that is scarce relative to potential uses is bought and sold in a market. We will also for the moment leave aside the possibility that the System is only partially self-regulating, or that it somehow combines a self-regulating sector with a non-self-regulating sector.[4]

(a) The first significant implication is in regard to people. In a Self-Regulating Market System the whole complex of personal life is irrelevant. Religious faith, social status, political belief, family life, loving, hating, gossiping, do not decide what shall be done, except as they are part of the complex of motives and emotions creating demand for products. On the contrary, the Self-Regulating Market, relieved of higher restraint, tends to govern the personal life. The demand for labor has a direct effect upon the locality in which one lives (where the job is), the kind of economic activity in which one engages (that for which the demand gives the highest return to one's talents), and the security of one's bodily survival. This last, being able to eat, sleep under cover, and keep warm, depends, in a Self-Regulating Market System, on there being a demand for labor great enough to provide a living wage. A failure of demand here means at best temporary disruption of the flow of life, and at worst starvation, whether because the sum of consumer and producer demand for goods falls, setting off a spiral of declining incomes and declining demand, as occurs in the wealthier western nations, or because there is so much labor that the gain in productivity of hiring another man is close to zero, as is the case in southeast Asia. Even without this kind of disaster, changes in relative demands may require the removal of labor from one place to another and result in changes in the relative income and social status of various segments of the labor force.

(b) Another significant implication is that in regard to non-economic political and social institutions. The management of the area and resources of the nation (the land market) and management of the productive resources of the nation (the capital market) are the result of the working of the Self-Regulating Market. When the Self-Regulating Market is international this severely limits the freedom of national action. On the social side family unity and community life are put in a constant state of flux since the personnel are so easily forced into movement.

(c) Therefore, a System of Self-Regulating Markets takes a large portion of human activity and sets it aside from all other activity, gives it a set of rules to live by—rules subject to no higher control—and permits the whole of this activity to be governed by the supply-demand-price mechanism. Because economic activities and other aspects of life are closely interrelated, a self-regulating market therefore tends to shape all other activity to a much greater degree than the economy would under other types of economic organization.

Markets in Economic History

No social institution is a perfect copy of its ideal, but the Self-Regulating Market System can be said to have existed in a workable approximation to the ideal type during the latter part of the nineteenth and the early part of the twentieth centuries. In many places, and in greater or less degree, it is still an appropriate model for the solution of many economic problems. By making allowances and recognizing limitations the economist still finds it the most useful tool for discussing problems of choice, economic efficiency, prices, the distribution of goods, and the particular uses to which resources are put. It is now our purpose to discuss other types of markets which are significantly different, some so different that they should never be thought of as markets in the senses we have been using.

As a first step, we shall distinguish between markets in the economist's sense and markets in the sense of market-place. In the former sense, a market need have no physical location, although of course it may. While the Chicago Board of Trade provides a room for transactions in grain, the international money market is a world-wide network of knowledge and communications between many centers and individuals. Unlike the Chicago Board of Trade it has no concrete geographical existence; it exists because there are many persons demanding and supplying foreign exchange. It is this sort of vague supply-demand-price mechanism of "no fixed address" which produces the phenomena known as world markets and world prices.

A Market Place is a very different matter. Here we have a specific location where people meet for the purpose of transferring goods from one to another. The term "exchange" really has three levels of meaning:*

1. Operationally defined, exchange includes any two way passing of goods—at a fixed price, or at an indeterminate or unknown ratio, such as Christmas presents. In this broad sense it includes reciprocity and redistribution. 2. In a more limited sense exchange means buying and selling at a definite or fixed price. The choice presented is whether or not to accept the option offered. This meaning includes: 3. Exchange used to describe buying and selling at a bargained price. Here there is an added element of freedom in the option; negotiating the price which provides the final option. This is the meaning of exchange in a self-regulating market system.

It now becomes clear that we can have "exchange" or a "market-place" in the first or second meanings of the term exchange, and not have markets in the economists' sense.

In a Market Place there is no necessity for a supply-demand-price mechanism. Whereas in the economist's markets individuals can be

* See above, pp. 254–5.

indiscriminately buyers and sellers, shifting from one side to the other,[5] this need not be the case in a Market Place. For instance, farmers could come to the town market only to sell food while the townsmen came only to buy. Furthermore, the farmers might bring a fixed quantity of food and sell it all no matter what the price, and townsmen buy no matter what the price. The price itself might be fixed by some official or simply be the traditional price. In these cases price would not determine either the amount supplied or the amount demanded. The medieval food market approximated this situation.

The Market Place need not even involve a price. For instance, there could be a meeting place simply for the transfer of one kind of goods from one group to another, which in turn would turn over another kind of goods to the first group. No element of barter need enter, for equivalence may be determined on entirely different principles. The fish-yams exchange of the Trobriand Islanders is of this nature. So are the meeting places of the Kula Ring. Clearly a Market Place of this kind has little in common with the supply-demand-price mechanism.

A Market Place can be of fixed location and open all the time, or it can be open only on certain days—market days in an English market town is an excellent example. Another example is the medieval fair, which met once a year. These example also provide a contrast between the Market Place which has physical equipment such as permanent stalls or a paved open space and the Market Place which reverts to countryside when the market is over.

The sort of market which occurs in a Market Place could occur in different locations at different times. Any particular market day would have to be in some specified place, but the place might vary from day to day, rotating among towns.

Again, a fair or different fairs involving the same personnel might travel from one fixed Market Place to another. This situation is typified by the autumnal agricultural fairs.

In all these cases of Market Place markets we have a meeting of persons for the transfer or exchange of goods, but we do not necessarily have a supply-demand-price mechanism. The Chicago Board of Trade, already mentioned, and the markets of English market towns of the last century and a half have operated with such a mechanism. But it is a question of historical fact whether or not a particular Market Place is also the physical seat of a supply-demand-price mechanism. The important thing is that the use of the term market in an historical document or current description *cannot be taken to imply that there is a supply-demand-price mechanism in operation.*

The difference between Self-Regulating Markets and other markets can be illustrated in several ways:

(a) The auction is a market with a supply, a group of people demanding and prices, but it is not a Self-Regulating Market. The supply is determined outside the economic system. For instance, the supply of war captives sold as slaves at auction is economically a fortuitous consequence of political action. The auction today of the household effects of the deceased is not a supply in response to a price resulting from demand and cost of production, but a chance supply caused by death. The point is that high prices at the auction will not call forth a larger supply (i.e., they will not cause more wars, and certainly not more victories, nor will they cause more deaths). On the demand side also the auction price has no repercussions (i.e., there is no long-run equilibrating mechanism). There is a "one-shot" chance at a particular batch of goods. In a Self-Regulating Market the existence of high prices induces demanders to shift to lower priced substitutes, or low prices induce an increased consumption of that good. There is a continuous process of adaptation among streams of goods. But this is not the case at the auction. There are no streams of goods coming along. One buys what one wants if one bids the highest, and that is the end of it, the consumer reverting after the auction to his normal sources of supply.

(b) Milk is sold for money in Indian villages. Women of cow-owning families bring to the Market Place the milk their families do not consume. As a rule the price for milk is a traditional price, and does not vary although the prices of other agricultural goods dealt with in the World Market fluctuate widely. It is also clear that the cow-owning families do not increase the number of their cows in response to changes in the difference between the traditional price and the cost of keeping cows.

(c) There are markets which more nearly approach the Self-Regulating Market, but are intermediate classifications (not stages). Thus one might have a market in which the price is fixed by official action and the supply and demand crowds adapt to the fixed price more or less as the economist would expect. Price control in war time illustrates this case, as did some mercantilist efforts to fix prices. Then one might have the demand occur independently of the economist's considerations, while prices and supply react as the economist would expect. An illustration is the "sky's the limit" demand of a government for armaments during a war with no price control, or United States strategic stockpile purchases on the international market. To some extent all government purchases on all markets have partaken of this character.

(d) There have beeen and are many examples of markets in which one or more of the economist's economic elements are governed by considerations outside the scope of the Self-Regulating Market. Illustrations are the politically determined unlimited demand at a specified price of the United States government for certain farm products and the Soviet demand for a minimum quantity of agricultural produce at a specified, low price.

(e) The Self-Regulating Market works only with demand, cost of supply, and prices, all reached by mutual interaction. This character may be destroyed by the introduction of outside elements affecting the equilibrating mechanism. Mercantilist governments of the sixteenth to eighteenth centuries altered the equilibrium at which the market acting alone would have arrived by subsidizing some industries, prohibiting the export of some goods and the import of others. Freedom to minimize costs was limited by government regulations of the techniques of production.

(f) These examples bring out a significant difference between Self-Regulating Markets and others. In a Self-Regulating Market the participants act on the basis of the relative prices arrived at by the supply-demand-price mechanism. If they are to survive in the market game they must follow the rule of maximizing return and minimizing cost. In non-Self-Regulating Markets the participants may act partly on "rational economic grounds" or relative prices, but they also reach decisions on the basis of other, different, or additional considerations.

Generally economists think of Self-Regulating Markets as being part of an all-embracing System of Self-Regulating Markets. Where some markets are Self-Regulating and others are not, it is correct to say that none of the markets can be truly Self-Regulating, for the limiting elements in the controlled markets will affect the working of all markets. Whether or not the limiting elements destroy the validity of analysis based on the assumption of Self-Regulating Markets is a question of how close an approximation to the ideal one requires and how frequent or widespread the limitations are. It is a matter of interest to the economic historian whether the markets at any particular time and place approximate Self-Regulating Markets or whether the limitations and interferences are so great as to make economic analysis inapplicable or applicable only with the greatest care. If the limitations upon Self-Regulation are great economic history must differentiate these markets from Self-Regulating markets, and establish their characteristics independently of the economist's deductions from the Self-Regulating Market.

The history of western Europe from the fifteenth to the nineteenth centuries has often been misread because of a failure to grasp the distinction between a Self-Regulating Market System and a number of markets more or less free to regulate themselves, but in sum not constituting a Self-Regulating System. An instance is the early English woollen market, where the international prices fluctuated, and merchants behaved much as modern merchants do. However, the production of wool from sheep farming was still in the hands of persons living under a feudal system of land tenure, while labor was organized in guilds and under the guilds in a strictly regulated hierarchy of apprentices and journeymen. Taking this period, usually called the Commercial Revolution and the Mercantile Period, we find that typically product markets tended insofar as they could to approximate the Self-Regulating Market, but were subject to controls of varying efficiency and importance, while Factor Markets in the economist's sense had not come into existence, except for the Capital Market.[6] The situation was logically (and in this case historically) a stage between non-supply-demand-price Market Places and a supply-demand-price Self-Regulating Market. For our purposes we may use it as an example of a System of Markets of a specific nature covering only a portion of the economy as distinct from a System of Self-Regulating Markets.

We have looked at an array of market types found in economic history. They may be ranged from:

(a) Self-Regulating Markets, where demand, price and cost mutually and exclusively determine what shall be produced, how it shall be produced, and to whom it shall be distributed,
to:

(b) Market Places, which have nothing in common with Self-Regulating Markets except that goods move from person to person. The varying systems of rules under which these Market Places operate is a subject for investigation to which the economist can contribute no more than anyone else, unless we emphasize his advantage in being able to utter warning when other unconsciously attribute Self-Regulating characteristics to these Market Places.

Between these two types are other markets having some of the characteristics of Self-Regulating Markets. They may be price-making markets in which considerations other than demand, price, and cost affect what is produced, how it is produced, and to whom it goes. They may be essentially Market Places which happen to make use of money but fix the prices. The closer these markets approach the price-making and self-regulatory types the more useful is economic theory, but economic theory has explanatory value only after the facts are established. It will not explain activity in a Market Place *a priori*.

For the economic historian a subject of special interest is the occurrence in Market Places of institutions or mechanisms resembling those in a Self-Regulating Market. Partly this interest arises from a desire to see how powerful these institutions and mechanisms are in forcing upon the economy other characteristics of Self-Regulating Markets; partly from a desire to see how these similar institutions can be made to operate in different ways and for different purposes from those we have come to expect of them as economists.

Another special interest of the economic historian is to see what other, nonmarket, ways have developed in the course of history to accomplish the same basic end as the Self-Regulating Market has accomplished for those of us who live in a market economy—namely, the provision of material means to satisfy our needs and wants; hence our interest in systems of Reciprocity and Redistribution.

As a final point it is probably fair to say that the social scientists writing this volume are at least tentatively committed to the view that Self-Regulating Markets are the exception rather than the rule—even to the view that they are unique to the nineteenth and twentieth centuries. Further, they regard price-making markets as the exceptional occurrence in history, and incline to the view that for most of its span man has lived with fixed price markets, non-price making Market Places, and perhaps mostly with economic systems best treated in terms of reciprocal or redistributive institutions whose essential character must be established independently of orthodox economic theory and with the help of other disciplines more familiar with nonmarket institutions.

Walter C. Neale

Notes to Chapter XVIII

1. Here and hereafter "goods" shall be used with the same meaning as the more cumbersome "goods and services." Also, when talking about nonmarket economies the technical term for a saleable commodity (i.e., "good") has been retained instead of using the more correct "material means of want satisfaction."

2. One may raise the question of an increase in supply when the price rises by citing the great and successful efforts to find more oil-bearing land after the usefulness of oil was discovered. However, here we have no increase in the supply of nature's resources, but only an increase in our knowledge about them and consequent increases in the price of land. In fact, this question illustrates the point: the oil-bearing land has always been an offer at some price, and that price has varied in response to a demand either ignorant of the uses of oil or cognizant of the uses and aware that the plot in question contained oil. The efforts at discovery, the analytic economist would say, were illustrations of the productivity of using capital resources to increase our knowledge.

3. The economist may think that short shrift is given to the range of economic theory. Our purpose, however, is to provide a picture of the formal characteristics of the genus "market" as understood in economic theory. There is no intention to imply that economics does not have much to contribute to analyses of markets which are not self-regulating or even not price-making. The important point is that economists begin with a model of the self-regulating system of markets and work from it, and our purpose here is to point out the limits of the concept, not its strengths.

4. Concrete meaning will be given to this possibility below under *Types of Markets: Historical Examples.*

5. In true speculative markets like the Stock Exchange and the Cotton Exchanges, each person has a price at or below which he will buy and another, *higher price,* at or above which he will sell.

6. Here again, there was not complete freedom of Self-Regulation since governments followed a bullionist policy of restricting the export of gold and silver in coin or bullion form, and during the earlier part of the period interest rates were by no means free of religious doctrine on usury and avarice, enforced by the governments.

Concluding Note

—————•—————

IN THE preface we spoke of this book as work-in-progress. Let us take a swift glance at the road we have traversed and at the position thus reached.

The fruits of the empirical research on trade and market institutions offered in Parts I and II admittedly provide but a slim foundation for the structure of theory and method erected in Part III. The historical and anthropological data of those parts fall short of exhausting the conceptual area marked out in the final section. We may thus appear to have been left with an array of untested tools.

Actually, however, those theoretical considerations and the facts that precede them are more closely linked than the subject matter of the loose sequence of chapters might indicate.

The authors see in the market bias the intellectual obstacle to that broadening of our vision in matters economic which they advocate. Adam Smith's discovery of the market as the pivot of the economy was more than a practical insight of superlative relevance; more than a pinpointing of the cell whence the emergent economic life could be theoretically mastered. His concept of the market as a spur to competition gave the decisive impetus for that view of society that was to arise from such an economy: a concept that was eventually regarded as an universal tool in the atomistically conceived history and theory of man. The market, then, shaped both the organization of our actual material existence and the perspectives from which we were allegedly enabled to grasp *all* forms of social organization.

And herein lies the key to unity in the argument of this book. The market envelopment of our own economy and society was seen as the major obstacle to understanding the economy in early societies. Only by a radical separation of the economic process from the market complex was it possible to proceed. The conceptual separation of trade from market institutions which might otherwise have appeared as merely pedantic, if not artificial, was justified by the uncovering of the "port of trade," that almost universal precursor of modern organs of foreign trade. Equivalencies, again, those antecedents of "prices," only became visible against this background. Similarly, regarding the purely theoretical question of what is and what is not "economic," what is and what is not a "surplus," and what is and what is not "scarce," the role which the market played in the evolution of our thinking emerged as the heart of the problem. Thus both in theory and in fact, detachment from the market context was the way to clarity.

The exploring of new paths, the inevitable testing of new tools along the way, does not, of course, amount to a general theory of the interaction of economy and society. No more can be claimed here than an approach that may help to produce identifiable elements in economic institutions without regard to "economic" motives or "economic" rationality. Yet, by providing this precondition of comparative and developmental studies in this field, the threshold of much more comprehensive research in the social sciences may well have been reached. For in some such way, we believe, will be built up in due course the valid contents of the reality of society that is replacing in our day the fading image of an individualistic atomism.

Index of Authors

Index of Topics

————•————